THE HIGHER EDUCATION MAN

G000155450

HIGHER EDUCATION DYNAMICS

VOLUME 3

Series Editor
Peter Maassen, *University of Oslo, Norway, and University of Twente, Enschede, The Netherlands*

Editorial Board
Alberto Amaral, *Universidade do Porto, Portugal*
Akira Arimoto, *Hiroshima University, Japan*
Nico Cloete, *CHET, Pretoria, South Africa*
David Dill, *University of North Carolina at Chapel Hill, USA*
Jürgen Enders, *University of Twente, Enschede, The Netherlands*
Oliver Fulton, *University of Lancaster, United Kingdom*
Patricia Gumport, *Stanford University, USA*
Glenn Jones, *University of Toronto, Canada*

SCOPE OF THE SERIES

Higher Education Dynamics is a bookseries intending to study adaptation processes and their outcomes in higher education at all relevant levels. In addition it wants to examine the way interactions between these levels affect adaptation processes. It aims at applying general social science concepts and theories as well as testing theories in the field of higher education research. It wants to do so in a manner that is of relevance to all those professionally involved in higher education, be it as ministers, policy-makers, politicians, institutional leaders or administrators, higher education researchers, members of the academic staff of universities and colleges, or students. It will include both mature and developing systems of higher education, covering public as well as private institutions.

The titles published in this series are listed at the end of this volume.

THE HIGHER EDUCATION MANAGERIAL REVOLUTION?

Edited by

ALBERTO AMARAL

Center for Higher Education Policy Studies,
Matosinhos, Portugal

V. LYNN MEEK

University of New England,
Armidale, Australia

and

INGVILD M. LARSEN

Norwegian Institute for Studies in Research in Higher Education,
Oslo, Norway

KLUWER ACADEMIC PUBLISHERS
DORDRECHT / BOSTON / LONDON

A C.I.P. Catalogue record for this book is available from the Library of Congress.

ISBN 1-4020-1575-5 (HB)
ISBN 1-4020-1586-0 (PB)

Published by Kluwer Academic Publishers,
P.O. Box 17, 3300 AA Dordrecht, The Netherlands.

Sold and distributed in North, Central and South America
by Kluwer Academic Publishers,
101 Philip Drive, Norwell, MA 02061, U.S.A.

In all other countries, sold and distributed
by Kluwer Academic Publishers,
P.O. Box 322, 3300 AH Dordrecht, The Netherlands.

Printed on acid-free paper

All Rights Reserved
© 2003 Kluwer Academic Publishers
No part of this work may be reproduced, stored in a retrieval system, or transmitted
in any form or by any means, electronic, mechanical, photocopying, microfilming, recording
or otherwise, without written permission from the Publisher, with the exception
of any material supplied specifically for the purpose of being entered
and executed on a computer system, for exclusive use by the purchaser of the work.

Printed in the Netherlands.

TABLE OF CONTENTS

LIST OF CONTRIBUTORS

ALBERTO AMARAL is professor at the University of Porto and director of CIPES. He is chair of the Board of CHER, vice-chair of EUA's steering committee on institutional evaluation, life member of IAUP, and a member of EAIR and IHME. Recent publications include articles in *Quality Assurance in Education, Higher Education Quarterly, Higher Education Policy, Higher Education in Europe* and *European Journal of Education.* He is editor and co-editor of several books, including *Governing Higher Education: National Perspectives on Institutional Governance,* the first volume in this series.

NICO CLOETE is the director of the Centre for Higher Education Transformation. He was research director of the National Commission of Higher Education appointed by the government after 1994 and served on the Minister's Advisory Council for Universities and Technikons. His research interests are in system and institutional reform in higher education. His most recent books are *Transformation in Higher Education: Global Pressures and Local Realities in South Africa.* Cape Town: Juta, 2002 (with R. Fehnel, P. Maassen, T. Moja, H. Perold and T. Gibbon); *Challenges of Globalisation: South African Debates with Manuel Castells.* Cape Town: Maskew Miller Longman, 2001 (with J. Muller and S. Badat); and *Higher Education Transformation: Assessing Performance in South Africa.* Pretoria: CHET, 2000 (with I. Bunting).

HARRY F. DE BOER is a senior research associate at the Center for Higher Education Policy Studies (CHEPS) of the University of Twente in the Netherlands. His research interests include university–government relations, steering models, institutional governance, management styles, leadership, strategic planning and models of decision-making. He has been a frequent contributor to the literature on these topics during the last few years, including recent articles in *Higher Education Policy, European Journal of Education* and *Tertiary Education and Management.* He has also been lecturing and tutoring in courses in higher education management.

OLIVER FULTON is professor of higher education at the Centre for the Study of Education and Training at Lancaster University, where he is also dean for the Associated Institutions. He has researched and published on many aspects of higher education policy and practice, including admissions and access, the academic profession and the organisation of academic work, implementing curriculum change, and policy formation and implementation at both governmental and institutional levels. From 1996–97 he was chair of the Society for Research into Higher Education and from 1998–2001 he was chair of the Board of the Consortium for Higher Education Researchers (CHER).

TEMBILE KULATI is the former Higher Education Policy Adviser to the Minister of Education in South Africa. Prior to that, Tembile worked as a Programme Manager at the Centre for Higher Education Transformation where he coordinated various research and capacity development projects on higher education management and leadership. He has been involved in several studies on the transformation of the South African higher education system, and his research interests and contributions have been in the area of higher education governance and leadership, the management of institutional change, and more recently on knowledge utilisation in higher education policy making. His most recent article is "From Protest to Challenge: Leadership and Higher Education Change in South Africa." *Tertiary Education and Management* 9.1 (2003): 13–17.

INGVILD MARHEIM LARSEN is a senior researcher at the Norwegian Institute for Studies in Research and Higher Education. Her main research interests are reform and change processes in higher education, more specifically, steering and organisation of the higher education system, leadership and management of higher education institutions, institutional response and adaptation to change, the role of the governing body in higher education institutions and the relationship between academic and administrative staff. Among her publications are "Between Control, Rituals and Politics: The Governing Board in Higher Education Institutions in Norway." In Amaral, A., G. Jones and B. Karseth (eds). *Governing Higher Education: National Perspectives on Institutional Governance.* Dordrecht: Kluwer Academic Publishers, 2002, 99–119; "Research Policy at Universities – Walking the Tightrope Between Internal and External Interests." *European Journal of Education,* 35.4 (2000): 385–402; and "The Bureaucratisation of Universities." *Minerva* 36.1 (1998): 21–47 (with Å. Gornitzka and S. Kyvik).

DENISE LEITE is professor at the Graduate Program on Education of the Federal University of Rio Grande do Sul, UFRGS, Brazil. She is a senior researcher, level 1, CNPq (National Research Council) and of the University Study Group of UFRGS, in charge of coordinating inter-institutional and international research projects about innovation, evaluation and university pedagogy in the public universities of Brazil, Uruguay, Argentina and Portugal. She is a member of the editorial board of *Evaluation* a reputed Brazilian journal edited by Unicamp and RAIES, the institutional evaluation net. Recently (2002) she took a post-doctoral degree at the Center of Social Studies at the University of Coimbra, Portugal. Among her publications are "Evaluation and Democracy: Counter-hegemonic Possibilities to the Capitalist Redesign of Universities." In Mollis, M. (ed.). *Latin American Universities: Reformed or Altered?* Argentina: Clacso, 2003; "The Evaluation Systems of Higher Education Institutions in Brazil." In Soares, S. (ed.). *Higher Education in Brazil.* UNESCO, 2002; "The Evaluation of Higher Education Systems in Latin America." In Cowen, R. (ed.). *World Yearbook of Education, 1996.* London: Kogan Page, 1996 (with Figueiredo, M.).

PETER MAASSEN is a senior researcher at the Faculty of Education, University of Oslo, where he is also the director of Hedda, a consortium of European centres on higher education research. He specialises in the public governance of higher education. In addition, he is a senior fellow at the Center for Higher Education Policy Studies (CHEPS), University of Twente, the Netherlands. He was the director of CHEPS from January 1997 to March 2000. He has published numerous books, book chapters and articles (in six languages) in journals of higher education, political science, management studies and policy analysis.

ANTÓNIO MAGALHÃES is assistant professor at the University of Porto and a senior researcher at CIPES. His main research interests are the regulation mechanisms of higher education and the relationships between the state and higher education. His recent publications include "The Emergent Role of External Stakeholders in European Higher Education Governance." In Amaral, A., G. Jones and B. Karseth (eds). *Governing Higher Education: National Perspectives and Institutional Governance.* Dordrecht: Kluwer Academic Publishers, 2002, 1–21 (with Alberto Amaral); "The Transformation of State Regulation and the Educational Systems." *Revista Crítica de Ciências Sociais* 59 (2001): 125–143 (in Portuguese); "On Markets, Autonomy and Regulation: The Janus Head Revisited." *Higher Education Policy* 14 (2001): 7–20 (with Alberto Amaral).

V. LYNN MEEK is professor and director of the Centre for Higher Education Management and Policy at the University of New England, Australia. Trained in the sociology of higher education at the University of Cambridge, his specific research interests include governance and management, research management, diversification of higher education institutions and systems, institutional amalgamations, organisational change and comparative study of higher education systems. Professor Meek has published 24 books and monographs and numerous scholarly articles and book chapters. He is on the editorial board of several international journals and book series, and has worked with such international agencies as UNESCO and the OECD.

HANS PECHAR is an associate professor at the Institute for Interdisciplinary Studies at Austrian Universities (IFF) and head of the Department for Higher Education Research at the IFF. He currently serves on the Board of the Consortium for Higher Education Researchers (CHER). Recent publications include "Accreditation in Higher Education in Britain and Austria: Two Cultures, Two Time-frames." *Tertiary Education and Management* 8 (2002): 231–242; "Promoting Innovation and Entrepreneurialism in the *Fachhochschulen* in Austria." *Higher Education Management* 13.1 (2001): 47–60 (with Tom Pfeffer and John Pratt); "The Enduring Myth of the Full-time Student: An Exploration of the Reality of Participation Patterns in Austrian Universities." In Schuetze, Hans G. and Maria Slowey (eds). *Higher Education and Lifelong Learners. International Perspectives on Change.* London: Routledge/Falmer, 2000, 27–47 (with A. Wroblewski).

GARY RHOADES is professor and director of the Center for the Study of Higher Education at the University of Arizona. He is also an editor for the international journal *Higher Education*. His research focuses on professional labour and the restructuring of higher education. His book, *Managed Professionals* (SUNY Press, 1998), concentrated on unionised faculty in the US. His forthcoming book is *Academic Capitalism and the New Economy*. Baltimore: Johns Hopkins University Press (with Sheila Slaughter).

ARI SALMINEN is professor of public administration at the Department of Public Management, University of Vaasa, Finland. He is former vice-rector and rector of his university. His special interests are theory and methodology of public administration and comparative administration and management. He is an author of several books, book chapters and articles on the development of the welfare state, market orientation in the public sector, transition theory and public sector ethics.

RUI SANTIAGO is assistant professor at the University of Aveiro, and a senior researcher at CIPES and RUDPKETS (Research Unit – Development of Pedagogic Knowledge in Education and Training Systems). He is the coordinator of the Master Program in Policy and Management in Higher Education at the University of Aveiro. Trained in educational psychology, his main research interests are organisation studies in higher education, organisation of academic work, academic success and the social representations of the school. His recent publications include *Failure at the First Year in Higher Education*. Aveiro: University of Aveiro, 2002 (with José Tavares); *Higher Education – Success/Failure*. Porto: Porto Editora, 2002 (in Portuguese); "Promoting the Academic Success by the Evaluation and the Intervention in the University." *Revista Avaliação* (Brazil) 6.3 (2001): 31–45 (with José Tavares); "The School as Organizational Learning System." In Alarcão, I. (ed.). *Reflexive School and Supervision*. Porto: Porto Editora, 2000, 25–43 (in Portuguese).

SHEILA SLAUGHTER is professor of higher education, Center for the Study of Higher Education, College of Education, University of Arizona, Tucson, Arizona. Her research areas are political economy of higher education, science and technology policy, academic freedom and women in higher education. Her recent publications include *Academic Capitalism and the New Economy*. Baltimore: Johns Hopkins University Press, forthcoming (with Gary Rhoades); "Universities in the Information Age: Changing Work, Organization, and Values in Academic Science and Engineering." *Bulletin of Science, Technology and Society* 21.2 (2001): 108–118 (with Jennifer Croissant and Gary Rhoades); "Problems in Comparative Higher Education: Political Economy, Political Sociology, Postmodernism." *Higher Education* 41 (2001): 389–412. Her most recent National Science Foundation grant, with Jennifer Croissant and Gary Rhoades, is "Universities in the Information Age: Changing Work, Organization and Values in Academic Science and Engineering" (1999–2002). She received the Association for the Study of Higher Education Research Achievement Award in 1998, and the American Educational Research Association Career Research Achievement Award in 2000.

PREFACE

Hedda, founded on 1 January 2001, is a consortium of nine European centres and institutes devoted to research on higher education (see web site: www.uv.uio.no/hedda). The consortium's aims are to strengthen the relationship between higher education research and practice, organise and support available academic expertise, and further knowledge on higher education in Europe in such a way that it becomes more accessible and visible at the supranational and international levels.

To contribute to the consortium's objectives CIPES, one of its member institutes, and *Hedda* have taken a new initiative in the field of research on higher education, that is, an annual seminar focused on one specific topic of research. The topic is determined by the *Hedda* Board from among the most burning issues of present day higher education policies. The first seminar was a four-day scientific event on *Governance Structures in Higher Education Institutions*. The seminar was held along the banks of the Douro River, Portugal, on 13–17 October 2001. The second seminar focused on the *Emergence of Managerialism in Higher Education Institutions* and took place at the same location on 4–9 October 2002. The theme of the third seminar is *Markets in Higher Education* to be held 2–6 October 2003.

Participation in the seminars is limited to select *Hedda* researchers and invited researchers of international standing, all of whom are active in the research theme of each particular seminar. The final product of each seminar will be a book in the Kluwer Academic Publishers series Higher Education Dynamics (HEDY). In order to make these annual books distinguishable within the HEDY series, they will be integrated as a 'series in the series' called the Douro Seminars on Higher Education Research (DOSHER). The name is inspired by the river that was the traditional highway for transportation of port wine from the interior region where grapes are grown – and where the seminars take place – to the caves located near the town of Porto.

The first Douro seminar (October 2001) was concerned with the changing governance of higher education in relation to changing state-society-university relationships. That seminar examined how changes in the wider social environment influenced transformations in power and authority relations within higher education institutions. *Hedda* considered it appropriate to focus the second Douro seminar more closely on the internal governance of higher education institutions; in particular, on questions related to the rise of management as an activity and managerialism as a set of practices and their accompanying ideologies. This focus led to lively presentations and discussions during the second Douro seminar and it provides the underlying framework for this book.

This second seminar emphasised that a number of trends have conspired, albeit in different balances across various higher education systems, to bring questions of institutional and sub-institutional management to the fore. First, in many European countries, the stepping back of state ministries from direct control and detailed regulation has in effect left a management vacuum which institutions have been expected to fill. This trend is generally linked to a shift in focus from input to output in governmental steering of higher education. In many countries this shift is accompanied by the introduction of contracts between ministries and individual higher education institutions. In other words, institutional autonomy has increased, but at the same time it has become more conditional. Second, throughout the last two decades the traditional pact between the university and society has been seriously questioned leading to changed expectations with respect to the socio-economic role of the university. The emphasis has clearly shifted from the social and cultural towards the economic function of the university. Third, in a number of countries public investment in higher education has decreased substantially with the accompanying requirement for the higher education institutions to find new, non-governmental sources of income.

The aims and expectations that underlie the enhancement of institutional management within higher education are not entirely coherent. There have been (and continue to be) attempts to reorient higher education institutions toward greater external economic effectiveness by increasing the entrepreneurial spirit of institutions in a more competitive environment, and by linking teaching programmes and research activities directly to economic needs. In addition, there are government concerns about greater internal effectiveness and efficiency through cost saving and performance monitoring; and about increasing accountability to a greater range of stakeholders than in the past. Simultaneously, there are pressures and expectations regarding maintaining academic standards and assuring or enhancing academic quality.

These trends have led in a variety of different contexts to a new or increased emphasis on the institution as a locus of power; on strategic decision-making at the institutional and sub-institutional levels; on the generation of non-state income; on resource management, including the management of staff as human resources; and on the management of academic work. The consequence in many countries has been the rise of managerialism in higher education, albeit in various forms sometimes categorised as 'soft' and 'hard', 'old' and 'new' etc. In other countries, the rise of managerialism has been termed the professionalisation of institutional administration.

The Douro 2 seminar provided an opportunity to further understanding of the rise of management and managerialism in higher education through documenting the range of experiences across different national and institutional settings and identifying the various aims and expectations of new management approaches. Evidence was examined about the way in which these new management practices have in fact penetrated the core business of higher education. These efforts are documented in this the second of the Douro books and cases are presented from eleven countries: Australia, Austria, Brazil, Finland, France, the Netherlands, Norway, Portugal, South Africa, UK and the USA.

We want to express our gratitude to all who have made the second Douro seminar and book possible, to begin with Amélia Veiga at CIPES and Therese Marie Uppstrøm at *Hedda*, without whom the Douro seminars could never have been organised. We are also grateful to Di Davies for her impressive editorial work that has made it possible to produce this volume in record time. We are indebted to all our colleagues for their timely contributions of papers, comments and editorial suggestions making possible the completion of a camera-ready version of the manuscript within very tight deadlines.

We want also to acknowledge the financial support from *Fundação para a Ciência e Tecnologia*, of the Portuguese Ministry for Science and Higher Education, making possible the organisation of this second Douro seminar. We are also grateful to the *Fundação Luso-Americana* that has supported the participation of Sheila Slaughter. Finally we record our appreciation to the management of Vintage House Hotel for providing the participants in the seminar with superb conditions propitious to intensive intellectual work.

Alberto Amaral
Matosinhos

and

Peter Maassen
Oslo

June 2003

V. LYNN MEEK

INTRODUCTION

Changed government perspectives on their role in system steering, changed community perceptions on the purpose of higher education, and changed economic conditions have impacted higher education institutions nearly everywhere. These developments have been studied and documented widely, both from a national as well as a cross-national perspective (Amaral, Jones and Karseth 2002; Goedegebuure et al. 1994; Marginson and Considine 2000; Meek et al. 1996; Neave and Van Vught 1991; Teichler 1988), focusing predominantly on the macro level. There is some agreement that the changing relationship between government and higher education is characterised by a common trend whereby governments increasingly refrain from detailed steering of their respective higher education systems in favour of more global policies that determine the boundary conditions under which institutions may operate.

Much less, however, is known about the effects of these shifts in governmental steering paradigms at the institutional level. Although claims are abundant that the academic ethos has been negatively affected through the imposition of corporate ideologies and bureaucratic reporting procedures, very little systematic study has been undertaken on the actual effects of these changes at the institutional (meso) or basic unit (micro) level. Notable exceptions are the study on innovations at the programmatic level (Van Vught 1989), the multi-national study initiated by the Carnegie Council on the changing conditions of the professoriate (Boyer, Altbach and Whitelaw 1994), and studies on the effects of quality assurance arrangements (Frederiks, Westerheijden and Weusthof 1993). This book too attempts to further understand the effect changes at the national policy level are having on patterns of institutional governance and management at the institutional level.

As explained in the preface, this is the second volume to result from the Douro River Seminar series. The first volume was concerned largely with the shifts in the relationships between universities and other institutions of higher education, and the state and society in general. That volume concentrated mainly on external governance issues as higher education institutions redefined themselves in relation to dramatic transformations in the control and coordination of higher education occurring in the external environment. This volume as well examines the response and adaptation of higher education institutions to their respective increasingly complex and turbulent external environments. But here the emphasis shifts more closely to the internal management and governance of higher education institutions. In the core chapters of this volume, national experts in the study of higher education

1

A. Amaral et al. (eds.), The Higher Education Managerial Revolution?, 1–29.
© 2003 *Kluwer Academic Publishers. Printed in the Netherlands.*

governance and management address the key question of how changes in management thinking and practice are affecting internal institutional dynamics. Answers to this question vary greatly across the various jurisdictions in which higher education institutions operate, though at the same time there appear to be some common trends.

Much of the previous volume examined the interactions of the major policy actors: government, government bureaucrats, university managers, academics, professions, learned associations, students, community lobby groups, etc. In the present exercise, we are not so much concerned with government and other external policy actors as with internal higher education dynamics and the institutions themselves. Universities and other higher education institutions, in line with the theoretical thinking of so-called new institutionalism (Hall and Taylor 1996; March and Olsen 1984), become themselves key policy actors with their own regulatory logic. According to Clark (2000: 36):

> National and state legislatures, executive departments, commissions, and councils can announce broad policies, but implementation lies squarely in the hands of the constituent universities and colleges ... The institutions have trajectories of their own; they have policies of their own, of which governmental dictates are only a part. *It is important analytically to pursue the ways that higher education operates as a 'self-guiding society' as well as to see it as composed of institutions dependent on certain main patrons* (emphasis provided).

The higher education institution itself, incorporating its governance and management control structures, plays an important role in the determination of social and political, as well as educational, outcomes. This research orientation is somewhat different from the 'classical' position adopted by scholars working in the field of public policy in general and higher education policy in particular. Premfors (1992: 1907), for example, maintains that "the *object* of policy analysis is public policies, that is, series of government actions and their effects in view of some goal or set of goals". While recognising the importance of public policy and changes in the way in which governments have approached the coordination and steering of higher education, the *object* of study in this volume is mainly the higher education institutions and their *response* to public policy/government actions and the interests of other external stakeholders. This distinction is particularly important in an increasingly deregulated and complex world where institutions have mounting discretion as to their response to government policy initiatives.

Institutions do not simply respond to pressures and directives arising from their external environment, but actively participate in shaping the environment in which they must function. In this respect, Becher and Kogan (1992) make the useful distinction between structure and process. From a broader sociological perspective, Giddens' construct of structuration (1979) also highlights the importance of a dynamic interaction between deterministic structures and intentional action – structure is both the medium and outcome of social interaction processes. What is required is a dynamic perspective on the issue of institutional governance and management whereby existing structures at any given point in time can be perceived as the resultant of interaction between the actors involved (i.e. the outcome), which in turn can give rise to further changes and adaptations (i.e. the medium). Such a non-static view appears appropriate in the light of the historical developments of higher education governance and management structures in relation to changing national policies. The country chapters in this volume should be read with this perspective in mind, thus helping to avoid an overly deterministic view of changes in higher education governance and management structures as merely the result of state intervention. More is said below about the hazards of simplistic determinism in comparative higher education research.

Approaching the higher education institution as a self-guiding society clearly focuses our attention on questions of governance and management at both the institutional level and within its various sub-divisions. A useful way of categorising the various levels of interaction is suggested by Clark (1983: 205–206) who concentrates on three authority levels: the understructure (basic academic or disciplinary units), the middle or enterprise structure (individual organisations in their entirety) and the superstructure (the vast array of government and other system regulatory mechanisms that relate organisations to one another). As indicated, the emphasis in this volume is on the interactions and dynamics at the understructure and enterprise levels, though it is fully recognised that all three levels must be understood in order to build a holistic picture of what is happening within particular higher education institutions and systems. Moreover, as also indicated above, there is a reciprocal process of action and re-action between all levels, and it would be a mistake to naively assume that academics residing within the understructure are totally at the mercy of the dictates of those who occupy the enterprise level and the superstructure. Trowler (1998: 142) maintains that "academics' responses themselves have effects on the direction of change just as much as formal policy does". In analysing recent changes in British higher education, Trowler goes on to argue that:

> It may be that we are merely seeing the first stage of the extension of control over and proletarianization of academics: what Derber (1983) calls 'ideological proletarianisation', to be followed at a later stage by 'technical proletarianisation'. Yet unalloyed images of 'traps' and 'decline' fail to take into account the resources that academics have to respond to curriculum and other forms of change which mitigate their effects or turn them to their own advantage.

At a relatively high level of generality, two broad and distinctive pressures that have brought about change in the way in which higher education institutions are governed and managed can be identified: the European/Continental model and the Anglo-Saxon model. With respect to the European situation, government has increasingly stepped back from the direct control of higher education institutions, forcing a corresponding need for increased management expertise at the enterprise level. This in turn can be seen as a strengthening of institutional autonomy. In contrast, the higher education systems shaped by Anglo-Saxon traditions have lost some of their institutional autonomy to governments intent upon introducing various quality control and accountability measures to better determine educational outputs. Of course, while governments in Europe have devolved somewhat direct control over higher education, they also have been very interested in quality assurance and other accountability measures.

Neither the pressures nor tempo of change in either the European or Anglo-Saxon contexts have been uniform across the various countries involved. As the chapters in this volume demonstrate, the consequences of these changes have also been just as varied. However, in the longer term, will the processes driving change in higher education force convergence on a new and universal mode of governance and management? Some students of higher education speculate that this has already happened, with changes in higher education merely being one derivative of the broader and universal new public sector management push (see below). The evidence presented in this volume would lead us to be more cautious about such a conclusion – a topic taken up in some detail in the final chapter.

Another broad trend affecting governance and management of higher education in several countries is the 'privatisation' of public higher education and the introduction of concepts of market steering. In some countries, this has also been coupled with the rise of a significant for-profit, fully-fledged private sector of higher education.

In examining the concept of the 'market' in relation to public higher education it is important to consider both its financial and ideological dimensions. In relation to the first dimension, an ongoing challenge faced by governments everywhere is how best to meet the costs of a mass system of higher education. A rather common (though not universal) policy response has been to pressure the higher education institutions themselves into seeking a greater proportion of their revenue from non-government sources through diversifying their funding base. To reinforce this shift in policy, governments have also sought to develop and implement mechanisms which can be used to differentially reward institutions on the basis of the amount of non-government funding secured. The second dimension of the 'market' as it applies to higher education is, however, far more complex, involving a redefinition of the basic ideological principles underpinning the relationship between higher education and the state, on the one hand, and higher education and society, in general, on the other. There is some evidence that market steering of higher education is fundamentally changing governance and management relationships at the base unit and enterprise levels and helping to redefine the academic profession (see Slaughter and Leslie 1997; and Meek this volume). However, as other chapters in this volume demonstrate, the consequences of market steering are neither universal nor at the same stage of development in all countries.

The final chapter to this volume will address in more detail the question of whether it makes sense to draw general/universal conclusions about contemporary changes to the governance and management of higher education across different national jurisdictions, or whether we need to be much more cautious and differentiated in our assessment of what is going on in the various countries. That analysis, of course, will be informed by a more thorough review of theoretical approaches to the study of higher education governance and management presented in chapter 1, along with the empirical evidence presented in the subsequent country chapters.

While a systematic discussion of the conceptual and theoretical bases to understanding recent changes in higher education governance and management is taken up in chapter 1 and the conclusion to this volume, it is important to note that a unified theoretical template has not been imposed on the country contributors. In our judgment, the cases are too diverse and the state of theoretical development in the field too meagre to warrant such a measure.

The remainder of this introduction will first present some cautionary words about the use of the comparative approach to higher education policy research, followed by an outline of the relationship between management practices and institutional autonomy and academic freedom. The next section provides a brief critique of new public management (NPM). A good deal of the writing on management in both the general public service and higher education sectors begs the question of whether NPM is actually a tangible phenomenon, or a set of value judgments designed to serve particular ideological interests. Thus, it is necessary to discuss the legitimacy of NPM in some detail. The following section looks at definitions and terminology, drawing a distinction between management as a technical activity and *managerialism* as a set of ideologically based prescriptions on how an institution should operate. Distinctions are also drawn between collegiality, governance, management, administration and leadership. The penultimate section presents an overview of the system characteristics of the countries examined in this volume, and the introduction concludes with a brief outline of what is to follow.

1. A CAUTIONARY NOTE ON COMPARATIVE RESEARCH

This book provides a critical analysis of changes and developments in the management of higher education institutions in a number of countries. In so doing, we attempt to avoid three common pitfalls in comparative discussions of higher education management.

The first pitfall common to many higher education discussions concerns the assumption that all national systems of higher education are experiencing the same changes and at the same pace. A related issue concerns the mistake of assuming that the language we use to discuss higher education management means the same thing in different national contexts. There has been a tendency to assume that higher education institutions everywhere are converging on a common organisational type in a post-modern, global society. The empirical evidence does not support such an assumption, particularly when we go beyond the superficiality of change in comparing specific countries.

Comparative higher education research continues to suffer from problems of mutual misunderstandings; in fact, it is exacerbated by the very global trends that seem to provide a familiarity if not unity to higher education reforms. As one Douro Seminar participant noted, it is easy and dangerous to gain a false impression that we are all talking about the same problems just because we are using the same words to describe them.

While strengthening management at the institutional level appears to be more or less a common theme amongst the countries examined in this volume, there is no assumption that the exact same factors have promoted the strengthening of higher education management in each national setting, that strengthening management involves exactly the same processes everywhere, or that management reform, even where it may follow a similar path, has the same consequences for each nation. If we compare Australia and Austria, for example, we see in Austria a very recent strengthening of university management that is generally regarded as having the potential to enhance institutional autonomy and the effectiveness of the academy generally. Australia, on the other hand, started its push towards management reform with considerable autonomy vested in individual universities, and management reform increasingly became tied to an ideological commitment by the national government to radical right, neo-liberal economic values and processes. In the overall context of higher education reform policy, Australian university managers increasingly toed the government line, which in turn considerably widened the gap between managers and the managed in Australian universities. While other countries may learn from the Australian experience, there is no expectation that it will be replicated in other nations. What we wish to stress in this volume is that we can learn as much if not more from the differences in management experiences amongst various higher education systems as from similarities. Some of the higher education literature assumes that common forces are driving higher education systems everywhere in the same direction. Except at the most general level of abstraction to be meaningless, the empirical evidence simply does not support such an assumption.

The second danger to avoid is treating all forms of management in a pejorative sense. Strong management is not necessarily the antithesis of collegial/professional autonomy of the faculty nor of academic freedom and institutional autonomy. In fact, there is some evidence to suggest that strong management at the institutional level is a prerequisite to academic freedom (Meek and Wood 1997). Moodie (1995: 21) states that:

> The relative weakness of academic administration is considered desirable by many faculty, and is not a serious disadvantage in a stable, benign environment. However, in an unstable and threatening environment strong professional academic management may be more effective in preserving academic values than reverting to a fictional ideal of 'collegiality'.

The third trap concerns assuming that the strengthening of higher education management at the institutional level is an entirely new phenomenon – quite the contrary in some countries. University/college presidents in the United States, for example, have for decades been renowned for the strength of leadership they bring to their roles. Historically and in contrast to the Continental system, higher education in the United States developed with a relatively politically and professionally weak faculty, and the president on occasion served as a buffer between both the faculty and the institution as a whole against powerful external forces that would unduly intrude in internal university affairs (Trow 1985). On the other hand, there have been occasions when both the ambitions of university presidents and the academic freedom of faculty have suffered at the hands of the institutions' boards of trustees claiming to be acting in the interests of the institution as a whole. The relationship between institutional autonomy and academic freedom is a complex one as is discussed below.

2. INSTITUTIONAL AUTONOMY AND ACADEMIC FREEDOM

Much of the recent changes in higher education management at the base unit and enterprise levels involve questions of institutional autonomy and academic freedom. However, the autonomy debate is not new nor is it restricted to any one country, except in its details (see Ashby 1966; Berdahl 1988). Moreover, debates about autonomy are often more emotive then they are analytically rigorous. The authors just cited along with many others have noted that if the issue of autonomy is going to be taken seriously, which indeed it should, then a distinction needs to be made between academic autonomy (maybe better phrased as 'scientific or academic freedom') and institutional autonomy. Drawing on Ashby (1966), Berdahl (1988: 7) defines academic freedom as the "freedom of the individual scholar in his/her teaching and research to pursue truth wherever it seems to lead without fear of punishment or termination of employment for having offended some political, religious or social orthodoxy".

In its literal sense, no higher education institution has complete autonomy; autonomy is not an all-or-nothing issue. Higher education institutions will always be subject to some demand to be publicly accountable, whether the institutions themselves are public or private. Society has too much of an interest in higher education to allow 'pure autonomy' (which always was probably myth) to prevail. According to Ashby (1966: 296), what is important is to examine the 'essential ingredients' of institutional autonomy:

1. Freedom to select staff and students and to determine the conditions under which they remain in the university.
2. Freedom to determine curriculum content and degree standards.
3. Freedom to allocate funds (within the amounts available) across different categories of expenditures.

Drawing again upon Ashby, Berdahl (1988: 7) further subdivides autonomy into substantive and procedural issues: "*substantive autonomy* is the power of the university or college in its corporate form to determine its own goals and programs ...; *procedural autonomy* is the power of the university or college in its corporate form to determine the means by which its goals and programs will be pursued ..." According to Berdahl (1988: 8–9), interference in procedural autonomy:

... (e.g. pre-audits, controls over purchasing, personnel, some aspects of capital construction) can be an enormous bother to Academe, and often even counter-productive to efficiency, but still usually do[es] not prevent universities or colleges from ultimately achieving their goals. In contrast, governmental actions that affect substantive goals affect the heart of Academe.

Generally, across the countries included in this volume, substantive autonomy has either been maintained, as in Australia and Britain, or is being substantially increased, as in Austria. The nature and details of procedural autonomy wax and wane in all of the countries to the great annoyance of institutional administrators.

Rather than viewing autonomy as an absolute, one can regard it as a relational issue involving the balance of power between institutions and government, on the one hand, and between management and the academic profession within institutions, on the other. Direct threats to academic freedom are more closely associated with the internal balance of power between executive and collegial governance than with external intervention, though the executive arm of the institution may act as a proxy for government bureaucrats. It is important to note that institutional autonomy provides no absolute protection of academic freedom.

3. NEW PUBLIC MANAGEMENT[1]

Any specific discussion of higher education management needs to be set within the broader context of NPM, if for no other reason than the prominence that both practitioners and policy makers have given the movement in recent years. NPM and related concepts, such as new managerialism and reinventing government (Osborne and Gaebler 1992), have dominated public sector reform over the last two decades as OECD governments respond to declining economic performance, fiscal deficits, changes in the patterns of demand for government services, greater consumer expectations about quality of service, and reduced community confidence in the ability of government to deliver services. As Denhardt and Denhardt (2000: 1) note: "The New Public Management has championed a vision of public managers as the entrepreneurs of a new, leaner, and increasingly privatised government, emulating not only the practices but also the values of business". Haque (2001: 65) puts the case in less charitable words:

> In recent years, the concern for ascertaining the status of public service as an authentic public domain seems to have diminished worldwide under the emerging market-driven mode of governance. Public service itself has undergone businesslike transformation, especially under the influence of current global reorientation of state policies toward deregulation, privatisation, and liberalisation.

One of the main principles behind NPM is that while public actors such as government should maintain core public service values they should place greater emphasis on achieving the desired results or outcomes of services rather than on the processes and rules of service delivery. It is assumed that efficiency and effectiveness of service delivery will be achieved through the use of private sector management techniques, such as specifying service objectives and competition for customers, performance measurement, decentralisation of decision making and the use of markets to deliver services. Based on public choice theory with its central tenet that all human behaviour is motivated by self-interest (Kamensky 1996), NPM assumes that market competition rather than centralised bureaucratic regulation will deliver to the public 'value for money' from public expenditures.

However, much of NPM is more a set of ideological assumptions about how public institutions *should* be run, than a well-thought through strategy for improving the efficiency and effectiveness of how they are actually managed (Pollitt and Bouckaert 2000). "The New Public Management is not just the implementation of new techniques, it carries with it a new set of values, specifically a set of values largely drawn from the private sector" (Denhardt and Denhardt 2000: 4). Moreover, in the literature, there is no consensus on a precise definition for NPM. The lack of consensus is, in part, due to countries and regions with different public institutional arrangements, different levels of public consultation in government decision making, and different public managerial abilities and historic patterns of public sector reform implementing NPM in various ways and degrees of intensity. It is also due to internal contradictions between some of the principles advanced by the movement's proponents.

While NPM has been characterised in a number of ways, Keating and Shand (1998: 13) succinctly summarise many of its purported key features:

- a focus on results in terms of efficiency, effectiveness, quality of service and whether the intended beneficiaries actually gain;
- a decentralised management environment which better matches authority and responsibility so that decisions on resource allocation and service delivery are made closer to the point of delivery, and provides scope for feedback from clients or other interested groups;
- a greater focus and provision for client choice through the creation of competitive environments within the public sector organisations and non-government competitors;
- the flexibility to explore more cost effective alternatives to direct public provision or regulation, including the use of market instruments, such as user charging, vouchers and sale of property rights; and
- accountability for results and for establishing due process rather than compliance with a particular set of rules, and a related change from risk avoidance to risk management.

Part of the criticism of NPM rests on deficiencies in the way in which it has been designed and implemented in different countries. Related to this criticism is the tendency for some countries, such as Australia, New Zealand and the United Kingdom, to implement the principles of NPM in a universal, hostile and ideologically motivated manner, rather than on a case-by-case assessment of whether the economic improvements of the services provided would outweigh the economic and social costs. Other criticisms are directed at perceived contradictions amongst the principles of NPM themselves. Decentralisation, for example, is an inherent aspect of NPM, as is rationalisation of bureaucratic decision making. But Williams (2000: 6) maintains that the two principles or themes are incompatible: "The effective use of rational decision making techniques relies on the existence of a strong centralised authority structure that can require that these techniques be used, assure that the outcomes of rational analysis lead to decisions, and prevent bureaucrats from subverting rational decisions while implementing policies". Another contradiction pointed out by Williams is that while proponents of NPM advocate the use of competition to reduce costs and improve quality of service, they also advocate a reduction in the duplication of the delivery of services.

Williams (2000) asks what is new about NPM, noting that the performance measurement literature begins in 1910 and performance budgeting in the 1950s; management by objectives was being discussed in the early 1960s, and "privatisation was in the governmental tool kit as early as the 16th century" (p. 10). Denhardt and Denhardt (2000: 2) outline some of the key criticisms of NPM arising from the literature:

Those challenging the New Public Management ... ask questions about the inherent contradictions in the movement (Fox 1996); the values promoted by it (deLeon and Denhardt 2000; Frederickson 1996; Schachter 1997); the tensions between the emphasis on decentralization promoted in the market model and the need for coordination in the

public sector (Peters and Savoie 1996); the implied roles and relationships of the
executive and legislative branches (Carroll and Lynn 1996); and the implications of the
privatisation movement for democratic values and the public interest (McCabe and
Vinzant 1999). Others have suggested that public entrepreneurship and what Terry
(1993, 1998) has called 'neomanagerialism' threaten to undermine democratic and
constitutional values such as fairness, justice, representation, and participation.

Although NPM and the reinventing government movement have dominated
management discussion in the public sector for the last two decades, NPM has failed
to deliver on many of its promises, and cracks are appearing in its intellectual and
ideological foundations. Initial success of NPM in delivering economic return, based
mainly on drastic reductions in the public service labour force, has not been
maintained across the board, and the wisdom of such strategies as privatisation (e.g.
electricity services in the UK and USA and railroads in the UK) is increasingly in
question. Moreover, the social costs of the movement are being brought into focus
as some argue that NPM's emphasis on productivity leads to decline in a sense of
community and public trust (Gregory 1999). Though NPM maintains a dominant
position in discussion on the way in which the public sector should be governed,
alternative 'paradigms' are starting to assert or reassert themselves. Denhardt and
Denhardt (2000), for example, propose New Public Service (NPS) as an alternative.[2]

Under NPM the public are clients of government, and administrators should seek
to deliver services that satisfy clients. In higher education, too, students are referred
to as customers or clients, and in most higher education systems a labyrinth of
quality assurance and accountability measures has been put in place to ensure that
academic provision meets client needs and expectations. According to Considine
(2001: 1), "universities are currently being 'enterprised' by a powerful logic of
managed performance, executive centralisation and a new code of corporate
governance".

The chapters contained in this volume examine the degree to which universities
in the various national systems of higher education are undergoing NPM reform.
The intensity of the reforms varies greatly amongst the different systems, with some
systems looking towards the hard, neo-liberal end of the managerial spectrum much
more so than others (see Trow 1994). Moreover, as indicated above, NPM is not a
coherent set of management prescriptions, and the way in which it is defined also
differs somewhat from country to country. One of the strengths of this volume is the
wide range of ways in which NPM has been conceptualised in the various countries.
Nonetheless, we also argue that the broad ideological context which has given NPM
such global prominence needs to be appreciated in order to judge its impact on
university governance and management in specific countries.

4. DEFINITIONS AND TERMINOLOGY

It was mentioned above that all attempts to strengthen institutional management
should not be regarded as a threat to the academic profession and its ability to look
after its own affairs. As universities increase in size and complexity on a corporate
scale, they require as much skill and expertise to operate as any major business
enterprise. In fact, legally, universities are a special form of corporation, and one of

the oldest forms in existence at that (Corcoran 1999). Though it can never be categorical, it is nonetheless worthwhile for analytical purposes to draw the distinction between management as a set of good or best practices in running an organisation and 'managerialism' as a set of ideological principles and values that one group of actors imposes on another in an attempt to control their behaviour. The 'ism' in managerialism, according to Trow (1994: 11), "points to an ideology, to a faith or belief in the truth of a set of ideas which are independent of specific institutions". That 'ism' becomes pejorative once it implies control over the academic products of the university by those not directly involved in their creation. Of course, management is never totally benign, and it behoves the researcher to discover the relationship with managerialism in day-to-day administrative practices. Nonetheless, unless we can distinguish between management as practice and management as ideology, there is no relationship to discover.

While once the intellectual products of the universities were regarded as public goods, increasingly, institutions have had to assert their intellectual property rights over the knowledge produced by their staff in order to survive financially in a highly competitive market. Based largely on the neo-liberal ideology of NPM (identified above), this movement, from the public good concept of knowledge to one of commercialisation and 'private' ownership, challenges many traditional academic values, particularly those associated with how the institution should be structured and controlled. This is one of the basic ways in which higher education institutions are moving from the realm of management as the effective and efficient administration of the institution to managerialism.

While we have distinguished between management as a set of practices and managerialism as ideologically driven, it is also necessary to draw a similar distinction between management and collegial authority or the notion of collegium. Collegial decision making can be regarded as a set of practices along the minimalist lines suggested by Kogan (1999: 263) who defines the collegium "as a group of academics of equal decision-making power acting together to determine standards of entry and accreditation, to share collective resources, and to determine divisions of labour and reward systems". But the notion of 'collegialism' also becomes ideologically embedded when defined as a "dynamic of consensus in a community of scholars" where "the collegial leader is expected to only facilitate the process of decision-making by consensus and not to lead, direct, or manage anything" (Moore and Langknecht 1986: 1). Collegialism thus defined becomes an attempted justification for a particular set of power relations that rarely if ever is reflected in how universities are actually run.

There has been no attempt to impose a single definition of management, managerialism or collegiality on our authors, although each contribution distinguishes between the concepts along the lines discussed above. Nor have the contributors been asked to adopt common definitions of 'management' and 'governance', though once again it is worthwhile to distinguish between the two concepts.

Often the terms 'governance' and 'management' are used interchangeably. But, as Gallagher notes, there are important distinctions between the two:

> Governance is the structure of relationships that bring out organisational coherence,
> authorise policies, plans and decisions, and account for their probity, responsiveness
> and cost-effectiveness ... Management is achieving intended outcomes through the
> allocation of responsibility, resources, and monitoring their efficiency and effectiveness
> (Gallagher 2001: 2, cited in *Meeting the Challenges* 2002: 14).

A distinction also needs to be made between 'management' and 'administration'. Administration can be defined as the process of interpreting and carrying out the goals and tasks of the organisation in line with established policies and procedures. Management, however, is much more than administration, since it involves leadership and a substantial measure of discretion in decision making and policy implementation; and the dividing line between policy development and management is often blurred. In many organisations, management contributes substantially to policy development at the most senior levels, while the task of management often includes a major policy-development and policy-choice role (Meek and Wood 1997).

While in some respects management and leadership are closely related concepts, academic leadership is often provided by staff holding neither formal management nor administrative positions. Leadership can be regarded as an individual capacity to effectively influence and motivate others with respect to the achievement of organisational goals, strategies and objectives. Whether or not an organisation's executive managers exercise leadership is an empirical question, not something that can be assumed by definition.

5. OVERVIEW OF NATIONAL SYSTEM CHARACTERISTICS[3]

The information provided in this section is not intended to be a detailed account of the structure and character of the different national systems contained in this volume. Nor is it intended to provide a comparative analysis of the convergent and divergent ways in which the countries have approached changes to higher education management. That task would take a book of its own. What is presented here is merely a brief account of the similarities and differences between the various systems with respect to a few key characteristics: size and shape of the system, formal authority/decision-making structures and recent system transformations. It is hoped that this background and contextual information will assist the reader to better assess the far more detailed accounts of managerial practices contained in the individual country chapters.

5.1. Size and Shape of the Higher Education Systems

The size and shape of the system varies markedly across the countries. Clearly, the largest and, in a number of ways, the most complex system is that of the United States, with over 14 million students and in excess of 3,500 higher education institutions of various kinds. The classifications used by the Carnegie Foundation (2000) give an idea of the range of different types of institutions found in the United States: doctoral/research universities – extensive; doctoral/research universities – intensive; masters colleges and universities I; masters colleges and universities II;

baccalaureate colleges – liberal arts; baccalaureate colleges – general; baccalaureate/ associates colleges; associates/community colleges; theological seminaries and other specialised faith-related institutions; medical schools and medical centres; other separate health profession schools; schools of engineering and technology; schools of business and management; schools of art, music and design; schools of law; teachers colleges; other specialised institutions (graduate centres, maritime academies, military institutes, etc.); and tribal colleges and universities. Moreover, each type of institution can be found in both the public and private sectors.

Brazil too is a very large country with a population in excess of 164 million inhabitants. Its higher education system comprises institutions of various types: universities, university centres, schools and institutes, education and technology centres. Each category of institution can be private not-for-profit, private for-profit, or public. Of the over three million students enrolled in higher education institutions of various types in 2001, about 70% were at institutions in the private sector. In the same year, the 71 public universities enrolled 816,913 students and the 85 private universities enrolled 1,139,629 students. The structure of Brazilian higher education is further complicated by the fact that public institutions are supported by either the federal government, the state government, or the municipal (local authority) government. Entrance to university is via a national examination (*Vestibular*).

Next in complexity in terms of sheer size would be the United Kingdom, with 111 universities (87 in England, 2 in Northern Ireland, 13 in Scotland and 9 in Wales), enrolling in excess of 1.75 million students. Universities in the UK can be distinguished by whether they are chartered universities or 'new' universities. Pre-1992 chartered universities' main structures are dictated by their charters, while the new or 'modern' universities' main structures are prescribed directly by comprehensive legislation in 1989 and 1992. Almost all of the latter universities are former polytechnics. The UK has one small private not-for-profit university. The colleges of higher education in the UK provide curricula and levels very similar to the new universities, but for the most part without their own degree-awarding powers (with a few exceptions, they teach for degrees which are awarded by a university with which they have an ongoing relationship). Colleges of further education provide a generally small range of higher education courses under similar arrangements to the colleges of higher education, but also provide vocational courses at sub-degree levels and academic and vocational courses for pupils aged 16–18 years. There is also a range of public and private (some for-profit) distance learning/correspondence course providers, mainly at sub-degree level, and specialist colleges (management, health professions, arts, etc.) analogous to colleges of higher education (mainly public but a few are private not-for-profit).

In 2002 there were nearly 800,000 students studying in Australian higher education institutions. The Australian higher education sector consists of 38 public universities, a number of specific purpose colleges (e.g. the Australian Maritime College, National Institute of Dramatic Art and the Batchelor Institute of Indigenous Tertiary Education) and two private universities. The specific purpose colleges and the private universities are quite small in terms of student numbers, while some of the public universities enrol nearly 40,000 students. Australia also has a postsecondary vocational education and training sector – Technical and Further

Education (TAFE) – which enrols around 1.5 million students, mostly for vocational qualifications, or at certificate or diploma level, or in secondary school courses, or general interest courses. A distinguishing feature of Australian higher education is that, while the states and territories have legislative responsibility for higher education, nearly all of the public funding comes from the federal government. Both financially and legally, the TAFE sector is mainly the responsibility of the states and territories and contains publicly funded as well as for-profit private institutions.

In the South African public sector of higher education there are 12 universities, 6 technikons (polytechnic-type institutions) and 5 comprehensive institutions which may become either a university or a technikon. There are approximately 111 registered private higher education institutions; 11 institutions are formed through a partnership between institutions in the public and private sectors. There are five foreign universities operating in South Africa. The South African universities enrol about 222,000 students, the technikons about 122,000 students, and the comprehensive institutions 301,000 students (225,000 of whom are studying in the distance education mode). Registered private higher education institutions enrol about 100,000 students and the private/public partnership institutions enrol approximately 50,000 students. Around 10,000 students are studying at the foreign universities operating in South Africa.

The other systems are more modest in terms of number of institutions and students. In Norway, for example, there are only four (research) universities, six specialised university colleges in agriculture, veterinary science, economics, sport science, architecture and music, as well as two art schools with the same status as a specialised university college. In addition, there are 26 state colleges in different regions of Norway. They are all public institutions. There are also 26 private colleges; with the exception of one they are small institutions most of which have religious affiliations. The one exception is a large private institution in business administration. In 2000 the four universities enrolled 75,000 students, the six specialised university colleges 7,000 students, the 26 state colleges 75,000 students, and the 26 private colleges 20,000 students.

Clearly, there is a relationship between size and the complexity of the management task. Small, elite systems of higher education of a previous era were simply easier to manage than the large, mass systems of today. However, size alone can be deceiving. While Norway, for example, has a relatively small system of higher education in terms of the overall number of students enrolled in universities, those students are concentrated in just a few institutions. The University of Oslo, for instance, has around 30,000 students, making that university as large and complex to manage as other universities in the much larger national systems of higher education.

Finland has 20 state-run universities, of which ten are multidisciplinary institutions, six are specialist institutions and four are art academies. University-level education is also provided by a military academy. Attempts have been made to construct a university network that covers the entire country, and in 2001 the number of university enrolments was approximately 163,000. In the early 1990s, Finland experimented with the creation of a binary system of higher education through the establishment of polytechnics based on upgrading and in several cases merging former postsecondary vocational institutions. There are now 29 polytechnics spread throughout the country, most of which are multidisciplinary institutions maintained by one or more municipalities and enrolling over 80,000 students (*Higher Education Policy in Finland* 2000).

Higher education in the Netherlands also consists of two types of institutions: 13 universities and about 55 polytechnic-type institutions (HBO institutions – *hogescholen*) offering higher professional education. Three of the 13 universities are legally private on a denominational basis, but are treated as being public institutions. In addition to the 13 traditional universities, the university sector also contains a private university for business administration, four theological schools and a humanistic university. The Open University offers courses that lead to either university degrees or higher vocational education (HBO) qualifications. Internationally, HBO institutions promote themselves as universities of professional education, while within the country they are not allowed to use the title 'university' (Boezerooy 2002: 12).

Of the 13 research-oriented Dutch universities, nine offer programmes in a wide range of disciplines, three concentrate on technological and engineering courses, and one specialises in agriculture. The HBO sector was reformed in the 1980s through the amalgamation of over 350 mainly small institutions belonging to what was then a quite diverse and fragmented vocational education sector. Presently, Dutch universities enrol about 164,000 students, while the HBO sector is considerably larger with over 300,000 students.

The public sector of Portuguese higher education consists of 13 universities, an open university (*Universidade Aberta*) and an independent institute (*Instituto Superior de Ciências do Trabalho* – ISCTE). There are also 16 polytechnics (the University of the Algarve and the University of Aveiro include some polytechnic schools within their structure) and 32 non-integrated schools. This subsystem also includes a network of nursing institutes, three institutes for the training of technicians for health services (Lisbon, Porto and Coimbra), a school of hostelry and tourism, and a school of art restoration. Public higher education is also provided for the armed forces and police forces (Military Academy, Air Force Academy, Naval School and the Higher School of Police). In the private for-profit sector there are presently 9 universities and 72 polytechnics (including non-integrated polytechnic schools). The Catholic University may be considered as a not-for-profit private institution. In the public sector, the universities enrol about 171,000 students and the polytechnics 108,000 students. Private sector universities enrol approximately 41,000 students and polytechnics enrol 60,000 students. There are around 10,000 students studying at the Catholic University.

In Austria, there are 18 public universities: 12 research universities (*Wissenschaftliche Universitäten*) and 6 universities for arts (*Universitäten der Künste*). By 2004 there will be 21 public universities and the medical schools of three research universities will be established as independent universities. Since the establishment of private universities was allowed in 1999, six not-for-profit private universities have been accredited. In terms of size, the research universities are clearly the dominate institutions with approximately 177,000 students. The universities for arts enrol about 7,500 students while the private universities are quite small.

Beside the universities, the other major component of Austrian higher education are the *Fachhochschulen* (polytechnics), established in 1993 and presently enrolling about 14,000 students. Though not formally considered part of the higher education sector, there are colleges for teacher training (*Pädagogische Akademien*), colleges for social workers (*Sozialakademien)* and schools for the paramedical professions (*MTD–Schulen*). All these institutions are in the public sector. Only universities have the right to establish doctoral programmes (*Doktoratsstudien*).

In Austria, as is the case with many Continental European universities, all universities are based on the principle of the 'unity of research and teaching'; teaching and basic research are supposed to have roughly the same importance. At *Fachhochschulen* (and the same could be said for polytechnics in Portugal, Finland and the Netherlands), the main emphasis is on teaching, though they also have a role in applied research. The schools for teacher training, social workers, and the paramedical professions are teaching institutions.

One of the interesting factors distinguishing some of the higher education systems is whether they have opted for a formally differentiated or unitary structure of higher education institutions. Both Australia and the United Kingdom in the late 1980s and early 1990s dissolved their so-called binary systems of higher education which distinguished universities from polytechnics in favour of a mainly unitary system in which all (or nearly all, in the UK) higher education institutions with degree-awarding powers were called universities. However, this is far from a universal trend. In South Africa, for example, the respective roles of universities and technikons continue to evolve. The Netherlands has strengthened its binary structure (though there are clear tendencies of academic and vocational drift), while Austria and Finland introduced a polytechnic-type sector in the early 1990s in response to perceived problems with their respective university sectors. Portugal has retained its binary structure of higher education which distinguishes between universities and polytechnics.

Until recently, Continental European universities could be distinguished from Anglo-Saxon universities by amongst other things their respective degree structures and the way in which students were admitted to degree programmes. In Australia, South Africa, the United Kingdom and the United States, the more or less common degree programme is a three- or four-year undergraduate bachelors degree, followed by a one- or two-year masters degree and a three-year doctoral degree. In most cases, entry to these degrees is both competitive and determined by each individual institution (entry requirements are not nationally prescribed), with universities setting quotas on student entry and prospective students ranked according to academic merit (though particularly in the United States, equity considerations may also play a role). The traditional first degree at European universities is considered to be equivalent to a masters degree (*Magister* in Austria; *Doctorandus* in the Netherlands), completed after four years and in some disciplines five years of study. Also, in most cases, prospective students who have successfully completed upper secondary education have automatic entry to university (Portugal requires a minimum mark on a national examination for entry to university by secondary school leavers). Traditionally, *numerus clausus* only applied in a few of the professional courses, such as medicine.

But the traditional Continental model is changing rapidly, and in some respects is starting to mirror that of the Anglo-Saxon model, particularly with respect to degree structure. One of the most significant initiatives potentially reshaping the structure if not the character of higher education in Western Europe in recent years has been the 1999 Bologna Declaration and subsequent amendments. Basically, the declaration imposes a two tier Anglo-Saxon structure of higher education (i.e. a three- to four-year bachelors degree, followed by a one- to two-year masters degree) on the whole of the European community.

The rate of adaptation to the Bologna Declaration amongst EU and other European countries is variable and the long-term consequences remain to be seen. Nonetheless, it appears that some countries, such as the Netherlands, are adopting the Bologna Declaration with gusto. In 2002, the Dutch government made it legally possible for higher education institutions to offer bachelors and masters degrees starting with the 2002–03 academic year. Interestingly, many of the institutions themselves started to implement the Bologna structure before it was sanctioned by the government. As Boezerooy (2002: 16) also notes, "in the Netherlands the Bachelor Master system (BM) is going to fully replace the current higher education system", while in some other EU countries, the new BM structure will be offered alongside the traditional one. According to Boezerooy, the Dutch government is promoting the BM structure as part of a general process to modernise the country's higher education system and make it more internationally competitive:

> The BM system is intended to make the Dutch higher education system more flexible and open, so that anticipating new societal developments, for instance internationalisation, globalisation and ICT developments, is simplified. The system should be flexible enough to meet the needs of students of all ages and open enough to all Dutch students to study abroad, as well as allowing foreign students to enter the Dutch system ... (Boezerooy 2002: 17).

Norway too is following a similar process to the Netherlands with respect to changes in the degree structure. Until 2003 the length of a lower university degree (*cand.mag*) was four years, and a higher degree (*hovedfag*) six years (which includes the four cand.mag years). The specialised university colleges mainly offer five-year degree courses (comparable to a masters degree level). The state colleges mainly offered two- to four-year vocationally oriented courses, as well as a range of programmes that corresponds to university subjects for lower degrees. A few subjects for higher degrees are offered at almost half of the colleges, mostly in cooperation with the universities. Universities, university colleges and a few state colleges also offer doctoral degree programmes with a length of three years.

From autumn 2003, a new degree structure will be introduced in Norway. It will involve an undergraduate degree on completion of three years of study (bachelors) and a higher degree building upon this to be awarded on completion of a further two years of study (masters). This reform encompasses most higher education institutions and most educational programmes, both in the public and private sector.

The first university degree in Finland already roughly corresponds to a three-year bachelors, which is followed by a two-year masters and then a four-year doctorate.

There are four university degree classifications in Portugal, two at undergraduate level and two at the postgraduate level. The first two are *bacharel* (short three-year programmes) and *licenciatura* (four- to six-year programmes depending on the discipline). This is followed by a two-year masters degree and then a three-year doctoral degree, both of which include a thesis. *Numerus clausus* applies in all cases. The Brazilian degree system is similar to that in the United States: four-year bachelors, two- to three -year masters and four-year PhD.

5.2. Authority/Decision-making Structures and Practices

The distinction between Anglo-Saxon and traditional Continental models of university governance and management structures with respect to institutional autonomy was alluded to above. But, as will become obvious from reading the various country chapters, each of the systems covered in this volume has its own particular characteristics in terms of management practices and authority/decision-making structures. A few examples will help illustrate further the complexity and diversity of the different systems. The discussion is confined solely to the university sector in each country.

In Finland, the "universities decide independently how their teaching and research are organised and on the formation of faculties and other teaching and research units" (*Higher Education Policy in Finland* 2000: 27). Faculties, senate and other similar entities are broadly representative, although external membership cannot exceed more than one-third of total membership. While there are national decrees on the duration, structure and main objectives of degrees, universities have full autonomy over content. Most of the funding of higher education is public, though based on a performance contract between each university and government.

In Norway, a university board has overall responsibility for academic as well as administrative affairs. As of 2003, the university board consists of an elected rector as chair, two representatives from the academic staff, one representative from the non-academic staff, one student representative and four external members. The universities' administration is headed by the university director and contains a number of administrative departments. The university director is appointed by the university board. The heads of central institutional administrative units are appointed by the university director. Each university has a slightly different central administrative structure.

At the faculty level in Norwegian universities, the highest body is the faculty board, which consists of elected academic representatives, student representatives and representatives of the technical/administrative staff. This board is chaired by a dean. The department (*institutt*) is the basic academic unit within Norwegian universities. Departments have traditionally been governed by a board chaired by the head of department. Up till 2003, deans and heads of department were elected. From 2003 the Ministry of Education has opened up the possibility for appointed heads, as is discussed further below and in detail in chapter 3.

Until 1997, the governance and management structures of Dutch universities were both highly representative and complex. At the central institutional level there existed the university council, the executive board, the board of deans and the *rector magnificus*. The university was governed by the university council and the executive board. The university council was a representative body consisting of 25 members drawn equally from and elected by academic staff, non-academic staff and students, with the provision to include up to five external lay members representing the broader community. The council elected the chair from its membership and had the final say with respect to budget, university plans and rules and regulations. The three member executive board consisted of the *rector magnificus* ex officio and two other members appointed by the Minister for Education, Culture and Science. In practice, ministerial appointments, including the rector, were drawn from nominations put forward by the university council and the board of deans. All powers not assigned to the university council were assigned to the executive board, which reported to government (Boezerooy 2002: 51).

At the faculty level, Dutch universities consisted of the faculty council, the faculty board, the dean and two standing committees – one for research and the other for teaching matters. The roles and relationship of the faculty council and board mirrored those at the central university level, although be it with respect to faculty matters. Elected from the full-time professors of the faculty, the dean chaired both the faculty council and board and held office for two or three years. At the departmental level, the disciplinary research group (DRG) was an important decision-making body, reporting to the faculty council on matters concerning course design and research programmes (Boezerooy 2002: 52). This participatory structure changed fundamentally in 1997. The basic principles altered in the direction of executive instead of representative leadership, as is explained further below and in detail in chapter 4.

In the Portuguese case, there are three main decision-making bodies and authority structures at central university level. First, there is the university assembly which has a large membership and only holds formal meetings on special occasions, namely for approval of the university's statutes and their alteration, and to elect the rector. Second, there is the senate which is the most important collective decision-making body, not only on academic matters but also on matters such as the approval of the budget, annual plans and strategic plans. The university, depending on its statutes, may decide to allow for external representation in the senate of up to 15% of total membership. The third most important authority/decision-making position is that of rector. The rector presides over the senate, and its power depends a lot on the rector's charisma and capacity of leadership. The rector appoints other high-level institutional officers, such as the vice-rectors and the pro-rectors.

In terms of basic academic units, Portuguese universities are divided into faculties, schools and/or departments. They have several governance bodies:

- Assembly of Representatives: approves the composition of the executive board and the annual activity plan.
- Executive Board: chaired by a professor – a dean – and consists of an equal number of professors and students, and non-academic staff (whose number of

representatives is half that of the number of professorial and student representatives).
- Scientific Council: composed of academics holding doctoral degrees who make decisions on scientific matters.
- Pedagogic Council: composed of an equal number of students and professors and has only an advisory capacity on pedagogical matters.

In Austria, like Norway, institutional governance and management structures are in a state of transition. Under the present situation, based on 1993 legislation, the academic senate has the main responsibility for academic matters at the university level and consists predominantly of representatives of professors, and a minority of junior faculty and student representatives. The university assembly (*Universitätsversammlung*) consists of one-quarter each of senior academics, junior academics, students and non-academic staff. It elects the rector (from those proposed by the academic senate) and the vice-rectors (on the recommendation of the rector), and it can recall the rector. The faculty senate (*Fakultätskollegium*) consists of representatives of senior academic staff (50%), junior academic staff (25%), and students (25%) and covers specific disciplinary areas. The faculty is run by a dean who is elected by the faculty senate. Institutes are the main disciplinary units. The institutes' council (*Institutskonferenz*) consists predominantly of senior academic staff, and representatives of junior academic staff and students. The council elects the head of institute. Compared to departments of Anglo-Saxon universities, most institutes are quite small. There is an advisory board (*Universitätsbeirat*) consisting of representatives from business, the region and alumni, but its function is purely advisory. The rector is appointed by the Minister on advice from the academic senate.

In some respects, the academic authority structure of Austrian and other Continental universities is not all that different from those in Australia, the United Kingdom and the United States. In these countries, there is a similar hierarchy of committee decision-making bodies flowing from departmental committees, faculty academic boards, and university academic boards (know as the senate in UK chartered universities). However, in Australia and the United Kingdom, the vice-chancellor (equivalent to the rector) is appointed by the institution and has greater executive authority, and recently deans are more likely to be appointed than elected, being assigned clear executive management responsibilities. In the United States, deans have traditionally had strong line-management responsibilities. Also in the United States, university/college presidents have had considerable power and authority over the institution. In all three countries, the president (vice-chancellor in Australia and the United Kingdom) would be appointed by a predominantly lay body (called board of regents, board of governors, board of trustees in the United States and council or board of governors in Australia and the United Kingdom) which has ultimate governance responsibility for the university. The decision-making authority structures of South African universities would be similar to those in Australia and the UK. A recent trend in the latter two countries has been the movement of small disciplinary-based departments to a much larger school (mega-department) structure.

5.3. System Transformations

All of the systems covered in this volume are dynamic in terms of change to their higher education systems. However, 'defining moments' with respect to change have not occurred at the same time nor to the same degree, either within or across the various systems. For example, the transformation of Australian and UK higher education systems from binary to unitary system occurred in the late 1980s and early 1990s. But change did not stop there. In early 2003, both the Australian and UK governments are contemplating allowing institutions to set tuition fees in response to market demand, with England also contemplating the introduction of a student tuition fee system similar to the Higher Education Contribution Scheme (HECS) that operates in Australia. The two countries continue down the road towards marketisation, including heightened competition for students and external funding, though Australia seems to be accelerating towards that goal at a faster pace than the UK.

At the end of 1999, the Finnish government outlined the priorities for higher education up to 2004. The objectives include education security (i.e. no tuition fees for any level of education); equity; lifelong learning; internationalisation and student mobility; quality assurance and evaluation of university performance; and the development of a "humane knowledge-based society through education and research" (*Higher Education Policy in Finland* 2000: 22). The main challenges in achieving these objectives are the professionalisation of management and leadership in universities and how to finance the considerable growth in student numbers.

In Austria, universities are about to receive (2004) a much greater degree of institutional autonomy. This will be coupled with the establishment of a new decision-making body (university council), which has no roots in the Austrian tradition, and the strengthening of the executive powers of the rector and the weakening of participation of junior academics and students. The Netherlands continues down a similar path of enhancing institutional autonomy and strengthening organisational executive management, but it is a journey which commenced in that country some years ago (see below). Prevailing trends in the United States which have the potential to significantly transform that system include the emergence of for-profit higher education (such as the University of Phoenix); reductions in allocations for higher education in state budgets; growth of adult education and certificate programmes; and the emergence of bachelors degree programmes at community colleges. Brazilian higher education is faced with significant issues concerning quality, particularly in the private for-profit sector, coupled with a need to substantially increase participation rates.

During the 1990s, Norwegian higher education experienced many changes, including dramatic growth in student numbers and the merger of 98 regional colleges into 26 state colleges with a governing system similar to that which prevails in the universities. Significant change continues with the implementation of the so-called quality reform of higher education in 2003. According to this reform the six specialised university colleges will be allowed to call themselves universities, and those state colleges that have the right to offer at least some masters and doctoral programmes will be able to apply for designation as universities. Other reforms include changes to the degree structure mentioned above and to management responsibilities and authority structures. Special powers will give more autonomy to the individual institution with regard to academic, financial, personnel and organisational issues. A new funding system will be introduced which will distinguish between funding of teaching and funding of research, with an element of funding based on output. Student financing also will change in the sense that part of the student loan will be converted to a grant when studies are completed (but still there will be no student fees). Finally, a new national accreditation body will be established.

While the governance and management of Norwegian universities are presently undergoing change, a rather dramatic transformation of the Dutch system commenced in 1997 with the introduction of the University Government Modernisation Act (MUB). In 1995, the government identified six main problems with respect to the then management and academic decision-making structures:

- the governance structure is inadequate with respect to the organisation of teaching;
- responsibilities with respect to teaching are not clear. Due to the collective mode of decision-making no individual seems to feel responsible. In addition, the structure is highly fragmented;
- the formal separation of powers with respect to governance on the one hand, and management on the other, is unsatisfactory, especially at the faculty level;
- as a result of the second and third point it is difficult to ascertain who is accountable for the quality of teaching;
- the strong orientation towards research at the expense of teaching has a negative impact on the quality of teaching;
- coherence and communication among the various levels [are] inadequate. This is in part the result of the ambiguous separation of powers between the key academic decision-making units (Boezerooy 2002: 52).

The new structures reduced the participation of staff and students in university management, and attempted to better clarify the responsibilities of the various decision-making bodies. According to Boezerooy (2002: 52), the main changes in the management structures of Dutch universities due to the launching of the new act on governance concerned:

1. the strengthening of executive positions *vis-à-vis* the position of councils at both the central and faculty levels;
2. the university and faculty councils becoming representative advisory bodies for students and employees instead of 'heavily equipped governing bodies';
3. the integration of governance and management/administration (the new structure combines governance and management functions in the one body), the abolition (at least formally) of the disciplinary research groups (DRGs), which until 1997 were quite powerful;
4. the increase in power of the dean at the faculty level; and
5. the introduction of a new governing body, the supervisory board (more or less comparable to a 'board of trustees').

It is also important to note that the legislation "explicitly gives several options to universities to create internal institutional arrangements to meet their own challenges".

The most important change in the Portuguese higher education system that had significant impact on governance and management is the 1988 University Autonomy Law. By giving institutions freedom to establish their statutes, together with scientific, pedagogical, administrative and financial autonomy, this policy instrument obliged institutions to deal with management and governance issues in an unprecedented way. In 1990, polytechnics were also given autonomy, but to a lesser extent than universities. Interestingly, except for matters relating to finance, private institutions (both universities and polytechnics) are less autonomous than the public sector institutions – for instance, they cannot commence new courses without ministerial permission.

Along with the Autonomy Law, the financing formula that was negotiated between the Council of Rectors of Portuguese Universities (CRUP) and the government also had an important impact on the governance and management of the institutions. Universities were given the right to buy and sell real estate, along with all the financial and legal responsibilities that that entailed. In addition, the funding formula through allocating budgets proportional to student enrolments promoted access to higher education since institutions wishing to increase their funding base needed to increase the number of student enrolments.

In 1994, the parliament approved Law 38/94 establishing the rules of the Portuguese quality assessment system for all institutions, both public and private. This law has had major consequences for the governance and management structures of higher education institutions. Even though there is no direct link between funding and quality assessment, quality has become a key issue for rectors and institutional managers.

Also in 1994, the Ministry increased tuition fees, an action which has had political consequences for the higher education institutions. Despite the fact that the increase was a modest one – fees are now around 300 Euros per year for the public sector – it increased demands by students and their parents for enhanced accountability, particularly with respect to the quality of teaching.

Since 1995, the financing and evaluation of research in Portuguese higher education institutions have been performed by the Foundation for Science and Technology, in the Ministry of Science and Technology. The funding of research is linked to the foundation's assessment of research output, focusing institutional attention on issues pertaining to research management and quality assurance.

In 2002, the Ministry of Education was reorganised and the Ministry of Science and Higher Education was created and separated from the Ministry of Education. The new arrangements are intended to restructure the entire research and higher education system and supposedly this will also bring about major changes to the way institutions are governed and managed, particularly with respect to institutional autonomy. But it is too early to assess the consequences of the new legislation for Portuguese higher education.

6. OUTLINE OF THE VOLUME

In the chapters that follow, the authors elucidate and analyse in detail the system changes briefly discussed above. The first chapter, however, rather than being country specific, provides a broad theoretical overview for interpreting changes in higher education governance and management. Peter Maassen analyses change in the various institutions used by the state to govern society and demonstrates how these broad social transformations are reproduced within higher education institutions. He suggests that students of higher education governance need to move beyond past conceptualisations of coordination in terms of state control and state steering models. He identifies two waves of governance reforms: the first largely driven by ideological justifications for market regulation and the second having a more pragmatic emphasis on outcomes and performance, especially in terms of quality and service. Our understanding of how these broad social shifts in governance arrangements are changing the patterns of higher education governance and management is just beginning.

The first country-specific study concerns changes to the governance and management of higher education institutions in Finland. In chapter 2, Ari Salminen examines the impact of NPM on the Finnish public sector, applying and exploring several of the concepts introduced in this introduction. He then turns his attention to higher education as a specific example of how NPM in Finland is affecting one of the nation's most important public sectors.

As mentioned above, the quality reform in Norwegian higher education to be implemented in 2003 includes changes to institutional governance and management structures. According to the new act for higher education institutions, the dean and heads of department can either be elected or appointed for a fixed term. It will be up to the institution to decide which approach to adopt. In chapter 3, Ingvild Marheim Larsen analyses staff opinion regarding the desirability of these changes. Adoption of the reforms is voluntary, and not surprisingly there appears to be mixed feelings as to their desirability and acceptability. The chapter focuses on the roles of academic leaders at the departmental level and analyses whether or not Norwegian universities are moving from a traditional model of governance based on collegial, democratic and political forms of decision making to a more corporate style of management.

In chapter 4, Harry de Boer analyses responses to institutional management reform across three countries: France, the Netherlands and Norway. He demonstrates that there is great variability in the degree to which the higher education institutions in these countries have adopted the so-called new managerialism. He draws the important conclusion that managerialism in higher education is neither universal nor one directional.

As already alluded to, changes to the legal base of Austrian universities initiated in 2002 will dramatically affect the way in which they are managed when implemented in 2004. Hans Pechar in chapter 5 outlines and analyses the most important changes resulting from the new law. These include the creation of a university board (*Universitätsbeirat*) that will act as a central decision-making body and which will appoint the rector. This is an entirely new development for Austria.

The rector will be given much greater executive responsibility, having authority over the employment of all university staff and responsibility for the budget which will be provided on a lump sum basis. The representation of junior academic staff and students in most collegial bodies will be reduced.

Chapter 6 examines to what extent the managerialist ideology has travelled to Portugal and what acceptance it is receiving in that country. Based on an ongoing empirical study of the rise of academic managerialism in Portugal, Alberto Amaral, António Magalhäes and Rui Santiago report the opinions and attitudes held by a number of significant stakeholders: former ministers, manager entrepreneurs and university professors on how Portuguese higher education should be managed. Analysis of the data shows no single or unitary interpretation by stakeholders in how universities should be run. While all interviewees favour competent administration of the academy, managerialism as a set of ideological principles on how universities should be managed has yet to become entrenched in that country.

The emergence of new managerialism in UK higher education is the subject of chapter 7 by Oliver Fulton. Based on an empirical study of the opinions and attitudes of manager academics from a wide range of institutions and levels within institutions, the study shows that the 'efficiency drive' has clearly affected management practices in UK higher education. However, the study also shows that the new managerialism has not colonised all in its path. What we find in UK higher education is a 'hybridised form of new managerialism', and one which in its implementation is less 'virulent' than in other public sectors, such as health.

V. Lynn Meek in chapter 8 analyses the continued push in Australia to transform university governance and management. One of the central arguments of the chapter is that concerns about university management are directly related to the centrality of higher education in the emerging knowledge-based, post-industrial economy. Powerful forces both within and without the academy are attempting to realign management practices to ensure that universities optimise the commercialisation of their intellectual products, including the training of the next generation of knowledge-workers. But the managerialist push in Australia appears to be taken to an extreme, producing a good deal of angst between managers and managed, and potentially becoming counterproductive as rank-and-file academic staff increasingly become alienated from their institutions.

One of the most important aspects of management in higher education is the management, control and ownership of knowledge. Where maybe once higher education institutions were committed to placing all of their knowledge wares in the public domain, now, operating within the context of a knowledge-based economy, this is no longer the case. Sheila Slaughter and Gary Rhoades in chapter 9 argue that in the United States "an academic public good knowledge regime is shifting to an academic capitalist knowledge regime". A key actor in this shift is the institution itself. Through case studies in California, Texas and Utah, the authors demonstrate how and with what consequences the university as an institution has become concerned with the appropriation of intellectual property rights for the purposes of securing and enhancing its financial security.

A consistent theme throughout this volume is that the governance and management of higher education cannot be understood outside the specific historical, political, constitutional and social contexts in which they occur. This is no more apparent than in South Africa where management practices in higher education have had to respond to dramatic transformation in the nation's political framework. In chapter 10, Nico Cloete and Tembile Kulati chart the complex evolution of South African higher education governance and management as the nation has gone from the apartheid to the modern political era. Whether or not all the governance and management changes within South African higher education institutions can be classified as the adoption of managerialism is quite a complex question. The answer to the question must take into account the interests and perspectives of a wide range of political actors both within and without the higher education institutions.

In the penultimate chapter, Denise Leite refers to the establishment of institutional evaluation systems in Latin America as a tool for what she calls the capitalist redesign of universities. By capitalist redesign, she means the implementation of institutional strategies internally directed to increased efficiency and effectiveness – or doing more with less – and externally directed to the new publics and to the market visibility of the institution. The changes are the result of several factors such as the governmental introduction of educational reforms, national evaluation and accreditation procedures, and pressures from international organisations. The author presents a general picture of the 1990 reforms of higher education in Latin America, followed by a more detailed description of the Brazilian situation and a case study of one university to illustrate the use of institutional evaluation as a tool for change.

In the last chapter, Alberto Amaral, Oliver Fulton and Ingvild Marheim Larsen attempt to bring together the various arguments presented in this volume to form a comprehensive final analysis of governance and management in higher education institutions. Through comparing and contrasting what is happening to higher education management in the various countries analysed in the earlier chapters, the authors are able to draw a number of conclusions. One of the most significant of these is that managerialism as an ideology is not imposing itself uniformly on all countries, and even in some places it appears to be mostly rejected. In the social science literature there is a prevalent assumption that public sector management everywhere is converging on the central principles of NPM. For instance, Lane's (2000: 2) argument is "that not only is there a new model of public sector management (NPM) but also that this model of public sector management will be more and more accepted in the countries of the world, whatever civilisation they adhere to". The evidence presented in this volume questions such an assumption. However, this does not mean that there are not some commonalities in management practice amongst many of the countries, such as centralisation of power, increasing tension between managers and managed, pressures to diversify budgets and the commodification of knowledge. However, as the authors demonstrate, a deep understanding of these and other themes is not possible in the absence of the consideration of the specific historical, political and cultural circumstances in which management practices operate. The chapter and the book concludes with the identification of areas and issues in need of much more research.

NOTES

[1] Thanks to Roger Carrington, research fellow, Centre for Higher Education Management and Policy, for assistance with this section.

[2] The main principles of NPS are:
- Serve, rather than steer. An increasingly important role of the public servant is to help citizens articulate and meet their shared interests, rather than to ... steer society in new directions.
- The public interest is the aim, not the by-product.
- Policies and programmes meeting public needs can be most effectively and responsibly achieved through collective efforts and collaborative processes.
- Serve citizens, not customers. The public interest results from a dialogue about shared values, rather than the aggregation of individual self-interests.
- Public servants should be attentive to more than the market; they should also attend to statutory and constitutional law, community values, political norms, professional standards, and citizen interests.
- Value people, not just productivity. Public organisations and the networks in which they participate are more likely to succeed in the long run if they are operated through processes of collaboration and shared leadership based on respect for all people.
- Value citizenship and public service above entrepreneurship. The public interest is better advanced by public servants and citizens committed to making meaningful contributions to society rather than by entrepreneurial managers acting as if public money were their own (extracted from Denhardt and Denhardt 2000: 9–15).

[3] Unless otherwise indicated, the discussion in this section is based on information provided by the individual country contributors to this volume.

REFERENCES

Amaral, Alberto, Glen A. Jones and Berit Karseth (eds). *Governing Higher Education: National Perspectives on Institutional Governance*. Dordrecht: Kluwer Academic Publishers, 2002.

Ashby, E. *Universities, British, Indian, African*. London: Weidenfield and Nicolson, 1966.

Becher, T. and M. Kogan. *Process and Structure in Higher Education*. 2nd edn. London: Routledge, 1992.

Berdahl, R. "Academic Freedom, Autonomy and Accountability in British Universities." Paper prepared for the *Conference of the Society for Research into Higher Education*, University of Surrey, 19–21 December, 1988.

Boezerooy, Petra. *Higher Education in the Netherlands*. Enschede: Centre for Higher Education Policy Studies – Higher Education Monitor, 2002.

Boyer, Ernst L., Philip G. Altbach and Mary Jean Whitelaw. *The Academic Profession: An International Perspective*. Princeton, NJ: Carnegie Foundation for the Advancement of Teaching, 1994.

Carnegie Foundation for the Advancement of Teaching. *The Carnegie Classification of Institutions of Higher Education*. 2000, http://www.carnegiefoundation.org/Classification/index.htm.

Carroll, James and Dahlia Bradshaw Lynn. "The Future of Federal Reinvention: Congressional Perspectives." *Public Administration Review* 56.3 (1996): 299–304.

Clark, Burton R. *The Higher Education System. Academic Organization in Cross-National Perspective*. Berkeley: University of California Press, 1983.

Clark, Burton R. "Developing a Career in the Study of Higher Education." In Smart, J. (ed.). *Higher Education: Handbook of Theory and Research*. vol. XV. New York: Agathon Press, 2000, 36–38.

Considine, Mark. "Commentary APSA Presidential Address 2000. The Tragedy of the Common-rooms? Political Science and the New University Governance." *Australian Journal of Political Science* 36.1 (2001): 1–13 (electronic version).

Corcoran, S. "Living on the Edge: Utopia University Ltd." *Federal Law Review* 27 (1999): 265–271.

deLeon, Linda and Robert B. Denhardt. "The Political Theory of Reinvention." *Public Administration Review* 60.2 (2000): 89–97.

Denhardt, Robert B. and Janet Denhardt. "The New Public Service: Serving Rather than Steering." *Public Administration Review* 60.6 (2000): 1–24 (electronic version).

Derber, C. "Managing Professionals: Ideological Proletarianization and Post-Industrial Labor." *Theory and Society* 12.3 (1983): 309–341.

Fox, Charles. "Reinventing Government as Postmodern Symbolic Politics." *Public Administration Review* 56.3 (1996): 256–261.

Frederickson, H. George. "Comparing the Reinventing Government Movement with the New Public Administration." *Public Administration Review* 56.3 (1996): 263–269.

Frederiks, M., D. Westerheijden and P. Weusthof. *De Effecten van Kwaliteitszorg* (The Effects of Quality Assurance). Zoetermeer: Ministerie van Onderwijs en Wetenschappen, 1993.

Gallagher, M. "Modern University Governance – A National Perspective." Paper presented at the *Conference on the Idea of a University: Enterprise or Academy?* The Australia Institute and Manning Clark House, Canberra, 26 July 2001.

Giddens, A. *Central Problems in Social Theory*. London: MacMillan Press, 1979.

Goedegebuure, L., E. Kaiser, P. Maassen, V.L. Meek, F. van Vught and E. de Weert (eds). *Higher Education Policy: An International Comparative Perspective*. Oxford: Pergamon, 1994.

Gregory, Robert J. "Social Capital Theory and Administrative Reform: Maintaining Ethical Probity in Public Service." *Public Administration Review* 59.1 (1999): 1–22 (electronic version).

Hall, Peter A. and Rosemary C.R. Taylor. "Political Science and the Three New Institutionalisms." *Political Studies* 44 (1996): 936–957.

Haque, M. Shamsul. "The Diminishing Publicness of Public Service under the Current Mode of Governance." *Public Administration Review* 61.1 (2001): 1–30 (electronic version).

Higher Education Policy in Finland. Helsinki: Ministry of Education, 2000.

Kamensky, John. "Role of Reinventing Government Movement in Federal Management Reform." *Public Administration Review* 56.3 (1996): 247–256.

Keating, M.S. and D.A. Shand. *Public Management Reform and Economic and Social Development*. Paris: OECD, 1998.

Kogan, Maurice. "Academic and Administrative Interface." In Henkel, M. and B. Little (eds). *Changing Relationships Between Higher Education and the State*. London: Jessica Kingsley, 1999, 263–279.

Lane, Jan-Erik. *New Public Management*. London: Routledge, 2000.

March, James and Johan Olsen. "The New Institutionalism: Organisational Factors in Political Life." *American Political Science Review* 78 (1984): 734–749.

Marginson, S. and M. Considine. *The Enterprise University*. Melbourne: Cambridge University Press, 2000.

McCabe, Barbara and Janet Vinzant. "Governance Lessons: The Case of Charter Schools." *Administration and Society* 31.3 (1999): 361–77.

Meek, V.L., Leo Goedegebuure, Osmo Kivinen and Risto Rinne (eds). *The Mockers and Mocked: Comparative Perspectives on Diversity, Differentiation and Convergence in Higher Education*. Oxford: Pergamon, 1996.

Meek, V.L. and F.Q. Wood. *Higher Education Governance and Management: An Australian Study*. Canberra: AGPS, 1997.

Meeting the Challenges: The Governance and Management of Universities. Canberra: Department of Education, Science and Training, 2002.

Moodie, Gavin. "The Professionalism of Australian Academic Administration." *The Australian Universities' Review* 38.1 (1995): 21–23.

Moore, John W. and Linda Langknecht. "Academic Planning in a Political System." *Planning for Higher Education* 14.1 (1986): 1–5.

Neave, Guy and F. van Vught (eds). *Prometheus Bound: The Changing Relationship Between Government and Higher Education in Western Europe*. Oxford: Pergamon, 1991.

Osborne, David and Ted Gaebler. *Reinventing Government*. Reading MA: Addison-Wesley, 1992.

Peters, B. Guy and Donald Savoie. "Managing Incoherence: The Coordination and Empowerment Conundrum." *Public Administration Review* 56.3 (1996): 281–289.

Pollitt, Christopher and Geert Bouckaert. *Public Management Reform: A Comparative Analysis*. Oxford: Oxford University Press, 2000.

Premfors, R. "Policy Analysis in Higher Education." In Clark, Burton R. and G. Neave (eds). *The Encyclopedia of Higher Education*. Oxford: Pergamon Press, 1992, 1907–1915.

Schachter, Hindy Lauer. *Reinventing Government or Reinventing Ourselves*. Albany, NY: State University of New York Press, 1997.

Slaughter, S. and L. Leslie. *Academic Capitalism: Politics, Policies and the Entrepreneurial University.* Baltimore: Johns Hopkins University Press, 1997.

Teichler, U. *Changing Patterns of the Higher Education System: The Experience of Three Decades.* London: Jessica Kingsley Publishers, 1988.

Terry, Larry D. "Why We Should Abandon the Misconceived Quest to Reconcile Public Entrepreneurship with Democracy." *Public Administration Review* 53.4 (1993): 393–395.

Terry, Larry D. "Administrative Leadership, Neo-Managerialism, and the Public Management Movement." *Public Administration Review* 58.3 (1998): 194–200.

Trow, M. "Comparative Reflections on Leadership in Higher Education." *European Journal of Education* 20.2–3 (1985): 143–159.

Trow, M. "Manageralism and the Academic Profession: The Case of England." *Higher Educational Policy* 7.2 (1994): 11–18.

Trowler, Paul R. *Academics Responding to Change: New Higher Education Frameworks and Academic Cultures.* Buckingham: Society for Research into Higher Education and Open University Press, 1998.

Van Vught, F. *Government Strategies and Innovation in Higher Education.* London: Jessica Kingsley Publishers, 1989.

Williams, Daniel W. "Reinventing the Proverbs of Government." *Public Administration Review* 60.6 (2000): 1–26 (electronic version).

PETER MAASSEN

SHIFTS IN GOVERNANCE ARRANGEMENTS

An Interpretation of the Introduction of New Management
Structures in Higher Education

1. INTRODUCTION

The introduction of new management structures in higher education can be discussed from various angles. In this chapter[1] the main angle used is that of the changing relationship between the state and the public sector, more specifically, the shifts in governance arrangements that are accompanying the changing relationship. As such this discussion can be regarded as a follow up to the first Douro volume that opened with the statement:

> A common theme in the dramatic restructuring of higher education throughout much of the world over the past few decades has been a shift in the relationships between universities, and other institutions of higher education, and the state (Reed, Meek and Jones 2002: xv).

Governance arrangements are interpreted here generally as the set of institutions which governments are using to govern society, that is, to "exercise collective control and influence over the societies for which they have been given responsibility" (Peters 2001: 1). Over the last two decades the traditional, national governance arrangements, as developed and used throughout most of the 20th century, have been heavily critiqued, and gradually replaced by alternative, multi-level arrangements. This reform process was driven both by ideological and pragmatic motives. However, the governance reform has not resulted in a new set of permanent and stable arrangements. In many ways it has led to continuous reform in the industrialised, Western democracies. Also in developing countries and the so-called emerging economies (e.g. in Central and Eastern Europe),[2] governance reform has been a frequent item on the political agenda, amongst other things, as a consequence of the pressure of international agencies, such as the World Bank (Torres and Schugurensky 2002).

This general pattern can also be observed with respect to higher education governance. Since the mid-1980s, reforming the governance relationship between the state and higher education has been a constant item on the political agenda of most countries. These reforms were initially ideologically driven, but gradually became more pragmatic. In this chapter, the first round of reforms will be discussed as well as the role public sector management played in these reforms. With respect to higher education, institutional management will be discussed without making a

A. Amaral et al. (eds.), The Higher Education Managerial Revolution?, 31–53.
© 2003 *Kluwer Academic Publishers. Printed in the Netherlands.*

distinction between academic and administrative management, unless indicated otherwise.

2. MANAGEMENT REFORM IN HIGHER EDUCATION

Governments at various levels are responsible for the regulatory frameworks within which higher education institutions are expected to perform and within which they have to manage their activities. Therefore, any discussion on changes in institutional management structures in higher education must include an interpretation of these frameworks and the way in which they regulate the management tasks of universities and colleges. Before starting this discussion the following questions are raised: What is meant by institutional management in higher education? How does it compare to related concepts referring to the task of running a higher education institution, more specifically, institutional leadership, governance and administration? In practice the activities covered by these concepts cannot always be distinguished from one another. Nonetheless, in the first Douro volume a useful attempt was made to discuss the differences between the related concepts (Reed, Meek and Jones 2002). Reed and his colleagues focused especially on governance and emphasised that a common element in the conceptualisation of governance in the various chapters of the book "is the notion of relationship or dynamic interaction of bodies and groups operating at different levels of a higher education system" (p. xxvii). Referring, amongst others, to Gallagher (2001: 1) they further suggest that, in higher education, institutional leadership is mainly about strategic direction giving and setting; management is about outcomes achievement and the monitoring of institutional effectiveness and efficiency in the distribution of resources; and administration is about the implementation of procedures. These interpretations are in line with the above starting-point that governance is about the frameworks in which universities and colleges manage themselves and about the processes and structures used to achieve the intended outcomes – in other words about *how* higher education institutions operate. This implies that governance is a "relational concept that can be considered to incorporate leadership, management, and administration" (Reed, Meek and Jones 2002: xxvii). This again shows the importance of discussing 'shifts in governance' for understanding the nature of changes in institutional management (and leadership and administrative) structures.

In examining the nature of the management reforms in higher education, it is of relevance to point to the general feeling that academic life is not what it used to be. Many changes, amongst other things the aftermath of the massification of higher education, have altered it beyond recognition. As a consequence, the question: "Who is actually in charge in a higher education institution?" has become very relevant. Anyone familiar with the complexity of current day higher education institutions will have to admit that it is not easy to give a straightforward answer to this question. Reflecting upon this complexity, many academics tend to refer to the good old days when decisions in academia were made in a collegial atmosphere without serious outside interference. These reflections are without any doubt nostalgic interpretations of a past that has become more and more idealised in comparison to the current situation in higher education. To summarise and paraphrase opinions often heard amongst academics: "When higher education institutions were run on the basis of the collegial model we were all better of in academia"; "The current university managers are more driven by economic than by academic considerations"; and "A higher education institution is not a shoe factory and therefore cannot be managed as a shoe factory". However, as is indicated by Kogan (1999: 264):

> This romantic view of academic government did not, however, show how essential collective decisions were reached. Later work showed how decisions made within diffuse sectors of the university became regularized as procedures and eventually structures, thus political and organizational models of decision making were bridged.

The main underlying worry is that external interests have become the driving force behind the reforms of the management structures of universities and colleges (Neave 1996: 404). In other words, the control by academics of the internal affairs of the university is threatened. What is the origin of this threat? How can it be interpreted?

Higher education has traditionally been a social institution allowed to govern its basic teaching and research activities through a form of collegial self-steering. In Continental Europe, for example, this implied for the universities that various intra-institutional governance bodies and an institutional leader (rector or president) (s)elected from among the highest professorial ranks, were seen as support structures for academic activities, teaching and research. Gradually the internally controlled, 'collegial' decision-making structures have been replaced by some form of externally oriented management structure. Already in the 1960s, reference was made in the USA to 'The Management Revolution in Higher Education' (Rourke and Brooks 1966; see also Keller 1983). This 'management revolution' consisted of a formal, internally and externally driven, strengthening of the management positions in public universities and colleges.

Throughout the 1980s, higher education in other countries, especially in Europe, Canada, Australia and New Zealand, entered the 'era' of management-driven higher education, later followed by most of the rest of the world. While this development is characterised by a great diversity between countries with respect to the nature of the changes in practice, one thing in common is the belief that the more government withdraws from steering higher education, the better the sector will perform (Goedegebuure et al. 1994; Meek 2002).

A concept often used to refer to the management reforms in the public sector is new public management (NPM), while with respect to higher education the term 'managerialism' is used more frequently to refer to the same phenomenon. However, we can wonder whether referring to the management developments in higher education by using these terms helps us to better understand this phenomenon, amongst other things, since both terms have multiple meanings, as is extensively discussed by Meek in the introduction to this book. They do not represent a particular narrow band of possible approaches for public management reform. With respect to higher education, the diversity in the nature of the strengthening of the management function, culture and structures is referred to, for example, by making a distinction between hard and soft managerialism. It will be clear that this conceptual homogenisation of a diverse and complex phenomenon affects the studies of higher education management considerably. A striking feature in this is that neither in management studies in general, nor in the literature on higher education management, has there been many convincing attempts to develop management theories other than by referring to economic theories such as public choice theory. Apart from these economic conceptualisations, the management literature consists in general of 'management recipes' or general explorations of new developments in management practice. This is contrary to the literature on governance, where many conceptualisations of 'governance' can be found as well as of related concepts, such as coordination. This difference between the 'management literature' and the 'governance literature' is another reason why in this chapter governance is used as the main concept for discussing the changes in institutional management structures in higher education.

3. ADAPTATION OF GOVERNANCE ARRANGEMENTS WITH RESPECT TO HIGHER EDUCATION

Over the last few decades, many countries around the world have undergone changes in the forms and mechanisms of governance, in the location of governance, in governing capabilities, and in styles of governance (Van Kersbergen and Van Waarden 2001; Peters 2001). For example, with respect to the location of governance, shifts have occurred vertically and horizontally, as well as by a combination of the two. With respect to higher education, vertical shifts can be observed from national to supranational public bodies such as the EU, or from national to sub-national and regional levels, for example, in France and Spain. Horizontally, shifts have taken place from public to semi-public or private forms of governance, for example, in the area of student support systems. Finally, an example of a mixed horizontal-vertical shift is the rise of international semi-public or private accreditation agencies in areas such as business administration.

Many authors have identified possible causes for the decrease in the effectiveness of traditional governance arrangements. Peters (2001), for example, points to the decreasing social and political homogeneity among individuals and groups in society. There is a growing 'lack of common ground' with respect to many issues. As a consequence, the traditional pattern of government-led negotiations between various interest groups has become problematic, while reaching social and political compromises has become more difficult. In addition, traditionally stable governance arrangements and organisations have destabilised making it more complicated for government to intervene in society (Cohen and Rogers 1994). These general developments can be observed worldwide, even though many smaller and larger variations can be found at the national level. For example, Van Kersbergen and Van Waarden (2001) mention a number of specific Dutch governance trends. First, they point to the growing importance of knowledge and information in the economy, polity and society. This trend leads to the growing importance, and consequently power of experts, as well as to the growing interdependence of public and private organisations. The second trend they identify is internationalisation and globalisation leading to multi-level governance arrangements. The third trend is the economisation of society, representing the growing importance of economic considerations and arguments in policy processes, for example, with respect to higher education. The final trend referred to is the individualisation of society, that is, the erosion of collective social identities. This is in line with the first cause identified by Peters, in the sense that individualisation is claimed to have made it more difficult for government to 'govern', while those who are 'governed' let themselves be governed less easily (Van Kersbergen and Van Waarden 2001).

With respect to most of these trends the 'chicken and egg' question can be asked concerning the underlying causal relationships between national politics and social trends. For example, did the rise of neo-liberal governments since the late 1970s lead to individualism and globalisation, or did political ideologies follow social and economic trends, such as individualism and globalisation?

Higher education offers interesting examples of governmental strategies for dealing with the 'governance crisis'. In general, governments have transferred parts of their authority with respect to higher education vertically towards the higher education institutions over the last ten to fifteen years. This shift has been interpreted, amongst other things, in the framework of what has been called a change in governmental steering strategies (Van Vught 1989; Maassen 1996), or an adaptation of the dominant state model with respect to higher education (Gornitzka and Maassen 2000). In this chapter, these two sets of interpretations will be taken as a starting-point for the discussion of changes in the relationship between the state and higher education, and especially the position of management reforms in these changes. As indicated, these management reforms will be analysed within the framework of recent shifts in governance arrangements (Peters 2001; see also Cloete et al. 2002).

After 1945 various developments, such as the massification of higher education, the democratisation movements of the 1960s, and the oil crises of the early 1970s, stimulated early efforts to adapt the governance arrangements with respect to the sector. On top of that came the general economic downturn of the 1980s that led governments around the world to emphasise the economic dimension in their higher education policies and to introduce further adaptations of governance arrangements with respect to higher education. While these shifts were part of a general reconfiguration of governance arrangements, both the high level of public expenditure on higher education, and the relatively low position of higher education on the political priority agenda, made higher education an obvious and relatively easy target for governance reform.

3.1. Aim of Governance Shifts

In the framework of this chapter, it is assumed that the ultimate aim of the shifts in governance is, in general, to influence the behaviour of individual citizens. With respect to higher education, this implies in the first place affecting the behaviour of the academic staff of universities and colleges (see Popper 1957; Maassen 1996).

The starting-point is that at a certain moment there is apparently enough agreement among involved stakeholders that a traditional governance arrangement is not sufficiently effective in 'steering' the behaviour of individual or collective human actors in such a way that specific social, political or economic goals can be achieved (Maassen and Van Vught 1989). Therefore, a new governance arrangement is needed that ultimately is expected to affect 'the human factor', that is, the aimed-at human actors, in such a way that their behaviour comes more in line with the underlying goals. With respect to higher education this implies that a new governance arrangement is expected to influence 'the academic human factor' accordingly.

What is meant by 'influencing the academic human factor'? In democracies the human factor in social institutions, such as universities and colleges, can never be controlled directly. As a consequence, governments in democracies try to realise certain changes in society not by attempting to influence and control individual citizens directly, but through adapting the governance arrangements with respect to the social institutional contexts of the citizens whose behaviour they would like to change. The success or failure of these adaptations can be tested by examining whether the 'citizens in question' have changed their behaviour – as well as their underlying values and beliefs – in the desired direction.

Applying this set of assumptions to higher education leads to the general interpretation that (supranational, national and sub-national) governments were at a certain moment not satisfied with the functioning of universities and colleges. Governments assumed that this functioning could not be influenced positively anymore by the governance arrangements used at that moment. Therefore new governance arrangements were introduced that were expected to change the social institutional contexts of academic staff in such a way that the functioning of the higher education institutions would change in the same direction (Maassen 1996).

The governance arrangement of greatest relevance here is the management structure of universities and colleges. Governments apparently were dissatisfied with the functioning of higher education institutions, as ultimately measured in the behaviour of the academic staff of these institutions, including their involvement in the institutional management structures. In order to stimulate a more satisfactory level of functioning, institutional management was changed from a 'necessary evil' to a self-justified activity (Becher and Kogan 1992: 181; see also section 5 below). The underlying assumption was that this new structure would influence the behaviour of academics in such a way that it would lead to a more satisfying level of functioning of the higher education institutions. As such, it meant that governmental steering towards higher education and governmental higher education policies became as much focused on the managing of higher education institutions as on the academic activities of these institutions.

In the remainder of the chapter this starting-point and the set of assumptions will be elaborated.

4. REFLECTIONS ON GOVERNANCE

4.1. New Models of Governance

Since the late 1980s, a number of higher education scholars have used state or steering models developed by other social scientists to analyse changes in the relationship between the state and higher education. Van Vught (1989) introduced, for example, a central planning model and a self-regulation model of government steering, later elaborated into state control and state supervision models (Neave and Van Vught 1991; Maassen and Van Vught 1994). These models were based on the work of classic social science authors, such as Meyerson and Banfield (1955), Ashby (1956), Lindblom (1959, 1965), Steinbrunner (1974) and Beer (1975). The implicit assumption in the state control/state supervision models was that a development from state control to state supervision was to be promoted, because a supervising role of the state would lead to a better performance of higher education than a controlling role. Van Vught and his colleagues presented the two models as being conceptually mutually exclusive, even though in the practice of higher education many hybrid forms of them can be observed (Maassen and Van Vught 1988; Neave 1998; Amaral and Magelhães 2001).

In the 1990s, a number of European higher education researchers (see e.g. Van Heffen, Verhoeven and De Wit 1999; Gornitzka and Maassen 2000) became inspired by the four so-called state models introduced by Olsen (1988): the sovereign (or unicentric) state, the institutional state, the segmented (or corporatist) state and the market state. Unlike the models introduced by Van Vught, these four models are not necessarily mutually exclusive. They represent different ways of organising the relationship between the state and society, that is, state dominance and control, state protection of specific social values and norms, the state as one of the involved interest groups, and a minimal state.[3]

Most analyses made in the 1980s and 1990s of the changes in the relationship between the state and higher education did not give much explicit attention to the effects of the changes on the management structures of the higher education institutions. In general, the authors in question did not go much beyond suggesting that some form of 'managerialism' had been introduced in higher education. The analyses were focused mainly on changes in the governmental steering such as the development of quality assessment systems and the adaptation of funding mechanisms; structural changes in higher education systems; curriculum innovations; efficiency issues; and institutional governance structures. The latter topic was closest to the issue of management structures, but the scholars involved did not in general conceptualise the differences between institutional governance and institutional management. This does not, of course, imply that there was no scholarly interest in institutional management in the field of higher education research. As the chapters in this book illustrate, there are many examples of major studies on institutional management (in addition to the studies presented in this book, see e.g. Birnbaum 1988). However, the nature of the changes in institutional management structures and practices up till now have seldom been examined in the broader framework of the changes in the relationship between the state and higher education.

The steering models introduced by Van Vught (1989) and the state models developed by Olsen (1988) reflected the governance changes of the 1980s. They represent the transition period in which new governance approaches were introduced without the old having been abolished completely. In line with the hybrid character of the steering models mentioned above, Maassen and Van Vught (1988, 1989) talk in this period about the *Janus-head* character of state governance with respect to higher education (see also Amaral and Magelhães 2001).

Governance, as discussed in this chapter, is a concept that refers to a higher education system as a whole. As a consequence 'shifts in governance' have to do with the system-level governance arrangements that provide more or less similar change conditions and expectations for all universities and colleges that formally are positioned within a specified higher education sector. However, this does not imply that all these organisations respond in the same way to external change and expectations. To examine these organisational responses in their own right, governance theories should be complemented by other theoretical approaches.

Neo-institutional theories, for example, can be relevant when interpreting the impact of governance shifts at the level of each individual university and college more closely. They can be helpful for understanding the differences between the responses of individual universities and colleges in the same higher education system to shifts in the system level governance model. From a sociological neo-institutional perspective, for example, both the concept of *sedimentation* and the processes of *deinstitutionalisation* and *reinstitutionalisation* contribute to a better understanding of the nature of management change processes in higher education.

Sedimentation refers to the "layers of values and understandings left from earlier times" (Peters 1999: 104) that can be found beneath the current practice in an organisation such as a university or college. Consequently, such an organisation is like a riverbed in which many layers of value and belief systems are deposited on top of each other (see Tolbert and Zucker 1996). Instead of change being abrupt, absolute and complete, change takes place through the development of "new understandings and symbols that are not incompatible with those that were in place before" (Peters 1999: 104).

A related argument is made by Trommel and Van der Veen (1997) who claim that, to understand the nature and effects of institutional change, it is necessary to take the process of institutional decline and reform seriously. They suggest that "the study of deinstitutionalization and reinstitutionalization reveals how institutions produce social and cognitive predispositions that in due course can foster their own decline or reform. It calls attention to the subtle ways in which old and new cognitive schemes compete, collapse and/or merge. In order to unravel this process of 'institutional resonance' institutional scholars must focus their attention on the micro level of institutional life" (Trommel and Van der Veen 1997: 61; see also Trommel 1995). Zucker (1991: 104) refers to this micro level as the black box in organisational studies. The various studies on management change in higher education presented in this book show the potential richness of this micro-level approach, even though not all authors refer explicitly to the underlying institutional dimension.

It goes beyond the scope of this chapter to discuss the relevance of these and other neo-institutional approaches, or other theoretical perspectives, in more detail. Instead, the focus is on governance shifts. However, this focus only allows for a general discussion of the possible consequences of certain system-level changes for the management structures, culture and function in universities and colleges. These system-level changes provide the frameworks within which these management dimensions have to be adapted. As such, the discussion in this chapter represents a first step in a more comprehensive examination of the management reforms in higher education. As indicated in any micro-level analysis of management changes in higher education, neo-institutionalism might provide relevant conceptualisations.

Below, the nature of alternative governance models and the expectations they have with respect to management functions will be discussed. In line with the neo-institutional perspectives mentioned above, it is not assumed that the traditional governance model is abolished completely; nor does the focus on alternative models and the interpretation and expectations they have with respect to the management function in higher education imply a judgment value of the actual appropriateness of the traditional model. Whether the traditional state model is 'effective' or 'ineffective', 'good' or 'bad' is not an issue in this chapter. The starting-point in this discussion is that it is not assumed that all new governance models with respect to higher education are market models, nor that all management developments in higher education institutions concern variations on NPM or new 'managerialism'.

We will start with Peters' (2001) general discussion of shifts in governance. His purpose was to "examine the ideas that motivate reform and that provide a diagnosis of the problems in the public sector as well as the basis for prescriptions to remedy the problems" (p. 2). Peters makes a distinction between the first waves of reforms of the traditional approach to governance that took place in the 1980s and early 1990s and were ideologically driven, and a recent, second, more pragmatic wave that combines further 'repair work' of the traditional model with attempts to deal with some of the flaws of the ideological reforms. In the first wave, four alternative models of governance emerged as alternatives to the traditional governance model, that is, the market model (or rather market models), the participatory state model, the flexible government model, and the deregulated government model. The ideological nature of the reforms was especially clear in the case of the market model that was introduced in many countries as an unquestioned improvement to the traditional governance approach. What do these models stand for? In line with Peters, each new model will be summarised on the basis of the following main features: problem diagnosis of the traditional governance model, structural implications, the position of public sector management, the nature of policy making, and the definition of the public interest (as summarised in Table 1).

As already indicated, the market model was the dominant new governance model in the 1980s and 1990s. The principal problem diagnosis with respect to the traditional state model is that a state monopoly does not provide enough incentives for the state's employees to work efficiently. The most important structural changes to implement as a consequence of this diagnosis are decentralisation of policy making and privatisation of public services. Further, it encourages the introduction of private sector management approaches and styles in public sector organisations, especially with respect to personnel and financial management. When it comes to policy making the market model suggests that autonomous organisations should make and implement policies for citizens who are seen primarily as consumers or customers. Finally, the public interest is assumed to benefit the most by the following outcomes of the use of market mechanisms in the public sector: low costs and more choice for citizens, and accountability taking place through market interactions, instead of through ministers and parliament.

Table 1. Summary of four alternative governance models

	Market government	*Participative government*	*Flexible government*	*Deregulated government*
Principal problem diagnosis	Monopoly	Hierarchy	Permanence	Internal regulation
Structure	Decentralisation	Flatter organisations	Virtual organisations	Power hierarchy
Management	Pay for performance; other private sector techniques	TQM; teams	Managing temporary personnel	Greater managerial freedom
Policy making	Internal markets; market incentives	Consultation; negotiation	Experimentation	Active bureaucracy
Public interest	Low cost	Involvement; consultation	Low cost; coordination	Creativity; activism

Source: Peters 2001: 21

The second model identified is the participative governance model. This model is almost the ideological antithesis of the market model. As indicated by Peters (2001: 50) "the political ideologies that most of its advocates use to justify their concept reject the market and search for more political, democratic and collective mechanisms for sending signals to government". Concerning the traditional governance model, the principal problem is perceived to be the hierarchical, top-down nature of traditional public sector bureaucracies and organisations. Further, it advocates the development of flatter organisational structures, and wants to stimulate the direct involvement of social interests of citizens in governance in general and organisational management in particular. Policy making is supposed to take place through consultation and negotiation, at various levels, including organisational policy-making processes. Finally, this model assumes that the public interest is served best through maximum involvement of citizens in policy making and management processes. This can take place through various mechanisms such as openness, bottom-up policy processes, and referenda. An interesting question in this respect is: Who is the 'public' in this?

The third alternative stands for a flexible government. According to Peters (2001: 77) "at a more basic level a flexible government is simply one that is capable

of responding effectively to new challenges and of surviving in the face of change".
At a more conceptual level it sees the permanence of public sector structures as the
main 'evil' of the traditional governance model. As a consequence, it promotes the
'frequent termination' of existing government agencies and organisations. Some
types of the structurally impermanent organisations that arise as a consequence have
been characterised as 'virtual organisations' (Bleecker 1994). According to
Bleecker, through the use of information, communication and technology,
corporations as well as public sectors will increasingly be defined by collaborative
networks linking many (up to tens of thousands) people together. Management in
this model is taking place through the use of temporary personnel. This has
advantages – cost reduction – but also potential disadvantages – reduced
commitment of personnel. With respect to policy making, an experimental approach
is advocated (see e.g. Campbell 1988). Since governments do not always know what
works and what does not work they may as well set up policy experiments. Finally,
with respect to the public interest, this model has the least explicit expression of
what the public interest stands for. It assumes that it is in the interest of the public
that management and personnel costs are low, that a flexible government is more
innovative, and communicates more effectively with the public.

The fourth and final model is the one advocating deregulation. The problem of
the traditional model that deregulation is supposed to address is that the "internal
regulation of government prevents it from achieving its purposes as efficiently or as
effectively as it might" (Peters 2001: 98). Concerning structure, the main aspect to
highlight is that, in the deregulation model, hierarchy is more important than in the
other three models, since this model puts a lot of value on strong management and
leadership that can rather autonomously and creatively benefit from the removal of
internal regulations. The consequences for policy making are a 'shift' in the
"procedures by which decisions are made and laws implemented" from the
politicians to the bureaucrats. This does not imply a diminished role for politicians,
but a different role. They would be responsible for determining the broad frames
within which policy would be made from the bottom up with an active role for civil
servants, because of their substantive knowledge and their close contacts with the
field. Finally, when it comes to the public interest the model assumes that
deregulation stimulates creativity, and promotes an active involvement in public
sector management and policy making of managers as well as individual citizens.

Even though there is some overlap in various bits and pieces among the four
models, they can be distinguished on the basis of their different problem diagnosis
with respect to the functioning of the traditional governance model and their ideas
about the nature of the governance reforms necessary to address the problems. What
is also of relevance for the discussion in this book is that, even though in governance
reforms one can observe various elements of different models implemented at the
same time, these combinations are not always compatible in practice (Peters 2001:
95).

A relevant example of the incompatibility of certain elements of the models is
that, with respect to the nature and role of public sector management, the market
model and the deregulation model appear to clash. The introduction of the market
model has led to a replacement of existing rules by new rules, for example,

procedural control rules 'copied' from private sector firms. For deregulators this is not acceptable, since different rules do not necessarily mean better rules. According to deregulators, public sector managers should be allowed to operate without externally imposed regulations, even though this might mean that they might make mistakes. Market proponents want to make sure that the market functions optimally. Therefore, they want to regulate the working of the market in the public arena and minimise the leeway for errors of public sector managers.

Another example concerns the incompatibility of the proposals regarding the structure of the market model and the ideas with respect to policy making of the deregulation model. Peters (2001: 110–111) even goes so far as claiming that "their simultaneous acceptance may be the worst of all possible worlds". Decentralised small organisational units (market model) that are not coordinated and have weak evaluation mechanisms and few ex ante controls (as would be the case in the deregulation model) will operate in a fragmented way and not as integrated government organisations.

How do Peters' 'first-wave governance models' compare to the 'state/higher education models' mentioned above? First, the terminology. Van Vught and his colleagues talked about steering models, Olsen and his followers referred to state models, while Peters focuses on governance. Without wanting to give too much meaning to the choice of terminology, the term steering was introduced at a time (1970s–1980s) when the belief in the 'makeability' of society was still supported by many political actors. A strong state was supposed to steer society in certain directions, either directly or indirectly. Olsen's discussion of state models (1988) came at a time when the belief in the 'makeability' of society was returning. There was a growing insight into the ineffectiveness of the way in which the traditional state operated. However, there was not yet enough knowledge available on the nature and effectiveness of alternative ways of organising the state's functions. This knowledge has become available throughout the 1990s and into the early part of this century. Consequently, a renewed scholarly interest in the governance of public sectors can be observed based on the new insights into the pros and cons of the new governance approaches, as well as the traditional governance model. This interest is now also beginning to infiltrate the field of higher education research.

Second, and more importantly, Peters' governance models are alternatives to the traditional governance approach, while in Van Vught's and Olsen's conceptualisations there was not yet the clear recognition that the traditional model was 'to be left behind'. Van Vught pointed to the self-regulation model as being more effective, but his arguments were mainly theoretical and, therefore, did not include other alternatives to the traditional model of central rational planning. Olsen did not present his models as alternatives to the traditional governance approach. He assumed that various combinations of the elements of his four models could be found in various countries over time.

Peters' analyses of the shifts in governance approaches can be related to the two models of Van Vught and the four models of Olsen (see Table 2). As indicated, Van Vught's central planning (or state control) model can be seen as referring to the traditional system-level governance approach in higher education. His self-regulation (or state supervision) model has most in common with the deregulation model, but also contains elements of the market approach. Olsen's sovereign state model as well as his institutional state model can be regarded as representing the traditional governance approach. His corporatist model has most in common with the participative governance model of Peters, while his (super)market model obviously can be seen as a variation of the market model that Peters described.

This comparison makes it clear that the more detailed and empirically better informed analysis of the introduction of alternatives to the traditional governance (steering, or state) model made in the late 1990s, early 2000s is also relevant to our examination of the governance changes in higher education, in general, and the management reforms, as discussed in this book, in particular. For example, in the models identified by Peters, management reforms are not isolated phenomena, they are part of governance reforms. In his models, Peters relates management reforms, amongst other things, to structural changes and changes in policy making. In addition, in order to understand the nature of management reforms, it is important to know the problem diagnosis with respect to the governance approach that is to be replaced.

Table 2. Higher education governance models compared

	State control (Neave and Van Vught 1991)	State supervision (Neave and Van Vught 1991)	Sovereign state (Olsen 1988)	Institutional state (Olsen 1988)	Corporate state (Olsen 1988)	Supermarket (Olsen 1988)
Nature of governance model	Traditional	Alternative (deregulation and market models)	Traditional	Traditional	Alternative (participative model)	Alternative (market models)
Main governance mechanism	State control	Self-regulation	State dominance	Institutional protection	Network consultation	Market
Main role of institutional management	Manage the institution as a state agency	Promote an optimal institution–environment relationship	Be accountable to state authorities	Promote the interests of the institution	Coordinate interests of involved stakeholders	Promote the interests of the market

4.2. Reflective Remarks

A number of final remarks before a more detailed discussion of the management part of the governance reforms will now be presented. First, Peters' conceptualisation of governance shifts suggests that the governance reforms that started 20 to 30 years ago have not yet reached their final stage. The initial, mainly ideological, reforms have developed into more pragmatic, continuing adaptations of public sector governance. Also with respect to higher education one can observe that there has not been a one-time-only introduction of new management structures, but a continuing adaptation of the way in which the management function in higher education institutions is organised.

Second, in Peters' work NPM is part of the market model. This would imply that not all the management reforms in higher education could be called examples of NPM. However, as discussed in more detail in the introduction to this book, it has to be recognised that NPM has been used in many different ways also in higher education. NPM has been used for a specific type of management innovation, for example, the application of specific private sector management tools in the public sector. However, NPM is also interpreted more ideologically to refer to all management reforms that have taken place in the framework of the replacement of the traditional governance approach. Therefore, in using the term NPM in the field of higher education, it is important to clarify what is being referred to, that is, a specific interpretation of the terms, or the broad, ideological meaning of them.

Third, different governance reform models imply different emphases on the main reform features. For example, the deregulation model as previously mentioned emphasises "the procedures by which decisions are made and laws implemented". It focuses mainly on the implications of reform policy making, and less on structure and management consequences. The participative model is most focused on the management and policy-making dimensions of governance, and less on structure. The market approach emphasises structure and management, and has apparent problems with the policy-making dimension in public governance. The latter is, amongst other things, related to the tension between coordination and control. Also the flexible government approach is least clear in its implications for policy making and most clear when it comes to structural and managerial consequences.

Finally, it has to be kept in mind that Peters' models are based on his analyses of governance shifts, in general, and not on the specific governance shifts with respect to higher education. As a consequence, some of the characteristics that he emphasises in the discussion of his models (see Table 1) do not seem to 'fit' the governance shifts with respect to higher education. For example, while the participative model is in many respects recognisable in certain higher education systems,[4] it did not lead to a management structure in which TQM was used prominently.

It can be argued that these four points relate to the issue that in governance – and with respect to management structures as part of governance models – 'one size does not fit all'. As is indicated by Peters (2001: 96) the 'one size fits all' approach to governance change, which is dominant even in the academic 'governance reform literature', represents "an oversimplification of the complex dynamics of the public sector and the efforts to make it work better".

As a transition to the next section on higher education management, an example of such a 'one size fits all' approach can be given from the well-known *Reinventing Government* book by Osborne and Gaebler (1993). According to these authors (p. 285):

> Markets are to social and economic activity what computers are to information: using prices as their primary mechanism, they send and receive signals almost instantaneously, processing millions of inputs efficiently and allowing millions of people to make decisions for themselves. Consider our higher education system:

> millions of students (and their parents) sift through volumes of information, compare prices, and finally choose their preferred schools. The colleges and universities do the same with student records, references and applications. And a match occurs. Would some kind of administrative mechanism – such as the assignment of students to the college nearest their home – work better?

This quote is in line with some of the arguments made above. First, the advantages of a market approach are almost unquestioned by its proponents. Second, in the management literature very few conceptualisation efforts can be found. Third, it is assumed that one specific model is best under all circumstances, in other words, one model fits all. Finally, the proponents of the market model assume that, with respect to any public service, information on all alternative options is available in an optimal and transparent way. Interestingly, it was this notion of rationality in governance that was rejected by Van Vught (1989) and other proponents of the self-regulation model in higher education.

5. HIGHER EDUCATION MANAGEMENT

How do the 'governance shifts' discussed above relate to the management reforms in higher education? Let us start with the specific literature on higher education management. In the USA, various authors starting with Rourke and Brooks (1966) have written since the end of the 1960s on the management revolution in higher education. Their message was that, as a result of some fundamental changes in American higher education, amongst other things the massification of higher education, higher education institutions were forced to develop an explicit management capacity. One of the most well-known authors in this was George Keller (1983) who promoted the use of strategic planning for academic management purposes. Keller's starting-point was that "American universities constitute one of the largest industries in the nation, but are among the least businesslike and well managed of all organizations" (Keller 1983). While Keller presented a detailed academic management model in his book, he did not analyse the nature of the underlying shifts in various governance, administrative and management structures in higher education. Why institutional management was regarded to be the answer to the administrative challenges of universities and colleges was not taken beyond the statement that, like any other business, higher education institutions should be managed professionally. Also, the question of why 'management' had never been an intrinsic part of the institutional structure in higher education was not addressed explicitly by Keller or any of his contemporary authors on management in higher education.

How is this question of the rise of institutional management dealt with in the 'classical' higher education literature? In his seminal book *The Higher Education System*, Clark (1983) does not refer to a 'management revolution' in higher education. However, he does indicate that the institutional administration is 'on the rise'. In his discussion of the cultural dimension in higher education he suggests that:

> least noticed in the subcultures of the academic enterprises and systems but of growing importance is the separation of administrative cultures from those of faculty and

students. As cadres of professional experts replace the professor-amateur, in campus,
provincial and national administration, a separate set of roles and interests emerge
around which separate definitions of the institution form (Clark 1983: 89).

A more explicit debate on the changes in the management structure and
functions in higher education can be found in Becher and Kogan's 1992 work
Process and Structure in Higher Education. Their discussion of institutional
management in higher education reflects the transition taking place in the 1980s
when management was changing from a second order set of activities into a self-
justifying activity (Becher and Kogan 1992: 181). Of relevance to the discussion in
this chapter is that Becher and Kogan explicitly relate the shift towards a self-
justified management function in higher education to the shift in system-level
governance of which the Jarratt Committee was a prominent symbol. They indicate
that:

> The Jarratt Report (1985) attempted to promote management into a self-justifying
> activity and allowed that it might take on imperatives of its own – with the implication
> that they could be endorsed separately from higher education's primary objectives, and
> could be distributed hierarchically (Becher and Kogan 1992: 181).

Becher and Kogan discuss the transition in the institutional management culture,
function and structures that Clark only referred to in 1983. In his 1998 book on
entrepreneurial higher education, Clark clearly shows the way the higher education
world has changed in the 15 years since the publication of *The Higher Education
System*. While in 1983 Clark points to the separation of academic and administrative
cultures and roles, in 1998 he discusses the importance of the intertwining of
managerial and academic values in what he calls the 'strengthened steering core' of
the entrepreneurial university (p. 137). The main challenge for current universities,
according to Clark (1998: 129–132), is the demand–response imbalance. The
traditional university governance structure, as part of a traditional government
governance approach, has become a constraint in responding to the growing external
demands with respect to higher education. Rigidity and maintenance of existing
structures are the result, instead of stimulating and supporting innovative behaviour.
Clark (1998: 131–132) indicates that the nature of the involvement of academics in
university decision making is to be blamed instead of the nature and role of the
management or administration:

> Elaborated collegial authority leads to sluggish decision-making: 50 to 100 and more
> central committees have the power to study, delay, and veto. The senate becomes more
> of a bottleneck than the administration. Evermore complex and specialized, elaborated
> basic units – faculties, schools, and departments – tend to become separate entities with
> individual privileges, shaping the university into a federation in which major and minor
> parts barely relate to one another.

Consequently, the starting-point for any university restructuring should be the
strengthening of the management, which in Clark's terms includes the fusion of
"new managerial values with traditional academic ones" (Clark 1998: 137). This
type of analysis, that is, a "strengthened administrative core, then, is a mandatory
feature of a heightened capability to confront the root imbalance of modern
universities" (Clark 1998: 138) was unthinkable for Clark and other 'classic' higher
education authors in the 1970s and early 1980s.

The reasons for this dramatic change can partly be found in the changes in the context of higher education. In addition, there are many internal factors that are of relevance for understanding the changes with respect to the management culture, function and structures in higher education institutions. It goes beyond the aims of this chapter to discuss and analyse all relevant factors. The changes in governance approaches with respect to higher education discussed here provide one contextual change that adds to our understanding of the nature of the management changes in higher education, even though it will be obvious that there is not a one-to-one relationship between shifts in governance and changes in institutional management in higher education. In the other chapters in this book, the interested reader will find discussions of other factors and perspectives of relevance for understanding the management changes in higher education institutions. In the remainder of this chapter, the so-called second round of governance reforms will be discussed briefly indicating the latest adaptations of governance models, in general, and their possible consequences for higher education, and higher education management in the years to come. In this, it has to be taken into account that we are still in the middle of this second round of reforms, so, contrary to the first round, there is not a lot of information available on the actual effects of the reforms in practice.

6. SECOND WAVE OF GOVERNANCE REFORMS

In the so-called second wave of governance reforms that, roughly speaking, started in the mid-1990s, the experiences from the first round of ideological reforms were taken into account. However, while the adaptations of the traditional governance approach continued in most countries, at least as important were the attempts to deal with the flaws of the alternative approaches (Peters 2001: 118–143). In this second round of reforms, emphasis seems to have shifted from promoting the use of 'markets' in public sector governance to measuring the performance and improving the accountability of public sector institutions. This implies in some respects a shift from mechanism, especially market, to outcome, especially performance or, in other terms, improving 'quality service' in the public sector. As such, the second round of reforms represents a shift from ideology driven reform to more pragmatic reforms of governance.

This also has implications for the nature of further management reforms in higher education. Instead of institutional managers being judged mainly on the basis of the way they have implemented their part of the governance reform as such, attention has shifted to the way in which the performance of the institutions for which they are responsible has improved. This performance orientation should not be mixed up with the introduction of formal quality assessment mechanisms in European higher education in the late 1980s and early 1990s. The latter were in general the outcomes of negotiations between government and higher education as part of the introduction of some form of self-regulation. These quality assessment mechanisms were not focused on performance of higher education per se, but rather represented a shift in the responsibility for guaranteeing the quality of higher education from the government to the higher education institutions. Initially, they had a mixed aim of assessing the quality of teaching or research programmes for the sake of quality improvement as well as for accountability reasons (Frederiks, Westerheijden and Weusthof 1994). In the course of the 1990s, national governments took a more explicit interest in the performance of the higher education institutions especially from a funding perspective. However, with the exception of the public funding of university research in the United Kingdom, the outcomes of quality assessment are not used directly in any of the European higher education systems as the basis for the funding of teaching or research in higher education.

Since these 'second wave' reforms are still going on, there is not as much empirical information on the nature of the changes and their implications as has become available with respect to the first round of reforms. However, despite the many positive outcomes of the first round of reforms also in higher education, the notion that it is necessary to keep on changing management structures in order to move closer to an optimum in management functioning is visible. As indicated by Peters (2001: 141):

> the concept of continual improvement appears to be firmly lodged in the thinking of many managers and reformers in government. Whether that idea will eventually lead to disillusionment as the possibilities for managerial improvements become exhausted has yet to be seen, as there appear to be ever more avenues for effective change.

This 'trend' of continuous adaptation of managerial functions, cultures and structures can also be observed in higher education. The chapters in this book give a rich insight into the practice of this continuous reform. However, what is complicating the situation in higher education in comparison with other public sectors is, first, that in higher education institutions management is as such a relatively new function that is internally embedded in a democratic governance structure and a traditional administrative structure. Despite recent adaptations of these governance structures (Amaral, Jones and Karseth 2002) and a professionalisation of the university administration (Gornitzka, Kyvik and Larsen 1998), institutional managers at various levels are still caught between the horizontal academic decision-making practices and the hierarchical administrative traditions.

Second, institutional management has become a self-justified activity not only in the eyes of the institutional managers, but also from the perspective of external stakeholders such as the state authorities. Since for most academic staff of higher education institutions, institutional management remains a 'necessary evil' that they would rather do without. Many clashes between these two sets of perspectives can be observed in the day-to-day practice of universities and colleges.

Nonetheless, as discussed by Reed (2002) and Fulton in his chapter in this book, the management reforms in European higher education institutions have not been as extreme as in other public sectors, such as health care. One important aspect in this is the recruitment of new managers. For example, contrary to the health care sector, external recruitment of managers is still relatively rare in higher education. The consequence of this is that higher education managers share certain sets of professional and academic values with their academic colleagues inside their institution. It also implies that the negative aspects of external recruitment, that is, lack of organisational memory, an increase of errors and reduction of predictability, and reduction of managerial commitment to the institution (Chapman 2000), are affecting higher education institutions far less than other public sector organisations. While other public sector organisations try to learn from this 'first round reform' experience with respect to external management recruitment, and are trying to find a better balance between the advantages of internal managers and the strengths of externally recruited managers, higher education institutions have kept the advantages of internal recruitment.

7. CONCLUSION

In this chapter, the changes in institutional management structures in higher education have been discussed from the perspective of shifts in system-level governance arrangements. This implies that management structures in higher education institutions have been identified as specific governance arrangements that can be influenced by external actors such as governments. However, this does not imply that the government is an almighty actor that can deterministically prescribe changes in the management structures, culture and function of higher education institutions. Instead, it is assumed that government introduces, implicitly or explicitly, the regulatory, policy and funding frameworks within which the public sector higher education institutions are expected to introduce, adapt or strengthen their management structures.

For understanding the actual relationships between these external change expectations and the changes in the management structures in universities and colleges in practice, an important first step is to examine these external change expectations in more detail. The first attempts in the field of higher education research to analyse governance reforms with respect to higher education did not pay attention explicitly to the expectations concerning institutional management (see e.g. Maassen and Van Vught 1989, 1994; Van Vught 1989; Neave and Van Vught 1991). In this chapter, these initial analyses have been taken one step further. Governance reforms have been examined by focusing on the underlying problem diagnosis, the expectations with respect to structures, public management, and policy, and the public interest links of specific governance models (Table 1). In this examination, various questions were raised. What kind of management reforms do governments have in mind when they introduce new governance models? In addition: How are these expectations operationalised in the form of formal and informal governance arrangements? How much leeway do the universities and colleges have in responding to the external expectations? And: How strict are governments in dealing with universities and colleges that do not live up to the change expectations?

For any given higher education system the answers to these kinds of questions will give an indication of the nature of the actual management changes in higher education institutions, as well as the variation between the institutions with regard to these changes.

One of the conclusions to be drawn on the basis of the discussion in this chapter is that market models of governance should not be identified with deregulation models of governance. In fact, Peters (2001) argues that these two models are even incompatible when it comes to public management as a specific governance arrangement. This conclusion is, amongst other things, of importance for understanding the frustrations many institutional leaders and managers in higher education have uttered over the last 15 years with respect to the interference by government in higher education management.

The initial wave of governance reforms in higher education carried a number of elements of the deregulation governance model, and these reforms were often characterised by publicly outspoken 'guarantees' of the involved government that one of the aims of the reform was to enlarge institutional autonomy. While in some countries this may initially indeed have been the case (Maassen and Van Vught 1989), the initial 'purely' higher education reforms were gradually integrated into the broader overall public sector governance reforms. In Europe, certainly at the beginning of the 1990s, these were characterised by an emphasis on market models of governance. The institutional leaders and managers in higher education still assumed that the 'deregulation governance shift' that they thought higher education was experiencing meant an enlargement of institutional autonomy or, more accurately, an authority shift from the government to the institutional leaders and managers. However, the use of market models of governance implied that the government was introducing new regulations for public sector management, including the management of higher education institutions. The main reason for this is that the involved governments wanted to minimise the risk of market failure, and therefore had to make sure that the public sector managers used their enlarged authority in line with market model expectations.

For more than two decades, many higher education systems around the globe have been experimenting with new management structures. We are only at the beginning of examining this experience more thoroughly. With respect to these new institutional management structures, three sets of valid research questions can be identified. The first set has to do with describing and analysing what is actually going on in practice. Examples are: "What is the nature of the 'management revolution' in higher education?" and "What are the basic characteristics of new management structures and practices introduced in higher education?" The second set of questions should focus on the impact of the shifts in governance on institutional management structures: "How do new system-level governance approaches relate to management changes in higher education institutions?" and "What other factors influence changes in management structures in higher education institutions?"

The third set relates to the difference management changes make: "Does the introduction of new management structures lead to the expected rise in effectiveness, efficiency, quality or responsiveness of universities and colleges?" and "Do the new management structures benefit higher education institutions and the general public more than the structures that are being abolished?"

The contributors to this book attempt to provide answers to these types of questions in various ways. It can be expected that these questions will be vigorously pursued by students of higher education management in the years to come, in the hope that their resolution will make continuing management reforms in higher education all the more effective.

NOTES

1   I am grateful to Alberto Amaral, Harry de Boer and Lynn Meek for helpful suggestions and comments to previous versions of this chapter.
2   The governance reform process in the new Central and Eastern European democracies has been characterised as a process continuously aimed at 'changing the changes' (see Maassen and Cloete 2002: 33–35).
3   For an elaborate discussion of the applicability of Olsen's state models in the field of higher education research, see Gornitzka (1999).
4   See, for example, the cooperative governance approach in post-1994 South African higher education as discussed in Cloete and Kulati's chapter in this book and in Cloete et al. (2002).

REFERENCES

Amaral, A., G.A. Jones and B. Karseth (eds). *Governing Higher Education: National Perspectives on Institutional Governance*. Dordrecht: Kluwer Academic Publishers, 2002.
Amaral, A. and A. Magalhães. "On Markets, Autonomy and Regulation. The Janus Head Revisited." *Higher Education Policy* 14 (2001): 1–14.
Ashby, W.R. *An Introduction to Cybernetics*. London: Chapman and Hall, 1956.
Becher, T. and M. Kogan. *Process and Structure in Higher Education*. 2nd edn. London: Routledge, 1992.
Beer, Stafford. *Platform for Change*. New York: John Wiley, 1975.
Birnbaum, R. *How Colleges Work: The Cybernetics of Academic Organization and Leadership*. San Francisco: Jossey-Bass, 1988.
Bleecker, S.E. "The Virtual Organization." *The Futurist* 28 (1994): 9–13.
Campbell, D.T. "The Experimenting Society." In Campbell, C. (edited by S. Overman). *Methodology and Epistemology in the Social Sciences: Selected Essays*. Chicago: University of Chicago Press, 1988, 290–315.
Chapman, R.A. *Public Service Ethics for a New Millennium*. Aldershot, UK: Dartmouth, 2000.
Clark, B.R. *The Higher Education System. Academic Organization in Cross-National Perspective*. Berkeley: University of California Press, 1983.
Clark, B.R. *Creating Entrepreneurial Universities: Organizational Pathways of Transformation*. Oxford: Pergamon Press, 1998.
Cloete, N., R. Fehnel, P. Maassen, T. Moja, H. Perold and T. Gibbon (eds). *Transformation in Higher Education. Global Pressures and Local Realities in South Africa*. Lansdowne, SA: Juta and Company, 2002.
Cohen, J. and J. Rogers. "Solidarity, Democracy, Association." *Politische Vierteljahrschrift Sonderheft* 25 (1994): 136–159.
Frederiks, M., D. Westerheijden and P. Weusthof. "Stakeholders in Quality. Improvement or Accountability in Five Quality Assessment Systems in Higher Education." In Goedegebuure, L. and F. van Vught (eds). *Comparative Policy Studies in Higher Education*. Utrecht: LEMMA, 1994, 95–127.
Gallagher, M. "Modern University Governance – A National Perspective." Paper presented at the *Conference on the Idea of the University: Enterprise or Academy?* The Australia Institute and Manning Clark House, Canberra, 26 July, 2001.
Goedegebuure, L., F. Kaiser, P. Maassen, V.L. Meek, F. van Vught and E. de Weert (eds). *Higher Education Policy: An International Comparative Perspective*. Oxford: Pergamon Press, 1994.
Gornitzka, Å. "Governmental Policies and Organisational Change in Higher Education." *Higher Education* 38 (1999): 5–31.
Gornitzka, Å., S. Kyvik and I.M. Larsen. "The Bureaucratisation of Universities." *Minerva* 36 (1998): 21–47.
Gornitzka, Å. and P. Maassen. "Hybrid Steering Approaches with Respect to European Higher Education." *Higher Education Policy* 13 (2000): 267–285.

Keller, G. *Academic Strategy: The Management Revolution in American Higher Education*. Baltimore: Johns Hopkins University Press, 1983.

Kogan, Maurice. "Academic and Administrative Interface." In Henkel, M. and B. Little (eds). *Changing Relationships Between Higher Education and the State*. London: Jessica Kingsley, 1999, 263–279.

Lindblom, Ch.E. "The Science of Muddling Through." *Public Administration* 19 (1959): 79–99.

Lindblom, Ch.E. *Intelligence of Democracy*. New York: Free Press, 1965.

Maassen, P. *Governmental Steering and the Academic Culture. The Intangibility of the Human Factor in Dutch and German Universities*. Utrecht: De Tijdstroom, 1996.

Maassen, P. and N. Cloete. "Global Reform Trends in Higher Education." In Cloete, N., R. Fehnel, P. Maassen, T. Moja, H. Perold and T. Gibbon (eds). *Transformation in Higher Education. Global Pressures and Local Realities in South Africa*. Lansdowne, SA: Juta and Company, 2002, 13–58.

Maassen, P. and F. van Vught. "An Intriguing Janus-Head. The Two Faces of the New Governmental Strategy for Higher Education in the Netherlands." *European Journal of Education* 23 (1988): 65–76.

Maassen, P. and F. van Vught. *Dutch Higher Education in Transition*. Culemborg: LEMMA, 1989.

Maassen, P. and F. van Vught. "Alternative Models of Governmental Steering in Higher Education. An Analysis of Steering Models and Policy-instruments in Five Countries." In Goedegebuure, L. and F. van Vught (eds). *Comparative Policy Studies in Higher Education*. Utrecht: LEMMA, 1994, 35–65.

Meek, V.L. "Changing Patterns in Modes of Co-ordination of Higher Education." In Enders, J. and O. Fulton (eds). *Higher Education in a Globalising World. International Trends and Mutual Observations. A Festschrift in Honour of Ulrich Teichler*. Dordrecht: Kluwer Academic Publishers, 2002, 53–73.

Meyerson, M. and E.C. Banfield. *Politics, Planning and the Public Interest*. Glencoe: Free Press, 1955.

Neave, G. "Higher Education Policy as an Exercise in Contemporary History." *Higher Education* 32 (1996): 403–415.

Neave, G. "The Evaluative State Reconsidered." *European Journal of Education* 33 (1998): 265–284.

Neave, G. and F. van Vught. *Prometheus Bound, The Changing Relationship Between Government and Higher Education in Western Europe*. Oxford: Pergamon Press, 1991.

Olsen, J.P. "Administrative Reform and Theories of Organization." In Campbell, C. and B.G. Peters (eds). *Organizing Governance, Governing Organizations*. Pittsburgh: University of Pittsburgh Press, 1988.

Osborne, D. and T. Gaebler. *Reinventing Government. How the Entrepreneurial Spirit is Transforming the Public Sector*. New York: Plume/Penguin, 1993.

Peters, B.G. *Institutional Theory in Political Science: The 'New Institutionalism'*. London: Continuum, 1999.

Peters, B.G. *The Future of Governing*. 2nd edn, revised. Lawrence, KS: University Press of Kansas, 2001.

Popper, K. *The Poverty of Historicism*. London: Routledge and Kegan Paul, 1957.

Reed, M.I. "New Managerialism, Professional Power and Organisational Governance in UK Universities: A Review and Assessment." In Amaral, A., G.A. Jones and B. Karseth (eds). *Governing Higher Education: National Perspectives on Institutional Governance*. Dordrecht: Kluwer Academic Publishers, 2002, 163–185.

Reed, M.I., V.L. Meek and G.A. Jones. "Introduction." In Amaral, A., G.A. Jones and B. Karseth (eds). *Governing Higher Education: National Perspectives on Institutional Governance*. Dordrecht: Kluwer Academic Publishers, 2002, xv–xxxi.

Rourke, F.E. and G.E. Brooks. *The Managerial Revolution in Higher Education*. Baltimore: The Johns Hopkins Press, 1966.

Steinbrunner, J.D. *The Cybernetic Theory of Decision: New Dimensions of Political Analysis*. Princeton: Princeton University Press, 1974.

Tolbert, P.S. and L.G. Zucker. "The Institutionalization of Institutional Theory." In Clegg, S., C. Hardy and W.R. Nord (eds). *Handbook of Organization Studies*, Thousand Oaks, CA: Sage, 1996, 175–190.

Torres, C.A. and D. Schugurensky. "The Political Economy of Higher Education in the Era of Neoliberal Globalization: Latin America in Comparative Perspective." *Higher Education* 43 (2002): 429–455.

Trommel, W.A. *Korter arbeidsleven: de wording van een rationale mythe (Shorter Working Life: The Birth of a Rational Myth)*. The Hague: SDU, 1995.

Trommel, W. and R. van der Veen. "Sociological Perspectives on Institutions and Neo-institutionalism." In Steunenberg, B. and F. van Vught (eds). *Public Institutions and Public Policy. Perspectives on European Decision Making.* Dordrecht: Kluwer Academic Publishers, 1997, 45–67.

Van Heffen, O., J. Verhoeven and K. de Wit. "Higher Education Policies and Institutional Response in Flanders: Instrumental Analysis and Cultural Theory." In Jongbloed, B., P. Maassen and G. Neave (eds). *From the Eye of the Storm. Higher Education's Changing Institution.* Dordrecht: Kluwer Academic Publishers, 1999, 263–295.

Van Kersbergen, K. and F. van Waarden. *Shifts in Governance: Problems of Legitimacy and Accountability.* Paper on the theme 'Shifts in Governance' as part of the Strategic Plan 2002–2005 of the Netherlands Organization for Scientific Research (NWO). The Hague: Netherlands Organization for Scientific Research (NWO), 2001.

Van Vught, F. (ed.). *Governmental Strategies and Innovation in Higher Education.* London: Jessica Kingsley, 1989.

Zucker, L.G. "Postscript: Microfoundations of Institutional Thought." In Powell, W.W. and P.J. DiMaggio (eds). *The New Institutionalism in Organizational Analysis.* Chicago: University of Chicago Press, 1991, 103–107.

ARI SALMINEN

NEW PUBLIC MANAGEMENT AND FINNISH PUBLIC SECTOR ORGANISATIONS: THE CASE OF UNIVERSITIES

1. INTRODUCTION

This chapter deals with the new public management (NPM) doctrine in Finnish public sector organisations with special emphasis on the higher education sector.

As several public administration scholars have stated, the rise of NPM is one of the most striking international megatrends in the contemporary public sector. NPM consists of several closely related administrative doctrines which have dominated the bureaucratic reform agenda in OECD countries for more than a decade. As Ingraham (1997) and Considine and Painter (1997) state, the term 'managerialism' is very close to the term 'new public management', particularly when considering public administration reforms after the late 1970s (see also Aucoin 1990; Pollitt 1990; Temmes 1998; Klausen and Ståhlberg 1998).

This is also the case in Finland. As many Finnish researchers emphasise, the essential reason for adopting NPM-type reform policy in Finland has been the need to be detached from the heavy, bureaucratic tradition of earlier years in order to improve efficiency, and to find more flexible ways to provide public services (Temmes 1998).

This chapter will explore a number of issues. Firstly, a short description of the core elements of NPM is given. Secondly, an analysis is undertaken of how these elements emerge in the Finnish public administration and how they impact on Finnish public sector organisations. The analysis of these issues is based mostly on my previous research.

Finally, NPM components are considered in relation to public administration. The context is Finnish higher education institutions which consist of universities and polytechnics. However, polytechnics are excluded from this analysis.

One central assumption of the analysis is that many of the changes in the structures, processes and organisational cultures of Finnish public administration are explained by the influence of the NPM doctrine. Therefore, it is necessary to begin with a short description of the doctrine.

2. NEW PUBLIC MANAGEMENT – WHAT IS IT ALL ABOUT?

A well-known definition of NPM has been presented by Christopher Hood (1991: 4–5). The definition covers the doctrine's main components which are: professional

A. Amaral et al. (eds.), The Higher Education Managerial Revolution?, 55–69.
© 2003 *Kluwer Academic Publishers. Printed in the Netherlands.*

management in the public sector; standards and measures of performance; output controls; emphasis on the shift to disaggregation of units in the public sector; competition; private sector management practice; and stress on discipline and parsimony in resource use. The NPM doctrine underlines, on the one hand, professional management and high discretionary power to achieve results ('empowerment of managers') and, on the other, the decentralisation of managerial authority over the use of allocated resources in the context of greater accountability for results (Aucoin 1995: 9).

The components of the NPM doctrine can be traced back to public choice theory. This theory has had a remarkable impact on critical thinking about governmental activities. For example, William Niskanen's (1971) idea of the 'budget-maximising bureaucrat' has been used to explain the uncontrolled growth of the state. The 'government that works better and costs less' slogan expressed efforts to reduce public spending (DeLeon and Denhardt 2000: 90).

NPM is no longer a newcomer among management doctrines. Another doctrine for new and future public service is presented in the literature on public administration (see Denhardt and Denhardt 2000; Ingraham, Selden and Moynihan 2000). The significant elements of the reforms in the public sector are the restructuring and reinventing of the government's role and improving services with fewer resources. Governments have to enhance new models for citizen participation. As discussed later, various criticisms have been directed at the values and normative elements of the doctrine.

As Peters and Savoie (1995) stress, citizens want more direct influence over policies. Claims for enhancing popular participation have become louder since the reinvention movement. Peters (1995) sees here some paradoxes: governments should attempt to be more efficient and more responsive to the market. On the one hand, governmental officials are told to be entrepreneurial and responsive to market signals and, on the other, the same leaders are being told to be more sensitive to public demands and to the wishes of lower echelon workers.

The critical notions of public choice theorists (e.g. Niskanen, Tullock, Downs) and others have been used as the 'scientific' basis for the ideologically grounded new right critique of government and public administration. This ideological change has occurred even in places where public service production has been highly valued, Finland included. The claimed inefficiency and unresponsiveness of state services should be met partly by an infusion of market concepts and disciplines in the public sector, and partly by transferring some tasks to the private sector (Self 2000; Brereton and Temple 1999).

Still, how do we understand the rise of the NPM doctrine? As shown in the case of Finland, one explanation is the emergence of strong stagflation in the late 1970s, combined with lower economic growth and rising public spending. We can assume that if the willingness to pay for public services diminishes, the legitimacy of 'big government' diminishes and public production of welfare becomes less popular. One can also then assume that market-based service production will replace public services (Salminen et al. 2000).

The Keynesian welfare state model emphasised the interventionist state and the expanded role of the public sector on welfare provision. Liberalism and right wing criticism claimed that welfare services produced by the state were not the most adequate way of providing welfare. These claims have been strengthened by various factors. One which has gained ground since the 1980s and promoted by Thatcherism and Reaganism is the powerful ideology of individualism and its stress on individual freedom.

The most obvious criticism of traditional public sector management practices is the rising cost of state welfare as a proportion of national income during a period of relative economic stagnation. As we have seen during the past decades, criticism of state welfare has had various implications for public sector governance such as provision–production split, downsizing of government activities, privatisation, re-regulation and the rather extensive use of market-type mechanisms (Brereton and Temple 1999: 456–457; Salminen and Niskanen 1996).

3. THE EMERGENCE OF PUBLIC SECTOR REFORMS IN FINLAND

3.1. The Welfare Model

How has NPM emerged in Finnish public administration? Obviously, the image of the Finnish welfare model remains far removed from the NPM model. As I have stated in my previous studies (e.g. Salminen 2001), the Finnish model in the European context has rested on such characteristics as democracy and parliamentarianism, a multi-party system and large majority political coalitions in government, as well as strong local self-government with municipalities playing a key role in welfare provision. A mixture of public services and social benefits is intended for the entire population. Publicly financed welfare services cover social security, health care and education, and include reallocative social benefits and high taxation.

The development of the Finnish welfare state has been a process of gradual evolution from the end of the 1950s to the beginning of the 1990s. Towards the latter part of this period, the welfare model faced many financial problems. The massive build-up of the welfare state from the 1960s to the end of the 1980s resulted in the growth of bureaucratic features in Finnish administration and management. Since the end of the 1980s, Finland's public administration has been affected by global managerial trends. The reform of Finnish public administration during the 1990s has more or less followed international trends (Temmes 1998: 448; see also Salminen 1991; Ahonen and Salminen 1997).

Public sector welfare functions have continually expanded. By the late 1990s, the growth of public expenditure in relation to the GNP increased to over 50%. The figures peaked at the beginning of the 1990s when public sector expenditure comprised more than 60% of GNP. The proportion of the labour force in the public sector was also rather high. In 1990, the total number of public sector personnel was 645,000 decreasing to 544,000 in 2000. The change in employment status of public sector personnel has been remarkable. Core staff dependent on the state budget have gradually decreased from 230,000 in the late 1980s to 125,000 at the beginning of 2000.

At its peak, nearly one in every four employed persons was working in the state government or a municipality. Taxation rates were high, as well. This was caused by the country's economic crises, unemployment and economic depression.

It should be noted that the implementation of reforms in Finland has taken place in the context of political and government policy consensus. For some time, new management reforms have been on the political agenda. Key concepts are reflected in programmes of the following governments: PM Holkeri (1987–1991), Aho (1991–1995) and Lipponen I (1995–1999) and Lipponen II (1999–2003). It needs to be realised that when governments have had significant differences of opinion on reforms, the aim has been to achieve a workable compromise. Otherwise it is not possible to understand the massive 'reform industry' during these years. Reform has clearly been a success story for those implementing and supporting it.

3.2. The Change

In considering the changes and reforms of the Finnish public sector since the late 1980s, several factors need to be identified. All of the administrative and managerial reforms are not directly connected to the doctrine of NPM. The main trends in the changes and reforms are presented in Figure 1.

The so-called background factors start with the formation of the welfare state and end with the liberalisation of the Finnish financial market. As Figure 1 illustrates, this change leads to particular outcomes in Finnish society. Taxes were on the rise; public sector expenditure was curtailed; competitiveness of the public sector was developed etc. The next level of the diagram shows the most important impacts on public administration, including such issues as the role of the state, privatisation, performance management and future public service policies. The last level indicates the main influences on the politics and administration of the public sector. New political governance was sought; citizens' expectations towards public administration were developed; and the entrepreneurial spirit was encouraged in public bureaucracies.

4. NEW PUBLIC MANAGEMENT ORIENTATION IN FINNISH PUBLIC SECTOR ORGANISATIONS

The general changes and reforms of the Finnish public sector were briefly summarised above. Now, we must ask ourselves: How to consider the NPM orientation in the Finnish public sector organisations in more detail? This can be done by focusing on particular administrative and managerial changes and reforms. Short definitions are given in the following sections.

4.1. Performance Efforts

This first issue, performance efforts, is summarised in Table 1. The other topics described later are market orientation and personnel policy. Since the university sector is an integral part of public administration, all government-wide management reforms will always have an effect on universities.

As Table 1 shows, performance efforts cover a large variety of activities in the public sector. Most of these efforts can be found in the university sector as well. Some are, of course, more important than others.

Figure 1. Premises for the change and reforms of the Finnish public sector in the 1990s

Background factors
Formation of the welfare state; globalisation; participation in European integration; economic recession; deregulation and the liberalisation of financial markets.

Outcomes
Rising taxes; expenditure cuts; competitiveness in the public sector; fulfilment of European Monetary Union criteria; market-orientation and decentralisation efforts; state activities in the markets.

Impacts on public administration
Discussion of the tasks of the large state; the abolishment of central government bodies; market-type mechanisms in the public sector, privatisation of state-owned companies and sales of state assets; reconsideration of state subsidies systems for the municipalities; frame budgeting; framework steering and performance management; personnel policy reforms.

Influences on politics and administration
Searching for political governance instead of old steering models; a bureaucracy more sensitive to the citizens' direct expectations; clear and open private sector influence on several fields of administration; efforts to move from traditional bureaucratic to modern market values; efforts to move from controlling bureaucrats to entrepreneurial public managers.

Source: Salminen 2001: 151

Table 1. A summary of the most significant efforts in the performance area

Areas	Performance Efforts
Quality strategies in the public sector	Quality and customer orientation in the public services; freedom of choice; substitutive and supplementary ways for public service delivery; cost-consciousness
Marketisation processes	Decrease of public personnel; privatisation; competition and profit making; new forms of public entrepreneurship; new proliferation in public organisations
New management techniques	Management culture; performance management; administrative cost awareness; accountability; control; reporting; public service ethics

Source: Adapted from Salminen and Lähdesmäki 1999

On the one hand, there are alternative ways of describing performance, all of which need to recognise the importance of quality strategies, corporatisation processes and various management techniques. On the other, performance efforts are connected to the issue of organisational efficiency. In general, performance is connected to the 3–Es:

- economy, minimising the consumption of inputs
- efficiency, the input-output relationships
- effectiveness, achieved outcomes to compared expectations.

4.2. Market Orientation

The process of market orientation has touched public sector organisations, including higher education organisations. Speaking very generally, the total process can be described at the government level as follows: public agencies have turned into state enterprises; state enterprises have been incorporated; and companies are partly or fully privatised.

Market orientation refers to the partial relinquishing of traditional political and administrative governance in public organisations. The traditional role of public power is weakened, but its position may be strengthened in new ways, tasks and contexts. Market orientation emphasises economic effectiveness as the criterion of organisational reform. In this sense, market orientation is a narrow reform strategy. The public sector is adapted to a new competitive context and new economic situation. Of course, it is possible that this strategy may limit the tasks of the public sector and also prepare the ground for a policy with no political alternatives.

As shown earlier (Salminen and Viinamäki 2001: 32–35, 37–39 and 60–70) the privatisation process can be described as a pragmatic process. No comprehensive privatisation programme has been drawn up in Finland. The creation of state enterprises has remained at an intermediate stage in Finland. The aim has been to implement privatisation on an organisational case-by-case basis. For example, at their peak in 1990, state enterprises employed over 67,000 people. By 1997 the number of employees in state enterprises was less than five thousand. The majority of this staff is now employed by state-owned companies and privatised organisations (see also Temmes and Kiviniemi 1997: 58–59; Meklin and Ahonen 1998; National Audit Office 1998).

Some other conclusions can be drawn from the analysis of Salminen and Viinamäki (2001: 70–71):

> Market orientation has so far been a pragmatic issue ... There have been no serious ideological conflicts in the political fields ... Market orientation is not a uniform procedure, but it includes several models of varying degrees and varying effects. Market orientation is a strategic issue of the public sector. It provides market oriented organisations with international competition and an ability to adapt to international markets as well as the freedom to act in the new environment ...
>
> The organisations of the public sector and their guidance relationships change with market orientation. At their best, the organisations change so that the public sector focuses on its core activities. Operational freedom increases, although in some cases the traditional responsibilities of the public sector are retained to varying degrees.
>
> The focusing of market oriented organisations on their core activities simultaneously means differentiation in the tasks of the authorities. Surprisingly and unintentionally, this has resulted in the establishment of new authority organisations in the Finnish public sector. The establishment of the new organisations fragments the structure of the public sector and conflicts with the goals of minimising and simplifying public administration.

4.3. Personnel Policy and Management

The third issue is personnel policy and management. Here I very much follow the text of my previous publication (see Salminen 2001: 144, 148–149). Compared to the NPM doctrine (cf. Hood 1991 and 1996), the Finnish reform process can be analysed by asking whether the reforms have, in fact, increased management freedom, performance efforts and empowerment in the newly profiled public administration. A few research findings could be summarised from this analysis.

One of the important questions, particularly in terms of personnel management, is: How is the performance management system functioning in public administration? As some Finnish analyses have indicated, the effectiveness of performance management varies from one administrative unit to another (Lumijärvi and Salo 1997; Klausen and Magnier 1998; Tulosohjausjärjestelmän toimivuus ministeriöissä ja laitoksissa 1998).

Another conclusion is that performance management has had many positive impacts on public administration. There has been increasing decentralisation in decision making and the freedom to manoeuvre within the agencies has improved. There have also been indications of strengthening result orientation and cost awareness (Temmes and Kiviniemi 1997; Temmes 1998). The government has encouraged the state and local administrations to implement market-oriented management styles. At the same time, evaluations of the changes to personnel policy and management culture are needed in order to reconsider the future of relevant administrative policies.

New management reforms emphasise the public managers' personal responsibilities with respect to accountability for their organisations' results. The analysis has also claimed that external evaluation, monitoring, follow-up and critical information concerning efficiency indicators should be included in the reforms of decision making and management processes (Temmes 1998).

Salminen, Viinamäki and Lähdesmäki (2002) analysed the development of human resources in the Finnish government. The main theme of the report is 'doing more with less', which refers to the performance and efficiency requirements set for the public sector. Special attention was paid to three cases: the creation of state enterprises, the amalgamation of administrative units, and the practices of performance management.

The creation of state enterprises has reinforced the pressures on government to continue public administrative and personnel reforms. Amalgamation has decreased the number of administrative units and public sector personnel. As a development strategy, amalgamation enhances expert capacity in public organisations. In order to function well, performance management requires an organisational culture based on results, and a personnel reward system. The managerial approach to human resources requires cost-effectiveness, customer-orientation, delegation of powers, accountability and the use of incentives. Each of the three cases has unique requirements for the development of human resources in the Finnish government. These requirements challenge government organisations to find unique solutions, organisation by organisation, to the issues of job occupation, salary and payments, competencies, training and commitment.

Management changes have their cultural aspect. For example, Virtanen (1998) has analysed the management culture in the Finnish public sector agencies by dividing the culture into a 'hard culture' and a 'soft culture'. The first refers to the employees' instrumental commitment to work and the latter to true commitment to work. Soft culture still prevails, but it has been forced to give way to many hard values. Often employees feel overworked. Dissatisfaction with the reward system has also increased.

5. THE IMPACT OF NEW PUBLIC MANAGEMENT ON FINNISH UNIVERSITIES

Having outlined the impact of NPM on the Finnish public sector in general, we will now turn our attention more specifically to how these broad trends are affecting the higher education sector. In the following, the analysis will be limited to a number of topics. Of several alternatives, the specific issues to be dealt with in this section are: evaluation of performance; managerial reform; and organisational culture and values.

With respect to higher education, the Finnish constitution secures the freedom of the sciences and the university act ensures the autonomy of the institutions. The university system in Finland is comprised of twenty state-run institutions. The total number of personnel in the Ministry of Education is approximately 33,000 with

20,000 employed in the university sector which is one of the largest branches in the central government.

As the strategic ministry, the Ministry of Education holds the steering and development role with respect to the governance of the higher education sector. Every university is responsible for basic research and graduate and postgraduate studies. The entire university system is coordinated by one single university act which provides substantial freedom to universities to make their own decisions on internal matters. The universities select their students independently and are responsible for effective student services and 'real time' learning.

The main managerial trend in Finnish higher education has been the delegation of power authority from the ministerial to university level. Administrative control mechanisms have changed during the delegation process. Universities hire their own personnel, set student numbers, select students, organise teaching and research, and determine the powers of administrative bodies. University degrees and fields of study are controlled by the Ministry of Education, but the content of degrees is determined by each university.

5.1. Evaluation of Performance

University expenditure is financed from the state budget and instruction is free of charge. Competition for student places is fierce and a *numerus clausus* applies to all subject fields. For example, in 1999 the number of university applicants was 66,000 of whom 23,000 were admitted (*Education in Finland, Statistics and Indicators* 1999). Demand is steadily increasing. In 2001 the total number of university students was 163,000.

In all universities, 'results agreements' have become important instruments for ministerial steering of higher education and form the basis for strategic decision making within universities. The universities are assured stable performance-based funding through the state budget. As many Finnish higher education researchers (e.g. Hölttä 1995, Kekäle 1997 and Malkki 1999) have pointed out, the university sector has been faced with pressure and challenges to change and reform. As far as the economy and efficiency and effectiveness of universities are concerned, several efforts have been made to improve university performance. Accountability is partly guaranteed by performance indicators. Evaluation of universities is formally set out in the university act.

Universities obtain most of their funding from the state budget. The amount of non-government resources varies from university to university. Universities are diversifying their funding base along the lines that Clark (2001: 12–13) identifies in his analysis of the entrepreneurial university. In some Finnish universities, external earnings are more than 40% of the total budget. In other universities external funding is more than 50%. Employment conditions are negotiated. The establishment of universities has been used as an instrument for regional policy and development.

Universities receive a lump sum budget from government. The level of funding is mostly based on targeted student load (graduate and postgraduate) weighted by field of study. Not meeting targets is also taken into account in the model. Basic funding accounts for 85–90% of public funding to the universities. In addition to this, there are earmarked funds for special purposes, project funding and performance-based funding (*Higher Education Policy in Finland* 2000).

Within the parameters outlined above, universities can allocate resources as they wish. Accountability criteria at universities are the same as for any public institution. Results agreements are part of the profiles universities negotiate with government. The way in which results are targeted and controlled is highly 'technical', and is based on setting numerical targets. 'Free hands' in universities encourage marketing efforts and restructuring.

5.2. Managerial Reform

The ministry anticipates mutual trust with the universities in achieving commonly set goals. Manifest and latent sanctions exist in the results agreement system. Collegial leadership in universities incorporates the accountability of rectors, deans, department heads and administrative officers. Correspondingly, the employees of universities are increasingly empowered by the use of such mechanisms as performance-related salaries.

The governance of universities is based on management by results/performance management steering, where the goals are collectively defined, resources are allocated to implement goals, and performance is measured in terms of outputs. The results agreements between the ministry and universities are public documents made for three-year periods. Results agreements can be seen as a compromise between centralised and regulated and decentralised and deregulated steering; they are not as binding and detailed as the former but not as loose as the latter form of steering.

In the university sector, the ministry formally encourages dialogue. Even so, a part of the 'control mentality' of the ministry still exists. For example, the role of project-based funding has increased, giving support to old steering approaches because each project is evaluated individually. Most of these projects remain nationally large, important and strategic (*Management by Results in Higher Education* 2001).

5.3. Organisational Culture and Values

As is commonly recognised, strategic management in universities involves cultural dimensions (cf. Ahonen 1998). One of the most well-known analysis comes from Clark (1983: 70–170). Clark (1983) differentiates between institutional and academic cultural dimensions of higher education. The academic, bureaucratic and managerial dimensions are more significant than entrepreneurial ones in publicly owned universities. From a contextual point of view, there are different ethics for different groups: academics, administrative personnel, other professional staff, students etc. Compared to other public sector organisations, universities are, in the first instance, professional organisations. The interrelationship of the various cultural dimensions that constitute the university organisation is illustrated in Figure 2.

Figure 2. Four dimensions of the value basis of higher education

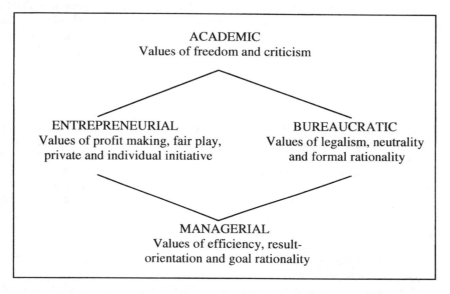

The academic dimension should be defined historically. It includes the traditional university mission (values of the Humboldtian 'Bildungsuniversität'). Universities help establish and preserve the cultural identity of a nation. Universities interpret, create and transfer knowledge. They focus on specialised and deep knowledge that is universal (Gerth 1992: 117). This is a special feature of the universities that must be taken into account with respect to their performance, effectiveness and quality. The academic dimension consists of such values as freedom, criticism and substantive rationality.

As with many other public sector organisations, universities also contain bureaucratic features and cultures, including such values as legalism, neutrality and formal rationality. A strong legal culture and tradition still exists in Finnish public administration, including the higher education sector (see Höltta 1995; Kekäle 1997; Temmes 1997).

As organisations, universities have to change from old to new management practices and processes. Trow (1994: 11) makes the distinction between soft and hard conceptions of managerialism:

> The soft concept sees managerial effectiveness as an important element in the provision of higher education of quality at its lowest cost; it is focused around the idea of improving the efficiency of the existing institutions. The hard conception elevates institutional and system management to a dominant position in higher education; its advocates argue that higher education must be reshaped and reformed by the

introduction of management systems which then become a continuing force ensuring
the steady improvement in the provision of higher education.

As far as the university context is concerned, efficiency, result orientation and
goal rationality can be considered managerial values. But contemporary universities
also learn to live with the private sector, including marketisation, commercialisation
and the like. Universities imitate entrepreneurial practices and adopt business values,
such as profit making, fair play and individualism (see also Clark 2001). The
'voices' of different stakeholders have become louder regarding the transfer of
scientific knowledge and economic exploitation of research and development.

6. CONCLUSION

The above description has its limitations. Past and future developments of the
university sector are not explained entirely by the doctrine of NPM. Still, some of
the core changes are understood by analysing them in terms of new managerial
issues such as performance and efficiency, market orientation, and new personnel
policy and management. Education is one of the most remarkable features of the
Finnish welfare state. With respect to the internationalisation of the Finnish
economy, education is seen as a central factor in improving the competitiveness of
the country. Universities play a key role in this process. Four conclusions can be
drawn from the analysis presented in this chapter.

First, the traditional approach to state steering of higher education is being
replaced by new approaches to performance management and control in the
ministry–university relationship. But, more efficiency and productivity are needed
and managerial capacities should be improved. The economic autonomy of
universities is being encouraged by alternative financial arrangements, including
market-oriented methods. Compared to other branches of public administration, the
higher education sector is rather decentralised, deregulated and autonomous
(particularly with respect to the universities).

Second, a key issue for the Finnish government is to encourage the development
of more professional management practices. Particular management reforms are also
an aspect of higher education. As the size of the sector increases so does the need for
more funding, particularly from external sources. Because of the massification of
universities and the increased complexity of university decision making,
management processes are much more complicated than previously. Performance
indicators, personnel policies and strategic choices have to be integrated in new
ways into management processes and practices in each university.

Third, as a result of these changes, the main challenge can be how to
professionalise management and encourage managers to adopt a new administrative
culture. Academic hierarchies are faced with change. In higher education
organisations, one of the immediate tasks is to effectively implement the systematic
development of professional academic management throughout the university
sector. In order to improve the strengths and to avoid the weaknesses of the present
performance management system, new professional leadership and managerial skills
are required in the administration of the universities.

Finally, one additional management challenge should be mentioned (it is already a legislative initiative). The challenge relates to a sort of entrepreneurial behaviour of universities and a new mission. Clearly, the two basic purposes of the universities are to perform scientific research and provide higher education training. But there is lively discussion in Finnish society concerning a third mission for the university sector. It is called a mission of 'service to society', implying a closer connection between research and the worlds of industry and commerce at local and regional levels. As far as I see it, the relationship between universities and polytechnics is being redefined in this process. From the managerial point of view, the new mission will make university management more complicated and more demanding. This also leads to the reconsideration of existing university strategies.

REFERENCES

Ahonen, Pertti. "Four Cultures in Strategic Leadership in the Universities." In Mälkiä, Matti and Jarmo Vakkuri (eds). *Strateginen johtaminen yliopistoissa* (*Strategic Leadership in the Universities*). Tampere: University of Tampere, 1998, 238–268.

Ahonen, Pertti and Ari Salminen. *Metamorphosis of the Administrative Welfare State: From Depoliticisation to Political Rationality*. Scandinavian University Studies in the Humanities and Social Sciences 14. Frankfurt am Main: Peter Lang, 1997.

Aucoin, Peter. "Administrative Reform in Public Management: Paradigms, Principles, Paradoxes and Pendulums." *Governance* 3.2 (1990): 115–137.

Aucoin, Peter. *The New Public Management. Canada in Comparative Perspective*. Ottawa: IRPP, 1995.

Brereton, Michael and Michael Temple. "The New Public Ethos: An Ethical Environment for Governance." *Public Administration* 77.3 (1999): 455–475.

Clark, Burton R. *The Higher Education System: Academic Organization in Cross-National Perspective*. Berkeley: University of California Press, 1983.

Clark, Burton R. "The Entrepreneurial University: New Foundations for Collegiality, Autonomy and Achievement." *Higher Education Management* 13.2 (2001): 9–24.

Considine, Mark and Martin Painter (eds). *Managerialism: The Great Debate*. Melbourne: Melbourne University Press, 1997.

DeLeon, Linda and Robert B. Denhardt. "The Political Theory of Reinvention." *Public Administration Review* 60.2 (2000): 89–97.

Denhardt, Robert B. and Janet Denhardt. "The New Public Service: Serving Rather Than Steering." *Public Administration Review* 60.6 (2000): 1–24 (electronic version).

Education in Finland, Statistics and Indicators. Helsinki: Statistics Finland, 1999.

Gerth, Donald. *University Management – Promise and Limitations. In Adaptation of University Management Structures and Strategies for New Requirements*. Paris: International Association of Universities, 1992.

Higher Education Policy in Finland. Helsinki: Ministry of Education, 2000.

Hölttä, Seppo. *Towards the Self-regulative University*. Publications in Social Sciences 23. Joensuu: University of Joensuu, 1995.

Hood, Christopher. "A Public Management for all Seasons?" *Public Administration* 69.2 (1991): 3–19.

Hood, Christopher. "Exploring Variations in Public Management Reform." In Bekke, Hans A.G.M., James L. Perry and Theo A.J. Toonen (eds). *Civil Service Systems in Comparative Perspective*. Indianapolis: Indiana University Press, 1996, 268–287.

Ingraham, Patricia. "Play it Again Sam: It's Still Not Right: Searching for the Right Notes in Administrative Reform." *Public Administration Review* 57.4 (1997): 325–331.

Ingraham, Patricia W., Sally Coleman Selden and Donald P. Moynihan. "People and Performance: Challenges for the Future Public Service – The Report from the Wye River Conference." *Public Administration Review* 60.1 (2000): 54–60.

Kekäle, Jouni. *Leadership Cultures in Academic Departments*. Publications in Social Sciences 26. Joensuu: University of Joensuu, 1997.

Klausen, Kurt Klaudi and Annick Magnier (eds). *The Anonymous Leader. Appointed CEOs in Western Local Government*. Odense: Odense University Press, 1998.

Klausen, Kurt Klaudi and Krister Ståhlberg. *New Public Management i Norden: Nye organisations- og lederformer i den centrale velfaerdssat (New Public Management in the Nordic Countries: New Organisation and Management Models in Decentralised Welfare States)*. Odense: Odense University Press, 1998.

Lumijärvi, Ismo and Sari Salo. *Steering and Auditing: Public Management Reform and the New Role of the Parliamentary Actors*. Bern: Peter Lang, 1997.

Malkki, Pertti. *Strategia-ajattelu yliopiston johtamisessa (Strategic Thinking in University Management)*. Kuopion yliopiston julkaisuja. Yhteiskuntatieteet 75, 1999.

Management by Results in Higher Education. Ministry of Education Publication Series. Helsinki: Department for Education and Science Policy, 2001.

Meklin, Pentti and Pertti Ahonen. "Finnish Government Owned Companies as Instruments of State Action." *Public Administration and Development* 18 (1998): 265–272.

National Audit Office. *Yhtiöittäminen – valtion virastojen, laitosten ja liikelaitosten tai niiden osien muuttaminen valtioenemmistöisiksi osakeyhtiöiksi (Incorporation – Changing State Agencies, Offices and Enterprises or Their Parts into Limited Companies With State Majority Ownership)*. Audit Report 16/98, 400/54/97. Helsinki, 1998.

Niskanen, William A. *Bureaucracy and Representative Government*. Chicago: Aldine-Atherton, 1971.

Peters, B. Guy. "Introducing the Topic." In Peters, B. Guy and Donald J. Savoie (eds). *Governance in a Changing Environment*. Canadian Centre for Management Development. Montreal and Kingston: McGill/Queen's University Press, 1995, 2–7.

Peters, B. Guy and Donald J. Savoie (eds). *Governance in a Changing Environment*. Canadian Centre for Management Development. Montreal and Kingston: McGill/Queen's University Press, 1995.

Pollitt, Christopher. *Managerialism and the Public Service: The Anglo-American Experience*. Oxford: Basil Blackwell, 1990.

Salminen, Ari. *Organized Welfare: The Case of Finland's Welfare Bureaucracy – A Nordic Comparison*. Frankfurt am Main: Peter Lang, 1991.

Salminen, Ari. "The Reform 'Industry' in the Finnish Government." In Peters, B. Guy and Jon Pierre (eds). *Politicians, Bureaucrats and Administrative Reform*. Studies in European Political Science. London: Routledge/ECPR 2001, 142–153.

Salminen, Ari, Esa Hyyryläinen, Kirsi Lähdesmäki and Olli-Pekka Viinamäki. "Striving for New Governance on the Premises of Contractual Governance in Finnish Higher Education and Road Administration." Paper presented at the *European Group of Public Administration Conference*, Glasgow, Scotland, 2000 (unpublished).

Salminen, Ari and Kirsi Lähdesmäki. "Strategies for Developing Public Sector Performance: Core Questions in the Administrative Reforms of the Late 80s and the 90s in Finland." IIAS Congeren in Portoroz, Slovenia, February 1999 (unpublished).

Salminen, Ari and Jouni Niskanen. *Markkinoiden ehdoilla? (On the Terms of the Market)*. Valtionvarainministeriö. Helsinki: Vaasan yliopisto, 1996.

Salminen, Ari and Olli-Pekka Viinamäki. *Market Orientation in the Finnish Public Sector. From Public Agency to Privatised Company*. Vaasa: Ministry of Finance/University of Vaasa, 2001.

Salminen, Ari, Olli-Pekka Viinamäki and Kirsi Lähdesmäki. *'Tehdä enemmän vähemmällä': Esimerkkejä uudistuvan valtion henkilöstöresurssien kehittämisestä ('Doing More with Less': Examples of Development of Human Resources within a Reforming Finnish Government)*. Vaasan yliopiston julkaisuja. Selvityksiä ja raportteja. Proceedings of the University of Vaasa. Reports 92, 2002.

Self, Peter. *Rolling Back the Market: Economic Dogma and Political Choice*. New York: St. Martin's Press, 2000.

Temmes, Markku. "Optimal Mix Between Managerialism and Legal–Administrative Regulatory System – The Finnish Case for the Reform of Regulatory System." *(Hallinnon tutkimus) Administrative Studies* 16.1 (1997): 70–79.

Temmes, Markku. "Finland and New Public Management." *International Review of Administrative Sciences* 64.3 (1998): 441–456.

Temmes, Markku and Markku Kiviniemi. *Suomen hallinnon muuttaminen 1987–1995 (Amending Finnish Administration 1987–1995)*. Ministry of Finance, University of Helsinki. Helsinki: Oy Edita Ab, 1997.

Trow, Martin. "Managerialism and the Academic Profession: The Case of England." *Higher Education Policy* 7.2 (1994): 11–18.

Tulosohjausjärjestelmän toimivuus ministeriöissä ja laitoksissa (*Performance Management and its Functionality in Ministries and Agencies*). Valtiovarainministeriön tutkimukset ja selvitykset 2/98. Helsinki, 1998.

Virtanen, Turo. *Johtamiskulttuurin muutos ja tuloksellisuus, Valtionhallinnon uudistumisen seurantatutkimus 1995–1998. Toinen väliraportti* (*Productivity and the Change of Management Culture*). Helsinki: Helsingin yliopisto, 1998.

INGVILD MARHEIM LARSEN

DEPARTMENTAL LEADERSHIP IN NORWEGIAN UNIVERSITIES – IN BETWEEN TWO MODELS OF GOVERNANCE?

1. INTRODUCTION

An accelerated pace of change is an obvious feature of university systems, putting questions of leadership and management of universities on the agenda. Change has also characterised the Norwegian higher education system since the 1980s. This trend will continue in the years to come as the higher education system in Norway faces a new comprehensive reform. A White Paper published in the spring of 2001 announced quality reform for higher education. The Ministry of Education and Research launched a number of major structural measures aimed at enhancing the ability and will to restructure higher education institutions. In order to secure and develop the quality of education and research and to increase control within educational institutions, the Ministry has proposed to strengthen academic leadership at the departmental level. The Ministry has recommended that heads of department should be appointed for a fixed term, and wants to give more power and instruments to the head of department. The intention is to give the head sufficient means to promote excellence in research. Consequently, the traditional leadership model, where the head of department is elected by and among academic staff and academic leadership is a temporary part-time job, is under pressure. However, the Ministry states that the adoption of this system should be voluntary. Since the new reform introduces a differentiated system of academic governance and management, the existing system (where the department head is elected) can carry on side-by-side with appointed leaders. If higher education institutions do choose the new system, this will mean a move from a collegial election system to appointed leaders approved at the institutional level. This is a development in line with international trends. The Netherlands, Sweden, Great Britain and Australia are examples of higher education systems that have moved from election to appointment of heads of department (Gulddahl Rasmussen 2002; Harman 2002; Henkel 2002).

The literature on leadership is overwhelming and there is no authoritative definition or understanding of what leadership actually comprises. Just as there are many definitions of leadership, so too there are many different approaches used to study leadership. The point of departure in this study is that leadership is concerned with influencing, and that leadership consists of a number of elements that constitute different roles. The amount of literature on leadership in higher education has also increased considerably. I will argue that studies and literature on leadership and

71

A. Amaral et al. (eds.), The Higher Education Managerial Revolution?, 71–88.
© 2003 *Kluwer Academic Publishers. Printed in the Netherlands.*

management in higher education often have a weak link to the primary tasks of the university, namely, teaching and research. My intention is to couple leadership to academic activities.

Based on empirical studies of academic leadership among heads of department and faculty staff, this chapter focuses on the roles of academic leaders at the departmental level in a period where leadership and management are coming increasingly into focus. The duties of heads of department are analysed through five roles based on activities and issues handled by the head with regard to teaching, research, personnel issues, political tasks and administration. These roles are used to try to identify the different elements departmental leadership consists of. The aim of this chapter is twofold. First, to shed light on staff expectations of departmental leadership: What do academic staff regard as being the duties and tasks of the head of department? Second, to explore the roles of the elected head of department in the present system: How do today's elected leaders interpret and describe their tasks and formal responsibilities? The underlying question of this analysis of leadership roles is: Are the universities moving from a traditional model of governance based on collegial, democratic and political characteristics to a more corporate style of management?

2. METHODOLOGY

The chapter draws on empirical data from different sources. First, from a survey conducted among tenured staff at the four Norwegian universities during the spring of 2001 (2,212 replies were received from 3,676 questionnaires distributed – a response rate of 60 per cent). Second, the chapter draws on interviews of 26 heads of department in six different disciplines at the four Norwegian universities in 2001. And third, the study is based on written material, primarily documents prepared by the Ministry of Education and Research.

The quality reform is expected to be implemented during 2003. Therefore, this study took place *prior* to the implementation of the reforms, and at a time when some of the proposed changes were already on the political agenda and being hotly debated. Thus, all heads of department in this study obtained their positions by election and were not appointed by institutional leadership. From 2003, higher education institutions can choose whether they want elected or appointed leaders and it remains to be seen what kind of arrangement will be preferred in different institutions – many faculty are divided on this issue. A survey conducted in 2001 among all tenured staff in the Norwegian universities showed that 40 per cent welcomed the appointment of heads of department, with 42 per cent against. Furthermore, the data showed that faculty were very negative to the head being appointed by institutional leadership. Less than 10 per cent were in favour of this procedure (Larsen 2002).

3. MODELS OF GOVERNANCE FOR HIGHER EDUCATION INSTITUTIONS

Understanding leadership in an academic organisation depends on the organisational images and conceptual lenses used. Different organisational models mean different roles of leadership and, to some extent, the role of leader is a consequence of the organisation's characteristics. Many labels are used to characterise universities: collegial, professional, loosely coupled, political and decentralised, as well as organised anarchy. Since leadership at the departmental level is explored in this chapter, models that describe academic activities and basic units will be used. Other models are more appropriate when the focus is on the institutional level (the relationship between the levels) or the administration level.

Two models on governance in universities will be presented and the way these lead to different leadership roles will be discussed. Firstly, is a traditional model that includes collegial as well as political elements. Traditional understanding of universities highlights the uniqueness of academic organisation. In a knowledge society with many other kinds of knowledge-based and complex organisations, there is reason to ask what distinguishes universities from other knowledge organisations with personnel with high formal skills. Therefore, the second model used in the analysis is a newer perspective that sees the university as a knowledge enterprise in line with other knowledge organisations.

The point of departure is that different models of academic governance lead to different leadership roles. The questions are: What kind of leadership role(s) can be expected from the different perspectives of academic organisations?; and, more specifically: According to the two models, to what extent can the head of department be expected to provide teaching, research and personnel leadership, as well as be a politician and administrator?

Leadership comprises the practice of legitimised authority (Byrkjeflot and Halvorsen 1997: 56). In order to be successful, a leader must have legitimacy among employees. There are several different sources of legitimacy in order to be able to practise leadership. There is a question of what provides leadership legitimacy within a university context when so many are sceptical of the concepts of management and leadership. The legitimacy of leadership is both a question of the leader's position, and the nature of the tasks to be pursued. Legitimacy can be based on legal or formal authority, authority based on expertise, or charismatic authority. The position as head of department, as a formal position, can contribute to legitimacy, but is no guarantee for leadership legitimacy (Birnbaum 1992: 14). Moreover, a distinction can be made between formal and informal leaders where those in a formal leadership role do not always practise leadership, and where those who do show leadership do not always hold the position of formal leader. The other question is *what* may legitimately be the object for leadership in an academic institution. Legitimacy both as a consequence of position and the nature of the tasks will be central topics in the presentation of the two governance models.

3.1. Leadership within a Traditional Perspective

A collegial university model highlights values such as academic freedom, critical reflection and local autonomy. These values run deep in the Norwegian universities, and are reflected in the way the system has been governed and organised. A collegial institution is also characterised by participatory democracy and committees. Leadership within this model is based on consultation and persuasion, and the leader's role is to promote consensus within the community, and to use consultative and democratic processes for decision making (Middlehurst 1993). According to this perspective strong academic leadership is neither wanted nor necessary. Furthermore, change occurs on the basis of consensus among the faculties, and emerges without any need for leadership (Dearlove 1995).

The collegial system means governance according to the norms and values in the scientific community. In such a system, authority is based on academic activities, primarily research. Furthermore, according to the collegial perspective, research is assessed by recognised academics in the same field. The ideal of academic freedom limits the possibilities of head of department to govern academic activities. This model sees universities as self-governing communities where leaders are often described as 'first among equals'. The collegial perspective tends to see the head as having the role of servant of the group and means a 'hands-off' approach to leading academic affairs (Bolton 2000).

The original collegial model was hierarchical in the sense that one professor led each department. From the end of the 1960s the former elite collegiality was replaced by a more democratic system where faculty staff at all levels, students and non-academic personnel took part in decision making. The new democracy was also characterised by a well-developed committee structure at all levels. Furthermore, an increase in the number of students and faculty members in the same period resulted in more professors in each department. More professors in the same discipline toned down the leadership function that was traditionally connected to the role of the professors and was an end to the department as a unit devoted to one subject and led by one professor (Kyvik and Larsen 1993; Gulddahl Rasmussen 2002).

Since a collegial perspective is based on a harmony model, and presumes that the members of the organisation agree or accept the result of decision-making processes, it is necessary to include a political perspective as an element of the traditional governance model. According to Baldridge (1971) universities can best be understood as 'politicised' organisations. The political image concentrates on features of differences of interests, values and norms (Middlehurst 1993). From a political perspective conflicts and competition within the institution are expected and are part of the daily life of the leadership. The perspective also emphasises that the organisation is fragmented, and characterised by unstable goals and coalitions between different individuals and groups. Furthermore, a political perspective highlights formal as well as informal leaders (Dearlove 1995).

The traditional precondition that individual freedom in academic affairs is necessary for doing research, and that leadership and scientific creativity is a contradiction, means resistance to what could traditionally be understood as leadership in more hierarchical organisations (Birnbaum 1988). Consequently, incentives and sanctions are not leadership tools in universities. In a collegial system, the formal position is not a guarantee for leadership of academic activities. It is academic activities which constitute legitimacy within a university context. The underlying legitimising principle is expertise within one's own field (Olsen 1987). In practice, it is research activities which will give the leader legitimacy as academic leader. A leader lacking the necessary academic skills will find it difficult to take advantage of the increased formal authority inherent in the position of institutional leader (Kekäle 1997). In a traditional system the head of department will be elected either because of academic authority among the staff, or because the position is not very attractive.

According to this traditional perspective on university governance – what is the latitude of the head of department with respect to teaching, research, personnel issues, political issues and administration? Leadership is without doubt difficult in a system that is described as individualistic (Eriksson 1997). The ideal of academic freedom limits the possibilities for leaders to manoeuvre in academic affairs. From a traditional perspective, leadership takes place according to the norms and values of the academic community. The leader is expected to be democratic and sensitive to colleagues' views, and the dominant leadership tools of influence are persuasion and argument. Primary tasks for department heads operating from this model are economic and administrative affairs and to create consensus among faculty. Following a traditional administrative role will scarcely present any problems in itself. It is expected that the leader will accept the main burden of administrative responsibility and restrict other academic staff from undertaking such tasks as far as possible (Gulbrandsen 2000: 165). Therefore, the role of administrator is vital for heads of department. To some extent the head also has to manage teaching according to this governing model. Some aspects of teaching are routinised activities; and traditionally the head coordinates teaching activities and handles timetabling and assigning teaching tasks. On the other hand, when it comes to the content of teaching, this is essentially individualised. To the extent that the head of department determines the content of the teaching programmes, the role of educational leader will immediately become more controversial. In accordance with the collegiate leadership model, directing research will be the most controversial area. Since academic freedom is regarded as a precondition for doing research, the head of department is not expected to provide research leadership. Furthermore, academics are individually responsible for their own career. Therefore, from a traditional perspective, staff development (in the sense that the head of department acts as support for competence and personal development) will not be regarded as a task belonging to the head of department. Consequently, personnel leadership will not be of great importance. Areas such as staff leadership and individual conferences with staff members, which are currently regarded as core functions of the leader's role in other sectors, may be regarded as inappropriate and artificial in the academic environment. According to the political elements in the traditional model, the head of department has to mediate between different interests among faculty staff and build coalitions. Regarding political leadership, we can distinguish between 'foreign policy' and 'domestic policy'. From a traditional point of view, the head will primarily focus on internal relationships.

Even though the traditional model is idealised by many academics, analysts of higher education systems often find it inadequate as a description of university governance (Henkel 2002: 30). Others point to the fact that the ideals connected to this model are coming under increasing pressure. It has been argued that traditional governance is slow and conservative, and that it ignores external signals (Dearlove 1995: 166). Mintzberg (1979) found that collegial-based institutions would experience problems with coordination, control and change. In a time of change, comprehensive reforms and increasing external expectations of higher education institutions, it can be questioned whether this governance model is appropriate and adequate.

3.2. Leadership in a Knowledge Enterprise

Reforms inspired by new public management (NPM) have introduced corporate enterprise principles into higher education institutions. Reforms and measures motivated by these ideas point in the direction of both centralisation and decentralisation (Christensen 1990). NPM places decision-making authority at the local level (decentralisation) according to goals set by the central authorities (centralisation). In Norway, user-orientation and result-oriented planning are two central steering mechanisms derived from NPM. A management-oriented governance system highlights the need for strong local leadership, incentives and control of results to assure quality and efficiency (Bleiklie, Høstaker and Vabø 2000). Consequently, NPM implies an extended leadership role.

Decentralisation is an international trend that expands the need and possibilities for leadership (Kekäle 1997). It is also the aim of many organisational changes in Norwegian higher education since the late 1980s (Gornitzka, Kyvik and Larsen 1998). Deregulation and decentralisation, in the sense of more use of lump sum funding and more freedom with regard to allocating funds, require strong leadership (Nordbäck, Nordberg and Olson 1999).

Universities as knowledge-based concerns mean professionalisation of the leadership role in terms of more formalised training of leaders. Furthermore, the user-orientation in this perspective makes external relationships vital. The leader is therefore expected to have an external role and represent the department in different arenas in order to ensure the unit's resources and survival. The 'external world' includes both other levels and other departments inside the university, administrative units at the university, and different milieus outside the university. Hence, external activities such as networking and entrepreneurship are central tasks for the head of department.

The introduction of NPM can also be interpreted as a renaissance of the bureaucratic model since hierarchy and control are preconditions for a result-oriented steering system. However, control of input is replaced by control of output. Moreover, while persuasion is the vital leadership tool to influence others, incentives and disincentives are important means to influence staff according to NPM.

It is not only management-inspired reforms that emphasise the need to strengthen the function of the leader and highlight the importance of the relationship between the universities and the environment. According to Kerr (1993) entrepreneurial leadership and stronger steering capacity are necessary if higher education institutions are to succeed in a highly competitive world. Clark (1995, 1998) has emphasised the connection between leadership and innovation. He points out that efforts to restructure universities require change-oriented leadership (Clark 1995: 7). In his study of European entrepreneurial universities, Clark (1998: 5) stated that universities "need to become quicker, more flexible, and especially more focused in reactions to expanding and changing demands". Clark's answer to this is that the universities need to strengthen their steering capability. Moreover, stronger line authority is required, and academics must accept that some will have stronger authority based on formal positions. Clark also recommended that universities be more focused, and he sees such profiling as a leadership task. On the other hand, Clark's recommendation is to maintain traditional academic values in conjunction with new managerial values (1998: 6).

Moreover, Gumport (2000) emphasises that the dominant legitimating idea of public higher education has changed from higher education as a social institution to higher education as an industry. According to Gumport, some of the reasons are to be found in what Kerr (2001) has called the 'multiversity'. A 'multiversity' faces increasingly complex and diverse demands and expectations from outside interests. Consequently, the services must correspond with different customers in the market such as students, parents, state legislators, employers and research funders (Gumport 2000: 71). When the university is understood as an industry, it is assumed that academics will be more productive through the use of incentives and sanctions. If universities do not take market forces into account, they will lose some legitimacy (Gumport 2000: 73).

If today's universities are to be understood as knowledge enterprises, the head of department has far-reaching academic, administrative and political tasks. Accordingly, the head's leadership role with regard to teaching, research and personnel, as well as being a politician and administrator is relevant.

4. DEPARTMENTAL LEADERSHIP – LEADING WHAT?

Different sources define which tasks the department head should perform. First, the Universities and Colleges Act states that the head of department is the chair of the department board and that the head's authority is delegated by the university board (Bernt 1996). In addition, some universities have developed their own instructions for heads of department which means that, with the exception of the task as chair of the board, there is no joint framework for departmental leadership in higher education in Norway. Consequently, what tasks and issues department heads will view as part of their duties will depend on the institution's guidelines and individual interpretations of formal instructions, tradition and individual ambitions. As in other sectors, leadership is not clearly defined, but more a case of 'muddling through'. Nevertheless, attention to leadership issues in Norwegian universities has increased.

This development has resulted in the training of elected leaders in the sense that most universities now offer courses in leadership to heads of department.

To picture what elected leaders at departmental level actually do, five possible leadership roles are examined with regard to teaching, research and personnel, as well as politicial issues and administration. How faculty assess the head of department's responsibility with regard to these roles will be discussed below.

4.1. Faculty Assessment of the Roles of the Head

Data from a survey among all faculty staff in Norwegian universities make it possible to illuminate academic personnel's view on what should be the head of department's responsibility. Table 1 gives an overview of tasks that could be related to the different leadership roles the head could hold.

Table 1. Faculty members' assessment of whether the head of department should have responsibility for the following tasks (N=1919–1931)

	Fully or partly agree %	Fully or partly disagree %	Neither agree nor disagree %
Should have the responsibility for quality assurance of teaching	71	14	15
Should have the responsibility for quality assurance of research	50	29	20
Should influence the department's academic profile	37	42	21
Should have the responsibility for professional development of the staff	46	36	18
Should be a spokesperson for the department	93	2	6
Should give strategic work priority	72	10	19

Starting with teaching leadership, different aspects related to teaching could be managed by the head of department. In the survey, responsibility for quality assurance is used as an indicator of the leadership role in this area. The survey results show that more than 70 per cent of faculty see quality assurance of teaching as the head's responsibility (Table 1). In this sense, leadership with regard to teaching is not a controversial matter among university staff. Both the traditional university governance model and the model of university as a knowledge enterprise include teaching leadership as a part of the head's responsibility. However, while quality assurance is emphasised in the knowledge-enterprise model, the traditional model underlines the head's responsibility for coordinating teaching.

If we move to research leadership, two indicators are used to shed light on how faculty see the head's responsibility with respect to research activities. In the survey, faculty were asked whether they saw quality assurance of research as the head's responsibility. Half the academic personnel fully or partly agreed that this was the head's responsibility, while nearly a third of faculty members disagreed (Table 1).

Whether the head of department should influence the academic profile is the second indicator used in this respect. The survey among faculty shows that almost 40 per cent of personnel suggest that the head should influence the profile of the department, and marginally more than 40 per cent disagree (Table 1).

The data show that academic personnel are much more divided when it comes to research leadership than teaching leadership. To some extent the results could be interpreted as a defence of the traditional model when it comes to research activities. However, the data also tell us that a significant proportion of personnel wants a stronger research leader than what can be deduced from the traditional model with regard to both quality assurance and influencing the department's academic profile. It is somewhat surprising that such a large proportion of personnel argued for stronger leadership in this sense since the norm of individual autonomy often dominates the Norwegian debate about university governance.

As for the roles of leadership with regard to teaching and research, personnel leadership also consists of different tasks. In the survey, the responsibility for professional development of staff is used as an indicator of personnel leadership. Almost half the academic staff agreed that the head should carry out staff development, while more than a third of personnel disagreed (Table 1). As with regard to research leadership, faculty are divided when it comes to the question of whether the head of department should have responsibility for the staff's professional career. According to a traditional perspective, faculty will have individual responsibility for their own career. However, almost half of faculty welcome more support and feedback in professional development than could be expected from the traditional model.

Being a spokesperson for the department is used as an indicator of the political aspects of the head's role. The survey results highly support the statement that the leader of the department should be a 'spokesperson' for the department's interests (Table 1). In general terms it could be argued that being a politician is not regarded as a controversial part of the head's role. However, other elements of this role could be much more problematic.

In recent years, the universities have faced increasing expectations regarding formulating plans and setting priorities. This also occurs at the departmental level. The survey among faculty shows that more than 70 per cent of academic personnel agree that the head of department should prioritise strategy issues (Table 1). Consequently, faculty staff see strategic planning as a key function for the department head. The question is formulated on a general level and not connected to specific issues, and as such is difficult to relate to the different roles. However, responsibility for preparing such documents could be regarded as a part of the administrative role. Another reasonable interpretation of the result could be that it is not controversial to set up such documents. On the other hand, to make them work is quiet another matter.

Based on faculty's view of the head's responsibility in different areas we move to the next topic: how the heads of department see themselves and their roles.

4.2. Teaching Leadership

As in the survey among faculty members, interviews with heads demonstrated that teaching leadership is not a controversial matter in Norwegian universities. Teaching leadership seems rather unproblematic and is an example of a matter that traditionally has been managed by departmental leadership. Despite the fact that managing teaching is formally the head's responsibility, it is quite common that the head of department delegates responsibility for teaching to the deputy department head. Even though the operative responsibility for teaching leadership is often delegated, most of the interviewed heads emphasise that they follow this work closely, and that the head of department has the formal responsibility. In addition, administrative staff are engaged in timetabling, the teaching budget and scheduling examinations.

Furthermore, most department heads emphasise that they play a central role when curricula are changed. Understandably, there are conflicts and different interests connected to revisions of curricula but, since such processes occur on a regular basis, there are procedures in place to handle them. This work frequently includes all academic personnel and could be characterised as a collective process. Teaching is described as both a manageable and hierarchically governed task. This is in line with the findings of Brunsson and Olsen (1990) who point to the fact that reforms and change processes that correspond with the institution's identity occur regularly and according to standard operating procedures.

In Norwegian universities, quality assurance of teaching mainly means student evaluation of individual courses. Some of the interviewed department heads see these evaluations as a useful tool for the head to further the development of the department's teaching activities; others view them as a tool for the individual teacher. Some of the heads also report that student recruitment is an issue they have to deal with. Since some disciplines have experienced decreasing numbers of students in recent years, some heads of department take part in recruitment procedures.

4.3. Research Leadership

Not surprisingly, the data show that leadership with regard to research activities seems to be a much more difficult and sensitive field than teaching leadership. The tradition of individual autonomy and responsibility in academic matters runs deep in Norwegian universities, and in contrast to teaching the head cannot instruct academic personnel when it comes to research. According to the informants, very few heads of department consider themselves as research leaders at the departmental level and most of the interviewed heads have no wish to determine the direction of research of their department. The majority of the interviewed heads stated that they are doing research in one sub-discipline, and consequently argued that it is impossible to be a leader in other sub-disciplines. Some perceived themselves as informal research directors for a smaller group inside their department, but not for the whole department as such. Within some departments there are other leaders and levels of leadership, often of a more informal nature, in addition to the leadership exercised by the head.

Excellence in research is a superior goal for universities. The question here is *if* and *what* role the head of department plays in quality assurance of research. Most of the interviewed heads do not see quality assurance of research and evaluating staff performance as their responsibility. They emphasise that quality assurance is taken care of by traditional peer review mechanisms, and they see no need for any supplementation of this established system. To give staff feedback on manuscripts to be submitted for publication is not normally a matter for the department head, rather, this is done by other colleagues or by the leader of the group.

So, what does it mean to be a leader of research when heads do not wish to influence the direction of research or to have any role in the quality assurance of research? These are issues that in most other sectors in society are central to the leadership role.

The data show that research leadership often means shielding faculty members from administrative tasks and improving the possibilities for doing research. Moreover, many of the informants stressed that selecting and recruiting staff as a leadership task was of great importance for the research activities of the department. However, because of a lack of resources in recent years many stated that vacancies for positions are not announced. Consequently, in many departments, recruitment is a sleeping leadership tool.

Since the beginning of the 1990s, more comprehensive planning processes have been established at Norwegian universities (Larsen 2000). Formulating strategies is also a task for department heads, and most departments have a strategy, which includes a strategy for academic activities. However, these strategies vary considerably. While some departments have profiled sub-disciplines of high quality, others focus on fields where competence is weak. In many cases the department's strategy also mirrors the strategy of the faculty, the university or priorities set by the Norwegian Research Council. To give priority to something at the expense of something else is not an easy task, and some departments have a strategy that includes all existing activities and research topics. Some heads stress that the purpose of a strategy is not to set priorities internally but to serve as an external policy instrument. Moreover, the interviews with heads of department show that plans are established in collaboration with staff.

Despite the fact that the norm of individual autonomy in research matters is strong in the university system in Norway, many of the interviewed leaders stated that academic staff need to cooperate more in research matters and concentrate their research efforts in selected research fields. As heads of department, most of the informants encourage group research. Different reasons and forces promote more teamwork. First, the funding system promotes development towards teamwork. Some of the informants see that, to be a competitive partner in the research market, more cooperation among staff is necessary. Second, several heads believe more teamwork will improve the academic milieu in the department, especially for young researchers and doctoral students. In this respect Norwegian universities are a part of a broader international trend. There are signs internationally that the department culture is slowly moving from an individualistic one towards being more group-oriented (Gulddahl Rasmussen 2002). Furthermore, Henkel (2002: 40) points to the fact that academic leaders in British universities agree that a stronger collective direction is needed.

Reduction in public funding is an international trend, followed by political emphasis on greater market responsiveness (Middlehurst and Elton 1992). Although basic appropriation through the state budget is the primary source of income for Norwegian universities, it is increasingly expected that higher education institutions supplement their resources with external research funding. Information about possible funding systems has to be collected and disseminated within the system. Some of the department heads see this as their responsibility; others hand this over to the administrative staff or see it as an individual responsibility. Some heads also encourage and assist staff with research grant applications. Only rarely does the head of department personally write applications for external funding on behalf of faculty.

Trends towards increased external funding, more group-orientation and need for stronger leadership are strongly connected. External funding often requires research teams, and formal responsibility for external projects requires leadership. To conclude this section we could claim that even though heads of department have no intention of formulating research issues for faculty members or being an instrument for quality assurance of research, other important tasks are included under the label of 'research leader'. Examples such as collectivisation of the research process and more externally funded projects are apparent and are trends that will have consequences both for the department's academic profile and the quality assurance system. Therefore, there is reason to argue that the head of department indirectly exercises leadership, which is understood as influencing the direction of academic activities and areas of study.

4.4. Personnel Leadership

A study of departments in Sweden and the Netherlands found that staff development is increasingly accepted by academics as a role of management. However, the leadership of the departments in this study does not appear to have yet reached that stage (Gulddahl Rasmussen 2002: 53). So, what is the present position of personnel leadership in Norwegian universities? Traditionally, faculty members are seen as competent individuals who manage their professional lives themselves. Several departments are breaking this tradition in the sense that the head of department regularly arranges formalised individual consultations about professional performance and development for academic personnel. It is emphasised that this is meant to be a dialogue about professional issues, not performance control. Most heads of department report that this arrangement is useful, but a very time-consuming activity. In some departments it is an institutionalised activity, in others a more hesitant attitude prevails. There are also heads who characterise such arrangements as absurd in a university, and turn it down as not befitting the academic culture. Others invite consultation only when problems or conflicts occur.

Some of the relatively young leaders report that they find it difficult to invite older colleagues to performance interviews.

Dealing with unsatisfactory faculty performance can be a part of personnel leadership. The interviews demonstrated that this is regarded as a very sensitive area. The expectation is that academics are self-motivated, and so far the department heads do little to stimulate research and publication by the staff when unsatisfactory performance is reported. However, not many heads reported unsatisfactory research and teaching performance as a problem among faculty. On the other hand, if department heads want to reward or punish faculty staff, they have very few tools to use. It could be argued that allocation of research resources is an important means to stimulate faculty staff. This is a question of both time resources and financial resources to run research projects. When it comes to money it is a question of distribution of scarce resources. The interviewed department heads report that the department's budget hardly covers salaries, and consequently there is little to distribute. But there are heads who admit that they use the scarce resources they have as a strategic means. When it comes to distribution of time, faculty staff in Norwegian universities traditionally have the right and duty to do both teaching and research. Nevertheless, some department heads see increased teaching loads as a possibility for staff who fail as researchers. But the heads doubt such a solution will be good for students, and so far time to conduct research is equally distributed.

Other studies have shown that staff career development is important for junior colleagues (Etzkowitz 1992; Henkel 2002). This was not the case in this study; the heads of department stated that in most instances junior colleagues meant doctoral students, and that it is their supervisors' responsibility to assist in their career plans. However, a few heads of department said that this responsibility should be more collectivised among faculty staff.

Several of the heads also pointed to the ceremonial function they serve *vis-à-vis* personnel. They see this function as an important contributor to the department's social environment. Dealing with personnel issues is reported as a time-consuming activity, particularly when personnel conflicts arise. It should also be mentioned that many of the interviewed heads find their responsibility in personnel issues unclear and vague.

4.5. A Political Role

Most of the informants reported that the political aspect of the head's role is of great importance. The head of department is a politician in different arenas and different political roles can be identified. First, as a politician in the domestic arena – namely the department. The leadership role that comes from being chair of the department board is a primary duty for the head: both setting the agenda and chairing the meetings are central duties. Second, the head of department plays a political role at the faculty level. Because resources are allocated at this level, most department heads see this as the most important political arena. In this respect, they are promoting the department's interests at this level. Many informants emphasised that to ensure their share of resources it is important to build alliances. Thus building coalitions is a central aspect of being head of department. Whether the leader also serves as a link to different groups outside the university is a third possible political role. The data show that the concern the head might have with being a 'foreign' minister outside the university varies considerably. On the other hand, being a foreign minister in the sense that the department leader is a spokesperson for the department does not appear to be controversial among faculty members (Table 1).

In leadership literature, change is a central topic. According to Middlehurst (1999: 308) "Leadership and governance functions are of major importance in interpreting the drivers of change, outlining potential scenarios, developing responses and making change happen". When questions about change are on the agenda in the interviews, the department head's first association is the workload caused by state reforms rather than their own possibilities to initiate change. Changes are often initiated by demands external to the department or the university itself. In other words, the heads of department see themselves as implementers of externally initiated change. When they are asked to consider their own possibilities to initiate and implement change, they regard traditional thinking by academic personnel as the most important obstacle to change. This indolence in the university system has to be taken into consideration when change processes are initiated and which result in broad democratic processes at the departmental level. Some of the leaders find such processes frustrating; others defend them and stress the legitimating function of the processes. Even though change is described as a time-consuming activity, many department heads emphasise their function as chair of the board as important in this respect: both setting the agenda and conducting the meetings provide opportunities for initiating change.

Despite the fact that many department leaders enhance the acceptability of proposals and changes by including faculty staff in broad decision-making processes, more heads of department also characterise the university as an arena for replays. As a politician, the head needs the ability to neutralise efforts from faculty members to reverse decisions. Some of the department heads find it frustrating that staff do not accept decisions taken according to formally correct procedures.

4.6. An Administrative Role

When the head of department is seen as administrator, the day-to-day running of the department is in focus. Working conditions (the physical character) are one aspect of the administrative role of the head of department. This includes such matters as offices, computers and furniture. The data show that there is considerable diversity as to whether heads of department see themselves as administrators. Even though heads of department report that they are involved in university administration, most heads acknowledge the support they receive from professional administrators. From the end of 1980s, the number of higher administrative positions in Norwegian universities increased considerably. The university departments absorbed the bulk of the new administrative officers and managers (Gornitzka, Kyvik and Larsen 1998). Even though this development is of great significance for the department heads, they are still involved to some extent in administrative matters and such tasks are often time-consuming. According to the informants, this is an area where many small issues become a large amount of work, and many complain about the amount of paperwork.

Moreover, administrative tasks relate to the leadership roles of teaching, research and personnel, and being a politician. The following examples illustrate the administrative elements in these roles. First, external funding brings about many administrative tasks both in relation to the application process, handling the contract and reporting. Correspondingly, there is a lot of administrative work connected to timetabling and curricula in teaching activities. Furthermore, there are administrative tasks connected to the political role of preparing documents for board meetings.

5. CONCLUDING REMARKS

A central question in this chapter is whether the universities are moving from a traditional model based on collegiate and political dimensions to a more corporate style of management. It could be argued that this study suggests that a collegial governance model still runs deep in Norwegian universities. First, department heads in Norwegian universities are defenders of democratic processes for decision making; they are promoters of consensus within the community and are sensitive to traditional values according to the collegial model including individual freedom in academic affairs. Second, the central leadership tools in Norwegian universities are still consultation and persuasion rather than the use of incentives. Furthermore, the data show that most department heads do not consider themselves as research leaders at the departmental level in the sense that they neither instruct academic personnel in research matters, nor desire any role in quality assurance of research. The analysis also demonstrates that department leaders in Norwegian universities carry out the role as politician/spokesperson for the department in different arenas inside the institution. As a result, this study has demonstrated that the traditional model in many respects is still applicable.

Even though the department heads are defenders of values connected to a traditional model to a considerable degree, there are some trends in the direction whereby the leader can no longer be regarded as the servant of the group. According to the traditional governance model, teaching is a task that has been managed by the departmental leadership. Research, on the other hand, has been more a minefield in this respect. There are signs that this is changing in Norwegian universities. For example, the data show that teamwork is widely promoted by the head. More group-oriented research at the departmental level can be seen as a break with the ideal of individual autonomy in research matters which puts academic individualism under pressure. However, more cooperation among colleagues inside the department can also be interpreted as a renaissance or strengthening of traditional collegiality. The efforts many heads of department make in terms of arranging individual conferences with staff members in order to stimulate professional performance and academic development can also be understood as a break with the traditional governance model. In addition, there are tendencies towards larger research projects inside the departments – a tendency that can claim strengthened leadership. On the other hand, there are other levels of leadership within departments in addition to those exercised by the head. Consequently, strengthened leadership does not necessarily mean a strengthening of the role of the head of department.

Staff expectations of leadership can also partly be interpreted as a break with the traditional governance model. The survey shows that a large number of faculty staff welcome a more extended leadership role than what may be deduced from the traditional model in the sense that relatively many faculty members at Norwegian universities regard quality assurance of academic activities and influencing the department's academic profile as the head's responsibility. This finding could open up possible changes in the roles of the head of department.

Since a more extended leadership role than what can be implied by the traditional governance model is observed, we could ask whether this can be regarded as support for a leadership role based on a model of universities as knowledge-based enterprises. More elements in today's leadership role point in this direction. According to this model we could expect that the heads of department have responsibility for far-reaching academic, administrative, political and personnel issues. The data have shown that department heads in Norwegian universities have tasks with regard to teaching, research, personnel issues, politics and administration. It could also be argued that training programmes for academic leaders mean a professionalisation of the role. Consultations about staff development, responsibility for external funding and promoting more group-oriented research are all elements that point in the direction of a more extensive leadership role in line with the enterprise model. However, the leadership praxis is not thorough or extensive enough to be in line with the enterprise model. Similar to studies from other countries (Gulddahl Rasmussen 2002: 52), it could be argued that we can observe a slow movement from a collegial governance model to a more knowledge-enterprise model and that the governance structure at the departmental level in Norwegian universities falls somewhere between these two leadership models. This study shows that the role of head of department is balanced between different models of governance.

It is also important to remember that the discretion of the position of head is great, and the interpretation the head applies to the duties of leadership is crucial. Where the ambiguity of departmental leadership renders the position complex, the very nature of the duties will attract candidates with a variety of skills and experiences to the position.

It is also necessary to pay some attention to the role concepts used. Five roles which heads of department might hold with regard to teaching, research, personnel issues, politics and administration are used in the analysis. Such distinctions may be useful as analytical tools, but the chapter also demonstrates that these are easily blurred empirically. Three examples will be given to demonstrate these unclear distinctions. First, professional development is regarded as a staff matter and treated as a part of the head's role as leader with regard to personnel. It could be argued that professional development largely touches upon both teaching and research leadership roles. Second, external funding is viewed as a part of the role of research leadership. Obviously, it could also be regarded as a relevant task for the head's leadership role in teaching since attempts to obtain more externally funded courses are one of the challenges the universities are facing. Third, as we saw in focusing the administrative role, there are administrative tasks connected to the other roles used in the analysis.

Universities can be understood in different ways – and this should be mirrored in the leadership role. Each perspective of organisation and leadership focuses on some aspects, while other aspects remain in the shadows. According to Morgan (1998) any realistic approaches to organisation must be broad and include an understanding that organisations are many things at once: they are complex, multifaceted and paradoxical (1998: 3). Accordingly, none of the models described in this chapter exist in pure form; a hybrid of different models is often the best description. That means that department heads must relate to different leadership models and that leadership and management in universities are grounded on a mix of different organisation models. Consequently, collegiate governing principles and political aspects must operate together with principles such as efficiency, effectiveness, quality assurance and quasi-market solutions. In such a situation leadership must relate to different leadership roles due to internal as well as external expectations. Since more models exist side-by-side, conflict and uncertainty must be expected. Moreover, the demands placed on the leaders will be numerous and sometimes incompatible and contradictory. In sum, this means that leadership in academic organisations is a balancing act between collegiality, hierarchy, politics and business where department heads need to find their role among different governing ideologies.

REFERENCES

Baldridge, J.V. *Power and Conflict in the University*. New York: Wiley, 1971.
Bernt, J.F. *Lov om universiteter og høgskoler. Med kommentarer*. Bergen: Alma Mater forlag, 1996.
Birnbaum, R. *How Colleges Work: The Cybernetics for Academic Organisation and Leadership*. San Francisco: Jossey-Bass, 1988.
Birnbaum, R. *How Academic Leadership Works. Understanding Success and Failure in the College Presidency*. San Francisco: Jossey-Bass, 1992.
Bleiklie, I., R. Høstaker and A. Vabø. *Policy and Practice in Higher Education: Reforming Higher Education*. Higher Education Policy Series 49. London: Jessica Kingsley, 2000.
Bolton, A. *Managing the Academic Unit*. Buckingham: Open University Press, 2000.
Brunsson, N. and J.P. Olsen. *Kan organisasjonsformer velges?* Bergen: LOS-notat 6, 1990.
Byrkjeflot, H. and T. Halvorsen. "Ledelse og kunnskap – angloamerikanske og tyske kontraster." In Byrkjeflot, H. (ed.). *Fra styring til ledelse*. Bergen: Fagbokforlaget, 1997.
Christensen, T. "Målstyringskonseptets begrensinger." *Norsk statsvitenskapelig tidsskrift* 1 (1990): 33–41.
Clark, B. "Leadership and Innovation in Universities: From Theory to Practice." *TEAM* 1.1 (1995): 7–11.
Clark, B. *Creating Entrepreneurial Universities. Organizational Pathways of Transformation*. Issues in Higher Education. Oxford: Pergamon, 1998.
Dearlove, J. "Collegiality, Managerialism and Leadership." *TEAM* 1 (1995): 161–169.
Eriksson, C.B. *Akademiskt ledarskap*. Uppsala: Uppsala University, 1997.
Etzkowitz, H. "Individual Investigators and Their Research Groups." *Minerva* 30 (1992): 28–50.
Gornitzka, Å., S. Kyvik and I.M. Larsen. "The Bureaucratisation of Universities." *Minerva* 36.1 (1998): 21–47.
Gulbrandsen, M. *Research Quality and Organisational Factors: An Investigation of the Relationship*. Dr. ing. thesis. Trondheim: NTNU, 2000.

Gulddahl Rasmussen, J. "Management Between the Shop Floor and the Corporate Level." *European Journal of Education* 37 (2002): 43–55.

Gumport, P. "Academic Restructuring: Organizational Change and Institutional Imperatives." *Higher Education* 39 (2000): 67–91.

Harman, G. "Academic Leaders or Corporate Managers: Deans and Heads in Australian Higher Education, 1977 to 1997." *Higher Education Management and Policy* 14 (2002): 53–69.

Henkel, M. "Emerging Concepts of Academic Leadership and Their Implications for Intra-institutional Roles and Relationships in Higher Education." *European Journal of Education* 37 (2002): 29–41.

Kekäle, J. *Leadership Cultures in Academic Departments*. Joensuu: Joensuu yliopisto, 1997.

Kerr, C. "Universal Issues in the Development of Higher Education." In Balderston, J.B. and F. Balderston (eds). *Higher Education in Indonesia: Evolution and Reform*. Berkeley, CA.: Center for Studies in Higher Education, University of California, 1993, 19–35.

Kerr, C. "The Uses of the University." The Godkin Lectures. Harvard University. 1963, 5th edn. Cambridge, Mass.: Harvard University Press, 2001.

Kyvik, S. and I.M. Larsen. *Nye styringsformer på instituttnivå*. Oslo: NAVFs utredningsinstitutt rapport 8, 1993.

Larsen, I.M. "Research Policy at Universities – Walking the Tightrope Between Internal and External Interests." *European Journal of Education* 35.4 (2000): 385–402.

Larsen, I.M. *Instituttleder – mellom amatøridealet og profesjonalisering*. Oslo: NIFU rapport 5, 2002.

Middlehurst, R. *Leading Academic*. London: Open University Press, 1993.

Middlehurst, R. "New Realities for Leadership and Governance in Higher Education." *Tertiary Education and Management* 5.4 (1999): 307–329.

Middlehurst, R. and L. Elton. "Leadership and Management in Higher Education." *Studies in Higher Education* 17 (1992): 251–264.

Mintzberg, H. *The Structuring of Organizations*. Englewood Cliffs, NJ: Prentice-Hall, 1979.

Morgan, G. *Images of Organization: The Executive Edition*. London: Sage, 1998.

Nordbäck, L.E., C. Nordberg and L.E. Olson. "National Devolution in Swedish Higher Education – A Quest for New Local Leadership. The Case of Leadership Development at Göteborg University." *Tertiary Education and Management* 5.3 (1999): 227–243.

Olsen, J.P. "Universitetet. Sentralisering, autonomi og markedsstyring." *Nytt norsk tidsskrift* 4 (1987): 16–26.

HARRY DE BOER

WHO'S AFRAID OF RED, YELLOW AND BLUE?

The Colourful World of Management Reforms

1. INTRODUCTION

The demand for efficient and effective management of higher education institutions
is a recurrent theme. At least for the last four decades of the 20th century,
institutions have attempted – voluntarily or otherwise – to adopt new management
ideologies, techniques and processes. As mentioned in the introduction to this
volume, much of the specific managerial push in higher education can be related to
the new public management (NPM) movement in general. But, as also mentioned,
NPM is not a coherent, clearly specified body of theories or practices. It has been
interpreted in a variety of different ways according to the ideological preferences of
the observer, while also expressing certain logical inconsistencies (see Hood 1995
for a critical overview). Nonetheless, NPM has had a significant impact on the
management practices of a variety of different types of public sector institutions in
numerous countries. And, in this respect, NPM has been more a source or fount of
new ideas and ideologies on management from which different public institutions
and systems have selectively borrowed, than a management blueprint that can be
implemented in its entirety.

The purpose of this chapter is not to critique all the ways in which NPM has
been interpreted and applied. Rather, the intention here is to identify, in the higher
education context, newly introduced management values that arguably have their
basis in the NPM movement, and to explore the degree to which these values and
ideologies are taking root in different types of higher education systems. In the
1980s and 1990s, several higher education reforms had the distinct flavour of a new
managerialism: performance appraisal, output budgeting, quality assurance,
decentralisation, accountability, outsourcing etc. But, while one can identify
commonalities in the ideological basis of the new managerialism in higher
education, it is an empirical question as to the extent (if at all) these ideologies are
accepted by specific systems with different historical foundations.

The focus of this chapter is on university management reforms and how these
reforms are perceived and adopted by universities and their members. The
successful implementation of a reform implies that a reform is applied in the daily
activities of organisational members. If this is not the case, the effects of the reform
have to be considered as marginal and, consequently, the influence of the underlying
ideology must be seriously questioned.

A. Amaral et al. (eds.), The Higher Education Managerial Revolution?, 89–108.
© 2003 *Kluwer Academic Publishers. Printed in the Netherlands.*

The analysis of the university management reforms will be carried out from an international comparative perspective. Responses of three universities from three different countries – France, the Netherlands and Norway – will be examined. The aim is to investigate the degree to which the acceptance of certain NPM practices and ideologies are being universally embraced by higher education institutions.

The next section of this chapter further clarifies the approach to managerialism that is being adopted. Section 3 explains why it makes sense to critically approach managerialism. Section 4 provides background information on the university management reforms in France, the Netherlands and Norway. Section 5 chiefly addresses various methodological issues: research design and data analysis. The empirical results are presented in section 6. Here, the perceptions of French, Dutch and Norwegian academics and managers with respect to certain aspects of the latest university management reforms in their country are presented. Finally, in the concluding section, the empirical findings are interpreted in relation to the main questions of this chapter: To what extent has the new managerialistic ideology and the reforms that accompany it produced 'real' changes in university life? And: To what extent have these changes been universal across universities in different higher education national contexts?

2. MANAGERIALISTIC REFORMS IN UNIVERSITY STRUCTURES

In this chapter, managerialism is regarded as an ideology, a set of by and large systematically ordered values, ideas and beliefs about the management of public organisations (Pollitt 1993). Frequently ideologies are not well defined or clearly specified, though there is some coherence. Managerialism as an ideology can be regarded as a subjective construction coloured by normative views of how public organisations are and should be managed. It is an attitude, expressing people's feelings, values, norms, beliefs and understandings of public management. The most obvious characteristic of this managerial ideology "is of management itself – it is not only important, it is also good. Better management will make institutions perform ..." (Pollitt 1993: 7). Consequently, it is argued that managers should be given the 'right to manage' in order to establish good management practices, which are assumed to be found in the private sector.

Generally speaking, for the effective discharge of the special role and function that according to the managerial ideology should be attributed to professional managers, the internal world of universities needed to be reformed. Prevailing rule structures of 'democratic' universities[1] prevented managers from using their expertise to realise the noble 3–E values: economy, efficiency and effectiveness. Thus, universities have been urged to move away from traditional models of participative management towards more executive models of management. In the 1990s, attempts were made to impose new rules for internal university management on universities in many Western countries, including France, the Netherlands and Norway (see Akkermans, Cohen and Donner 1996; Askling and Henkel 2000; Bauer et al. 1999; De Boer and Denters 1999; De Boer, Denters and Goedegebuure 1998; De Boer and Goedegebuure 2001; Braun and Merrien 1999; Dimmen and Kyvik

1998; De Groof, Neave and Svec 1998; Halsey 1992; Henkel 2000; Larsen 2001; Meek and Wood 1997; Merrien and Musselin 1999; Mignot-Gérard 2003; Shattock 2002).[2]

The reforms of university management in the 1990s, in line with managerial ideas and values, attempted a redistribution of authority between the various levels in the higher education systems. The balance of power between the nation state, the central management level of the universities and its basic units (departments and chairs) have shifted. National governments, main players in many higher education systems, have encouraged a strengthening of institutional management by changing the composition of governing bodies, streamlining decision making within universities, providing greater power and authority to institutional executives, and altering the role of democratically elected senates and councils. Collegial decision-making bodies, such as these committees, are now largely advisory rather than vested with specific decision-making powers. Compared to the past, universities have been reshaped around a command structure with increased powers of executives and clear line management. Generally, there are tendencies for decision making with respect to teaching and, to a lesser extent, research to be centralised, whilst decision making on issues such as finance and personnel has been devolved. In these new university structures, here described in broad terms and somewhat stereotyped,[3] one can recognise core values of the managerialistic ideology.

The value of the 'right to manage', to use the managerial jargon, can also be seen in the expectations of those filling the new management positions inside universities. Traditionally, the university functions of scholarship, administration and leadership were interwoven. Leaders and managers in higher education were academics; academics controlled the main decision arenas, at least to a large extent. In the new structures of university governance and management, leaders are no longer expected to combine academic and administrative work as in the past. They are first and foremost full-time managers, no longer involved in the implementation of teaching and research programmes. They are supposed to be professionals in the art of governing, not in the primary academic processes.[4] A consequence of the managerial reforms should be the establishment of new patterns between 'policy entrepreneurs' ('the new managers') and employees ('academic and non-academic staff') (Exworthy and Halford 1999). A key element in the new interactions seems to be the tendency to increase the powers of the policy entrepreneurs, that is, the executives at top and middle level. They appear to be given 'the right to manage'.

Many seem firmly of the opinion that the managerial ideology has contributed to the establishment of broadly similar kinds of institutional structures 'everywhere'. The rationale of managerialism seems so convincing that it is hard to escape from it. But as will be pointed out in the next section there are several reasons to question the universal impact of this modern management 'remedy'.

3. QUESTIONING MANAGERIALISM AND ITS REFORMS

There are a number of reasons for questioning and investigating managerial reforms in higher education. First, as argued above, the concept of managerialism remains ill-defined and much more work is required in order to provide it with theoretical rigor and internal consistency. The second reason to question managerialism and its universality is that universities have different backgrounds and histories, especially when they are located in different countries. History matters, in particular when it comes to governance and management (De Groof, Neave and Svec 1998; Neave and Van Vught 1991). Under the assumption that institutional designs are path dependent, the same phenomenon may turn out differently from one place to another. Path dependency means that today's options are restricted by past choices. The repertory of designs and responses is limited; not all universities, given their past, have the same options. Why should, for instance, English, German and French universities respond to managerialism in the same way? And, suppose they want to respond in similar ways, do they have the (same) means and opportunities to do so? An educated guess based on the notion of path dependency would be that they do not.

The third point does not relate to the managerial ideology per se but to the implementation of its accompanying reforms. Reforms do not by definition lead to the intended results (Pressman and Wildavsky 1974).[5] One of the problems reformers have is that they have to rely on people who hold specific knowledge of the rules and have specific experience that can be acquired only through a long and costly learning process (Lanzara 1998). This knowledge and experience is a valuable commodity, required in order to implement new rules successfully. Otherwise the reform will fail. Many reforms are seen as 'old wine in new bottles', but probably even more frequently reforms are 'new wine in old bottles'. And these 'old bottles' tend to implant most of the old rules, practices and habits, if given the opportunity. Often people have this opportunity. Reformers are dependent on 'the old boys' knowledge'. They have a certain degree of autonomy, even when they are expected to play prescribed roles (Wippler 1983).[6] This autonomy can be exerted to maintain the status quo; performing the roles one knows best instead of applying new rules. New rules have to be learned and increase uncertainty. Thus, those charged with implementing new rules and ideas have strong predilections to resist change. Consequently, the result of the reform "starts to look strangely similar to what the innovators wanted to get rid off" (Lanzara 1998).[7] There is no reason why university reforms will not suffer the same problems with respect to their implementation.

The argument concerning doubts about intended outcomes of reforms needs special consideration when reforms are externally enforced. 'Forced' reforms tend to increase resistance to change even further, especially when they go against the wishes of those undergoing the reform. Most of the reforms of university management in the 1990s were initiated by national governments and were usually legally imposed on universities. This does not necessarily mean that the reforms were implemented against the will of all members of the universities. Nonetheless, the acceptance and impact of the reforms require critical analysis.

Formal change imposed by national legislators (and their accompanying rhetoric) and day-to-day practices may diverge significantly.[8] How deep have restructuring processes actually penetrated into university life, if they have penetrated at all? Universities and their members may have developed an array of plans, strategies and visions as a matter of symbolic compliance or legitimation. It may look like they are playing the game by the book. But have practices really been transformed? How is the redistribution of power perceived inside the universities? And are there differences in responses and perceptions within and between universities? Or are the managerial-based reforms so compelling and universal that they mould perceptions in the same way everywhere? The basic questions are: How are these reforms and their effects perceived? And: To what extent do they make a difference in daily activities? Do they affect people's behaviour in universities? If this is not the case, the effects of reforms are marginal and, consequently, the acceptability of the managerial ideology is questionable.

4. REFORMS OF UNIVERSITY MANAGEMENT STRUCTURES IN FRANCE, THE NETHERLANDS AND NORWAY

As stated above, in the late 1980s and 1990s the formal internal 'rules of the game' of universities changed in many Western countries, among them France, the Netherlands and Norway. At first glance all these reforms seem to be inspired by a common managerial ideology. From a distance they all look alike. But differences become apparent when a closer look is taken. To better understand what is happening, it is necessary to look at the reforms in detail. First, however, a few words about the similarities and differences of the three higher education systems prior to the reforms will be presented.

The case studies concern three universities belonging to what is traditionally known as the Continental system (Clark 1983). This model highlights important past features of the three higher education systems relevant to the understanding of subsequent shifts in university management. One of the central features of the ideal type Continental system is an authority distribution in which both the academic guild and the state bureaucracy have substantial powers. As a consequence the top level of the universities is rather weak. This top level of the university was regarded as the 'middleman' relaying information both top down and bottom up. Thus, in the traditional ideal type Continental structure, substantial powers were vested at the bottom, in the academic guild, and at the top of the system, that is, the ministerial bureaucracy (Clark 1983: 127).

In addition to sharing some common aspects of the Continental model of higher education, the three countries also experienced in the late 1960s and early 1970s similar social pressures to democratise internal university decision-making structures. 'Paris 1968' is a household word, not only in France but also in Norwegian and Dutch higher education. In all three countries the movement to increase student and non-professorial staff participation in higher education decision making had substantial effects inside universities, both in structural and cultural ways. A participatory decision-making style was enhanced with many factions of the university community granted rights to participate in decision making at various organisational levels.[9]

Having identified, at least superficially, some past higher education management commonalities amongst the three countries, the chapter will now examine how universities in these countries are responding to more recent pressures for management reform.

4.1. France

French higher education has a long and turbulent history that has left deep marks on its higher education institutions. The French system is still quite centralised and has a diversified structure. It is fragmented into diverse sectors with specialised functions, mainly for historical reasons (for a detailed overview of the system see Kaiser 2001). A striking feature of the fragmented French system is that public universities have never been institutions solely for the upper class (Merrien and Musselin 1999).

Until at least 1968, the state bureaucracy and the faculty guild were seen as the two dominant pillars in terms of governance and management. At the institutional level, the university itself hardly participated in governance (Merrien and Musselin 1999). 1968 is regarded as a turning point, though the extent of substantial change might be questioned. Merrien and Musselin (1999) drew the following conclusion. On the one hand, French universities had become more autonomous, while on the other hand, actual changes were seriously constrained because of path dependencies. For historical reasons, French universities look to the state as well as the academic corporation.

In 1984, the Savary Act was passed by national parliament, aimed at strengthening the autonomy of universities and providing more coherence at the institutional level. This act was not a radical change but more or less in keeping with the main ideas of the late 1960s. The university governing bodies remained as the office of the president and the two university councils (the *Conseil d'Administration* and the *Conseil Scientifique*). A third advisory body was introduced, the *Conseil des Études et de la Vie Universitaire* (CEVU). This 'democratic' structure soon attracted criticism. Some believed that this mode of governance allowed too many opportunities to politicise debates, while others believed that it prevented effective and strong leadership, encouraging 'fuzzy' balances of power among the main players.

In the late 1980s and early 1990s, French universities were confronted with a new policy that affected their governance. This 'contractual policy' was not aimed at university reform, yet ironically it introduced some profound and successful changes to the French university governance model (Mignot-Gérard 2003). It was not the contracts but the policy objectives that were important, including increasing internal institutional dynamics, strengthening the president's role, and modifying the state-university relationship (Merrien and Musselin 1999). This contractual policy clearly stated, among other things, that universities needed to strengthen and update their management tools in order to prepare strategic documents for negotiation processes with the ministry. It became necessary and possible at the institutional level to consider decisions that would not have appeared on the agenda previously. In these contractual processes, presidents discovered they could do more than simply represent their institution. Increasingly, presidents appear to have taken the opportunity to exercise their powers.

4.2. The Netherlands

Prior to the 1970s, Dutch university management was, in some respects, comparable to the French structure, dominated by state bureaucrats and academics. Authorities of academic and non-academic affairs were clearly separated in different bodies. At the universities, the nation state was represented by a board of curators, responsible for upholding laws and regulations, personnel policies and the administration of the university finances. The other pillar in this pre-1970 structure was the senate consisting of all full professors. This senate epitomised academic self-governance.

During the 1960s, there was a growing concern regarding the effectiveness and efficiency of traditional forms of university governance. These concerns were overshadowed by demands for more democratic participation, as was happening in France and Norway. This democratic movement fermented discontent in higher education resulting in a new act of university governance, *Wet op de Universitaire Bestuurshervorming* (WUB).

In this new WUB-Act of 1970, the emphasis was upon external and internal democratisation, though there were other, mostly forgotten, objectives including effectiveness and efficiency. The WUB-Act abolished both the senate and the board of curators. They were replaced by a system of functional representation through university and faculty councils. Academics (professors and other academic staff), non-academics and students were given the right to elect representatives to these legislative bodies. In addition, a limited number of lay members representing the general public were appointed to the council (for further information see De Boer and Denters 1999; De Boer, Denters and Goedegebuure 1998; De Boer, Maassen and De Weert 1999). The WUB-Act has attracted criticism from the beginning, but it constituted the formal governance framework of universities up till 1997.

In the mid-1990s, interrelated problems regarding the prevailing governance system were identified by an *ad hoc* committee chaired by the Minister of Education, Culture and Science. These problems were: 1) the inadequacy of the governance structure pertaining to the organisation of teaching; 2) the lack of clarity regarding responsibilities (in collective decision making, individuals did not seem to accept personal responsibility); 3) the dispersal of authority; 4) the bicephalic structure, particularly at the faculty level; 5) the strong orientation towards research at the expense of teaching; and 6) the inadequacy and incoherence of communication between the various organisational levels. These issues at the time were of concern to a wide audience. They contributed to a new act in 1997.

The introduction of the 1997 Act 'Modernising University's Governance Structures' (MUB) indicated substantial change, though the magnitude of change is debatable (e.g. De Boer, Denters and Goedegebuure 1998). The reform promoted efficiency and effectiveness in university decision making, and was in line with the overall governmental steering strategy that aimed to enhance institutional autonomy.

It abolished the system of 'co-determination' by board and council and the system of power fusion. Most powers regarding academic and non-academic affairs were allocated to executive positions at central and faculty levels. In addition, the structure became less decentralised in several ways such as through the abolition of the organisational third layer – the previously powerful *vakgroepen* ('departments'). From 1997 on, the dean has been given the authority 'to arrange the faculty's organisation'.

For the first time in their history, Dutch universities got a monocephalic structure. The new governing bodies comprise a system where executive and legislative powers are concentrated. Compared to the past, the academic community has little formal say in final decisions. All members of the crucial governing bodies, *raad van toezicht* ('supervisory board'), *college van bestuur* ('executive board'), and *decaan* ('dean'), are appointed by the body above it. Thus a new hierarchical management system based on appointments replaced the old, democratic system.

4.3. Norway

The Norwegian university sector is relatively young and the number of institutions in the university and college sector is rather small. Norwegian higher education is traditionally a public affair. The ministry has overall responsibility for higher education and research. Until the 1980s, the state bureaucracy used detailed regulations in determining the framework for universities.[10] However, for many years there was no general law governing all institutions. Instead most universities and institutions with university status had separate laws.[11] It was not until 1989 that institutions came under the umbrella of one legal authority.

A further salient feature of Norwegian university governance is the relatively long tradition of democratic participation. Since the beginning of the 20th century there has been a general tendency to broaden participation in university government. For many decades, students and academics were represented within universities in a form accepted by these groups themselves (Midgaard 1982: 290–294).[12] However, for several reasons things changed from the late 1960s onwards.

In the 1960s, university governance was reassessed. The reform processes began with the establishment of the Organisation Committee in 1967, and was further fuelled by the events in 1968 concerning the lack of 'democracy' in institutional governance. The student agitation did not result from resentment due to blocked participation in university affairs. New ideas speedily appeared, however, creating new structures and situations (Midgaard 1982: 320). After years of discussion, experiments and incremental adaptations, the new act was adopted in 1976, and was put into effect in 1977. In sum, the reform validated a three-level university structure (central level, faculties and departments), and a broadened composition of the collegiate bodies substituting representation with elections (Midgaard 1982). The reform meant that in university management both students and non-academic personnel should hold seats in the governing bodies (proportional representation). From the end of the 1960s, the former elite collegial structure in which full-time professors dominated was replaced by a more democratic system where other faculty staff, students and non-academic personnel also had opportunities to participate in formal decision making (Larsen 2002).

Further changes in university management occurred in 1989, 1996 and 2003. In 1989, parliament passed an act affecting the four universities and the six university-level colleges. This act strengthened institutional autonomy by shifting decision-making authority for many issues from the government to the institutions.

The 1996 Act provided a common framework for the governance and management structures of universities, colleges with university status, and non-university level state colleges. This contributed two major changes to the former steering principles: increased emphasis on stronger academic and administrative leadership of institutions and a definite division of responsibility between academic and administrative leaders. The first change has been referred to as initiating managerialism, through granting the central board and rector more power and authority, giving elected deans and chairs stronger academic leadership roles, and giving the administrative director a stronger formal role in institution management and greater regulative authority over all administrative levels (Dimmen and Kyvik 1998). The second change is labelled as divided leadership, by developing a tangible boundary between academic and administrative activities (Dimmen and Kyvik 1998). At the end of the 1990s, all higher education institutions had a differentiated governing structure at the central, faculty and department level and academic leaders had less administrative power and were developing a more political role. In addition, the central board had to appoint two to four external members – an initiative which initially met with much scepticism, but was later assessed as 'constructive' (Larsen 2001).

The elected leaders at a particular level are not superior to administrative leaders at the same level. The administrative director appointed by the central board heads the administrative side of the institution and has the authority to instruct and direct all administrative personnel. During the last 10 to 15 years, administrative director positions have been established at the faculty and department levels (Gornitzka, Kyvik and Larsen 1998), though not all departments have one. They are accountable to the central director. In this sense, the university is regarded as a single entity rather than a collection of faculties. The administrative director is accountable to the minister and is responsible for preparing proposals for governing body meetings and ensuring they are implemented according to established legal rules and practices. Norwegian institutions clearly have bicephalic structures where academic and non-academic affairs are separated.

In 2003, as Larsen analyses in this volume, Norwegian universities and colleges will face a new comprehensive reform entitled 'Quality Reform for Higher Education'. Initiated by the Norwegian government, and specified in a white paper, the reform allows for unitary leadership at faculty and department level, making academic leaders superior to administrative personnel. It is intended to strengthen academic leadership at the lower levels of the university by introducing appointed leadership for a fixed term and increasing the powers of department heads. This traditional model of elected leadership is under pressure, though the new reforms are not being forced upon the universities. Within the legal framework, the universities are granted ample room to choose their own structures. At the institutional level, for instance, it is no longer obligatory to have a university council.

5. METHODOLOGY

This chapter regards managerialism as an ideology with an almost unconditional trust in management itself as the paramount value. According to this ideology, managers should be granted reasonable 'room to manoeuvre' and have the right to manage. But what does 'the right to manage' mean? How can the realities underlying this slogan be measured?

In the case studies, two aspects of the reforms have been identified. The first aspect relates to the decline of the traditional features of a university as an organisation. For years, universities have been characterised by being loosely coupled, bottom heavy, dominated by academics, and having dispersed powers and fluid structures. The slogan 'the right to manage' is associated with top-down decision making, hierarchy, centralisation, dominance by managers etc. Therefore, the degree of acceptance of the ideology behind the slogan 'the right to manage' can be measured through university staff's perceptions with respect to questions such as "Do you perceive a strengthening of institutional leadership?", "Have decision-making structures become more hierarchical?", "Are powers more concentrated compared to the past?" and "Has the role of professionals changed in favour of managers?"

The second indicator for change concerns the selection mechanism for those who are granted the right to manage. As described in the previous section, the universities in all three countries have a longstanding tradition of elected academic leadership.[13] The alternative to elected leadership is of course appointed leadership. In the latter case, leaders are allocated to a community by means of appointment from above. The legitimacy of a leader, their role, position and functionality may be differentiated by the type of selection mechanism. The 'right to manage' is associated with appointed leadership. However, appointed leadership is not traditionally characteristic of universities. Therefore, the acceptance of appointed leadership would be a good indicator for measuring substantial change in university management.

To explore how people inside universities experience the changed governance structures of their institutions, empirical evidence from a larger study has been analysed (Currie et al. 2003). Between 1998 and 2001, four case studies were conducted of four universities in four different countries. In this chapter, the cases of the University of Avignon (France), the University of Oslo (Norway) and the University of Twente (the Netherlands)[14] will be taken into consideration with respect to issues of governance and management.[15]

For each university a trend report has been written. These trend reports are the sources for the analyses. There are three types of evidence and evaluation in each report. First, university documents, national statistics, reports and historical and contemporary accounts have been analysed. On the basis of these background materials, the three universities have been contextualised within their national settings. Second, face-to-face interviews were conducted with senior administrators and academic staff. Due to time constraints, students and non-academic staff were not interviewed. The sample included 94 persons (31 from Oslo, 31 from Twente and 32 from Avignon). The length of the interviews ranged from 30 to 60 minutes. The respondents were asked a similar set of about twenty questions, including aspects of governance and management. They gave their opinions and thoughts about what was occurring at their universities. Finally, the trend report of each university was checked by a local key respondent and sent to each participant. (For more details about this study see Currie et al. 2003.)

The three case studies are addressed in the next section. Each case starts with a brief description of the university followed by the respondents' perceptions.

6. THREE CASE STUDIES

6.1. University of Avignon

6.1.1. Introduction
The original institution was founded in the 14th century, but was abolished during the French Revolution. It was reconstituted after World War II. The University of Avignon is one of the newest and smallest of France's 90 universities, though it has grown considerably (within 13 years, it increased student numbers from approximately 2,500 in 1985 to 6,480 in 1998). Today, there is a new campus at the University of Avignon that accommodates four faculties and two technology institutes.

The academics have permanent civil service status. Their recruitment and promotion are decided by nationally determined panels, guidelines and authority. In general, the structure of French universities remains primarily a bureaucratic, public service model. Along with its public service model, the French higher education system is rooted in the democratic traditions of the French Revolution, therefore also adopting a fairly collegial approach. However, without as much autonomy as Dutch or Norwegian universities, French universities have power over a much smaller budget and make fewer employment and curricular decisions.

At the end of the 20th century, the French higher education system compared to other systems remains quite centralised with a diversified structure. An important organisational feature, deeply historically embedded, is the prominence of the faculty as an organisational unit in relation to the university as a whole. Deans are powerful persons and remain in office for a considerable length of time. Several initiatives have been taken to strengthen institutional leadership. It seems only recently that these initiatives have started to succeed.

6.1.2. French Perceptions
The French respondents argued that managerialism has not yet entered their university structure. Their perceptions are completely different from those of their

colleagues at the Universities of Oslo and Twente. Only a few of the Avignon respondents suggested that there has been a shift towards a managerial approach. Many perceived collegiality as the main feature (particularly at the lower levels). About a third mentioned the bureaucracy as a dominant characteristic. Perceptions of increased bureaucracy might be due to the growth of the university. Many respondents referred to blends of collegial, bureaucratic and managerial elements.

Generally, the Avignon case does not suggest major changes in the area of governance structures. The most often mentioned change is the arrival of new leaders, not of a change in rules and structures. New leaders may of course make a difference, but they do not necessarily transform rules and structures.

It can be concluded that the Avignon respondents did not perceive a fundamental change in the role of academics in decision making. Approximately one-third observed no change at all in this respect. Many of those who did perceive change expressed positive feelings with respect to increased openness, collegiality and information exchange. There were also some negative feelings regarding less freedom and academic autonomy and the imposition of reforms upon academics.

In Avignon, leaders are elected and almost all respondents approved of this. Democracy is normatively appealing to them, involving intrinsic values traditionally held by French society and dating from the days of the French Revolution. This is illustrated in the following quote when a respondent was asked if he preferred elected leadership.

> It goes without saying. We didn't go through the whole French Revolution and cut off the heads of our kings only to end up today with a system where the former President chooses the next one. Heavens no, this is absolutely unthinkable!

Other positive effects of electing leaders, according to the Avignon respondents, include better choice of leaders, enhanced solidarity among academic staff and leaders, the development of a sense of responsibility and mutual trust and respect.

6.2. University of Oslo

6.2.1. Introduction
Initially, the University of Oslo had four faculties; today there are eight. Teaching staff are civil servants, with life tenure, and are appointed by the university. In 1998, student enrolments totalled 34,450.

The university draws its ethos and mission from the Humboldt tradition, stressing dedication to pure research, and freedom to criticise all established truths and societal institutions. In addition, academics are given much autonomy, many preferring to work on questions of curiosity rather than being overly involved with questions of community relevance or applied research.

A common characteristic of the university's governing system is its colleague-based decision making, evident at each level: central, faculty and department. Each level has a parallel administrative leadership. The University of Oslo is regarded as democratic, holding elections for important academic positions at least every three years. The boards and councils are specifically constituted to ensure that all groups are represented. Since 1996, external representation, from state bureaucracy and corporate life, has been required on university boards. The university board decides most strategic research issues, though the National Research Council, through its funding programmes, influences the direction of strategic research in Norwegian universities.

6.2.2. Norwegian Perceptions

The majority of the respondents in Oslo perceived a shift towards 'managerialism', by and large, similar to the University of Twente (see section 6.3.2). The assessment of this shift is split unevenly with approximately half expressing negative perceptions, a quarter positive ones, and a quarter having mixed feelings. The most frequently mentioned change at the top level of the University of Oslo concerned increased bureaucracy and smaller governing bodies with more external representation. Bureaucracy in this context implies increased control, emphasising transparency and accountability and strengthening central steering capacity and centralising power. After the 1996 reform, the rector, deans and heads of departments were supposed to have more responsibilities.

At the lower levels of the University of Oslo, respondents reported increased power for the deans and heads of departments, the need to economise due to budget cuts and, to a lesser extent, the restructuring of faculties and departments into larger units. However, despite the perceived trend toward managerialism and increased bureaucratisation, many respondents indicated that there remains a strong culture of democracy and collegiality. This feeling is well reflected in the following quote by a senior social scientist:

> There is a managerial culture, the administrative culture, and the academic culture. And I would still think that by and large the academic culture prevails. I think in the central administration there is some move towards professional managerialism, but once you move out of that building you would still see the other culture prevailing. The academic culture is very, very strong.

Nevertheless, most of the Oslo respondents believed that the role of academics in decision making has diminished, without suggesting that they have been sidelined. About a quarter of the respondents did not perceive significant changes in this respect. Most of the respondents, believing that the academic's role in university decision making has declined, assessed this decline negatively. A few mentioned positive effects such as increased efficiency and greater accountability.

At the University of Oslo leaders are elected.[16] As in Avignon, the respondents at the University of Oslo are keen to preserve this tradition.[17] Democracy is valued for its own sake. In addition to the reasons mentioned in the French case, the respondents see elections as a desirable mechanism because it may stimulate internal discussion between candidates running for office. And competence is used as an argument: those who work at a university are more capable of saying who will be the best leader than an external committee appointing someone. This final point is an intriguing one. The 'competence argument' is used elsewhere to draw the opposite conclusion. In the case of the centrally managed university of Boston College and, to a lesser extent, at the University of Twente, it was argued that while the most popular person will win the elections, this most popular person may not have the management skills to do the job. Beliefs about the consequences of a selection mechanism could not differ more.

6.3. University of Twente

6.3.1. Introduction
The University of Twente is one of the youngest and smallest of the 13 Dutch universities, founded and established in 1961, in an area that was economically depressed, near the eastern region of the German border. During the 1980s, enrolment increased, followed by a slight decline of student numbers to 6,383 in 1993 and 5,515 in 1998. By 2000, most staff (80 per cent) were full-time, permanent civil servants.

In the mission statement, Twente describes itself as "an entrepreneurial university for academic education and research, offering training courses in both technical and social disciplines". This organisational saga of being entrepreneurial dates back to the early 1980s in the Netherlands because of Twente's success in developing links to regional industries. The University of Twente had 10 faculties up till September 2002 after which the number was reduced to five.

Because of the imposed MUB-Act, the University of Twente established new governing bodies in 1997 and 1998 (De Boer and Goedegebuure 2001) such as the supervisory board (a central management team composed of the central executive board and the deans).[18] The central executive board, including the *rector magnificus*, has increased its power. In December 1997, the university council was dissolved, and in its place a new council of staff and student representatives was established.[19] This representative advisory council lost many powers compared to the former university council, including budgetary powers.

6.3.2. Dutch Perceptions
An overwhelming majority of the respondents at the University of Twente indicated that there had been a shift towards managerialism. In particular, they mentioned the centralisation of decision making. About half the respondents valued this positively, while the other half raised objections. But it needs to be noted that there are differences between formal rules and informal practices, as some of the answers clearly indicated:

> In theory we have become more managerial, but in practice we haven't.

> In a formal sense there is more line management but in practice I think the decision-making system remained highly collegial.

The respondents were nearly unanimous on the issue of increased hierarchy and the introduction of a top-down structure, which according to their answers had clearly been the case since 1997, the year of the governance reform. It should be taken into account, however, that the structure of the University of Twente prior to

1997 was known to be very decentralised, which implies that a change by and large 'automatically' means more centralisation.

The position of the executive at the middle level – the dean – is perceived in various ways. It is not denied that the power of the dean's position has increased. However, the exercise of these extended powers is perceived differently: some stressed the formal position of the new deans, whereas others observed that the changes were not as dramatic as they first appeared because deans realise that consultancy and commitment are needed to achieve good results and to keep the faculty viable.

What then are the perceptions of the role of academics in decision making? Approximately half of the 'Twentonians' believed that the role of academics in decision making had changed over the past years. This is a remarkably low number considering the implementation of the 1997 Act on governance and the fact that nearly all respondents reported a shift towards more managerialism.

Many respondents did not perceive dramatic changes to the academic's role in decision making. Most of the respondents who perceived changes to academic roles indicated that these roles have generally been diminished, but not necessarily in a negative way. Increased transparency, efficiency and less gratuitous interference with detailed decision making were mentioned as gains. On the other hand, the loss of collegiality, potential power concentration and greater difficulty of being involved and well informed were reported as negative effects.

The selection mechanism for leaders such as rectors, deans and heads of departments is a difficult item to analyse in Twente. Formally, there is no tradition in the Netherlands to elect leaders, at least not directly. However, prior to 1997 the governance structure as such was regarded as democratic (representatives of the powerful councils were chosen by the various factions and these councils had a say in the selection of the leaders. This situation is not very different from the French structure where elected representatives choose the president and the deans). Since 1997 all executives are appointed; right of nomination and the like are formally not now in the hands of representative councils.

About a third of the Twente respondents do not prefer elected leadership, whereas the others would like to have some kind of democracy, but without direct elections for rectors and deans. Democracy is valued for instrumental reasons. The following quote illustrates this point:

> I think for the best functioning of the academic environment it would be good to have academic staff have a say in the way the university is being managed. And the electoral process may be a very good mechanism for that.

Those in Twente who did not support elections for executives argued that elections might politicise internal decision making further; it is less efficient; and, the most often mentioned reason: it is too difficult to find suitable candidates to run for a position. In other words, it is hard to organise meaningful elections. It has to be kept in mind, as some of the respondents state, that appointing leaders may be less undemocratic than it looks. It does not by definition exclude the involvement of various members of the university community. A frequently used informal system of consultation appears to be an important aspect of decision making at the University of Twente.

7. CONCLUSION

A common assumption is that the rationale for the push towards a new managerialism in higher education is so powerful that all institutions must accept it. But the empirical evidence presented in this chapter questions the universal applicability and impact of the managerialistic ideology. In order to assess the universal applicability of the managerialistic ideology, it was assumed that its accompanying reforms must have produced the intended effects in day-to-day practices. The key questions are: Have the managerialistically driven reforms been taken up inside universities? Do university members perceive changes? and, related to the universal claims of the managerial ideology: Are these perceptions at different locations proceeding in the same direction? How are changes attributed to managerialism perceived in reality?

The classic answer regarding the appraisal of reforms such as managerialism obviously is that it depends on the perspective of the observer. There are both similarities and differences in the perceptions of the respondents to the case studies with respect to the new management regimes. Differences depend in part if one focuses on formal or informal rules and regulations. If formal rules are taken as the point of departure, clearly, changes associated with various aspects of the managerial ideology are occurring in the different higher education systems. In all three countries previously classified as Continental systems of higher education, managerialism seems to have influenced public management thinking. Examples include structural reforms of formal university management; the introduction of contractual policies in France; the 1996 reform of the national higher education act in Norway; and the 1997 'modernisation' of Dutch university governance. If, however, informal rules and daily practices are taken into account the conclusions may be different, as the respondents have clearly indicated.

As the case studies demonstrate, changes relating to the managerialistic ideology and university management reforms are perceived in various ways. There is a wide variety in perceptions within and between universities. Moreover, the case studies support the idea that, in the area of management, history matters. This is clearly evident with respect to the selection of leaders. Apart from other benefits and costs of a new management ideology, in Avignon and Oslo change to the election mechanism seems out of the question according to the respondents.[20] These respondents have never experienced or imagined an alternative. As one of the French respondents said:

> This is the only system we know, and quite honestly this is the only one I can imagine.

Similar responses came from Oslo and Twente.[21] The Twente case is somewhat confusing. Most of the Twente respondents appear to prefer to stick to their tradition of being involved in the process of appointments without the necessity of electing leaders.

The case studies also indicate that people have incentives to be conservative towards change. Consequently, the outcomes of reforms or the institutionalisation of change may differ from the intentions. The Norwegian case, for instance, shows that managerial ideas might have had some impact but that a culture of democracy persists. This outcome is supported by Larsen (2002) who suggests that a collegial governance model still runs deep in Norwegian universities. It is also clear that there are several opportunities for people inside universities to continue with old, informal rules and to preserve habits and customs. For example, why the degree of perceived change is limited in the Netherlands may be due to the fact that the 'new boys' are still the 'old deans'. It will be interesting to see what happens when the next generation of new managers are installed.

This chapter will conclude with a metaphor to summarise the findings (see Currie et al. 2003). Suppose that red, yellow and blue university structures are exposed to the very same black reform. What will be the action of black on the three other colours? The first conclusion is that each university's colour will change. The second conclusion will be that they will change in the same direction: all universities developing darker colours. The third conclusion to be drawn, however, is that the universities continue to have different colours! Red and black do not yield the same colour as the yellow and black mixture. The ultimate colour of a university depends, of course, on the precise composition of the mixture of colours. If you were to add enough black, the other colours would disappear. That is the fear of those who see the threat of managerialism to traditional values in universities.

Based on the interpretation of the case study respondents' answers, we can conclude that the intensity of the managerial ideology and its impact differ from one university to another (a little more black is spotted at some places and is nowhere totally dominant). In the end, the three universities still have many differences in their governing styles and structures. Thus, adding one single colour has not (yet) resulted worldwide in one grey institutional structure for universities.

NOTES

[1] A democratically structured university refers in a general sense to a university structure in which many factions of a university community have the opportunity to speak up and to promote their interests (for instance, by means of being represented by elected representatives on commissions, councils, boards and so on). For an analytical discussion of this concept see De Boer and Denters (1999).

[2] Note that managerialistic ideology and the structural reforms of university management have been separated from each other for analytical reasons. One might also argue that structural reforms are a fundamental part of managerialism. In that case, managerialism is not seen solely as an ideology, but as a bundle of instruments, techniques, methods and so on. That is not the position adopted here.

[3] By way of introduction to the three case studies that will be presented in this chapter, a more detailed description of the university reforms in France, the Netherlands and Norway follows in the next section.

[4] This is a general and over-simplified picture of modern university management practices. It is clear that several 'managers' such as deans are still connected to and familiar with teaching and research. There is, however, a noticeable shift in terms of role expectations and the interpretation of the management positions.

5   This becomes immediately evident when one reads the (sub)title of Pressman and Wildavsky's classic Implementation: *How Great Expectations in Washington are Dashed in Oakland; Or, Why It's Amazing That Federal Programs Work at All.*

6   Different interpretations of rules, the ambiguity of some rules, and multiple, and sometimes conflicting rules to adhere to, may cause situations in which people chose not to follow the rules as was intended by the reformers, even when these people in principle are willing to contribute to the reform.

7   This argument begs the question of what the meaning and content of change actually is but, in this chapter, this interesting question will not be addressed.

8   This does not necessarily imply that people break the law. As described above, laws, rules and procedures leave considerable room for people to manoeuvre. As a consequence, rules can be by-passed, can have side effects, or can be moulded instead of broken.

9   For more details see Currie el al. (2003) and Daalder and Shils (1982).

10 Concurrently, universities clearly needed and had considerable academic autonomy, for instance, professors had substantial power and freedom regarding teaching and research (Midgaard 1982).

11 Due to the lack of a comprehensive higher education law stipulating university governance and the fact that two of the four universities had to start from scratch, there are substantial differences between Norwegian universities. This section outlines the main changes focusing largely on the University of Oslo.

12 Midgaard (1982: 293) concludes for instance that in the (early) 1960s "Student leaders involved in the governing bodies of the university and the Student Welfare Organisation hardly had the feeling that barriers must be broken down to give them a say in affairs of central interest to the students".

13 This of course is not the same as democratic leadership. It depends on who belongs to the electorate. In the past, these rights were usually granted to full professors only (De Boer and Denters 1999).

14 Boston College (US), which was included in the original study, is excluded from the analyses here. In this chapter, I want to focus on Continental European structures of higher education, because of their similarity in background, at least to some extent. As is well known, the structure and history of higher education in the United States is completely different. For those interested in the contrasting case of Boston College, see the larger study of Currie et al. (2003).

15 Other issues that have been analysed in the study of Currie et al. (2003) are privatisation, competition and entrepreneurialism, accountability, employment flexibility and new technology.

16 One of the changes of the quality reform in 2003 is that universities have the opportunity to change the election system by replacing it with an appointed system for leaders (see Larsen 2002). This change was, however, not under discussion when the empirical data were gathered. Consequently, in this section, it is assumed by respondents that leaders are elected, though that mechanism may have been replaced at some universities since 2003.

17 The perceptions about elected leadership may have changed after the publication of the government's white paper 'Quality Reform for Higher Education'. See Larsen's contribution in this volume.

18 This management team is not a legal entity, but is nevertheless a powerful body within the new governance setting.

19 Originally two separate advisory councils were established; one for students and one for staff. After two years, it was decided to merge these two councils of representatives into one. The same development has taken place at the faculty level.

20 This conclusion is based on the outcomes of surveys that were conducted in 1998 and 1999. As mentioned earlier, the election mechanism in Norwegian university management structures, and the perceptions of it, may have changed after the 2003 reform.

21 Similar acceptance of the prevailing status quo was also found in the (not presented) case of Boston College, where leaders are appointed. Take, for instance, the following quotes: "Oh gosh. It seems so remote I can't even imagine it" or "Quite honestly the idea is so foreign to me that I find it hard to even contemplate how that would occur".

REFERENCES

Akkermans, P.W.C., M.J. Cohen and J. Donner. *Een nieuwe universitaire bestuursvorm.* Deventer: W.E.J. Tjeenk Willink, 1996.

Askling, B. and M. Henkel. "Higher Education Institutions." In Kogan, M., M. Bauer, I. Bleiklie and M. Henkel (eds). *Transforming Higher Education. A Comparative Study.* London: Jessica Kingsley, 2000, 109–127.

Bauer, M., B. Askling, S.G. Marton and F. Marton. *Transforming Universities; Changing Patterns of Governance, Structure and Learning in Swedish Higher Education.* London: Jessica Kingsley, 1999.

Braun, D. and F.-X. Merrien. "Governance of Universities and Modernisation of the State: Analytical Aspects." In Braun, D. and F.-X. Merrien (eds). *Towards a New Model of Governance for Universities? A Comparative View.* London: Jessica Kingsley, 1999, 9–33.

Clark, B.R. *The Higher Education System: Academic Organization in Cross-National Perspective.* Berkeley, CA: University of California Press, 1983.

Currie, J., R. DeAngelis, H. de Boer, J. Huisman and C. Lacotte. *Globalizing Practices and University Responses. European and Anglo-American Differences.* Westport, CT: Praeger, 2003.

Daalder, H. and E. Shils. *Universities, Politicians, and Bureaucrats: Europe and the United States.* Cambridge and New York: Cambridge University Press, 1982.

De Boer, H. and B. Denters. "Analysis of Institutions of University Governance: A Classification Scheme Applied to Postwar Changes in Dutch Higher Education." In Jongbloed, B., P. Maassen and G. Neave (eds). *From the Eye of the Storm. Higher Education's Changing Institution.* Dordrecht: Kluwer Academic Publishers, 1999, 211–233.

De Boer, H., B. Denters and L. Goedegebuure. "On Boards and Councils; Shaky Balances Considered. The Governance of Dutch Universities." *Higher Education Policy* 11.2/3 (1998): 153–164.

De Boer, H. and L. Goedegebuure. "On Limitations and Consequences of Change: Dutch University Governance in Transition." *Tertiary Education and Management* 7.2 (2001): 163–180.

De Boer, H., P. Maassen and E. de Weert. "The Troublesome Dutch University and its Route 66 Towards a New Governance Structure." *Higher Education Policy* 12.4 (1999): 329–342.

De Groof, J., G. Neave and J. Svec. *Democracy and Governance in Higher Education.* The Hague/London/Boston: Kluwer Law International, 1998.

Dimmen, A. and S. Kyvik. "Recent Changes in the Governance of Higher Education Institutions in Norway." *Higher Education Policy* 11.2/3 (1998): 217–228.

Exworthy, M. and S. Halford. "Professionals and Managers in a Changing Public Sector: Conflict, Compromise and Collaboration?" In Exworthy, M. and S. Halford (eds). *Professionals and the New Managerialism in the Public Sector.* Buckingham/Philadelphia: Open University Press, 1999, 1–17.

Gornitzka, Å., S. Kyvik and I.M. Larsen. "The Bureaucratisation of Universities." *Minerva* 36 (1998): 21–47.

Halsey, A.H. *Decline of Donnish Dominion: The British Academic Professions in the Twentieth Century.* Oxford: Clarendon Press, 1992.

Henkel, M. *Academic Identities and Policy Change in Higher Education.* London: Jessica Kingsley, 2000.

Hood, C. "Contemporary Public Management: A New Global Paradigm?" *Public Policy and Administration Journal* 10.2 (1995): 104–117.

Kaiser, F. *France: Country Report.* CHEPS Higher Education Monitor. Enschede: University of Twente, 2001.

Lanzara, G.F. "Self-destructive Processes in Institution Building and Some Modest Countervailing Mechanisms." *European Journal of Political Research* 33.1 (1998): 1–40.

Larsen, I.M. "The Role of the Governing Board in Higher Education Institutions." Paper prepared for the *Seminar on Governance Structures in Higher Education Institutions,* CIPES/HEDDA, Pinhao, Portugal, 2001.

Larsen, I.M. "Between Control, Rituals and Politics: The Governing Board in Higher Education Institutions in Norway." In Amaral, A., G. Jones and B. Karseth (eds). *Governing Higher Education: National Perspectives on Institutional Governance.* Dordrecht: Kluwer Academic Publishers, 2002, 99–119.

Meek, V.L. and F. Wood. *Higher Education Governance and Management: An Australian Study.* Canberra: AGPS, 1997.

Merrien, F.-X. and C. Musselin. "Are French Universities Finally Emerging? Path Dependency Phenomena and Innovative Reforms in France." In Braun, D. and F.-X. Merrien (eds). *Towards a New Model of Governance for Universities? A Comparative View.* London: Jessica Kingsley, 1999, 220–238.

Midgaard, K. "Norway: The Interplay of Local and Central Decisions." In Daalder, H. and Edward Shils (eds). *Universities, Politicians, and Bureaucrats. Europe and the United States.* Cambridge: Cambridge University Press, 1982, 275–328.

Mignot-Gérard, S. "Who are the Actors in the Government of French Universities? The Paradoxical Victory of Deliberative Leadership." *Higher Education* 45.1 (2003): 71–89.

Neave, G. and F.A. van Vught. *Prometheus Bound. The Changing Relationship Between Government and Higher Education in Western Europe.* Oxford: Pergamon Press, 1991.

Ostrom, E. "An Agenda for the Study of Institutions." *Public Choice* 48 (1986): 3–25.

Pollitt, C. *Managerialism and the Public Services. Cuts or Cultural Change in the 1990s?* 2nd edn. Oxford: Blackwell Publishers, 1993.

Pressman, J.L. and A. Wildavsky. *Implementation: How Great Expectations in Washington are Dashed in Oakland; Or, Why It's Amazing That Federal Programs Work At All.* Berkeley: University of California Press, 1974.

Shattock, M. "Re-balancing Modern Concepts of University Governance." *Higher Education Quarterly* 56.3 (2002): 235–244.

Wildavsky, A. "If Planning is Everything, Maybe it's Nothing." *Policy Sciences* 4 (1973): 127–153.

Wippler, R. "De plaats van roltheoretische ideeën in de sociologie." In Visser, A.P., E. van der Vliert, E.J.H. ter Heine and J.A.M. Winnubst (eds). *Rollen; Persoonlijke en sociale invloeden op het gedrag.* Amsterdam/Meppel: Boom, 1983, 61–82.

HANS PECHAR

IN SEARCH OF A NEW PROFESSION

Transformation of Academic Management in Austrian Universities

1. INTRODUCTION

It could be that future historians of Austrian higher education will consider the early years of the new millennium as equally important as the aftermath of the revolution in 1848, when Austria embraced the Humboldtian model. Commencing in 2004, Austrian universities will cease to be state agencies and will acquire a kind of corporate autonomy unparalleled in the last 400 years.[1] This chapter looks at this radical change from the perspective of management issues: What are the consequences of this reform for academic leadership? Under what conditions will the new managers be able to cope with their tremendously increased responsibilities? The chapter is divided into three sections. The first two are analytical and descriptive: What are the roots of Austrian universities? What traditions shaped them? What were the reasons for, and the steps of, change? The third section has a rather normative approach: What can be considered as 'good practice' for academic management in a period of transition?

2. THE STARTING POINT: UNIVERSITIES AS STATE AGENCIES

Nearly everywhere, universities are going through fundamental change driven mainly by the persistent growth of participation rates on the one hand, and the emergence of new general policy paradigms on the other. Governments have strengthened their demands of accountability due to increasing public expenditure for higher education. Declining public expenditure per student has forced universities to enhance their efficiency and to look for other sources of income. As a consequence, universities have experienced significant pressure on their organisation and decision-making structures. The traditional self-governing bodies have lost influence while leadership at the top of the institution has been strengthened. This is the general background for the 'managerial revolution' in higher education.

There are, however, some characteristic features of that change in Austrian higher education. In a nutshell: reforms came later to Austria than to most comparable nations but, when they arrived, they were rapidly promoted. What can be labelled as the 'state model' (referring to 'Clark's triangle') was until the early 1990s strongly developed in Austria. Correspondingly, the sense of the corporate autonomy of the university was very weak, even weaker than in some other

A. Amaral et al. (eds.), The Higher Education Managerial Revolution?, 109–129.
© 2003 *Kluwer Academic Publishers. Printed in the Netherlands.*

countries of the Humboldtian tradition. The traditional pattern can be characterised by a dualism between administrative and academic issues: the university as an organisational unit was subject to centralised decision making by legislation and state bureaucracy while all issues regarding teaching and research were in the hands of the academic oligarchy – each chairholder in charge of their own specialised field of research.

This dualism was also reflected in the internal organisation of the university, in a parallel leadership structure. There was an academic hierarchy (rector, dean, head of institute) on the one hand, and a hierarchy of administrative functions on the other. The head of university administration (*Universitätsdirektor*) was neither appointed by the rector nor elected by the collegial bodies; the head was appointed by the Minister and in most matters responsible to the Minister.

This dualism goes back to the mid 19th century, when the Humboldtian system was established in Austria (Cohen 1996). Academics usually did not strive for corporate autonomy of the university, rather the opposite; it was a relief not to be in charge of trivial matters. The educated elite regarded it as a cultural obligation of the enlightened secular state (*Kulturstaat*) to provide beneficial circumstances for academic life. The state was seen mainly as a power to protect the integrity and autonomy of universities, not as a potential threat to their independence. Academics were civil servants with lifelong tenure. This status was supposed to secure academic freedom against pressure from outside, in particular from the Roman Catholic Church which up to the 20th century had a strained relationship with the modern concept of autonomous science. Of course, there were occasional conflicts between politicians and bureaucrats[2] on the one hand, and academics on the other; but, for most of the time, the relationship was based on mutual respect and trust.

At the institutional level, the university as an organisation was weak. The most important issues were directly dealt with between the chair-holding professors and the state bureaucracy. The corporative structures at the university and faculty levels had merely a symbolic function. It was the self-image of the university to be a self-governing community of scholars held together by common values. The rector was regarded as *primus inter pares* to represent the university, not to govern, let alone manage it. The administration of the institutions was regarded as a trivial issue; it was the responsibility of a senior administrative civil servant (*Universitätsdirektor*) who was not of equal academic rank, but subordinate to the Minister.

This pattern was maintained longer in Austria than in most comparable countries. Its basic structures even survived a first cycle of reforms during the late 1960s and 1970s, when policy makers tried to modernise the higher education system. Since it was now regarded as an important goal to raise the qualifications of the workforce, the whole education system, including higher education, caught the attention of policy makers. The government set the course for educational expansion and modified the traditional chair system (*Ordinarienuniversität*). In the course of these reforms, students and junior faculty acquired new rights, but that was not accompanied by a strengthening of the corporate rights of the university; on the contrary, this was the heyday of state regulation. During that period the mutual trust and respect between academics and policy makers started to erode. A majority of the academic oligarchy opposed the higher education reforms, so the government had to enforce it by legislation and other means of regulation.

During the 1980s, universities slowly got used to the new model of decision making. There was some complaint, but the majority of the academics, and even a large proportion of professors, accepted the idea of the university as a corporate body. In some ways, the early 1980s was a time of consolidation in higher education policy. In other ways, however, it was also a time of change, though unspectacular. Student numbers continued to grow and exceeded the levels which had been forecast only a few years earlier. However, due to fiscal consolidation, public expenditure on universities could not keep pace with the growth of student numbers.

During the late 1980s, a dramatic shift of paradigms in higher education policy took place. Up to that time, the key actors in the political and administrative system supported the tradition of stringent state regulation of all kinds of education institutions, universities included. During the late 1980s, trust in the traditional patterns of maintenance and funding gradually eroded. This was caused by a variety of factors, the two most important being the crisis of central steering and the crisis of public finance.

- *The crisis of central steering.* The expansion of higher education significantly increased the complexity of the system. This undermined the Austrian tradition of central steering of the education system, which was based on the assumption that the key actors of the system share some common visions about the 'one best system' (or at least that they share the belief that one such best system does exist); and that the most powerful actors at the top of the system have the necessary means (sufficient information and influence to motivate actors at lower levels) to implement the 'best solution'. First doubts on that approach appeared in Austria during the 1970s. During the 1980s, the legitimacy of the central steering approach was gradually undermined. The dominant view was that universities were bound by a rigid state bureaucracy and hence could not develop their creativity. At the end of the 1980s, even some policy makers and top civil servants shared those views. As soon as the key actors stopped believing in them, the 'etatist'[3] traditions in educational steering could not be perpetuated.

- *The crisis of public finance.* Fiscal consolidation, which became a priority of government in the late 1980s, had severe consequences for higher education policy. As long as politicians and senior civil servants had sufficient funds to distribute, they were quite eager to influence in some detail how that money was to be spent. When fiscal stringency brought an end to those 'golden years', political and administrative decision makers increasingly had to refuse applications for additional funding or – even more embarrassing – had to decide upon cuts. Life became more difficult for all stakeholders and relations between the representatives of the government and the higher education community deteriorated. The former had no interest in being engaged in the ugly details of executing cuts and became quite sympathetic to the arguments for increasing the autonomy of higher education institutions.

3. FROM STATE AGENCIES TO PUBLIC ENTERPRISES

The change in the underlying paradigms of higher education policy gave rise to a new reform cycle. Within only a few years the architecture of Austrian higher education was fundamentally changed. In the early 1990s, a non-university sector (NUS) was established in order to provide a new educational profile (short-term studies, clear vocational orientation). With respect to management issues, *Fachhochschulen* were an unexpected break with the tradition of state agencies. In 1993, at the time of their establishment they were in many respects regarded as a model for universities. At the same time an initial attempt was made to fundamentally restructure organisation and decision making at universities. This latter reform proved to be much more difficult than the former. The initial reform goal of the government was too ambitious; the University Organisation Act of 1993 (UOG 1993) was a compromise. However, it was easy to foresee that the UOG 1993 was not more than an intermediary stage with a short lifespan of less than ten years. In 2002, a new act was passed (University Act 2002 (UG 2002)) which finally realised and even radicalised the original intentions of the reform initiative of the early 1990s.

3.1. Fachhochschulen *as Pioneers of Managerialism*

In 1990, a new coalition government (social democrats and conservatives) took over and announced two major higher education reforms for the next term. The first reform was the establishment of a *Fachhochschul* sector. Compared to other OECD countries, the establishment of a NUS in the 1990s was rather late. Earlier attempts in the late 1960s had failed (Lassnigg and Pechar 1988). From today's perspective, the reasons for that delay are difficult to understand. There was a strange alliance between conservatives and social democrats to prevent the establishment of a NUS. Conservatives opposed further growth of higher education. In their view, a NUS would facilitate access and thus be a 'catalyst' to expand postsecondary education. Social democrats, on the other hand, were sceptical of all plans to diversify the system of higher education. In their view, any kind of diversification would lead to the re-introduction of elite structures with the unavoidable consequence that students from the lower social strata would be excluded from the prestigious university sector and be pushed aside to a sector of less quality and esteem. Only in the late 1980s did the resistance against a NUS begin to ease.

One way to establish a NUS would have been to upgrade existing institutions either at the secondary or postsecondary level. For all kinds of vested interests, this approach was not chosen. The *Fachhochschul* sector was established with completely new institutions. This has the important implication that the sector will remain, in the short to medium term, much smaller than the university sector.

The late establishment of the NUS at least partly explains the peculiar role *Fachhochschulen* play within Austrian higher education. If Austria had established *Fachhochschulen* in the late 1960s or early 1970s, this sector would have been funded and organised on similar lines to the universities, as state agencies with line-by-line budgets. However, in the early 1990s, when the new sector was planned and organised, the policy context had changed.

We have already pointed to the resistance of universities to the new policy approach of the government. In some respects it is easier to build new structures than to change existing ones: there are no vested interests at stake. For that reason the *Fachhochschul* policy was a more radical departure from Austrian traditions than UOG 1993 (Pratt and Hackl 1999). The difference between *Fachhochschulen* and universities, as they were in the early 1990s, is striking:

- Both sectors were regulated by federal law. However, the function of this legal basis and the range of the respective acts differ fundamentally from each other. In the university sector there was a large number of acts, many of them voluminous; their function being tight regulation of organisation, personnel and study courses. For the *Fachhochschul* sector only one act existed, consisting of a few paragraphs, which provided a fairly open legal framework for the activities of the single institutions.
- Universities had been federal state agencies, governed by the ministry. For the *Fachhochschul* sector there were no legal ownership restrictions. All institutions were owned by 'quasi-private' associations or corporations and governed by a professional management.
- All academic and non-academic staff at university were employed by the federal state; faculty members were usually civil servants. The academic and non-academic staff of *Fachhochschulen* were employed and appointed by the institution.
- In the university sector, admission of students was (and still is) regulated by federal law. Graduates of the secondary elite-track were entitled to enrol at any Austrian university: there was open access regardless of resources. In the *Fachhochschul* sector students were admitted by the institution in accordance with available study places.
- At the universities, study courses were regulated by four steps: two federal laws, a ministerial decree and a final 'fine-tuning' by the university itself. This strong ex-ante control by federal law was considered to guarantee equal status and standards of quality. At the *Fachhochschulen*, decisions on the curriculum were made by the responsible academics in cooperation with institutional management. The final responsibility for quality in the *Fachhochschul* sector was in the hands of an external professional body, the *Fachhochschulrat*. The *Fachhochschulrat* guaranteed minimal standards of quality. Furthermore, *Fachhochschulen* were expected to vary widely in terms of profile and quality of their education.
- Universities were funded by the federal government in the form of an earmarked grant, whereas *Fachhochschulen* received a lump sum based on student numbers. All public funding for universities came from the federal state, while *Fachhochschulen* received funds from multiple public sources; besides the federal state, provinces and municipalities, and in some cases chambers, played a significant role.

At first glance, it is obvious that the *Fachhochschul* policy follows the broad global trends and fashions of the late 1980s and 1990s to be found in the higher education literature or in the recommendations of international organisations like the OECD. The buzz words of these trends are deregulation, efficiency, institutional autonomy etc. The important aspect in our context is that *Fachhochschulen*, from the very beginning, were designed as an alternative to universities; an alternative not only with respect to their educational profile, but also with respect to the management, administration and funding of the institutions. The meaning of 'alternative' was ambiguous from the beginning. At first, representatives of the universities hoped that the establishment of such an alternative would strengthen their elite status and shield their institutions from demands for more efficiency. But, in the public debate, the success of *Fachhochschulen* had the opposite effect: the new institutions served as a role model which increased the pressure for change on universities. The *Fachhochschulen* proved that an alternative which in some respects seemed to be preferable to universities was possible.

The *Fachhochschul* reform was by no means a 'harmonious' effort; rather, it was accompanied by serious political controversies, which is not surprising given the magnitude of change. Yet the kind of conflict aroused by the government's *Fachhochschul* policy was relatively easy to deal with. There was no strong resistance from the higher education community. Academics at universities, if they paid attention at all, unanimously supported the establishment of *Fachhochschulen* at that time. Some school teachers, in particular at the 'higher vocational schools', had a less positive attitude; but this group did not have a voice powerful enough to shape higher education policy. The only serious opposition came from within the political sector; it was a conflict among politicians about the amount and mode of political control of the *Fachhochschul* sector. And not even this conflict can be described in terms of the traditional right/left polarisation. Rather, it was a conflict about 'modern' and 'traditional' policy concepts. Looking back after ten years, the *Fachhochschul* reform can certainly be regarded as a success story of higher education policy in the 1990s.

3.2. A First Step to Managerialism at Universities (UOG 1993)

The second major topic of the new government's higher education policy was a reform of universities with a focus on autonomy and efficiency. In October 1991, the ministry presented guidelines for a new organisational act (Green Paper, BMWF 1991). Its most important purpose was to complement and balance the traditional collegial decision-making structure (academic senate chaired by the rector) with a parallel managerial structure. At the institutional level it was proposed that this would be the *Präsidium*, an executive body chaired by a president who would be appointed by the Minister. This strengthening of decision making would enable the university to receive and handle lump sum budgets. It was proposed to exempt public expenditure for universities from the normal fiscal regulations for the public sector (*Kameralistik*) and to leave it to the *Präsidium* to spend the money according to its own priorities. Each university would have an external board (*Kuratorium*) which would, however, not be a governing body but rather have advisory functions. There would be two types of academic personnel: the traditional category of civil servants would be supplemented by academics who would be employed by the university on the basis of private contracts.

The Green Paper was met with uncompromising rejection by all groups of the university. There was hardly any support from academics which was strange because only a few months before the Green Paper was published, an academic association which was quite influential within the professoriate made a similar proposal (Österreichische Forschungsgemeinschaft 1991). There were two main sources of resistance to the new managerial policy: one was left wing, the other had rather conservative implications. Students and a majority of junior faculty opposed strong academic leadership on the grounds that it implied an authoritarian backlash of the democratic reforms of the 1970s. Most professors and a minority of junior faculty rejected the new proposals on the grounds that a professional academic management would endanger the status and privileges of the academic oligarchy. Both positions were legitimised using the rhetoric of autonomy of universities.

Autonomy of universities can be interpreted in totally different ways by different actors. During the reform debate, three concepts of autonomy clashed:

- In the Humboldtian tradition, autonomy is mainly used as a synonym for academic freedom of the individual academic, that is to say, mainly the full professor. Many professors saw this kind of autonomy endangered, on the one hand, by state intervention and, on the other, by academic co-determination of students and *Mittelbau* (junior faculty). From their perspective, autonomy became a buzz word for a kind of restoration of the 'old regime' of academic oligarchy, of the *Ordinarienuniversität*.
- Junior faculty and students mainly favoured the concept of the autonomous collegial university. In their view, the focus of autonomy was not the individual academic but the collegial bodies in which they had some representation (after the democratic reforms of the 1970s). Those collegial bodies should govern the university without any interference from the state. Sufficient and unconditional funding by the government was simply taken for granted.
- Politicians and state bureaucrats advocated the concept of institutional autonomy; they wanted to turn universities into enterprises which were self-governed with respect to not only academic, but also financial and administrative affairs. They had serious doubts that the existing decision-making structures would be sufficient for the new tasks. They argued that increased institutional autonomy must go hand-in-hand with the development of a professional management (Bast 1990; Höllinger 1992).

It is easy to see that neither the concept of individual autonomy nor the concept of the autonomous collegial university is compatible with the ministerial reform approach. For a couple of months the Austrian public witnessed an uncommon passionate debate in which the multiple opponents imploringly referred to the same keyword 'autonomy' without any clarification or moderation of argument. As a response to this strong opposition, the Minister installed a project team which tried to reach a compromise between the ministry's proposal and the ideas of the different actors of the university. In May 1992, the Orange Paper was published which clearly softened the managerial approach of the first reform draft (BMWF 1992a). There was still a division of collegial and managerial elements. However, there was a shift of power to the former. The executive body (*Präsidium*) was now to be chaired by the rector who was to be elected by the collegium (*Universitätsversammlung*). The external board for each university now had less responsibility than proposed in the Green Paper. Instead, there was now more emphasis on the system level: a buffer body was to be created between the ministry and the universities (*Universitätenkuratorium*). There was still the proposal of some kind of lump sum budget for the whole university system which would now be distributed by the *Universitätenkuratorium*.

The Orange Paper was still rejected by the interest groups of academics and students. They argued that even the softened managerial approach was in conflict with the idea of the university. In December 1992, a draft for a new organisational act (White Paper, BMWF 1992b) was published which withdrew some elements of the Orange Paper. The traditional chair structure in a multitude of small institutes, many of them with only one professor, basically remained unchanged. The concept of lump sum budgets was weakened; the Ministry of Finance was strongly opposed to giving a lump sum to universities on the grounds that managerial power and the responsibility of persons in leadership positions were not sufficient. After a review process which resulted only in minor changes, the new act (UOG 1993) was passed by Parliament in October 1993. Like its predecessor, the UOG 1975, it was one of the most divisive and heatedly discussed acts in Austria. In the academic year 1994–95, the UOG 1993 was implemented in five universities, in 1995–96 at the next five, and in 1996–97 the remaining universities started to implement the new act. In the large universities with a traditional faculty structure (Vienna, Graz, Innsbruck and Salzburg) the implementation was not finished until 1999.

3.3. Completion of the Managerial Revolution: Full Legal Entity for Universities

During the process of implementation, some groups at the universities started to complain that the UOG 1993 was only a half-measure, merely a first step which omitted some of the most important factors. What they wanted was in many respects the same as the government intended with its first draft (Green Paper) for the UOG 1993: full legal entity for universities and a lump sum budget which would relieve universities of the state accountancy (*Kameralistik*). The centre of this movement was the new rectors, who in some universities managed to build influential networks of senior academics.

The emergence of this new group of academics, which was small but quite influential, changed the power relations in the reform debate significantly. The initiative of this reform came from a group of academics (even if it was a small group and many other academics opposed the initiative), not from the government (even if it was easy to remember that the government pursued similar goals a few years before). When the government took up this initiative and started to develop a new reform strategy it was not in the uncomfortable position of fighting alone against a united front of academic estates; rather, it had a powerful ally within the university (who at least strove for the same goals).

A first draft for full legal entity of universities was issued in 1998 by a government consisting of a coalition between the social democrats and conservatives (bm:wv 1998). This draft was in line with the Austrian tradition of consensus politics: it left sufficient room for debate[4] and negotiations. The cornerstones of this draft were:

- Universities should be relieved from the fiscal regulations of the federal budget and instead receive a lump sum budget for their own discretion. However, there was no intention to base the block grants on indicators; rather, the available resources for higher education should be allocated on the basis of a mixture of incremental budgeting (85% of the budget) and performance contracts.
- The establishment of a Board of Regents (*Universitätsrat*) for each university, consisting of 10 members, five of whom should be elected by the academic senate, and the other five appointed by the Minister.
- The strengthening of the position of the rector, who now was to be elected by the board and thus independent of all collegial academic bodies.
- The new act should not prescribe the internal organisation of universities other than the general regulations regarding the decision-making structure. The organisational details should be determined by a statute (*Satzung*) decided by the academic senate.
- Taking part in the reform would be voluntary (at least during the initial phase); each university would be free to stay with the old organisational model if the majority of the academic senate decided to do so. This should help to relax some of the most fundamental controversies. Some small and flexible universities which already impatiently wanted to move ahead could do so while the large universities which – due to the complexity of their decision-making structure – were more rigid, could wait and see.
- It came as no surprise that the draft was criticised by the academics. However, this was not a unanimous refusal of the draft (as was the case during the debate of the UOG 1993), rather, one can distinguish two sides of the critique:
- The draft was refused flatly by the interest groups of students and junior faculty and by a large number of individual academics. Those people complained about being permanently involved in badly conceived and never-ending reform activities.[5] And they were strongly opposed to the basic tendency of the draft: the strengthening of managerial functions. This kind of critique reflected an unconditional disapproval of any step to give more institutional autonomy to universities.

- On the other hand, there was a more pragmatic (or constructive) critique which basically agreed with the overall goals of such a reform but rejected particular elements of the draft. This was the position of most rectors and their networks. The emphasis of this group was that the draft, in particular the funding arrangement, was not sufficiently reasoned. With respect to the performance contracts, the rectors' criticism was that the ministry, instead of measuring output, wanted to intrude in the process of teaching and research. In addition, there was concern that the government wanted to pass some 'hidden costs' of the reform on to the universities. In order to built an alliance with the Rectors Conference, the ministry agreed to fund a project which would clarify those objections and deepen the expertise with respect to the financial, legal and organisational aspects of the reform.

However, by the time the Rectors Conference working group presented the outcomes of this project to the public in the summer of 2000 (Titscher et al. 2000), the political situation had changed. Austria was no longer governed by a coalition of social democrats and conservatives; the new government was a coalition of conservatives and the right wing populist 'Freedom Party'. This new government can be characterised by a fundamental change not only in political direction but also in the style of policy making: in order to foster radical change in a short time it took leave from the traditional consensus politics which were regarded as too ponderous. The new trademark, proudly announced by some leading politicians, was: 'speed kills'.

In September 2000, the government for the first time applied the 'speed kills' approach to higher education by introducing tuition fees without any consultation and only two weeks after the Minister had categorically ruled out the possibility of fees during her term. A few weeks later (December 2000) the ministry announced a new initiative towards organisational reform. This time, however, it was not an invitation to a debate but a straightforward timetable without any possibility to opt out of the reform process. A first draft for the new act was published in August 2001 (bm:bwk 2001); in many respects it picked up the thread of the earlier draft (1998), but it unmistakably also showed the new government's hand:

- The 'speed kills' philosophy demanded a tight schedule: the new act should become effective as from October 2002 and should be implemented immediately and simultaneously by all universities.
- The governing board should consist of only five persons, a majority of whom would be appointed by the ministry. The functions of this body were vastly extended, partly overlapping with executive functions.
- The new draft put stronger emphasis on managerial functions: collegial bodies were thrust into the background and lost almost any significance. Leadership functions in all organisational units[6] are to be appointed by the rector.[7] The only collegial body with decision-making power should be the academic senate, but even the function of the senate was devalued.

- The new draft put very strong emphasis on formal hierarchies. Participation of junior faculty[8] in the academic senate was strongly restricted; junior faculty members were excluded from any executive function even at the institute level.
- The allocation of the federal budget should be based on performance contracts. As in the earlier draft (1998), the ministry avoided specifying any quantitative indicators as a basis for the allocation process.

As with the former draft, the critique from the academic side was passionate but there were different kinds of critique. Most important were the objections of those who basically agreed with the goals of the reform (Österreichische Rektorenkonferenz 2001). The emphasis of their critique was:

- While the draft is based on the principles of 'new public management', the government has neglected to clarify its own strategic goals in higher education policy.
- The governing board's competencies are too far-reaching. The functions of the board should be limited, its size should be enlarged (up to 11 members).
- The academic senate should play a more eminent role. In addition to the senate, collegial bodies on lower levels with decision-making power are crucial for the life of a university.
- The concept of the performance contract is not sufficiently elaborated. The legal obligations which result from that contract are not symmetrically balanced.
- There is uncertainty whether higher education institutions will be sufficiently compensated for the increase of personnel cost, due to the change from public to private contracts (contributions for pension).

As a result of the negotiations, the government changed its draft on some minor points. The substance of the new organisational act (Sebök 2002) can be summarised as follows:

- Universities are no longer agencies of the state without legal capacity, but they remain in the domain of the public law,[9] they are 'legal persons under public law' (*Körperschaften öffentlichen Rechts*).
- The federal government keeps the responsibility for basic funding; resources are allocated on the basis of performance contracts. Twenty per cent of the budget allocation must be based on indicators.[10]
- The size of the governing board (*Universitätsrat*) is to vary between five and nine members, according to the statute. Compared with the first draft, the spectrum of functions of the board was limited towards a supervisory profile.
- The executive board (*Rektorat*) is to consist of a rector and up to four vice-rectors. The rector is elected by the governing board from a proposal by the academic senate.

- The size of the academic senate is to vary between 12 and 24 academics, according to the statute. Full professors must have a majority. The senate has the power to establish committees for *Habilitation*, appointments and study affairs.
- All academic personnel are to be employed by the university on the basis of private contracts.[11] Only two types of academic personnel exist: full professors and other academic personnel.

For better or worse, the new act probably makes Austria a leader in the 'managerial revolution' on the European continent. Policy makers will regard this as a success. Academics, even academics in leadership positions who basically support the reform, have mixed feelings. One of the concerns is the pace of reform. Compared with other countries of similar tradition, the change in academic leadership from the 'pre-managerial' age to modern higher education management has to be accommodated in a very short time.

4. CHALLENGES FOR ACADEMIC LEADERS: OPPORTUNITIES AND RESTRICTION IN VARIOUS FIELDS

The new legislation on higher education has significantly changed the rules of the game. In retrospect, the UOG 1993 can be interpreted as a kind of moratorium, a phase of transition, which gave universities and their leaders a chance to adapt to the harsh realities of academic managerialism.[12] One might argue that the lifespan of this act was too brief to be effective in this respect. After all, in the large universities it was implemented only in the late 1990s. At any rate, the UG 2002, which must be implemented in October 2004 in all universities, definitely brings an end to that transition period. Being forced to implement such a fundamental change within only a few months puts enormous pressure on the new higher education managers. What are the main challenges they are confronted with? This section discusses a number of issues which will be decisive for the success or failure of the reform.

4.1. Higher Education Management as a New Territory

Persons involved in higher education management are pioneers, they enter a new field of activity. The routines in which universities used to be led and administered have lost their validity; new practices have to emerge, but it is not yet clear how they will look. It is not possible to rely on experience. All actors feel a high level of uncertainty. This is inevitable and not really surprising concomitants of a transformation period; but it is useful to pay attention to them, because this situation will strongly affect the implementation of higher education management in Austria.

Pioneering can be a very stimulating and rewarding activity. It gives a person or a group of people the feeling of being actively involved in new developments, of 'shaping history'. However, to be successful as a pioneer requires, on the one hand, extraordinary abilities and, on the other, a very high commitment. This is necessary to master the high level of uncertainty and to compensate for lack of experience.

Only a very limited number of available people meet these criteria. Of course it could be claimed that this is the standard situation for all leadership positions: they always require rare abilities. And one could argue that even in countries with a long tradition in academic management, academic leadership is full of uncertainty. As Fisher and Koch (1996) write about the American university president: "Practically, the only person who approaches the office with any real knowledge is someone who has previously held a successful presidency, but one presidency is usually enough for most people. For most presidents, the first venture into that fascinating and lonely office is a situation worlds apart from anything they have experienced before". Even in a country like the USA, academic managers are regarded as amateurs compared with the standards of the corporate world.

From that perspective, there would be nothing unusual in the Austrian situation. Yet I think there is an obvious difference. American novices can be guided and informed by role models, they can rely on a huge body of literature,[13] and most importantly they have a chance to choose from a broad range of education and training opportunities.

It would be desirable to establish new routines, to 'normalise' the new area as soon as possible. One way to do this is to professionalise higher education management by developing education and training opportunities at various levels, starting with short seminars and proceeding to degree courses.[14] Many initiatives to develop such courses are evolving. However, this requires a great deal of energy. Although there is the widespread assumption among experts that there is a significant demand for such training opportunities it is not clear to what extent they would be actually used. After all, the traditional view of academics is that they need no formal education and training for the self-governance of their institution. A reasonable way to reduce the risk for the suppliers is to cooperate and develop, at least as a first step, joint courses, with modules coming from different universities or groups of academics. Since the situation in other German speaking countries is similar, it would be useful to extend the cooperation across national borders.

4.2. Strategic Management

The UG 2002 will tremendously increase the discretionary power of university leadership to shape the profile of their institutions. Many areas which were formerly prescribed either by legislation or by ministerial decree can now be formed according to the concepts of the managers. In the old regime each university used to be an embodiment of the prototype of the 'Austrian university' which was laid down in the extensive paragraphs of the University Organisation Act.[15] A uniform system was never the reality, but for some decades it was the assumed norm. This has changed. Now the normative goes in the opposite direction: each institution should have its distinctive profile. This will foster competition and enhance consumer choice. Now universities have the right to deliberately shape the organisational features of their institution, for example, how to sub-divide the university into faculties/schools, departments or institutes; the size of the academic senate. Universities are no longer obliged to offer standardised programmes defined by study acts and study regulations; they are free to determine the range of subjects they want to offer to shape the curriculum their own way.

As a matter of fact, universities not only have the right, but they are forced to make these kinds of decisions. In the past, strategic planning of a university was limited to the total requests of all individual academic units. Conflict regarding how to distribute limited resources or how to restrict incoherent plans was avoided. It was always easier to blame the ministry. This is no longer possible; for that reason strategic management is one of the key tasks for the new academic leaders.

How can a distinctive profile emerge? The literature on management places a high value on the development of a mission statement (*Leitbild*). Already, on the basis of the UOG 1993, some universities have had their first experiences with mission statements. A mission statement, in any case, is part of the symbolic dimension of leadership (cf. Trow 1984: 13); it would be naïve to expect the mission statement to contain concrete/precise steps of the day-to-day management of institutions. The crucial question, however, is whether this statement is just rhetoric or a tool of strategic management. There are mixed views about the experience of mission statements in Austrian and German universities (Nickel 2000). The aspect of involvement and participation of the faculty at all levels is crucial. Is the mission statement the personal vision of the rector and a small circle of his/her confidants? Or is it the result of an organisational process which aims at integrating the expertise and ambitions of the decentralised units of the university into a coherent statement of the organisation as a whole? Only in the latter case will it be possible to connect the symbolic dimension with the managerial and academic dimension of leadership.

Another set of questions arises with respect to the substance of the special features: in what direction should institutions strive for their distinctive profile? What paths would allow them to improve the position of their own institution? At present, Austria has a binary system of higher education, with an extremely diverse *Fachhochschul* sector[16] and a relatively uniform university sector. What kind of differentiation would be possible? Which one would be desirable? Theoretically, one could make the distinction between horizontal vs vertical differentiation. First signs of both exist in the present system. A certain level of specialisation was always taken for granted, but in the past the tendency was to weaken this kind of differentiation rather than to emphasise it.[17] It was equally obvious that some universities have a greater reputation than others, however, it was rather taboo to address that openly. Moreover, the quality differentiation was rather flat and reliable knowledge about it did not exist.

Should universities look for niches (horizontal differentiation) or should they try to be better than their direct competitors (vertical differentiation)? Recently, interest in both modes of differentiation has increased: government has a strong interest in setting priorities (*Schwerpunktbildung*) for efficiency gains at the system level. As well, there are several attempts to increase the importance and popularity of rankings (cf. CHE).[18]

One main difficulty universities will experience is the lack of strategic planning by government. In the Austrian context, it is said that NPM is an abbreviation for 'no public management', rather than for 'new public management' (Zechlin 2002).

4.3. Resource Management

As a state agency, each university received earmarked grants as part of the public budget. During the 1970s and 1980s the rigid restrictions of the traditional public accountancy (*Kameralistik*) were a major source of dissatisfaction and conflict with the ministry. UOG 1993 allowed greater flexibility, but universities still received earmarked grants. UG 2002 brings about the major change that has been sought by universities for so long. In terms of funding, universities have full legal responsibility for their state budget allocation; basic funding still comes from the federal budget, but universities now get a block grant based on performance contracts.

The rationale for the reform was the expectation of efficiency gains at the institutional level. Policy makers have realised that in higher education a central agency is not able to make wise decisions on the internal distribution of resources. As a matter of fact, many aspects of the present situation can be characterised as a coincidence of shortage and wastage (e.g. insufficient use of rooms and teaching capacity). The ministry was not able to intervene effectively in vested interests; new management is expected to make better use of the existing resources.

The new legislation increases the discretion of management, but at the same time internalises many conflicts which formerly were fought between the university (or individual academics) and the ministry. The loosely united community of scholars lose, at least partly, a powerful external enemy. This might have a deep impact on the organisational culture. Will an institution develop proper procedures to handle internal conflict?[19] Some academics fear that the university as an organisation is too fragile to master such conflict in a productive manner. As a consequence there could be substantial disturbance which could adversely affect the cohesion and productivity of the organisation. It will be an urgent task of the new leadership to take care of the 'conflict culture', not only between the different levels of hierarchy but also among colleagues.

The key issue is the development of transparent procedures for the internal allocation of resources. On the one hand, this requires a substantial improvement of the statistical/empirical basis for such decisions. Sure, there are plenty of statistics, but few contain relevant information which could support decisions on allocation. In the past, academic units cultivated tremendous skills to hide important information; the ministry had neither appropriate sticks (academic freedom!) nor carrots (was there any reward for honest reporting?) to get that information. Internal academic managers are in a different position. They have better access to some of the secrets of this complex organisation and, in many aspects, they might be perceived as less of a threat than the ministry (in some respects, however, it might be the opposite). During the period of the UOG 1993, many of the new rectors took their first steps to develop a data warehouse.

However, internal resource allocation can never be completely driven by formulae. Good academic leaders pursue an active policy; they set priorities which are to be reflected in the allocation of the budget. This is why resource allocation has to be linked to the mission statement and other instruments of strategic management. This is also the test of whether the mission statement contains just nice words or is an effective management tool. To link the conflict aroused by resource allocation with strategic issues requires not only substantial skill but also a proper understanding of the insoluble tensions of academic life; for example, equity vs excellence, external demands vs academic curiosity etc. Academic leaders have to balance these tensions in a way which is not regarded as arbitrary by the faculty.

4.4. Personnel Management and the Influence of Collegial Bodies

So long as the university was a state agency, the government was the employer of academic and non-academic staff; only temporary staff were employed on the basis of private contracts, usually within the scope of 'third party projects'. The civil servant status of academics with lifelong tenure was supposed to secure academic freedom against pressure from outside. In addition, the majority of non-academic staff had permanent positions.

In general, the traditional view of this employment pattern emphasised the advantage of a 'principal' being distant from the sphere of academic work; distant in the sense of space, but also with respect to professional competence. Personnel management is a good example of the dualistic nature of the traditional university as a state agency on the one hand, and a sphere of academic autonomy on the other. The status of civil service did not only guarantee lifelong job security for academics, it also offered an opportunity for academic self-governance. Only formal aspects of personnel management which could be executed by bureaucratic procedures were handled by the ministry, which was the 'principal' in the legal sense. All aspects of personnel management related to academic work were delegated to collegial decision making in self-governing bodies of the university.

In the traditional chair system (*Ordinarienuniversität*) self-governance was restricted to the small group of full professors. The situation of junior faculty was then characterised by personal dependency on the chairholders. The university as a whole was an assembly of many small 'principalities', each of them managed and controlled by a full professor. In the course of expansion of higher education, non-professorial academic staff took on an increasing range of academic functions, many of them independently, without the guidance of a professor. The traditional assumption of the junior faculty of mere assistance to the professor could no longer be maintained. As a consequence, junior faculty was partly included in self-governing bodies and collegial decision making.

The co-determination of a wider range of academics softened the authoritarian structure of the traditional university,[20] but it created problems of a new kind. Collegial bodies are based on the assumption of equality of its members (respectively the members of each status group). As a consequence, they emphasise equal treatment of all staff and equal distribution of resources. In other words, the equal treatment of academics by the ministry which was inherent to their status as civil servants (no merit pay, advancement based on seniority) was paralleled by collegial bodies which in many respects acted like faculty unions.

The new university with full legal entity is the employer of all academic and non-academic staff.[21] This is one of the most positive aspects of the reform; it will definitely strengthen the university as an organisation. It will bring an end to the paradoxical dualism in which the ministry is responsible for the formal aspects of personnel management (making contracts, paying wages) without being able to supervise the quality of academic work; and the university as an autonomous, self-governed organisation which is responsible for guidance and monitoring of academic work without being able to effectively use incentives or negative sanctions. Even in large and complex universities the institutional management will be much closer to the basic academic units and their work than the bureaucracy of the government; closer in terms of space, professional competence and shared academic values. Under the new conditions, universities can no longer afford to leave it to the individual responsibility of senior academic staff to take care of staff development.

While this is good news from the perspective of the university as an organisation, it might be seen as a threat from the perspective of the individual academic. It means that the 'principal' comes closer to the 'agent', possibly close enough to effectively influence their work. Not surprisingly, there is a lot of suspicion among academics of the organisational change and the corresponding decision-making structures. Rectors were regarded as *primus inter pares*, now they are 'bosses', 'superiors'; this is at odds with the traditional concept of academic autonomy which means: no subordination, no formal responsibilities, in particular for the members of the guild, the chairholders.

However, even in an 'entrepreneurial university' the relation between the 'principal' and the 'agent' is extremely complex and sensitive. The university is a 'bottom heavy' expert system; academic leadership at each level needs support from the decentralised units. Rectors will depend on permanent consultation with faculty in order to strengthen their position. It will be one of the most urgent tasks of the new academic management to quieten the mistrust which was aroused during the recent reform debates. Many academics think that the new legislation has imposed the decision-making structures of the corporate world onto universities. They fear and expect a sharp hierarchy which will not leave sufficient room for collegial bodies; an authoritarian mode of leadership which will not allow appropriate faculty influence.

The mistrust mainly among junior faculty was enhanced by government legislation in 2001 to regulate terms of employment; in addition, during the debate of the UG 2002, representatives of government and ministry emphasised the importance of academic hierarchy and autocratic management. It will be important that the new rectors demonstrate the superiority of participative management.

4.5. Teaching and Research as a Management Task

Whatever the achievements will be with respect to strategic, or resource, or personnel management, what counts in the end are the outcomes, the 'products'. The success of the new academic management will finally depend on how the stakeholders assess the performance of a university in teaching and research. The performance of the whole institution in teaching and research will increasingly become a concern of academic leadership.

This is a severe break with the Humboldtian legacy: the university as a whole used to be a fragile bundle of individuals and small units, striving in different, sometimes opposite directions, integrated by a common ethos and other rather symbolic mechanisms.[22] In each specialised field teaching and research were shaped by the ambitions and interests of the single chairholder.

With respect to teaching, the Humboldtian tradition has strongly shaped the curriculum of Austrian universities. Until recently, an undergraduate curriculum in a strict sense did not exist. The first degree (*Magister* or *Diplomingenieur*) would be roughly comparable to the masters degree in the Anglo-Saxon tradition, which is already a graduate degree.[23] This has implications for the whole concept of university education, for the culture of teaching and learning (Pechar 2002). From the very first semester, students are assumed to be 'apprentice researchers' who are capable of conducting their studies in a completely independent way. This is reflected in a sharp distinction between the culture of learning at universities on the one hand, and other types of postsecondary education and schools on the other.

At universities, a need for guidance and monitoring by the staff is not seen. Students are not supposed to be school children who need help, they should be mature persons who are able to learn independently. This makes it very easy for academics not to care about student needs. As a matter of fact, the laissez faire conditions for students are matched by laissez faire conditions for academics. Neither side has formal obligations *vis-à-vis* the other as they are experienced in some other higher education systems, mainly in the Anglo-Saxon world. Academics and students likewise are obsessed with the danger of a 'school-like' curriculum (*Verschulung*). In a sense, this is the core of the Humboldtian ideal of a university. The question of whether this is still a proper concept for mass higher education was never addressed in Austria.

High drop out rates and very long durations of study are consequences of this lack of attention to student needs (with respect to both indicators, Austria belongs to the countries with the worst performance, cf. OECD 2002). During the last two decades, this unfavourable picture has increasingly caught the attention of external stakeholders, who have called for improvements. Representatives of universities were not at all impressed by such reproaches and emphasised the unfavourable conditions of universities (decreasing per capita funding, open access policy).[24] These claims are in part factually correct, but this can be no excuse for neglecting efficient teaching. Under the new conditions it will be necessary to take external demands much more seriously.

Research is not the subject of public debate to the same extent as is teaching; but research performance will be crucial for the reputation of a university in the academic hierarchy. The fiction of equal quality and position of all Austrian universities is likely to diminish. On the one hand, pressure by stakeholders and consumers will make already existing differences more transparent; on the other hand, the trend to emphasise distinct profiles and competition is likely to increase such differences.

Academic reputation will be decisive for the ability of universities to generate additional research income. In this context, it will be important for the university as an organisation to develop a coherent research strategy. This strategy must be based on an assessment of the strengths and weaknesses of its research capacities and should lead to a realistic number of research priorities. Under the circumstances of increased competition for research funds at national and European levels, it does not make sense to try everything at the same time. Rather, it would be useful to strengthen some areas; each institution needs at least some priority areas in which it is able to compete successfully for research funds at the European level.

5. CONCLUSION

One of the most depressing outcomes of a quarter century of higher education reform in Austria is the continuous erosion of trust between the main actors involved in the process. In the early 1970s, the tradition of the benevolent state (*Kulturstaat*) was still alive. Government then was regarded as a 'friend of the universities'. That situation has changed dramatically.

There are many reasons why the mutual respect between the universities and the state has eroded. The high degree of suspicion on both sides works against achieving even minimum cooperation for pursuing common goals. In the absence of mutual respect and cooperation, state controlled governance of universities could not be maintained. With ministries shifting from being a patron to an enemy of the universities (at least in the minds of the academics), the universities are better off becoming legally independent and distanced from government.

However, even with universities gaining legal independence, lack of trust and suspicion does not disappear. Rather, the erosion of trust shifts to a different level, with internal relations within higher education institutions burdened with new problems. Although the state was regarded as the external enemy in control of the universities, it nonetheless shielded academics from a variety of potential internal conflicts. With the demise of state controlled governance of the universities, the external enemy is being replaced by a new class of institutional managers, which in turn is regarded with hostility and suspicion by large groups of academics. The worst case scenario for the future development of Austrian universities is for the former angst between the universities and the state to be reproduced and entrenched in terms of hostility and mistrust between institutional managers and academics. Hopefully, rectors and other senior university managers will see it as their first priority to convince their respective academic communities that such mistrust is not inevitable and that in fact management is the friend of their institution.

NOTES

[1] During the late 16th century, Jesuits made Austrian universities a cornerstone of counter-reformation; when the Jesuit dominance was abolished during the 18th century, universities became agencies of the 'enlightened state'.

[2] It would be an exaggeration to call them 'policy makers' before the mid 20th century.

[3] The term 'etatist' refers to the dominant role of the government in Austrian society.

[4] Formally, this first paper by the government was not described as a legal draft but rather as a contribution/blueprint for debate. This was a clear indication that the government was ready to make compromises.

[5] A popular slogan was: 'Leave us alone and let us do our academic work' (Laßt die Universitäten in Ruhe arbeiten!).

[6] The structure and size of these organisational units depend on the statute. Most but not all universities will have faculties headed by deans; some universities will probably stick to the tradition of small institutes, others will change to departments.

[7] As a principle, all leadership positions would be based on the principle of 'double legitimacy', which is to say that both higher and lower hierarchical levels would be included in the decision process.

[8] Junior faculty (*Mittelbau*) is all academic personnel below the rank of full professor. One problem of the academic workplace in Austria is the unfavourable quantitative relationship between professors and junior faculty which allows only a minority of the latter to proceed to professorship. Presently, Austria has about 2,000 professors compared to roughly 6,700 junior faculty. The corresponding figures for Germany would be 24,100 professors and 14,200 junior faculty.

[9] An alternative concept, pushed forward by the Ministry of Finance, was the private limited liability company (*Ges.m.b.H.*).

[10] This provision was got through by a joint effort of the Rectors Conference and the Ministry of Finance. Up to the end, the Ministry of Education wanted to prevent the use of indicators for resource allocation.

[11] Academics who already are civil servants keep that status.

[12] This is not to insinuate that such a moratorium was deliberately planned by the ministry or any other master mind. The (rapid) succession of university organisation acts was rather a result of political power struggle and the necessary compromises.

[13] The literature on higher education management in the German language is still sparse; among the pioneers are Hanft 2000 and Hanft 2001.

[14] The same is true for Germany. In March 2002 the German *Stifterverband* invited tenders for the development of a masters programme for higher education management. The rationale read: "It would be useful to establish higher education management as a profession in its own right with special requirements on education and training".

[15] Of course this is an exaggeration, although only a slight one. Firstly there have always been different types of universities, for example, specialised institutions such as technical universities. Secondly, each institution had its peculiarities, shaped by history, links with the region etc. This was simply beyond the reach of legislation.

[16] This diversity is a result of the broad variety of ownership and maintenance in this sector.

[17] Only in 1975 most specialised institutions (e.g. technical universities) gained university status. In 1998 the former colleges for fine arts and music gained university status. This standardisation on the legal and organisational level was often accompanied by a widening of the range of courses (e.g. social sciences at technical universities).

[18] The German 'Centrum für Hochschulentwicklung' (CHE), a higher education think tank funded by the Bertelsmann Stiftung, has launched a ranking which has uncommon high acceptance within the academic community (http://www.stern.de/hochschul-ranking/jsp/ranking/frame.jsp).

[19] Of course, conflict in universities is omnipresent. However, many conflicts can be resolved by the use of the 'exit option': if an agreement is impossible, each opponent can go their own way. This is one of the benefits of a 'loosely coupled organisation' and one of the driving forces of fragmentation. However, many of the new conflicts cannot be handled this way.

[20] Still, junior faculty was dependent on professors with respect to the advancement in their professional career; 'staff development' was an individual responsibility of professors.

[21] To be precise, this change will be rather gradual. The legal status of the 'old' staff will not change, only new staff will be employed by private contracts. For a period of approximately 30 years there will be two categories of staff, which will not make things easier.

[22] A sharp tongue might add: in recent times the academic community was mainly integrated by common enemies, such as the ministry and other external stakeholders.

[23] Since Austria has joined the Bologna process, a new degree structure with the bachelor as the first degree will gradually be implemented in Austrian universities. However, there is a lot of resistance among academics and for that reason this process is very slow. In particular, there is little awareness that undergraduate education needs a new culture of teaching and learning.

[24] Austrian universities are not allowed to reject students due to limited resources. There is no *numerus clausus* which would allow to link the number of students to the number of staff and other resources. The concept of 'study place' which takes that dependency into account is not familiar at Austrian

universities. This makes it easy for the government to adhere to an open access policy without feeling too much of an obligation to carry the financial consequences. In particular the teacher-student ratio has dramatically deteriorated over the last two decades.

REFERENCES

Bast, Gerald. "Ordinarienuniversität, Gruppenuniversität - und weiter?" In *BMWF: Universitäts-Management*. Wien: BMWF, 1990, 7–10.

bm:bwk. "Die volle Rechtsfähigkeit der Universitäten. Gestaltungsvorschlag für die Regelung der Autonomie." Mimeo. Wien, 2001.

BMWF. *Die neue Universitätsstruktur. Reformkonzept* (Green Paper). Wien: BMWF, 1991.

BMWF. *Vorschläge des Projektsteams "Universitätsreform"* (Orange Paper). Wien: BMWF, 1992a.

BMWF. *Universitätsorganisationsgesetz '93. Entwurf, Erläuterungen, Kostenberechnung* (White Paper). Wien: BMWF, 1992b.

bm:wv. "Vollrechtsfähigkeit von Universitäten. Diskussionspapier für ein Bundesgesetz über vollrechtsfähige Universitäten." Mimeo. Wien, 1998.

Cohen, Gary B. *Education and Middle-Class Society in Imperial Austria, 1848-1918*. West Lafayette, Indiana: Purdue University Press, 1996.

Fisher, James L. and James V. Koch. *Presidential Leadership: Making a Difference*. American Council on Education. Phoenix: Oryx Press, 1996.

Hanft, Anke (Hrsg). *Hochschulen managen? Zur Reformierbarkeit der Hochschulen nach Managementprinzipien*. Neuwied: Luchterhand, 2000.

Hanft, Anke (Hrsg). *Grundbegriffe des Hochschulmanagements*. Neuwied: Luchterhand, 2001.

Höllinger, Sigurd. *Universität ohne Heiligenschein. Aus dem 19. ins 21. Jahrhundert*. Wien: Passagen, 1992.

Lassnigg, Lorenz and Hans Pechar. *Alternatives to Universities in Higher Education. Country Study: Austria*. Paris: OECD, 1988.

Nickel, Sigrun. "Zielvereinbarungen als partizipatives Management – ein Anwendungsmodell." In Hanft, Anke (Hrsg) (ed.). *Hochschulen managen? Zur Reformierbarkeit der Hochschulen nach Managementprinzipien*. Neuwied: Luchterhand, 2000, 153–169.

OECD. *Education at a Glance*. OECD Indicators. Paris: OECD, 2002.

Österreichische Forschungsgemeinschaft. *Universitätsreform. Ziele, Prioritäten und Vorschläge*. Wien: Österreichische Forschungsgemeinschaft, 1991.

Österreichische Rektorenkonferenz. "Elemente der Universitätsautonomie. Stellungnahme zum Gestaltungsvorschlag einer Arbeitsgruppe des." Mimeo. bm:bwk, 2001.

Pechar, Hans. "Studienabbruch und Hochschulkultur." Paper presented at the *Conference Studienabbruch*, University of Vienna, 2002, http://www.soz.univie.ac.at/lehre/pool/kolland/teil2.pdf.

Pratt, John and Elsa Hackl. "Breaking the Mould in Austrian Higher Education." *Higher Education Review* 32.1 (1999): 34–54.

Sebök, Martha. *Universitätsgesetz 2002. Gesetzestext und Kommentar*. Wien: WUV Universitätsverlag, 2002.

Titscher et al. *Universitäten im Wettbewerb. Zur Neustrukturierung österreichischer Universitäten*. München/Mering: Rainer Hampp Verlag, 2000.

Trow, Martin. "The University Presidency: Comparative Reflections on Leadership." Ninth David D. Henry Lecture. Urbana, Illinois: University of Illinois at Urbana-Champain, 1984.

Zechlin, Lothar. "University Reform in Austria: Quick Change, No Public Management." Paper presented at the *15th CHER Annual Conference*, Vienna, 2002.

ALBERTO AMARAL, ANTÓNIO MAGALHÃES AND
RUI SANTIAGO

THE RISE OF ACADEMIC MANAGERIALISM
IN PORTUGAL

1. INTRODUCTION

Under the convergent effects of financial restrictions resulting partly from the rolling-back of the welfare state, rising expectations and social demand, mandates of the new economy and a weakening of its symbolic capital, higher education has been exposed to the influence of strong outside pressures, only paralleled by those of the Napoleonic and Humboldtian reforms in the 19th century.

The emergence of neo-liberal ideologies seems to combine the 'market', 'performativity' and 'managerialism' to offer an answer to the triple crisis of the university – a crisis of social legitimacy, a crisis of hegemony in terms of knowledge production and an institutional crisis (Santos 1994). The influence of neo-liberal ideologies over the behaviour of higher education institutions combined with mimetic pressures from the myth of private management efficiency gives rise to the strong establishment and development (Reed 2002) of 'narratives of strategic change', of 'new organisational forms' and of 'micro management control techniques' characteristic of 'new managerialism' as a redeeming, universal, totalising and unquestionable answer.

It is important to distinguish between 'managerialism' as ideology for strategic change of public services that will liberate public sector initiative from 'the dead weight of professional mendacity and bureaucratic mediocrity' (Reed 2002) and the need to provide institutions with management instruments and processes allowing for a more flexible and effective administration. In the latter case, the management tools and processes will remain instruments at the service of the institution and its leadership, without assuming a dominant role as determinants of the institution's objectives and strategies. And it is useful to consider the development of 'managerialism' at two different levels: the level of the political steering of the system and the level of institutional governance.

The Centre for Research into Higher Education Policies (CIPES) Portugal is developing a research project entitled 'The rise of academic managerialism in Portugal' which aims at understanding how far 'managerialism' has become important in the Portuguese higher education, both at system and institutional levels. This is a multidisciplinary project conducted by a team of researchers of CIPES and initiated in October 2001. The research is based on data sources both internal and external to higher education institutions. Data external to institutions were collected

131

A. Amaral et al. (eds.), The Higher Education Managerial Revolution?, 131–153.
© 2003 *Kluwer Academic Publishers. Printed in the Netherlands.*

in interviews with politicians and political decision makers and with private managers/entrepreneurs, as well as gathered from political statements, legislation, government programmes, political party programmes, books written by politicians and other relevant documentation. Research material internal to institutions was collected in interviews with rectors/presidents and senior administrators of six universities and six polytechnics, as well as from documentary analysis of institutions' statutes, strategic plans, annual reports and other relevant documentation, and in the analysis of the changes of composition of the administrative staff of those institutions over a period of 20 years.

This chapter intends to be a preliminary account of the analysis of the interviews of external actors. The interviewees were managers/entrepreneurs (8), and politicians and political decision makers (8), whose selection was made on the basis of their importance as social actors in the Portuguese context, rather than on the basis of statistical representation of the population to which they belong. The sample can be characterised as a careful choice of active actors (interviewees) with real decision power over the higher education system (eight former Ministers of Education) and of actors relevant within the context of the Portuguese economy (presidents of industrial and commercial associations and some of the more important Portuguese private entrepreneurs). Indeed, instead of interviewing a large number of minor actors, there was a choice of interviewing actors with a very significant role in defining higher education policies (e.g. eight former Ministers of Education), who played a decisive role in the development of the system and were active witnesses of the system's transformation and of the efforts of higher education institutions to adapt and change in answer to those developments, and of interviewing actors with a relevant role in the Portuguese economy who frequently made public statements on the role and mission of higher education.

Table 1. The interviewees' profile

	Former Minister	Manager/ Entrepreneur	University Professor	Academic Background
A	X		X	Sciences
B	X		X	Sciences
C	X		X	Engineering
D	X		X	Engineering
E	X		X	Engineering
F	X		X	Engineering
G	X		X	Sociology
H	X	X		Engineering
I		X		Engineering
J		X		Engineering
K		X		Economics
L		X	X	Engineering
M		X		Engineering
N		X		Engineering
O		X	X	Sciences

Table 1 summarises the individual characteristics of the interviewees. It is interesting to note that seven of the former Ministers of Education are university professors, the eighth being a private manager and member of the board of an industrial association. Seven of the former ministers hold university degrees in engineering (5) or science (2), and one is a sociologist. All the managers/entrepreneurs hold higher education degrees (six engineers, one scientist and one economist), and two of them teach occasionally in universities.

In this text, three related terms are used: government, governance and management. It is considered that the 'government' of an institution or university includes a 'governance' component in the sense of predominantly 'political decision making', as well as a 'management' component in the sense of achieving intended outcomes through the allocation of responsibilities and resources, and monitoring their efficiency and effectiveness.

2. MANAGERIALISM AS A TRAVELLING IDEOLOGY

The basic assumption of the project is that there is a 'travelling ideology' which is becoming central in the political discourses on higher education political steering and institutional government. One calls it 'travelling' because it is pervading not only the political discourses in countries in which higher education was consolidated as a mass system but also in countries where such expansion has been recent. In fact managerialism, as it is characterised in this text (see below), emerged in the Anglo-Saxon countries during the eighties and nineties apparently as the result of the transformation of public sector institutions by "the dismantling of 'bureau-professional' organisational regimes and their replacement with market-entrepreneurial regimes" (Clarke and Newman 1992, cited in Ball 1998).

Managerialism also played a visible role in eroding the authority and autonomy of professions, and transforming occupational ideologies and professional identities (Reed 2002). The traditional concept of profession, based on a strong core of professional and ethical norms, is associated with the surrender of market benefits in exchange for a monopoly of professional exercise. Professionals claim to be guided by the ideals of public service and altruism (the Hippocratic oath is a good example of this) and they do not seek to maximise profits, considering the interests of clients and community as paramount. No ideal could be further alien to the new ideology based on market values, relevance for the labour market, operational efficiency and entrepreneurship. It is no wonder that the new ideology of public management proclaims the need to destroy, or at least weaken, the sclerotic professional monopolies and the corporative bureaucracies that have created alliances to control public life.

As for higher education, the expansion of the systems took place in a context in which the welfare state and welfare devices began to, according to some interpretations, 'hold the line' (Scott 1995), and to retreat, according to others. Thatcherism in Europe and Reaganism in the US started this trend in the 1980s and its consequences were not yet fully evaluated and understood, namely in relation to higher education which has remained a relatively neglected research theme (Reed

2002). These two processes (the expansion of higher education systems and the dismantling of the welfare state) provide the main context in which managerialism made its appearance.

Managerialism is generally presented as a technical approach both to systems' political steering and to institutional governance. However, this assumption is based on a set of *implicit assertions* which transforms the managerial account into an ideological perspective:

a) market and market-like environments are more effective as instances of regulation than state;
b) market organisations – the firms – and market-like organisations are more efficient than their public sector counterparts;
c) organisations must be responsive to environmental changes;
d) market mechanisms rely heavily upon the merits of individual choice and the emphasis on unrestricted individualism as the main characteristic of the self-sufficient, competitive institution.

It is also important to establish managerialism clearly as a governing concept in higher education. The conception of system and organisational problems can be characterised as 'technical' issues, meaning that they depend on a set of identifiable variables, and as such they can be dealt with by developing strategic actions. That is why managerialism enhances the separation between 'governance' and 'management'. This approach aims at efficiency (reaching the maximum *output* by using the minimum *input*), and consequently 'performance' (either individual or institutional) is its main concern. Only performance can be approached in those terms and 'technically' evaluated. That is why decision-making processes become, in this paradigm, 'non-political', technically neutral. Consequently, managerialism – as an ideal type – insists not only on professionalised management, but also on professionalised governance. Simultaneously, it is assumed that collegial decision-making processes are to be abandoned on charges of corporativism and inefficiency.

Rosemary Deem articulates in what she calls 'new-managerialism' the change in the way "publicly funded institutions are managed, following the widespread restructuring of welfare services in Western societies" (2001: 10), and she stresses also that 'new managerialism' is both an 'ideology' and a set of management practices and techniques applied to the public sector:

> Those promoting new managerial discourses, whether politicians, management gurus or managers themselves, frequently claim that the ideas of new managerialism are purely based on an objective search for efficiency, effectiveness and excellence, with assumptions about continuous improvement of organisations often a further underlying theme. New managerialism is used to refer to the desirability of a variety of organisational changes (2001: 10).

Since the 1980s a large number of states, mainly in Western Europe, have adopted forms of higher education regulation that apparently reflect these assumptions. According to several authors, political steering in Europe has been emphasising institutional self-regulation against state control, the only apparent exception being the UK[1] (Maassen and Van Vught 1988; Goedegebuure et al. 1993;

Goedegebuure and Van Vught 1994; Amaral and Magalhães 2001; Magalhães 1998). And at the same time that market-like (or rather market-friendly) devices were developed – such as autonomy – states assumed remote control of the system and of institutions by developing evaluation mechanisms (Neave and Van Vught 1991), which are other manifestations of the insertion of a 'cult of excellence' into the public sector (Ball 1998).

It is in this context that managerialism emerges and is assuming an increasingly relevant position in the discourses on higher education. Market and market-like environments are presented as THE effective and relevant response to the crisis of higher education. Hence, the managerial account appears as a universal response not only to the problems of effective systems regulation and of institutional 'government', but also as carrying out an implicit idea of university and higher education. (This second aspect will not be developed in this chapter.) It is in this sense that managerialism travels as an ideology. And, as such, its features are often more implicit than explicit, for instance, with regard to assumptions taking for granted the efficiency of market and market-like organisations, regulation devices and environments. To understand how far managerialism has travelled in the Portuguese higher education system is the aim of this research project.

3. MANAGERIALISM IN PORTUGAL

The 1974 revolution installed a revolutionary and socialist climate which pervaded both government policies and national institutions. The revolutionary period (1974–76) was characterised by a total opening up of the higher education system to all citizens who wished to enrol; and the role of education in general was seen as a path leading to a new society and a new humanism, while refusing to be an instrument for cultural and capitalist exploitation. It is obvious that in this context traditional forms of authority were replaced by forms of participative democracy, sometimes on the verge of 'anarchy'.

The ten-year period from 1976 to 1986 could be described as the 'normalisation' period of higher education. The binary system was consolidated, and government policies began to move away from centralised control towards less restrictive steering of higher education institutions. As well, the governance system moved away from 'anarchy' by creating democratic collective decision-making bodies at all levels within higher education institutions with strong participation of students and non-academic staff and where election became the main source of legitimation.

From 1986 to 1989, the main features were the consolidation of the private/public duality of the system and the conferring of autonomy by the government on higher education public institutions. The Autonomy Act for universities (Law 108/88, of 24 September) gave institutions freedom to establish their statutes, together with scientific, pedagogical, administrative and financial autonomy, as well as the power to act in matters of academic discipline. In general the new law consolidated the 'democratic rule' within the academy while at the same time transferring vast powers to the institutions.

To understand the Portuguese case it is important to have a good knowledge of the national system of university government resulting from the Autonomy Law. There are three main decision-making bodies at central (university) level: the University Assembly, the Senate and the Rector. The University Assembly has a large membership and only holds formal meetings on special occasions, namely for the approval of university statutes and their alterations and to elect the Rector. The Senate is the most important collective decision-making body, not only on academic matters but also on matters such as the approval of the budget, annual plans and strategic plans that, in other countries (e.g. the UK), are within the legal authority of a council. The university may decide to allow for external representation in the Senate of up to 15% of the total membership. The Senate is presided over by the Rector whose power depends a lot on his/her charisma and capacity of leadership.

Schools have several government bodies: Assembly of Representatives, Executive Board, Scientific Council and Pedagogical Council. The Assembly does not convene very often and approves the composition of the Executive Board and the annual activity plan and budget. The Executive Board is presided over by a professor and is composed of an equal number of professors and students with the non-academic staff being represented by half that number. The Scientific Council is composed of academics holding a doctoral degree who make decisions on scientific matters. The Pedagogical Council is composed of an equal number of students and professors and has only an advisory capacity on pedagogical matters. It is possible that some decisions made by the Scientific Council (for instance hiring new professors) are vetoed by the Executive Board with the argument of lack of funds – this is just one example of possible conflicts arising between the two more important decision-making bodies of a school.

From 1989 to 1999 institutional autonomy was reinforced while two coordinating bodies, namely the Council of Rectors of the Portuguese Universities (CRUP) and its homologous organisation for polytechnics (the CCISP), emerged as important actors (more the former than the latter) in the definition of higher education policies. This was the time for agreement over a funding formula for higher education institutions and for quality. In 1994 Parliament approved Law 38/94, of 21 November, establishing the rules of the Portuguese quality assessment system, the whole implementation of this process being far more academically driven (by CRUP, mainly) than government driven. In 1997 a new decree largely increased the financial autonomy of universities and transferred all real estate to them.

The present research project aims at identifying the emergence of the characteristics of managerialism in the Portuguese context. While some research has focused on the narrative account on which managerialism is based (Magalhães 2001), this project intends to go further and to locate not only the ideological features (the managerial narrative) of managerialism but also some of its specific proposals on the discourses on higher education.

The managerial discourse has explicitly emerged in the context of Portuguese education at both the system and institutional levels. At the system level it is echoed in the policies aiming to steer the sector, and at the institutional level it is present in the issues of institutional governance and management.

At the first level, it appeared in the mid-1980s promoted by Roberto Carneiro under the aegis of the thesis, which underlined the need to assimilate firms to schools and schools to firms (1988: 18). In Portugal, therefore, this phenomenon is contemporary with the rise of a new regulation mode of the higher education system, referred to as the supervisory model (see Neave and Van Vught 1991). This model, based on the principle of deregulation, is justified by the awareness that it is impossible for the state to efficiently regulate the processes at system and institutional levels within a 'centralised control' logic. In a number of Western European countries the rise of managerialism appears to be linked to the need – given the pressure of social demand for education and the financial stringency due to welfare dismantling – to regulate national systems differently.

Therefore, it is important to mention that the emergence of the managerial discourse in Portugal is linked to the approval and implementation of the 1988 University Autonomy Act. Managerialism eventually became more visible during the 1990s as a conception of institutional governance and linked to a new political discourse that associated the new institutional autonomy with the need to demonstrate that higher education institutions were well run. However, it is only in the late 1990s, early 2000s that the traditional collegial forms of academic management have come under more visible public attack. This may be due to several factors, such as:

- until the late 1990s the governance structures resulting from the Autonomy Act were in an experimental phase;
- recent economic difficulties have put in jeopardy the funding formula and looking for alternative funds has become more imperative;
- decreasing birth rates have resulted in lower number of candidates to higher education, thus initiating a competition of institutions for students;
- quite recently a more neo-liberal government has been elected.

However, for a better understanding of the Portuguese situation it is also important to identify some peculiarities of a society that has emerged from a dictatorial regime less than 30 years ago. A Portuguese sociologist, Boaventura de Sousa Santos (1993, 1994), identifies those characteristics as pertaining to a 'heterogeneous state' and to a 'parallel state'. After the 1974 revolution, Portugal emerged from decades of isolation and in a few years "the Portuguese corporative state went through a transition to socialism, a Fordist regulation and a Welfare State regulation, and even a neo-liberal regulation. The structure of the state presents, in each moment, a geological composition with several layers, sedimented in different forms, some old, some recent, each one with its own internal logic and its own strategical orientation. This is the meaning of the heterogeneous state" (Santos 1993: 41). It is also true that the new Constitution approved in 1996 had a very strong left-wing influence and was indeed a detailed programme for building a socialist country. However, none of the governments elected after the Constitution was approved could be considered Marxist or extreme-leftist. This has resulted in a gap between the objectives and intentions of legislation and the social and political issue that they intend to regulate. Over the years, many laws have fallen into oblivion without producing effects while the Constitution was progressively amended to eliminate the more obvious ornaments of a socialist ideology. This is what Santos (1994: 63) calls the 'parallel state'.

It is perhaps the parallel and heterogeneous character of the Portuguese state that explains the rhetorical character of the political agency in general and higher education in particular as these characteristics lead to weak central government regulation.

4. THE ACTORS' DISCOURSES: AUTONOMY, COLLEGIALITY AND CHANGES OF THE DECISION-MAKING PROCESSES AND STRUCTURES

The initial analysis of the interviews that support the research results presented in this chapter was based on four broad dimensions of organisation of the social actors' discourses:

a) the purposes of higher education;
b) the relationship between institutions and the state;
c) the operation and internal organisation of institutions;
d) the relationship of institutions with the outside environment.

From this initial analysis it can be discerned that the interviewees' main perceptions were centred on the following themes: the corporativist 'perversion' of the present model of university governance and management; and change proposals of this model, namely of the legal authority and formation of institutional government bodies and of the allocation of decision-making powers among those bodies. These two themes were analysed to find out to what extend they are permeated by the managerial rhetoric on markets which imposes efficiency as an unquestionable institutional goal (Deem 1998, 2001; Bostock 1998; Fitzsimons 2000; Reed 2002; Meek 2002), a goal that is to be attained under the inspired guidance of a strong and professionalised technical authority (Edwards 2001), presented as politically neutral. With regard to this main purpose, one analysis – more specifically the actors' perceptions that the present combination of the exercise of political-collegial power legitimised by democratic representation of all institutional bodies (students, academic and non-academic staff) in governance – can be interpreted within the managerial logic as a barrier to developing new systems of authority. This interpretation is corroborated by the following assumptions:

a) reinforcement of the power mechanisms of central administration (concentration on top management to define the main political and management orientations);
b) professionalisation of management and separation between management and academic activities;
c) resort to management and strategic planning as a goal in itself and as a source of legitimacy for a new ethical-ideological discourse;

d) strong reinforcement of the representation of external constituencies (economic, social and cultural) in the institutional governance bodies at the expense of the representation of academics and other institutional bodies (students and non-academic staff).

After a general approach to the 'corporativist perversion' of the present model of the governance and management of universities, and taking into account the different themes, an analysis is presented of the change proposals formulated by the actors *apropos* of decision-making structures and processes.

4.1. A Critique of Corporativism

With regard to institutional autonomy, the analysis of the interviews suggests strong criticism of the present university model of governance and management, with stronger emphasis being placed more on its 'corporativist perversion' than on its lack of efficiency.

The collective governance bodies, particularly the Senate, would represent only corporative interests, and their membership gives excessive weight to the representation of the different internal bodies, more conspicuously in the case of students and non-academic staff. These corporative interests are sometimes visible in *ad hoc* alliances and coalitions established among academics, or sometimes between academics and the students and impact negatively on university governance.

These critiques however take on different meaning according to the relative proximity of the actors to the managerial rhetoric. For those actors closer to the managerial rhetoric, the disparaging remarks on collegiality are developed from an instrumental vision of the reorganisation of the decision-making power and processes that is self-explained by the functionality of market-friendly devices. For the other actors, criticism of collegiality remains within the boundaries of the debate over the grounds for legitimacy of the exercise of decision-making power. In some sense the key to the resolution of the university's problems would depend on the redefinition of that legitimacy at the different decision levels within the institution.

For the first group of actors (mainly managers/entrepreneurs) with discourses that are closer to the managerial rhetoric, emphasis is placed on the necessity of reallocating and resignifying the legal capacity of governance and management bodies in order to achieve increased efficiency and effectiveness – collegial governance bodies would play only an advisory role, the university's central administration would be similar to private business administrative boards and the Rector would be an efficient manager able to transform the university into a credible institution:

> ... the university Autonomy Act needs revision. (...) this act was a mistake because it confers an excessive weight to students and non-academic staff for the election of management bodies. It is fundamental to increase the weight given to professors (at the pedagogical level)... it is quite absurd to allow students to participate in management. (H)[2]

> (…) the university collegiality has the same meaning, the same feeling of pure and hard academic over-protectiveness and not the material organisation of the system of management… (I)

For the second group of actors (mainly those ministers and political decision makers with a university job) the criticism of corporativism emerges as an opportunity to legitimise changes in power allocation between university governance and management structures, within a post-Weberian perspective where the legitimacy of hierarchical authority is resignified in the light of the new challenges facing the universities. The collegial model is mixed up with corporative interests and commitments celebrated among academics, which hinder the university's adaptation to the real interests of the nation, the economy and society. In other cases it is assumed that the political-collegial model prevents higher education institutions from taking on increased responsibilities *vis-à-vis* their external stakeholders and from defining a strategic vision that would be implemented through strategic planning and strategic management. A collection of opinions is thus revealed in the actors' discourses which insists on the necessity of a general redefinition of power allocation and of the relative weight of the different internal institutional actors, and of the external stakeholders in decision-making bodies and decision-making processes:

> The model of academic power that emerged inside public higher education institutions, shared by professors, students and non-academic staff is completely worn out and is no longer adequate to answer the challenges from society. (…) there is a common element to all these (collegial) forms represented by the almost absolute victory of corporativism dominated by the *status quo* conservatism and by internal commitments which exercise an absolute power dominated as a rule by personal and sporadic interests. (…) the present model of power tolerates an irrational use of human and material resources (…) and to make things worse it is never associated with a plan and a medium and long term strategic vision identifying each institution's mission. (A)

> (…) it is a power that should not be delegated in schools or in their governance bodies (…) the job (of the members of Parliament) was not done under those conditions of impartiality, of detachment, of rigour, of objectivity that would take precautions against all consequences. (…) there is a power that was granted and which is not being properly used… (C)

> (the Senate) (…) has become a very powerful body inside the institution, which is a corporation, and sometimes acts to protect and to maintain its own interests. This power needs to be broken… (F)

Taking this initial approach to the analysis of the social actors' discourses, some diversity of opinion can be found both in those discourses close to the managerial rhetoric as well as in those more distant from it. However, some common features are evident in almost every discourse: the need of centralisation of the decision-making power and the redefinition of the range of influence of internal institutional bodies and of external stakeholders. It is true that in those discourses closer to the managerial rhetoric, these features are derived from (private) management imperatives that can be identified with the application of principles of economic and technical rationality aimed at obtaining efficiency. On the other hand, in the other discourses emphasis is placed either on the definition of a new legitimacy of power (and on subsidiary reinforcement of management), or on the internal redefinition of that legitimacy which reinforces hierarchical authority by recommending changes in the formation of academic boards and presidencies based on the limitation of the democratic principle of election as a source of legitimacy.

4.2. University Governance and Management Structures and Processes

The proposals made for improving institutional governance and management present considerable diversity. What emerges clearly from the actors' improvement proposals are different representations of institutional autonomy, of legitimacy of the exercise of power, of external mitigation of this exercise, of the relationship between (professionalised) management structures and academics, and of participation of internal institutional bodies – namely the academics – in the decision-making process. The diversity as well as the ambiguity of the proposals is evident for instance in those aiming at preventing institutional corporativism. On the one hand, some actors suggest that the election of the Rector should be replaced by appointment in order to protect the Rector from becoming a hostage of the electoral process and electoral compromises. On the other hand, other actors propose an increase of the Rector's power, sometimes at the expense of students' participation in decision making. There are also diversified proposals for changing the legitimacy and legal capacity of governance and management bodies such as restricting the role of the Rector to that of a mere executive; limiting the role of the Senate to that of an advisory body to the Rector; concentrating power in the Rector assisted by a Board of Trustees; subordinating the Rector to the Board of Trustees; strongly limiting the power of collegial decision-making bodies; or creating General Councils while downgrading the role of the Senate.

The actors' views on increased participation of outside constituencies – external stakeholders – in university governance and management are more consensual. Only two actors are against this increased participation, especially when it includes an executive role. Their defence is that universities have their own culture that needs to be protected from colonisation by alien cultures and that the business sector (or the market) has in general only short-term visions, which are not compatible with university governance. Neither institutional autonomy nor (sometimes) even its reinforcement is put in question. However, most managers/entrepreneurs (5) support market regulation mechanisms while the other actors (including two entrepreneurs) either bluntly reject the market's intervention or would prefer to see a more strategic role played by the state (quality assessment, performance indices, management and financial indices, state planning, accreditation, more generalised accountability) with protection of areas deemed important for national culture and identity, or protection of the university's core values – higher education institutions' soul.

The diversity of opinion formulated on changes for improving university governance and management made it necessary to carry out a more detailed analysis of the actors' discourses in order to find out if those opinions could eventually be aggregated into more sharply defined specific themes allowing for a more logical interpretation of those proposals. These specific themes are the following:

a) predominance of management over governance;
b) functionality of management and the reinforcement of academic power;
c) social and institutional consensuality;
d) internal redefinition of the legitimacy of institutional power.

4.2.1. Predominance of Management Over Governance

Four actors (three managers and a former minister) formulated proposals about changes of governance and management processes and models in the Portuguese universities that are close to an idea of the 'market', which does not really result from individual rational choices but from the activities of entrepreneurial organisations. For one actor (a former minister) university regulation would thus depend, in the last resort, on the nature of the inputs from the business world, from the techno-rational nature of processes and from the alignment of outputs with presumed labour market demands. Efficiency is identified with the management processes of private enterprises taking for granted that they imply a better technical rationality and a better clarification of power and decision-making systems.

The arrangement would be completed with professionalised management and strong participation of external stakeholders in university governance:

> Universities should follow a management model as any enterprise. (…) universities need to behave like enterprises. (…) university's central management and departments instead of dealing with money (…) should only worry about (…) academic questions: how good are classes (…) if professors do not miss their classes (…) listen to students' opinions by means of permanent inquiries (…) it is important to think about study programmes and their pedagogical contents with help from the business world. (…) the rector and his team should stop doing financial management, which is a job for a professional manager… (…) within a principle of management rationality I debate curricular contents with teaching staff and if necessary also with external entrepreneurs. (H)

> It is a long time since I started to dislike the system. I would very much prefer a professionalised management (…) I believe that university management needs to be taken seriously instead of asking who is going to be the manager of this institution? A rector? I consider that this is a very bad example for management because it is very difficult to find an academic with a very good curriculum that is able to get involved with management problems with the pragmatism that good management demands… (I)

> In the case of university government as well as in general government systems, I could see some advantage in at least testing as soon as possible a system allowing for the participation of outside people with better training for this kind of job. (…) they would create less internal discord, they are not acquainted with professors, and they can provide a method of curricular analysis that will differ substantially from that provided by those inside the institution… (I)

> It is necessary to create appropriate conditions for university autonomy that would allow them to behave like enterprises while retaining their condition of public universities; they have their own specific products, the students (…) It is important that universities realise this, that they are 'product' enterprises, quality products (…) it is fundamental to develop a concept of management and efficiency inside the university and the institution needs to be profitable, it needs to become economically sustainable… (M)

Most change proposals reveal, however, some unusual characteristics. It is true that they favour separation of management from pedagogic and academic matters, but the institutional authority system relies strongly on management. Put in different words, the separation of management from governance becomes blurred; management is assumed as the real way of governing, supported by an efficiency concept with a meaning that conforms with prescriptions of technical and economic rationality referred to practical skills imported from business practices. More than being an explicit statement of a technical device, neutral and depoliticised, or of a mere magical recipe, the management change proposals emerge in these actors' discourses as real governance devices or as a governance rationality that is signified in the context of institutional culture and of its own governance structures. This position becomes further evident as proposals also include important changes of the management's professionalisation and of the governance bodies' operation, that should also take place at the same time, as well as changes of the relative weight (number and status) of the representation of external stakeholders (economic, social and cultural) in university governance.

According to these four actors, changes at the level of management professionalisation should comprise the recruitment of professional managers to stimulate a more entrepreneurial management of universities, eventually under the control of governance bodies:

> I would recruit, just like any other enterprise, a professional manager (…) from inside or outside the organisation (…) there are management schools with very good managers that can be hired (…) to provide entrepreneurial management (but answering to a collective body or to the rector) (…) this can be seen as having central management as a non-executive board of administration (…) but I do not agree with the creation of 'university managers' because there are no specific managements. There is management 'tout court'. A good manager can manage a university, or a hospital, or an enterprise. (H)

> University managers, although some could be academics, should be recruited because of their management capacity, of their capacity of taking decisions and defending them (…) In this area of university management, involving enormous sums of money, sometimes with managers who do not really know the meaning of managing (…) It is obvious that no one will ignore that the academic area must be protected. (I)

> Who runs the university must be someone with competence, and competence means a lot of things such as accountancy, capacity to choose the necessary instruments to work with the raw materials entering the university – the students, those young people. (M)

This vision of professionalised management is not restricted to mere reinforcement of the administrative structure or to power reallocation between what can be identified as management and governance. It can be interpreted as integrating a managerial rhetoric where the vision is signified as the introduction of a strong element of 'rationality' into the 'irrationality' of 'traditional' academic management. Management professionalisation thus seems to be fundamentally assimilated to a change of the power system at the institutional top level, probably in the sense of professionalising governance through management and/or of legitimising management as a rational form of governance.

The actors' discourses on professionalised management are in some way consistent with their discourses on the operation of governance bodies and the reallocation of the relative weight of the representation of external stakeholders (economic, social and cultural) in those bodies. In general, these actors assume the position that governance bodies need restructuring, their composition needs revision and that eventually they can coexist with or be replaced by a 'Board of Trustees'.

The convergence of opinion is more evident regarding the reinforcement of the representation of external stakeholders (from the business world) and the reduction of the weight of the internal bodies, namely students and non-academic staff. Sometimes, there is also some convergence of proposals for reducing the power of the Rector's role, changing its legitimacy source or restricting its legal authority to academic problems:

> (...) I consider that the Senate's legal requirements as prescribed by the university's Autonomy Act need revision because its membership is so vast that it is good for nothing (...) its membership should be drastically reduced and should become an effective advisory board of the university with a significant participation of economic activities, to introduce what is the effervescence of economy ... (...) central administration should become an administrative (...) board and one or two entrepreneurs should participate in this central body (...) but it is necessary to be careful to avoid importing into the university more sins than those that are already there. (H)

> I would like to see the users of the university's products being invited and staying effectively inside the university or participating in a legal body capable of assuming responsibility for its opinions and for the selection of candidates (new students). (...) they should participate while users (...) individual entrepreneurs should not formulate their opinions. This should be the task of entrepreneurial associations worthy of credit...
> (I)

> Monarchy does not renovate itself by doing very good things. So the way to create some inquietude is by introducing some outside members with a different life background (...) it is necessary to give some status to those outside people (...) those people need to be permanently available to reflect on problems and to offer their contributions; it is not enough to rely only on outside people's hunches! (J)

One of the interviewed actors (an entrepreneur) assumes a rather peculiar position by agreeing on the one hand with participation of students, academics and non-academic staff in university governance bodies in their shareholder capacity, and on the other hand by accepting government interference in the elections for those bodies again in its capacity as major shareholder of public universities:

> The electors are the shareholders and it is necessary to have a General Assembly [as in shareholding societies] that elects its administrative board (...) I would say that in the case of state universities the government should have the power to elect because he is the most important shareholder and as such must assume this responsibility (...) I do not believe in anything which does not have a boss and I consider that the state as boss/manager is not a bad boss but it is certainly a bad manager... [and that is why it is important to create a General Council equivalent to a General Assembly] (...) that would act as a body of supervision and as the guardian of the university's development and of its future... [but a Council appointed by the state], (...) [Universities would be financed] only by state capital in a transition phase, later also by private capital... (M)

4.2.2. Functionality of Management and the Reinforcement of Academic Power

Some actors (three political decision makers and entrepreneurs) emphasise the necessity of reinforcing the functionality of university management and governance, together with a reinforcement of the professors' power at the expense of students and non-academic staff. One actor (a former Minister of Education) stresses that the democratic legitimacy of university governance bodies (Senate and Rector) should be reconstructed without paying heed to the principle of equity which imposes parity of all institutional bodies' representation, thus eliminating the present populism that confers on students a disproportionate power in decision making and in the Rector's election:

> I would not allow any place for students' participation in management (...) I have the strongest scepticism about the participation of students in management. (N)

> It is obvious today that in Portugal the university's democratic governance cannot be made by reproducing inside the institution the logic of (numerical) equity of the different bodies and within the bodies the logic of the majority of voters. This is the case even for the systems for choosing a new rector as well as for the systems for choosing executive boards, scientific councils or pedagogic councils. There is a lot to be made, namely, by eliminating some of the populism still present and which places the rectors under an excessive dependency on the students' votes. (L)

In what concerns the professionalisation of the administrative structure, the actors note that it should be merely functional and pragmatic, always subordinated to academic power and designed to liberate academics of the more technical activities of day-to-day management, including financial management:

> I believe that the techno structure of universities needs more professionalisation, and this means technical staff in the strong meaning of the word – in support of elected management (...) we need to reform the university governance system in the sense of making more clear what is 'direction', which are the sources of legitimacy of this 'direction', and what it is day-to-day and professional management of university matters. We still confuse what it means to manage and what it means to govern a higher education institution. That is why collegial bodies do not produce a substantial amount of strategic management while at the same time paralysing day-to-day management. (G)

> ... it is possible that there is a double control of universities: the administrative component (...) while organisation and management of all finances, is a job that requires training; the rector should assume legal capacity on academic matters, as well as contacts with society and with the region where [the institution] is established. (...) I think that more professional management is necessary, I believe that it is necessary to find some platform for concentration of points of view (...) allowing for regular meetings of academics, the leadership of the different schools, the rector, some representative leaders of the region (...) to devise ways of opening windows without subverting the institution. (L)

> Speaking of management (...) in constructions, in classes, etc. that is pure management and this management needs to be professional (...) the educative process is a complex process, even without massification (...) and this is something different from the other management. (...) [management] needs to be professionalised but it has two completely different aspects. (...) to safeguard these two management components (academic and material) they need certainly to be balanced because it may happen that someone is the manager of the educative process and needs the money for this but someone else holds the keys of the safe. (N)

The actors' position with respect to participation of external stakeholders (economic, social and cultural) converge in recommending their reinforced presence, but essentially as 'resource' people supporting academic leadership or as a model for increasing institutional democracy:

> ... thinking in terms of democratic legitimacy means opening [the institution] to the presence, to the participation with an active voice and deliberative power to representatives of the community (...) a democracy restricted to the internal bodies is a weak democracy. (G)

> ... a Board of Trustees makes complete sense as it relieves the rector of some areas that eventually bother him or wear him out, because he has not appropriate training for dealing with them, making him waste his time and eventually providing a bad service (...) I would not feel at all disturbed by an executive administrative board taking care of financial management and relieving rectors and academics for more relevant functions that would obviously include all the academic matters but also and mainly the research of new areas. (N)

One of the actors (an entrepreneur and simultaneously a part-time professor in a university) raises some doubts about participation of external stakeholders in the management and governance of universities, namely about those representing the business sector. He claims that this participation can be as pernicious as the participation of students:

> That [external participation] is a very complex process. If on the one hand I think that the university cannot be kept closed inside its ivory tower, cut-off from society, on the other hand the university needs to be ahead [of other institutions] and because of that the presence of people from industry may be extremely pernicious. It is a process that I consider desirable but needs to be implemented very carefully (...) and the same is valid for the process of students' participation. (N)

Although revealing some characteristics of managerialism, the previous statements neither dramatise these characteristics nor appeal to them for an assumption of a notion of efficiency implying the idea of a 'magical recipe', the only one capable of solving the problems faced by universities. They raise however the question of determining if managerialism is capable of offering some 'exclusively technical' contribution for improving the rationality of the governance and management of universities.

4.2.3. Social and Institutional Consensuality

Two former Ministers of Education place special emphasis on changes to governance conferring considerable centralism on the idea of rebuilding institutional autonomy around a 'Council' or 'Board of Trustees'. For one actor this new body is institutionally consensual as it originates from the institution's traditional governance bodies; for the other actor the new body represents a social commitment due to the substantial (majority) involvement of organised outside interests (economic, social and cultural).

These actors reject the professionalisation of academic boards based upon the outside recruitment of managers. At the same time, they agree to professional governance support for academics. Thus, in reality, the idea that the Rector's position (and other academic bodies) should be professionalised is emphasised within the context of redefinition of the legitimacy and range of exercise of its institutional power. The election of the Rector (who is always an academic) is replaced by appointment (legitimation through nomination) by a 'Board of Trustees'.

For one of the former ministers the Rector's legal capacity and powers should be contractualised. The 'Board of Trustees' (with a majority of external members) holds the power of deciding the contexts of management and governance as well as the new Rector's recruitment profile:

> Today I would propose a different management model (...) or more precisely a governance model, as management is something different, (...) where the rector or the university president (...) would be chosen by a body with a majority of outside representatives and a minority of internal representatives (...). (...) this (body) should be a General Council or a Curator's Council with representatives from the state (assuming the role of champions of the national interest), from genuine economic interests, from business associations, from trade unions, from local government, from cultural interests, from the main foundations, etc. The General Council would define the university's strategic plan and then look for the person (rector) with the best profile to carry out its implementation. The rector would sign a contract, a five-year contract of government to fulfil all those goals and objectives (...). (The General Council) evaluates and controls the implementation of the plan (...). However, the fundamental feature of this governance model (...) would be giving additional weight to concerns that are external to the university (...) [in the present situation] the weight of academics is overwhelming (...) it represents only the weight of corporative interests (...) which determine the choice of the president or rector (...) this person is an academic, not a manager... (E)

For the other former minister the Rector's legal capacity should be a matter for negotiation with the Board of Trustees. The 'Board of Trustees' should contemplate a very strong external representation, all the members being there on an individual capacity. The main role of the Board should be regulatory providing approval of proposals and projects submitted by the Rector and/or the academic bodies. Moreover, as the initiative for the creation of the Board of Trustees originates from the present institutional governance bodies and not from the state or the business sector it gains its legitimacy on a consensual basis:

> My proposal is to have the rectors and the deans of faculties chosen by a 'Board of Trustees' (...) that should express the external weight, where people are not the representatives of ... but are there on their own individual capacity. So I do not see representatives of industries, of political power or of local power inside the university... (...) People who are members of the Board ... are the guardians of the university's operation, ensuring that the objectives pursued by the university are adequate. There is also an internal representation from the University, which must have an active presence (...) It is the 'Board of Trustees' that must appreciate and approve the institutional projects submitted by the rector and the deans... It is not necessary to have professionalisation in the sense of recruiting an outside manager; the area of recruitment of rectors may be enlarged, for instance by stating that the rector can be a professor from any university instead of a full professor of that university. (...) it is important to find a legitimation instrument for the Board of Trustees. Of course it cannot be appointed by Parliament or by the Prime Minister, or by a group of enterprises (...) however, the institution has its own legitimate bodies, it has an elected rector, it has a Senate, it has faculties, it has an Assembly of Representatives. There is a legitimacy that was conferred upon these bodies and they have capacity for saying – we want a system like this, and the transition system is... (F)

In any case, internal actors (professors, students and non-academic staff) are divested of a substantial share of political power and of participation in decision making, at both the management and governance levels of the universities. It is true that the seat of political and institutional control is referred to as a 'General Council' or a 'Board of Trustees' that becomes the guardian of institutional autonomy (societal autonomy as it is stressed by one of the interviewees) and a 'mediator' between the state and the institution. This new body concentrates vast powers at the expense of the Rector's power, that is now seen as only an 'executive power' with very limited space for political intervention. There is not a depolitisation of university management and governance but quite to the contrary there is a real resignification of political power and of legitimacy, which gives the Board of Trustees a very strong supervisory power. This process combines new forms of institutional and social control, supported by a new rationality and it is backed by management tools (contracts, strategic management and strategic planning) inspired by managerial rhetoric.

The role of the members of the Board of Trustees corresponds to what Amaral and Magalhães (2002: 1–21) have called 'Form 2 external stakeholders' and it

> is to represent the broader and long-term interests of society and this role corresponds to the notion of higher education as a public good. Their role is not to promote market values *à outrance*, but to ensure that externalities and the core values of the university are not jeopardised by institutional attitudes that emphasize short-term market values while ignoring the university's social role. This is the traditional ideal role of the trustees of American universities: to represent the interest of society but at the same time to uphold the core values of the institution as seen by society and defined in the institution's statutes and mission statement.

4.2.4. Internal Redefinition of the Legitimacy of Institutional Power

Three actors (two former ministers and a manager) have discourses that are mainly centred on the problem of reinforcement and clarification of the legitimacy of internal power systems in universities. Their positions also present some diversity. For one actor more power should be conferred on the Rector by changing the position's source of legitimacy. The Rector would be appointed by the Minister from a list of names proposed by the university professors. This would obviously entail a decrease of the power of collective decision-making bodies; the deans of faculties would also be appointed and, like the Rector, their decision-making power would be less dependent on scientific and pedagogical councils; students would lose their power, even if they kept the same level of representation in pedagogical councils:

> It is not possible to manage the university with the present system where there is a multiplicity of decision-making centres and where no one has effective power to speak in the name of the university... (...) The decision-making body of the university needs to have more capacity and pedagogic-scientific knowledge to decide in the name of the university and this is not the case of a body (Senate) with a very heterogeneous composition (...), very disperse and without an important centre of power... I would reinforce the rector and his team's decision capacity by downgrading the position of the Senate – if not regarding the important questions and the general orientations then at least regarding daily administration. (...) I would give more power to rectors (...) and also to deans of faculties while taking some administrative authority away from the multiple management boards subsisting in the system. (B)

> I do not believe an election of the political-democratic type to be the more adequate for this kind of person (academic boards/rector). In this case the person remains subdued, it

becomes a prisoner, a prisoner of commitments... (...) an appointment is less prone
than an election to originating mistakes in the type of person chosen for some bodies.
(...) the appointment must however be internal (...) but through a process that is not an
electoral process based on partisan support of any kind... (C)

Using the same logic of centralisation and reinforcement of institutional power,
one interviewee (a former Minister of Education) assumes the position that
management should be reinforced within the hierarchical structure of the
universities: management should integrate a new model of institutional power more
hierarchical and less dichotomised or dispersed. This model does not seem to
represent an approximation to the 'market' notion. As stated in the introduction to
this chapter, it is important to distinguish between 'managerialism' as an ideological
tool aiming at redefining the mission of higher education and the pragmatic use of
management tools to improve the efficiency and effectiveness of institutional
operations. In the latter case, it is a tool that is at the service of academics and not a
device aiming at an ideological reconstruction of the university. Instead of a tool for
changing the 'political-bureaucratic-collegial' model of universities, it is interpreted
as a process of modernisation or restructuring that model, which includes the
downgrading of collegial power in decision-making bodies:

> The alternative model [to the present model] demands that universities do not have a
> dichotomic vision of their unity of power. (...) the dichotomy (of the present model) is
> such that governance is impossible because scientific bodies have an opinion, executive
> boards have a different opinion, they start quarrelling and there is no decision-making
> capacity.
>
> (...) moreover, the (present) model of power is never associated with a plan and with a
> medium and long-term strategic vision, which identifies the mission of each institution
> (...). (...) That is why in my opinion the model of hierarchical management needs to be
> reinforced without effectively giving up academic power exercised through the rector as
> the main authority. (B)

Actors more removed from the managerial rhetoric reject the introduction of the
idea of the 'market' in higher education and a professionalised management
supported by the recruitment of external professional managers (both academic and
non-academic):

> I believe that imposing someone coming from outside to replace an academic will not
> work (...) because academics are also relatively complicated people, or because the
> university system is relatively complex (...) university administrations need to have
> good knowledge of the university so maybe they should be recruited among university
> professors... (B)
>
> To manage an institution of this nature [university] presumes a good internal
> knowledge... (...) [I wonder if] the insertion of people from outside the university in
> decision-making bodies will ever be useful or relevant. I do not believe in genius of
> economics or of finances (...) and I do not believe that the recruitment of some genius
> from those areas will change the life of universities. (C)

However, this convergence of stakeholders in decision-making bodies no longer
exists. One of the interviewees (a former minister) considers that this presence
should become more visible without giving them majority control over academics:

> (...) advisory boards (...) have relatively low efficiency because advisors are not
> involved and, because of that, I would rather have an acceptable number, not a majority,

> of outsiders in those bodies, which are more important for decision-making and taking
> the burden of responsibility for university life. I also consider students among outside
> people as they are outsiders relative to the administration (...) and not only students but
> also employers as people from the social environment (...) what I do not accept is a
> parity representation, which may block the system. (B)

Another former minister rejects this participation or even the creation of a Board of Trustees with the argument that the university must above all rely on its internal members because it has the 'best brains' in the country:

> If the universities adopt a less corporative attitude, less exclusive, more responsive to
> external information (...) they do not need additional elements. By definition the 'best
> brains' in the country are in universities and if this is not the case then something is
> wrong (...) with enough capacity for recognising what needs to be done and how it must
> be done (...). In our case I do not foresee the arrival of boards of trustees (...) I share
> the opinion that it is better to rely on people from the universities with its own
> mysticism and resources (...) the university has a vision of itself, its own culture, and an
> organisational culture... (C)

Lastly, yet another former minister only mentions that the percentage of social representatives should be relevant and given specific powers:

> (...) it is essential to change this [present] model of power to allow for clear
> identification of obligations and prerogatives, with relevant participation of social
> representatives – collective, cultural, economic, socio-professional and even from local
> power – with specific powers and not only in an advisory capacity. (A)

5. PRELIMINARY CONCLUSIONS

Some preliminary conclusions can be drawn based on the analysis of the interviews with political decision makers and managers/entrepreneurs despite their very heterogeneous positions and proposals.

The main conclusion is quite broad and deals with the very existence of managerialism in Portugal. It is obvious from the actors' discourses that the emergence of managerialism is not yet established in Portuguese higher education. This is confirmed by the absence of legislation imposing a 'market' or 'market-like' behaviour on public universities, despite the presence of an important private higher education sector and some opinions and comments propagated by the more neo-liberal press. It can thus be claimed that, if managerialism exists, it is present at a rhetorical level.

In the discourses of seven of the former ministers – the only exception being a former minister who is also a professional manager – the managerial rhetoric appears so mitigated and intertwined with other types of discourses that one feels tempted to doubt the existence of strong managerialism in the Portuguese higher education context.

What is perhaps more surprising is that among the managers/entrepreneurs only four (and this includes the former minister already mentioned) express positions that are more clearly closer to the managerial rhetoric, and even so the most radical managerialist of our interviewees makes appeals to state regulation. One has a feeling that entrepreneurs feel uncomfortable in openly criticising the university or in imposing their own values and culture on an institution, which is quite alien to most of them. The fact that the fast development of a university private sector has produced mainly low quality institutions, which survive by political lobbying and by offering courses in disciplines of low investment/low running costs, does not encourage the unfettered promotion of the market as provider of high quality higher education.

It is possible to argue that a clear presence of the managerial paradigm both in discourses and in steering and governance practices in the Portuguese context cannot be found. Only hybrid approaches in which different elements coming from diverse paradigms can be found. The model of state supervision and remote control, and even elements of state control, as regulation devices, can be found in the discourses of the interviewees, together with some market-friendly elements.

The third conclusion is that among interviewees there is an almost generalised consensus in criticising the corporative nature of the present collegial model of university governance and management. From the interviews analysed in this research project it becomes evident that the criticism assumes different meanings for different actors (managers/entrepreneurs and political decision makers). Most actors agree that universities must change their organisational structures and their governance and management processes, namely by restricting collegial decision making and by professionalising management. However, the logic of change and its extent depends on how the discourses of the actors are framed around concepts of organisation and operation of universities, some of which are more removed than others from that of managerialism as defined in this chapter.

For those actors with rhetoric closer to managerialism – whose proposals were analysed in 4.2.1 – management should be reinforced in institutional governance by means of an increased entrepreneurial character of management, by increased professionalisation of management as well as through an increased representation of external constituencies entrusted with more decision-making power.

Those actors more distant from the managerial rhetoric present a diversity of opinion, which can be systematised in the following way: reinforcement of the technical aspects of management but under the control of academics; reinforcement of the Rector's power by changing the election system to an appointment system; and increase of the external representation but under the overall control of academics.

Despite the diversity of these actors' position, it is possible to infer that what seems to emerge from their discourses are concerns that are fundamentally related to rationalisation (and efficiency) of academic activities and management and planning in what can be interpreted as a neo-Taylorist/Fordist vision of institutional organisation and operation, possibly close to the old managerial ideologies (Reed 2002), but within a logic of public service. The concentration of power in academic presidencies does not imply, from a market perspective, the convenience of having a single unified institutional voice which can be a better proclaimer of institutional competence when looking for external riches (Slaughter and Leslie 1997), or a mechanism aiming at control and homogenisation of management processes, and harmonisation of institutional postures, but implies instead the necessity of bureaucratic and political elucidation of the power mechanisms. The authority of academic presidencies needs to be assured and their legitimacy needs to be restored by increasing academic power to the disadvantage of other institutional bodies (students and non-academic staff), while simultaneously reducing the number of decision-making bodies and limiting collegial decisions to the appointment of academic presidencies (at the level of the institution and its units). In some cases it is recommended that the professionalisation of the techno structure be increased in order to reinforce the legitimacy of its decisions.

The complexity and heterogeneity of the actors' proposals in regard to the management and governance models for Portuguese higher education institutions are mainly due to the historical development of the system in the last thirty years. Portugal came out of a dictatorial regime in which higher education's political steering was very rigid and centralised. This rigidity and centralisation meant not only legal homogeneity but also a very strictly controlled decision-making process. With the 1974 revolution, institutional governance was redesigned in the opposite direction: the academic community (students and non-academic staff included) became a central source of decision making. In the following years (see Amaral et al. 2002) attempts were made to 'normalise' the functioning of the system and institutions, and in 1988 the University Autonomy Act legitimated the governance processes.

However, the centralist and democratic ingredients – now eventually merged in the discourses on governance and management – are apparently still present with their specific logics. It is our contention that the way these ingredients developed is also crucial in understanding the nuances in the interviewees' discourses and the divides between them, that is, their interpretation of this 30-year period impinges on their proposals for redesigning the governance and management of the Portuguese higher education system. Interestingly enough, even the most managerialist-driven discourses claim that the legitimacy of their proposals stands not only on the managerial narrative – which in fact is its core – but also on the specificity of the Portuguese context.

NOTES

[1] While in Continental Europe there is a general movement from state control to state supervision with increasing levels of autonomy being conferred upon universities over the last decades, in the UK the traditional high level of institutional autonomy is being corroded by government.

[2] Interviewees are identified in Table 1.

REFERENCES

Amaral, A., F. Correia, A. Magalhães, M.J. Rosa, R. Santiago and P. Teixeira. *O Ensino Superior pela Mão da Economia.* Porto: CIPES, 2002.

Amaral, A. and A. Magalhães. "On Markets, Autonomy and Regulation: The Janus-Head Revisited." *Higher Education Policy* 14.1 (2001): 7–20.

Amaral, A. and A. Magalhães. "The Emergent Role of External Stakeholders in European Higher Education Governance." In Amaral, A., G.A. Jones and B. Karseth (eds). *Governing Higher Education: National Perspectives on Institutional Governance.* Dordrecht: Kluwer Academic Publishers, 2002, 1–21.

Ball, S.J. "Big Policies/Small World: An Introduction to International Perspectives in Education Policy." *Comparative Education* 34.2 (1998): 119–130.

Bostock, W.W. "The Global Corporativisation of Universities: Causes and Consequences." Paper presented at the 15th ISSED Seminar, *Higher Education and Social Conscience,* University of Scranton, Pennsylvania, 1998.

Carneiro, R. *Portugal: os Próximos 20 Anos: Educação e Emprego em Portugal, uma Leitura da Modernização.* Lisbon: Fundação Calouste Gulbenkian, 1988.

Clarke, J. and J. Newman. "Managing to Survive: Dilemmas of Changing Organisational Forms in the Public Sector." Paper presented at the *Social Policy Association Conference,* University of Nottingham, Nottinghamshire, 1992 (unpublished).

Deem, R. "'New Managerialism' and Higher Education: The Management of Performances and Cultures in Universities in the United Kingdom." *International Studies in Sociology of Education* 8.1 (1998): 47–70.

Deem, R. "Globalisation, New Managerialism, Academic Capitalism and Entrepreneurialism in Universities: Is the Local Dimension Important?" *Comparative Education* 1 (2001): 7–20.

Edwards, J.D. "Managerial Influences in Public Administration." Department of Political Science, University of Tennessee, 2001, http://www.ute.edu/umpa/managerialism.htm.

Fitzsimons, P. "Neoliberalism and Social Capital: Reinventing Community." Paper presented at the *AEREA Conference,* New Orleans, 2000.

Goedegebuure, L., F. Kaiser, P. Maassen, V.L. Meek, F. van Vught and E. de Weert (eds). *Higher Education Policy: An International Comparative Perspective.* Oxford: Pergamon, 1993.

Goedegebuure, L. and F. van Vught (eds). *Comparative Policy Studies in Higher Education.* Enschede: CHEPS, 1994.

Maassen, P. and F. van Vught. "An Intriguing Janus-head: The Two Faces of the New Governmental Strategy for Higher Education in the Netherlands." *European Journal of Education* 23.1 (1988): 65–76.

Magalhães, A. "The Changing Relationship Between Government and Higher Education: The Portuguese Case." Paper presented at the *Alpha Bracara Conference,* Recife, 1998.

Magalhães, A. *Higher Education Dilemmas and the Quest for Identity: Politics, Knowledge and Education in an Era of Transition.* Enschede: University of Twente Press, 2001.

Meek, V.L. "On the Road to Mediocrity? Governance and Management of Australian Higher Education in the Market Place." In Amaral, A., G.A. Jones and B. Karseth (eds). *Governing Higher Education: National Perspectives on Institutional Governance.* Dordrecht: Kluwer Academic Publishers, 2002, 235–260.

Neave, G. and F. van Vught (eds). *Prometheus Bound: The Changing Relationship Between Government and Higher Education in Western Europe.* Oxford: Pergamon, 1991.

Reed, M. "New Managerialism, Professional Power and Organisational Governance in UK Universities: A Review and Assessment." In Amaral, A., G. Jones and B. Karseth (eds). *Governing Higher Education: National Perspectives on Institutional Governance.* Dordrecht: Kluwer Academic Publishers, 2002, 163–185.

Santos, B.S. *Portugal, um retrato singular.* Porto: Afrontamento, 1993.

Santos, B.S. *Pela Mão de Alice.* Porto: Afrontamento, 1994.

Scott, P. *The Meanings of Mass Higher Education.* Buckingham: SRHE and Open University Press, 1995.

Slaughter, S. and L. Leslie. *Academic Capitalism: Politics, Policies and the Entrepreneurial University.* Baltimore: John Hopkins Press, 1997.

OLIVER FULTON

MANAGERIALISM IN UK UNIVERSITIES: UNSTABLE HYBRIDITY AND THE COMPLICATIONS OF IMPLEMENTATION[1]

1. INTRODUCTION

It is common ground in this volume that 'managerialism' constitutes, not so much a single, distinctive and fundamentally technically defined approach to management, as a bundle or cluster of ideologies and practices, loosely and indeed contingently linked. This chapter aims to analyse the gradual emergence and evolution of a local embodiment of what has come to be known in the specifically British (or even English) context as 'new' managerialism in higher education. To do so, it sketches a theoretical account of 'new managerialism' (section 2); outlines a recent analysis of different facets of new managerialism/new public management and compares these with policy developments in the UK (section 3); reviews some relevant literature on the changing nature of academic work and discusses how this might affect its management (section 4); and reports some findings of a recent research project on the internal management of UK universities and its consequences for those working in them, whether as 'managers' or 'managed' (section 5).[2]

2. BACKGROUND: THEORETICAL APPROACH

Much of the theoretical background to this project was laid out in Michael Reed's paper for the first Douro Seminar (Reed 2002). In summary, the research set out to explore the extent to which narratives, forms and technologies of 'new managerialism' (Clarke and Newman 1997) had, or were perceived to have, permeated UK universities. The imposition of new managerialism has been studied in UK public services from health (Ferlie et al. 1996) to local government and schools (Exworthy and Halford 1999) but has been relatively little examined in higher education in the UK.

We defined the concept of new managerialism which informed our research in relation to three overlapping elements. First, as a generic *narrative* of strategic change which may be used "to persuade others towards certain understandings and actions" (Barry and Elmes 1997: 433) in relation to the established governance and management of universities. Second, as an emergent *organisational form* that may provide the administrative mechanisms and managerial processes through which change is to be realised. Third, as a practical *control technology* through which strategic policies and their organisational forms may be translated into practices,

A. Amaral et al. (eds.), The Higher Education Managerial Revolution?, 155–178.
© 2003 *Kluwer Academic Publishers. Printed in the Netherlands.*

techniques and devices that challenge the established systems of 'bureau-professionalism' (Clarke and Newman 1997: 68–70).

Reed's contention is that if, or when, fully implemented as "a package of cultural, organisational and managerial interventions", 'new managerialism' would constitute a distinctive,

> alternative model of governmental and institutional order for higher education within the UK to that which has existed under the traditional compromise between corporate bureaucracy and professional association from the mid-1940s onwards ... [That compromise] shaped the post-Second World War development of British higher education to the extent that it facilitated a viable trade-off between managerial control and professional autonomy, as exemplified in the organisational logic and practice of 'professional bureaucracy' (Mintzberg 1979). 'New managerialism' ... radically questions ... the terms on which that ... trade-off ... was struck, [through its] ... critique of existing ... structures' ... endemic lack of external accountability, internal managerial discipline and routine operational efficiency (Reed 2002: 165).

Potentially, he continues, new managerialism:

> entail[s] a number of interrelated changes in structural design and operating systems [which in turn enable] a more tightly integrated internal regime of managerial discipline and control: [a] radical ... depart[ure] from the untidy but stabilising compromises of bureau-professionalism (Reed 2002: 166).

However, as Ferlie et al. (1996) pointed out in relation to the National Health Service in the UK, what was at first described as 'the new public management' did not in fact arrive as a full-blown, coherent model either of ideology or of practice, and it is possible to discern within it a number of internal tensions and even contradictions (see also Meek in the introduction to this volume). Some of these tensions relate to the ambiguous relationship between discourse and ideology, on one hand, and structures, forms and practices on the other, which we took as a significant feature for investigation in our own research study; some also relate to the evident gradual evolution over time both of the ideas of new managerialism and of their implementation. Some, however, may indicate more irreconcilable difficulties.

Ferlie and his colleagues, writing in 1996, distinguished four different 'models' of new managerialism, which they placed on a rough evolutionary time-line. In the following section we describe each of these four models briefly, and discuss their relevance to the changing context of management thinking and management practice in UK higher education. However, it will be apparent that the suspicion of inconsistency relates not only to differences between the models but also to problems within them. Although each 'model' may appear to have a certain intuitive coherence, the first two, at least, are better seen as clusters of rather loosely connected ideologies and prescriptions than as a tightly knit and consistent package.

3. THE EMERGENCE OF NEW MANAGERIALISM IN UK HIGHER EDUCATION

3.1. The Efficiency Drive

3.1.1. General Description

Ferlie et al. (1996) labelled the first of their models 'the efficiency drive'. This model took as its starting point its diagnosis of the alleged problem: the internal, and to a certain extent external, inefficiency of services provided by the public sector. The public sector was described as insufficiently 'business-like', both literally in its organisational forms and metaphorically in its values and practices, as witnessed by the absence of the 'bottom line' of profit-and-loss accounting and hence of the profit motive. Obviously, therefore, the remedy must be a good dose of firm and effective management and discipline, such as could only be found in the private sector. The key themes of this model included improved financial control, a greater emphasis on value for money and the imposition of 'efficiency gains' – requiring the public service in question to 'do more with less'. In support of this there was also a drive towards improving management information with a view to 'benchmarking', performance management and more transparent target-setting and monitoring, and the extension of audit activities to cover substantive as well as financial performance. Underpinning these processes came the promotion of strengthened and more directive and hierarchical management; with the clear intention of reducing the power and range of professional self-regulation (Ferlie et al. 1996: 10–11).

3.1.2. Implementation in UK Higher Education

In the higher education context, there is no question that the drive for efficiency – doing more with less – was eagerly adopted by the British government, which presided over reductions in unit costs per student of 36 per cent in funding per student between 1989 and 1997 alone (DfES 2003: 18). As to management processes, there is a good example of the early promotion of this approach in the Jarratt Report of 1985 (see e.g. Fulton 2002: 193; Kogan and Hanney 2000: 185–187). The Jarratt Committee, although commissioned by the universities themselves (albeit under pressure from government) was chaired by a prominent industrialist (but also included "leading academics from strong universities" (Kogan and Hanney 2000: 187)). Its prescriptions laid particular emphasis on aligning university management processes with conventional approaches to management in the private sector, by improving internal management controls, strengthening line-management hierarchy and reducing academic power, which was described as 'conservative' and liable to self-interest. Some of the Jarratt proposals (e.g. the transfer of decision-making power from basic units to the central institution and the creation of budgetary 'cost centres' at the departmental level) seem to have been fairly quickly adopted or absorbed by institutions aspiring to be regarded as competently managed: indeed, Kogan and Hanney describe senior university managers as regarding much of the report as little more than 'commonsense' (2000: 187). But, not surprisingly, there was also resistance to attempts to impose directive management which excluded academic staff, with critics such as Shattock (1994) pointing out that nearly all of those universities which had experienced serious difficulties in recent years had in fact been characterised not by the traditional and so-called 'inefficient' structures of academic self-government, but by strong central management supported by lay governors. Nevertheless, there has been a persistent strain of official criticism of the alleged poor quality of university management, echoed even in the latest White Paper (DfES 2003), which again emphasises the need for improved management and leadership and greater financial efficiency (paragraphs 7.12–7.13) – despite the sector's apparent success in coping with the per-capita funding reductions referred to above. Supposedly well-informed press commentary on the White Paper has frequently reported the view of treasury ministers that many universities, not least Oxford, Cambridge and the large civic universities, are still poorly governed and managed (e.g. THES 7 March 2003: 16).

Turning to other aspects of the efficiency model, or cluster, of approaches to managerialism, external audit mechanisms grew steadily in prominence, especially in the years following the unification of the UK system in 1992. These mechanisms included, notably, the UK's national research assessment and teaching quality assessment exercises (Fulton 2002: 196–197). The former, which had begun in the mid-1980s, was designed not only for the explicit and manifest purpose of providing retrospective public accountability for general state funding for research, but also to serve other functions: notably to provide both a method of, and the legitimation for, differential prospective financial allocation to institutions and departments based on their assessed research performance. The national system of teaching quality assessment was first introduced in the years after 1992, following the merger of the former polytechnics and universities into a single university system, and it made use of (and imposed on the 'old' universities) a number of features borrowed from the quality assurance arrangements of the former polytechnic sector. It too served multiple purposes, being ostensibly designed to provide not only accountability for the use of public funds but also public information to guide prospective students. (One consequence of this multiplicity was a long-running debate over whether the assessment results should be ungraded, simply containing qualitative and descriptive information and an assurance that national standards had been attained, or should be graded to provide more information to the marketplace and hence incentives for improvement. Unlike the research assessments, teaching assessments were not (except in Scotland) directly linked to financial allocations.) A key latent function was undoubtedly to avoid the suspicion of declining quality at a time of fast-declining per-student funding – or at least to ensure that the risk was carried by institutions and not by government. I discuss some of the consequences of these audit and assessment processes for institutions' internal management in section 5 below.

In summary, one might characterise the 'efficiency drive', as applied to British universities, as reflecting an ambiguous balance, both in discourse and in practice. On the one hand we can see elements of what Reed (2002: 172) summarises as "neo-Taylorist/Fordist control systems … [which] did not threaten professional … power or autonomy in any direct way", but simply sought to deliver better use of resources for purposes which were still professionally determined. On the other hand, the increasing use of audit mechanisms, combined with constant questioning of professionals' competence and an attempted redefinition of academic and other professionals as self-interested 'producers', signalled a more interventionist and considerably less trustful approach, which was not afraid to challenge practices which had hitherto been seen as reserved for professional expertise.

This tension is best exemplified in two areas. The first of these is institutional governance, where there has been a three- or four-way contest for power between 'lay' members, institutional managers, academic staff and, perhaps, students (Fulton 2002), with academic staff gradually losing control over all but a shrinking core of academic processes. The second illustration is provided by long-running struggles for control of the criteria and procedures to be used for the national assessments of teaching and research, and indeed for membership of the assessment panels themselves. Here the battle has been more evenly balanced and, in the case of both teaching and research, academic power has regularly been reasserted to considerable effect.

3.2. Downsizing, Decentralisation and the Market

3.2.1. General Description

Ferlie and his colleagues distinguished the 'efficiency drive' from a second cluster of practices and associated ideologies which they labelled 'downsizing and decentralisation'. Some of the prescriptions of the efficiency cluster may well have represented, in the UK context, an inescapable and irreversible imperative – not least the fundamental requirement to 'do more with less' in a public sector for which the UK government was increasingly keen to shed some of its financial responsibility. But its more conventionally managerial elements were not so self-evidently desirable. As Ferlie et al. pointed out, in the business world, fashion was already swinging in the 1980s against large, vertically integrated organisations with strong hierarchical management, in favour of 'leaner' and more flexible 'post-Fordist' structures. They saw the key features of this second model, as applied to the public sector, as a reversal of conventional strong management approaches. Notably, it encompassed a shift from top-down planning to increasingly elaborate market or quasi-market mechanisms; the creation of more loosely coupled organisations, managed by contract rather than by hierarchy; and a split between a small strategic core and an operational periphery, with contracting-out of 'non-essential' functions: all leading to a process of delayering and downsizing, with flatter organisational structures characterised by new forms of coordination and management based on influence and networks rather than command and control (Ferlie et al. 1996: 12–13). Again, it is not necessarily the case that all of these elements form a coherent approach to management – here too there are elements of tension or even contradiction. But the general espousal of flatter structures and market-like resource allocation does appear to have constituted a consistent approach, at least at the discursive or ideological level, in other parts of the public sector in the UK.

3.2.2. Implementation in UK Higher Education

It can of course be argued that universities, with their commitment to networked and expertise-based collegiality, have long been prime examples of successfully flexible organisations – and that, in a peculiarly British irony, business enterprises had finally begun to learn from the strengths of traditional, loosely coupled university organisation, and to decentralise and flatten their structures, just at the moment when these strengths were under threat in universities from the imposition of traditional, and inappropriate, neo-Taylorist models of management. Whatever the prescriptions of the advocates of 'management power', it is certainly the case that in British higher education efficiency expectations have been further tightened in recent years, and that the imperatives of financial survival (and the examples of a succession of near-disasters) have led some institutions to impose much tighter central control of expenditure, and more systematic and centrally controlled management of their academic staff (hiring, promotion and even performance), than had been the custom in the past. However, if only in search of additional resources, these restrictions have been mitigated or overlaid by an increasing emphasis on market responsiveness and entrepreneurialism. We referred above to the Jarrett Committee's recommendation of devolved budgeting to departmental or faculty 'cost centres', as an example of a management practice designed to increase control and accountability, and hence to improve efficiency in the use of resources. However, devolved budgeting, which appears to have been almost universally adopted, can work in different ways (Jarzabkowski 2002), including providing powerful incentives to sub-units to act independently by diversifying their activities to increase their income, not always in the collective interests of the institution as a whole. As Meek points out (in the introduction to this volume), there is an inherent tension between the needs of effective and efficient central management on the one hand and decentralisation on the other: as I show in section 5, this tension can often be experienced within devolved budgetary units as a set of contradictory demands and constraints.

Historically, of course, British universities were well protected from the market. The planning and funding systems, which were embodied up to 1989 in very different ways in the academic 'buffer' of the University Grants Committee (Moodie 1983; Fulton 2002) and in the more short-lived and evolutionary arrangements for national-local direction of the polytechnic sector (Pratt 1997; Fulton 2002), had favoured the other two points of Clark's triangle by emphasising, respectively, academic priorities and governmental policy concerns in preference to market forces. However, the conservative administrations of the 1980s were not only attracted ideologically or intellectually by market mechanisms, but also made the practical discovery that higher education institutions could be tempted by market opportunities (and by squeezing their resources) into actions which they would certainly have resisted if directly imposed upon them. In the case of the old universities, the temptation had been the institution of so-called 'full cost' fees for overseas students; in the case of the polytechnics it was the adoption of a *de facto* price-competitive mechanism for funding new student places (Fulton 1991). New national funding methodologies which were first tried out in the years after 1989 represented a deliberate and self-conscious switch at national level to quasi-market mechanisms: the new national funding bodies were formally debarred from institutional planning.

Under these methodologies, although teaching and research funding are still handed over to universities as a single lump sum, the resource flows are earned by sub-units, to which the earnings are publicly attributed. In the case of research, funding is proportional to a disciplinary area's (normally an academic department's) grading in the national research assessment system (see above); for teaching, universities receive per-student income on the basis of their student number contracts at prices fixed by the funding agency (the Higher Education Funding Councils for England, Wales and Scotland): under-recruitment is penalised, and there is thus a direct incentive to maximise numbers up to the contract ceiling. Contracts and funding formulae specify broad disciplinary areas, but most universities allocate both contracts and funding to departmental units and therefore pass on the market pressures (both incentives and risks) to departments. In these ways, what had previously been treated as 'cost' centres have now become budget or even *de facto* profit centres.

As Reed (2002: 166) suggests, the introduction of market mechanisms has generally been seen – by policy makers and analysts alike – as the crucial 'solvent', both at the ideological level and in practice, of entrenched professional and bureaucratic rigidity. The belief is that the imperatives of institutional and personal survival in the newly competitive environment will inexorably convert academics from professionals operating in the protective 'cocoon' of the public sector, into self-monitoring and self-managing competitive agents – once the necessary techniques (financial monitoring, quality audit, performance measurement and work rationalisation) have been put in place (Reed 2002: 168). The essence of 'new managerialism', in this version, is that the key features of marketisation (including of course the substitution of private funds for state support) and external accountability have produced a series of interconnected, even if not wholly coherent, strategies and practices for restructuring the public services at large, not only from without but from within. They have led directly to work intensification and service commodification; and indirectly to a series of other internal changes, which might not be consistent across services, nor even across institutions within a given service, but which amount in effect to a form of 'control at a distance' by the state.

3.3. Other Models of 'New Public Management'

Ferlie et al. (1996) also identified two further models of 'new' public management. It cannot be said that either of these have played a prominent part in discussions of the governance and management of higher education, so far as official thinking or national debates are concerned: each of them is largely a product of prescriptive writing and debate within management theory as a whole, and they have not been widely applied to higher education. However, this would not necessarily preclude their application to higher education, either on a national scale or, more plausibly, within specific institutions, and they are therefore briefly described here.

3.4. In Search of Excellence

3.4.1. General Description

Ferlie et al. (1996: 13–14) defined a third strand in management thinking which they saw as at least potentially applicable to UK health service reforms. This was derived from 'human relations' and 'cultural' approaches to organisations within management theory, including the 'learning organisation movement' with its emphases on building strong collective cultures and values and cultural approaches to strategic change. They suggested that this might come in two forms: a 'bottom-up' and humanistic approach which emphasises teamwork and the empowerment of employees, accompanied by radical decentralisation; and a 'top-down' approach which involves an emphasis on charismatic management and leadership, corporate training and the building of corporate identities and cultures, in other words explicit attempts to engineer cultural change.

3.4.2. Implementation in UK Higher Education

No doubt government agencies and institutional leaders in higher education, as in other public services, have been conscious of this approach – or movement. There has not been any clear or explicit endorsement of it at national level as applicable, let alone desirable, in the university context: the official demands for better management, in so far as they can be decoded into specific, positive prescriptions as opposed to general-purpose negative comments on the culture and practices of academia, seem to fall much more neatly into one or other of the first two approaches, or perhaps a hybrid of the two. However, 'learning organisation', corporate transformation and cultural change approaches have featured for many years in popular books on management, and it would not be surprising to find these picked up and echoed, however diffusely, by managers at various levels within higher education. As we have seen, Reed (2002) argues that the ultimate goal of new managerialism is to engineer a profound change in the culture and values, as well as the practices, of academic staff. In so far as the 'new managers' are the front-line troops in this re-engineering process, one might well expect them to be attracted by the possibility of deliberate, top-down cultural and organisational change.

3.5. Public Service Orientation

3.5.1. General Description

The final 'model' in Ferlie et al.'s (1996: 14–15) list was, as they admitted, the 'least developed' in their typology at that time – indeed, it was derived almost entirely from the prescriptions of a small number of writers on the public sector, and specifically on services provided in the UK by local government. It consisted of an attempt to fuse the best elements of private and public sector practices and techniques, combining a strong emphasis on service quality (to be promoted using quality management techniques invented in the private sector) with a recognition of the distinctive mission of the public services. With strong resemblances to the Blair-

Giddens 'third way' ideology which was briefly popularised in the first years of the 'New Labour' government after 1997, it aimed to borrow 'best practice' techniques, regardless of their origins, so as to maximise efficiency and quality, and at the same time to reorient the public sector away from supplying 'consumers' in the market and towards responding to a wider community of 'users' as a collectivity. Users' needs were to be defined, not just through the market but by providing better accountability to communities, including through elected representative bodies at local as well as national level: in other words, by shifting direction from customer exit to user voice.

3.5.2. Implementation in UK Higher Education

It cannot however be said that there has been any strong official pressure on higher education to move in this direction. The New Labour government's 'third way' rhetoric, in so far as it has achieved any kind of operational reality, has not taken higher education as one of its major targets. The nearest approach has probably been that of the Dearing Committee which called for a 'new compact' between higher education, society and individuals, which were invited to recognise their 'interdependence' and mutual obligations: if higher education were prepared to deliver the required services, 'adaptively and proactively', society should reciprocate with recognition, respect and financial support (NCIHE 1997: 11–12). However, the Committee's recommendations on management and governance (NCIHE 1997: 228–247) are narrowly technical and can hardly be said to embody even the rather etiolated vision implied by the proposed 'compact'.

4. NEW MANAGERIALISM AND ACADEMIC WORK

Recent analytic work on the academic profession in Europe (Ender 2001; Enders and Teichler 1997) and OECD countries (Kogan, Moses and El-Khawas 1994; Altbach 1996) has focused on two central themes: the changing environment for higher education and its consequences for academic work and culture, and internal differentiation within the 'profession'. Leaving aside for the moment any question of managerialism in the strong sense, as ideology or policy, other aspects of the external environment have obvious implications for the management of higher education. The relevant issues include massification; resource constraints and the quest for efficiency; the increase in audit and assessment; technological change; and globalisation.

4.1. Massification and Other Aspects of the Environment

The consequences of massification have been widely analysed since Trow (1974) first drew systematic attention to the phenomenon. It is certainly plausible that, as Trow implies, the 'market turn', and especially the rise of consumerist expectations in students, are consequences not so much of an ideological shift, either at governmental level (see above) or in general social and economic attitudes (Reed 2002; Keat, Whiteley and Abercrombie 1994) as of the changed relationship between university teachers and students brought about by the increased scale of higher education, and the consequent shift in its central tasks from elite socialisation to professional and vocational training for a wider occupational range. By the same token, massification has also led to the recruitment of new students with much more diverse needs for learning and non-academic support. It has broken the previously unquestioned linkage between teaching and research, and diminished the status of the profession (Halsey 1992) as well as its morale (Fulton 1996; Enders 2001). Resource constraints, arguably an inevitable consequence of massification, have led to lower per-student expenditure and thus increased staff-student ratios, a relative decline in salaries, poorer working conditions and fewer tenured or indefinite appointments.

Whether or not they are attributed to a broad ideological shift, the post-1992 audit and assessment regimes are frequently described as key elements of an experienced loss of autonomy for the traditional self-regulating academic, leading to claims of de-professionalisation or 'proletarianisation' of the academic profession (Halsey 1992) and routinisation of its labour process (Winter 1995). Such experiences, it can be argued, can only be further reinforced by the increasing use of information and communications technology for teaching and learning, reducing academic staff to quasi-technicians (course material writers, learning facilitators), and by the globalisation of knowledge with further threats of commodification.

However, these trends, whether functional or ideological in origin, might well be both incomplete and contested. Reed (2002) quotes Webb (1999: 757) who predicted "the emergence of schisms within the public service class between 'old style' professionals who use the language of welfare and care and 'new style' senior managers and professionals who use the language of markets and efficiency"; and in the UK a recent case study of a 'new' university (former polytechnic) uncovered a wide variety of responses to top-down change from academic staff, ranging through resistance, distortion, compliance and enthusiasm (Trowler 1998). Others suggest that British academics are engaged in a process of 'reprofessionalisation' in which certain core and unifying values around the centrality of research and the value of teaching are being re-articulated and strengthened (Henkel 2000). In schools, Gewirtz, Ball and Bowe (1995: 96–109) have followed early work by Clarke and Newman by suggesting that senior teachers can often practise a form of 'bi-lingualism', using both of Webb's kinds of language in different contexts. One could also reasonably hypothesise that resistance may be strengthened by the market power and potential of some universities and academics. Clark (1998) describes 'entrepreneurial' universities which foster a high level of academic autonomy within a context of central 'steering'; Slaughter and Leslie (1997) have argued that university research is so central to globalising knowledge economies that the most successful research academics have become 'capitalists' whose market power challenges the capacities of their employing universities to manage them.

There is therefore a choice of competing hypotheses, and the research project to which I turn in section 5 was in part designed to test these rival interpretations as they are perceived by both managers and the staff they manage, and played out both in their practices and in new organisational forms.

4.2. Structured Differentiation

The higher education literature points to the likelihood of structured differentiation (Fulton 1998). Many commentators (notably Clark 1983, and his later amplifications; Becher and Trowler 2001, and Becher's earlier work referenced therein) have pointed to academic disciplines as a highly significant differentiating factor: not only do important aspects of working practices and cultures vary by discipline, but so too do funding regimes, costs and market position. However, the evidence from recent quantitative and qualitative data in the UK is surprisingly inconclusive, suggesting that despite these differences, other professional values, especially about the balance of teaching and research, and attitudes to and views of institutional management and governance, are remarkably constant across disciplines (Fulton 1998; Henkel 2000).

The other key component of Clark's (1983) 'master matrix' of differentiation is institutional type. In the British context there was of course a history of strong differentiation between the former university and polytechnic sectors including not only their academic mission but also governance, management and working conditions (see e.g. Fulton 2002 for governance and related issues). Although some differences in working conditions still exist between the pre- and post-1992 institutions, the unified and formally competitive national regime which was instituted in 1992 has created and reinforced strong pressures for convergence and isomorphism, while leaving a strong institutional hierarchy virtually unaffected (Fulton 1996). Thus differences in mission have persisted, chiefly supported by the differential funding and status conveyed by the research assessment system, and by the conversion of this and other status differences into market advantage in recruiting students. Indeed, the latest government White Paper (DfES 2003) has in effect acknowledged the inevitability of hierarchy, and made it plain that for the future only a minority of academic staff in leading research departments can ever expect to receive state support for their research; and it makes a series of other proposals for structured differentiation between the work of staff in institutions with different missions (e.g. through variable involvement in technology transfer and regional engagement). Finally, British higher education operates, as it has done for many years, national pay scales for academic staff, with very little latitude for systematic differentiation by academic discipline or by institution (Fulton and Holland 2001).[3] Some commentators have argued that the absence of differential pay and conditions across institutions (and disciplines) of different status and market position is both indefensible and damaging to the profession as a whole (e.g. Shattock 2001). The new White Paper apparently endorses this view by arguing for a much greater degree of market-related pay determination.

These aspects of differentiation also invite investigation through research into staff and their managers' experience. In our research project we aimed to analyse how tendencies towards new managerialism might be mediated across disciplines and between the former sectors.

4.3. Individual-level Differentiation

Finally, we were interested in new forms of differentiation at the individual level. For example, the recent White Paper (DfES 2003) argues not only for market-related salaries but for individual determination of performance-related pay. (There have been earlier attempts to introduce a performance element, and it is now common at the top of the career grade, i.e. for full professors; for other grades, however, the national scales and national union-employer agreements have kept any performance element to a minimum.) Pay aside, the separation of resource flows for teaching and research has certainly enabled, if not required, the double scrutiny of individual academics' performance in each of these two areas of activity. Financial pressures have also led to an increase in short-term hiring and thus a shift in the balance between core/permanent staff and those on the periphery. (Indeed, the increasing complexity of work in the contexts of mass higher education has changed the nature of core and periphery in other ways, by rendering simple distinctions between 'academic', 'administrative' and 'support' staff increasingly untenable (Cuthbert 1996).) All of these trends create issues for managers of individual work allocation, closer monitoring and performance management, including more sharply differentiated reward structures (Fulton and Holland 2001). Moreover, academic careers take longer to establish and more preparation is being required for teaching as well as for research. This too suggests that manager-academics are liable to be drawn much further into active performance management of academic staff (Fulton and Holland 2001; Enders 2001). A further complication is the increasing awareness of issues of equity. Social origin and prior educational experience have always been significant determinants of academic careers (Halsey 1992), even if this has not always been seen as problematic; but inequalities of gender and ethnicity have now become highly visible, culminating in public recognition of the issue in salary terms (Bett Report 1999) as well as in relation to management (Deem 1998; Deem 1999), and demands for determined action to eliminate unfair practices.

Thus from a functional, technocratic point of view alone, there must be plenty of new work for managers to do. Our project was designed to explore the extent to which managers did indeed find themselves drawn into the direct and differential 'line' management of individuals, in contrast to the assumptions of traditional values and practices which privilege individual autonomy and the right and obligation of all staff to engage in both teaching and research – and the assumption that any differentiation should be democratically arrived at rather than imposed from above.

5. THE 'NEW MANAGERIALISM' RESEARCH PROJECT

5.1. Methods

Details of the project's research design are given in the appendix. In outline, the project was organised in three phases. Phase 1 involved 12 focus group discussions with academics, manager-academics and administrators from different UK-wide learned societies and representative bodies, and was designed to gather views and perceptions not only of managerialism and management but also of changes to the context of UK higher education. The second phase consisted of semi-structured interviews with a range of manager-academics from heads of department or school, through deans up to pro vice-chancellors and vice-chancellors, at each of 12 UK universities. These covered academic and management careers (including selection for their current post), training and support for management, management practices and routines, views about change, work anxieties and pleasures, views about the institution and about recent developments in the external context of UK higher education, work life and home life, and issues related to management and gender processes. Phase 3 focused on a further four institutions for more detailed study, and included interviews with manager-academics as in phase 2, interviews and focus groups with a broad range of university staff, analysis of documentation and observation. In total we carried out 135 usable interviews with manager-academics across our 16 sample universities.

5.2. Results

5.2.1. Environmental Change and Managerial Narrative
The first stage of our research, which relied on focus groups with manager-academics, other academics and administrators, suggested that respondents did indeed feel strongly that the UK higher education system was not only much more managed but also more bureaucratic than previously. New modes of management were seen as consistent with ideas about efficiency, performance monitoring, target setting, private sector models of running organisations and a decline in trust and discretion. In respondents' views, these developments were closely, and most of them functionally, related to significant changes to the environment of higher education, notably the massification of student intake, the very sharp decline in the unit of resource for teaching, and the national schemes of assessment of teaching and research quality. People talked of higher workloads and long hours; of finance driving almost all decisions; of greater pressure for internal and external accountability; but also of senior management teams (generally at a higher level than their own) which were remote from other staff and students. There were widely held perceptions that collegiality as previously understood was being replaced by more overt line management, although some respondents, particularly in those disciplines where the 'lone scholar' approach was still dominant, also felt that teaching and research quality reviews had brought about more teamwork, albeit in response to threat.

The focus groups thus provided evidence of perceived changes in all three aspects of theoretical interest. There were references to strategic and cultural change; descriptions of the organisational forms which supported this, notably the widespread use of devolved financial responsibility through faculty or departmental cost centres; and some illustrations of control technologies. The latter included reference to both informal and formal performance review through target-setting, performance appraisal and the use of external monitoring mechanisms, notably the national research assessment exercise, for internal management purposes. Broadly speaking, however, the general impression was that conventional, strong-management and efficiency approaches predominated, as opposed to devolved or self-management approaches in a genuinely marketised environment. One further outcome of the focus groups was some evidence of 'bilingualism'. In the course of these sometimes lengthy conversations, members of these groups not only displayed a collective ambivalence about the desirability of the changes which they perceived but even, in some cases, an ability to switch between a broadly favourable identification with managerial imperatives and identities and a more sceptical posture identified with traditional academic values.

The interviews were designed to explore both the larger themes which were touched on in the focus groups and also experiences, practices and perceptions at a more personalised level. The great majority of interviewees gave accounts of the external changes to the environment of higher education which were similar to those noted in the focus groups (notably funding, massification, research assessment and teaching quality review), and then described the effects of these factors on their institutions and their own posts, their daily practices and routines, anxieties and pleasures – including how their work impacted upon their home life – and their vision for the future. Respondents were also asked about their own career trajectories, their routes into management roles, how they had learned to be managers, what support they received for their management roles; and what kinds of management approaches are effective with academics.

5.3. The Manager-Academic Identity and Career

In their self-descriptions of their present identity, we were struck by the way in which our respondents described their personal biographies in terms which are common to academics of all kinds: many of the elements which Henkel (2000), Altbach (1996) and others note about academic identities (especially the continued commitment to both teaching and research, and the identification with disciplines) were strongly evident. Nor, generally, did these identities disappear once an interviewee had embarked on major management roles: almost all our respondents, whether they had experienced a distinguished research career or were still in the apprenticeship stages of research, held on to their research as generally a central, and always at least a parallel, strand of their academic identity.

We noted three typical routes into management. The first was the career track route, where a young lecturer decides early on in their career that they want to pursue a management role (a minority of our respondents and typically found in the post-1992 institutions. This group was the most likely to identify themselves unambiguously as managers, whereas others generally defined themselves as managers but academic 'leaders' too). Their motivations for becoming a career-track manager included an enjoyment of management tasks, liking power, thriving on institutional politics, becoming bored with teaching and sometimes also with research, and seeing management as a way to achieve a higher salary than as an academic.

The second route was the 'reluctant manager' route, especially typical of heads of department in the pre-1992 institutions, where such roles are usually temporary and rotate around senior staff in departments, some of whom may 'give in' largely because (they say) they fear that someone else may make a worse head of department than themselves. Finally there is what we termed the 'good citizen' route, where an individual chooses to take on a more senior management role (e.g. at pro vice-chancellor level) often quite late in their careers, in order, so they say, to give something back to their institutions and because they see themselves as having an obligation to do so. This last route, however, may be in decline, as people begin to reach manager-academic roles earlier in their careers and as more emphasis is placed, at least in some institutions, on the importance of selecting people with clearly identified skills for management posts.

Gender processes, however, were also important in shaping careers, with nearly two-thirds of respondents believing that gender had affected their own careers – and also that gender was relevant to the management approaches adopted by women and men.

5.4. Management Practices and Mechanisms

Manager-academics' lives were described to us as packed with meetings – from large formal committees to one-to-one encounters, mountains of paperwork and email, the constant hunt for new resources (some pro vice-chancellors e.g. did nothing else but bid for money, often relatively small amounts) and, most importantly, motivating and persuading colleagues. Few reported sufficient time to think, reflect or plan. It was noticeable that many reported extremely long hours of work (over 65 hours a week was common) and that whilst academics have always worked long hours on their own research, much of the time was allegedly being spent on management and not on research or teaching preparation.

The long hours seem directly attributable to several factors. The first is, ironically, the extent to which academic autonomy remains in place despite apparent changes to the working conditions of academics. Hence manager-academics have to spend long hours persuading academics to do things they may not want to do; even though external forms of assessment have provided more leverage for this task, it remains hard – presumably unlike most other occupations except perhaps for a small range of creative knowledge workers. The techniques used at the individual level range from formal appraisal processes, through one-to-one meetings with staff, the deliberate use of manager-academics as role models for other staff, to staff meetings in which those failing to achieve the required standards in teaching and research are exposed to peer scrutiny. They also include the setting of income and other targets (notably the achievement of particular scores in research assessments) and the measurement of departmental units or even individuals against these: senior manager-academics in a minority of institutions described using performance measurement techniques for research activity which forced those older staff less successful in research to 'choose' between early retirement and teaching-only contracts.

However, such techniques did not work so well for teaching and indeed were much less used. After all, it is one thing to get an academic to do more teaching and another to get them to do it well. In any event, heads of department in particular described serious tensions between what academics needed to do to retain and develop good teaching and student contact, and the increasing requirement for all academics to do well in research: it was the managers who had to sort out the day-to-day implications of these tensions and of the competition for people's energy and time.

Thus negotiation, persuasion and motivation still played a central role in manager-academics' daily lives, not least because there are very few dependable rewards for good work at their disposal. Even though almost all respondents declared that carrots work better than sticks in motivating academics, there are very few carrots available. Where there are rewards, as some interviewees noted, these are more likely to be for research than for teaching or administration, even in those institutions less oriented to overall achievement in research.

It should be added that an additional factor leading to long hours of work seems to be an embedded cultural emphasis on the long working day and week, although traditionally in higher education the hours have been spent on research, not management. Some respondents, particularly in more senior posts, believed strongly that the job cannot be done without long hours, even while acknowledging the damage to home and family life and even health that this can cause; this view may well impact not only on the effectiveness of those who become manager-academics but also on who is attracted to the role.

5.5. Organisational Forms

We collected little data to suggest that there are particular ways of organising academic activity in universities that are thought more effective, or more attuned to current expectations, than others, though amongst our respondents there were clearly some approaches (e.g. merging smaller departments into schools) which were gaining in popularity. Incoming vice-chancellors, it appears, often undertake organisational restructuring (delayering was indeed a favourite phrase in some interviews) but often it was perceived by others that the layers or previous structures crept back in again. All sixteen institutions studied used some version of department and/or school organisation and the majority retained faculties also. All had some form of devolved resource model, with departments and sometimes even individual programmes and research groups being treated as cost centres. There was a widespread perception, however, that institutions which purported to use devolved models claimed, when it suited them, that cost centres made their own decisions but, in other circumstances, insisted that they did not have the power to do so. Thus, for example, it was common for devolved budget mechanisms to exclude any right to hire new staff without central permission, a point which some manager-academics made to us with evident resentment. This is a clear example of the tension which we identified earlier between decentralisation and control from the top: sub-units are expected to earn resources for themselves and are held responsible for any shortfall, but they are not often fully trusted or empowered to invest any 'surplus' they may create.

Perhaps unexpectedly, if structural differences were hard to detect, cultural variations between institutions were felt to be stronger than we had expected. Institutional history, perceived niche and mission, absolute size and the existence of multi-sites were key factors. In fact we saw no indications of the cultural isomorphism in universities which some new managerialism theorists see as being imposed on public service organisations by explicit policies, funding mechanisms, the use of a small pool of consultants and the selection or socialisation of new recruits to the profession (Powell and DiMaggio 1991; Clarke and Newman 1997).

5.6. Selection and Training of Manager-Academics

Two factors which emerged as of considerable significance in our study were variations in the selection processes used to place academics in management roles and the support for their learning and development once in the post.

The selection of manager-academics varied considerably as between pre- and post-1992 institutions. In the latter, a formal appointment process (often following external advertisement) was common practice for all levels of management post, while in the pre-1992 universities a mix of colleague consultation (usually followed by confirmation at senior level), and simply picking individuals believed to have the relevant skills, was more common (we found almost no examples of genuine colleague-constituency-based elections to posts). These patterns are not unrelated to tenure of office, since in the post-1992 sector most management roles were permanent, whereas temporary and rotating posts were more usual in the pre-1992 sector (although fixed-term posts were found at pro vice-chancellor level in both pre- and post-1992 institutions). We suspect that the more informal selection mechanisms may, even if not intentionally, exclude some of those who would bring considerable talent and skill to management posts, and perhaps particularly women. It was notable that the small number of women in appointed posts above head of department level had only reached those posts very late in their careers, and thus were not always in a position to proceed further (for example to vice-chancellor posts). The issue of temporary and permanent management positions is also important, though the implications of each are quite complex. Permanent posts have the apparent advantage of recruiting willing applicants, properly remunerated for their work, who can build on their acquisition of skills and knowledge and need not be distracted by pursuing a parallel career in research (although almost all of them still tried to do so). However, permanent incumbents are not always perceived by other staff as providing a good basis for accountability; and permanent managers who do not move on to higher posts may suffer burn-out, stop innovating and come to be a liability. Temporary posts allow academics to try out management – we found that some initially reluctant recruits became enthusiastic later – and to return to their purely academic duties if they wish. They are more likely to be perceived by colleagues as remaining accountable to peers and students.

What both categories of manager-academics appear to lack is support for and recognition of the realities of their own learning. It is often argued by both UK politicians and funding bodies that manager-academics are poorly prepared and trained for their roles (and this was a view shared by some managed staff). It was indeed the case that only about a third of our sample had received any significant formal training for their role (and many of them were at best ambivalent about the benefits of this kind of training) – and even fewer felt they had received adequate feedback on their own performance. However, this does not mean that manager-academics had not engaged in significant informal learning, along the lines of the processes described by Lave and Wenger (1991) in their study of how professional and occupational skills are passed on in communities of practice. Respondents explained how early experiences of running courses or research groups, or having some other administrative roles, had helped them prepare for more onerous posts later; and individuals also drew on the particular strengths, skills and knowledge involved in their own disciplines as support for management roles. Some also pointed out that even if being an academic expert in a narrow field, or being a superb teacher of undergraduate students, are not in themselves obvious experiences which prepare for management, manager-academics have to manage people who do these things, and can benefit from inside knowledge as well as credibility. It was also noticeable that, where their institution did not provide such opportunities, many of our sample consciously sought out informal occasions and encounters where they could meet and exchange experiences with others in management roles.

Finally, in the detailed case studies we noted that there were some sharp contrasts between the often quite optimistic and positive stories of achievement and change told by manager-academics, especially at senior levels, and the accounts given by ordinary academics, support staff and student union officers. Although both sides recounted high workloads and increasing emphasis on individual responsibility, managed staff and students talked of poor communication, failure of senior management to listen, slow decision making, absence of clear policies and growing gaps between senior management teams and the rest of the institution. Furthermore new technologies were seen as exacerbating such gaps. What managed staff appeared to want was not mechanistic but cultural change.

6. CONCLUSION: A NEW MANAGERIALISM?

If we return now to the four models used by Ferlie et al. (1996), there is no question that the first of these – 'the efficiency drive' – was perceived by almost all our respondents as having permeated higher education very significantly. Financial considerations, and doing more with less, were, if not a constant preoccupation, the backdrop and rationale for much of daily practice. Manager-academics at the departmental level may not themselves have relied on management information for decision making, but they saw themselves as working in institutions where demands for information were unrelenting, and the use of target setting and monitoring from above were steadily increasing. And the consequences of assessment systems for research and teaching were everywhere. What was missing, however, for nearly all of them, was a clear identification for themselves with strong and directive top-down management, partly for lack of adequate levers but also because of their continued espousal of an academic identity.

The second model was concerned with 'downsizing and decentralisation'. There was no evidence of downsizing in absolute terms at the time of our fieldwork, although the higher education sector in the UK may now be beginning to see this, as undergraduate places remain unfilled and the government's ambitious expansion targets prove hard to achieve. Nor was there evidence of down-sizing through contracting-out, unless one includes in this the increasing use of short-term and part-time contracts for academic staff (which undoubtedly increases some management burdens even if it eases financial difficulties). We certainly found evidence of decentralisation – devolved budgets, internal markets for space and various services – but these were often only partially realised, especially since central managers generally retained veto power on major spending decisions such as the appointment of new staff. The national policy environment – notably, the process of national assessment of both research and teaching quality at departmental/disciplinary unit level – has probably been much more powerful in enhancing the roles and responsibilities of unit-level managers than any consciously managerialist decision at the institutional level.

Where the model fits most clearly, however, is firstly in the persistence (rather than the new espousal) of loosely coupled forms of control, and secondly and particularly in the increasing importance of market mechanisms: the markets for students, for research and for service income have grown steadily in importance, and in a steadily tightening resource environment, failure in the market place has consequences from which not even high quality public assessments can protect an institution or its departments. Most of the managers we interviewed were acutely conscious of these pressures.

The third model 'in search of excellence' is essentially that of the learning organisation. Respondents in all three phases reported perceived or actual attempts at top-down cultural change, including themselves among its intended recipients. Some people in senior posts also claimed to be engaged themselves in strategic activity designed to bring about cultural change, though some recent research which compared the proclaimed priorities of vice-chancellors in interviews with work-shadowing of their actual practices suggests that these claims could well be overstated (Bargh et al. 2000). Teamwork was mentioned a good deal in the focus groups but somewhat less in individual interviews; and empowerment was scarcely mentioned by any respondent, although some 'managed' staff told us that they felt they had become 'responsibilised' without the power or back-up to go with it.

The final model, which could be described as an endeavour to provide a new value base for public services and greater involvement of service users in deciding what should be provided, was not mentioned by any respondent and we found no other evidence of its existence.

To summarise these outcomes, we would place particular emphasis on the apparent emergence of a specifically hybridised form of new managerialism (see also Reed 2002). Unlike the British National Health Service, where early reforms introduced massive organisational changes, in universities new managerialism has developed within existing organisational forms. Furthermore, unlike those public services where new managerialism has grown out of the introduction of general managers without experience of the particular service, this has not happened in universities. In addition, there has been no very overt introduction of new managerialist practices from outside (e.g. we found very few manager-academics or administrators with significant experience of industry). Rather, the mechanisms used to get academics and support staff to perform at the required level have been quite subtle (the encouragement of what is still largely self-regulation of research and teaching performance) or appear coincidental (e.g. higher workloads).

Nor have academics and manager-academics easily absorbed new managerialism – for each one who had, we found three who felt uncomfortable. At least within the confines of a single interview, there was little evidence of the strong bilingualism found amongst head teachers after school reform – where a new language of targets, customers and quasi-markets was used in some contexts and the old one of teaching, learning, pupils and social justice retained elsewhere (Gewirtz, Ball and Bowe 1995). So far as we could tell, manager-academics either (though unusually) fully embraced the language of business or did not do so at all. When they did speak approvingly of new management practices, they generally referred to the practical and in their view functional necessities of adaptation to a more challenging environment, rather than to wholesale change.

Table 1. Homo Academicus and institutional management

Homo Academicus	Institutional Manager
Deeply socialised professionals	Symbolic representative
Lazy professors	Powerful controller
Homo Economicus	Cost-centre manager
Differentiated academic staff	Soft supervisor

Source: Adapted from Enders 2001: 6, Fig. 1.2

In conclusion, we return to two fundamental issues. The first of these concerns ideology. In a recent chapter entitled 'Between State Control and Academic Capitalism', Jürgen Enders (2001) suggested that, comparing countries and over time, one can detect four different concepts of 'homo academicus' and of the corresponding form of institutional management [though Enders refers to 'leadership'] which each concept evokes (Table 1). The analysis of public policy and managers' narratives within this chapter suggests that the UK offers a powerful example, within a single country, of how each of these potentially competing discourses still has resonance, both at the level of official policy discourse and in the narratives of manager-academics themselves. It seems clear that this indicates, not a successful hybridisation, but a contested and still unpredictable discursive struggle between competing views of university-based knowledge workers.

The second issue is severely practical. Our study of those who currently occupy management positions in British universities has revealed a whole set of organisational tensions and dilemmas, ranging from the functional (How might future managers be selected and trained?) to the personal (How could their jobs be made less difficult? How might they be helped to survive?). Their present working and living conditions confirm yet again that policy makers – and ideologues – ignore the unforeseen and unintended consequences of policy change at their peril.

NOTES

[1]   Part of this chapter is adapted from the End of Award report of a (UK) Economic and Social Research Council project: ROO237661, 'New Managerialism and the Management of UK Universities' (Deem et al. 2001). I acknowledge the contributions both of these colleagues and of Rachel Johnson and Sam Hillyard: all errors and omissions in this paper are my own responsibility.

[2]   The chapter reports some outcomes of a substantial research project based at Lancaster University and conducted in UK universities between 1998–2000. The research aimed to explore the extent to which recent theories about 'new managerialism' in public sector organisations matched the situation found in UK higher education institutions. The research involved talking to 'manager-academics', professional administrator-managers and academic and non-academic staff, in sixteen UK universities and in a number of learned societies, about their views, perceptions and practices with regard to the running of higher education institutions. The project had four primary research objectives:

- to acquire knowledge about how university academic managers perceive, and tell narratives about, current and recent university management;
- to illustrate the range of management practices and mechanisms currently found in different UK higher education institutions;
- to describe and explain the current organisational forms in a number of case study institutions; and
- to develop theory about 'new managerialism' consistent with the empirical results.

[3]   The two former sectors (pre-1992 universities and former polytechnics/colleges) have different grade and salary structures, but since 1992 there have been considerable pressures for harmonisation.

REFERENCES

Altbach, P. (ed.). *The International Academic Profession: Portraits of Fourteen Countries*. Princeton: Carnegie Foundation for the Advancement of Teaching, 1996.

Amaral, A., G. Jones and B. Karseth (eds). *Governing Higher Education: National Perspectives on Institutional Governance*. Dordrecht: Kluwer Academic Publishers, 2002.

Bargh, C., J. Bocock, P. Scott and D. Smith. *University Leadership: The Role of the Chief Executive*. Buckingham: Open University Press, 2000.

Barry, D. and M. Elmes. "Strategy Retold: A Narrative View of Strategic Discourse." *Academy of Management Review* 22.2 (1997): 429–452.

Becher, T. and P. Trowler. *Academic Tribes and Territories*. 2nd edn. Buckingham: Open University Press, 2001.

Bett Report. *Independent Review of Higher Education Pay and Conditions: Report of a Committee Chaired by Sir Michael Bett*. London: The Stationery Office, 1999.

Clark, B.R. *The Higher Education System: Academic Organization in Cross-National Perspective*. Berkeley: University of California Press, 1983.

Clark, B.R. *Creating Entrepreneurial Universities: Organisational Pathways of Transformation*. Oxford: IAU/Pergamon, 1998.

Clarke, J. and J. Newman. *The Managerial State: Power, Politics and Ideology in the Remaking of Social Welfare*. London: Sage, 1997.

Cuthbert, R. (ed.). *Working in Higher Education*. Buckingham: Open University Press, 1996.

Deem, R. "New Managerialism in Higher Education: The Management of Performances and Cultures in Universities." *International Studies in the Sociology of Education* 8.1 (1998): 47–70.

Deem, R. "Power and Resistance in the Academy – The Case of Women Academic Managers." In Whitehead, S. and R. Moodley (eds). *Transforming Managers: Engendering Change in the Public Sector.* London: Falmer Press, 1999, 66–83.

Deem, R., O. Fulton, M. Reed and S. Watson. "New Managerialism and the Management of UK Universities." End of Award Report to ESRC on Award R000237661, 2001.

(DfES) Department for Education and Skills. *The Future of Higher Education* (White Paper). London: Her Majesty's Stationery Office (HMSO), Cm 5735, 2003.

Enders, J. "Between State Control and Academic Capitalism: A Comparative Perspective on Academic Staff in Europe." In Enders, J. (ed.). *Academic Staff in Europe: Changing Contexts and Conditions.* Westport: Greenwood Press, 2001, 1–23.

Enders, J. and U. Teichler. "A Victim of Their Own Success? Employment and Working Conditions of Academic Staff in Comparative Perspective." *Higher Education* (Special Issue on the Academic Profession, A. Welch (ed.)) 34.3 (1997): 347–372.

Exworthy, M. and S. Halford (eds). *Professionals and the New Managerialism in the Public Sector.* Buckingham: Open University Press, 1999.

Ferlie, E., L. Ashburner, L. Fitzgerald and A. Pettigrew. *The New Public Management in Action.* London: Sage, 1996.

Fulton, O. "Slouching Towards a Mass System: Society, Government and Institutions in the United Kingdom." *Higher Education* 21.4 (1991): 589–605.

Fulton, O. "Mass Access and the End of Diversity? The Academic Profession in England on the Eve of Structural Reform." In Altbach, P. (ed.). *The International Academic Profession: Portraits of Fourteen Countries.* Princeton: Carnegie Foundation for the Advancement of Teaching, 1996, 391–437.

Fulton, O. "Unity or Fragmentation, Convergence or Diversity? The Academic Profession in Comparative Perspective in the Era of Mass Higher Education." In Bowen, W. and H. Shapiro (eds). *Universities and their Leadership.* Princeton: Princeton University Press, 1998, 173–198.

Fulton, O. "Higher Education Governance in the UK: Change and Continuity." In Amaral, A., G. Jones and B. Karseth (eds). *Governing Higher Education: National Perspectives on Institutional Governance.* Dordrecht: Kluwer Academic Publishers, 2002, 187–211.

Fulton, O. and C. Holland. "Profession or Proletariat: Academic Staff in the United Kingdom after Two Decades of Change." In Enders, J. (ed.). *Academic Staff in Europe: Changing Contexts and Conditions.* Westport: Greenwood Press, 2001, 301–322.

Gewirtz, S., S. Ball and R. Bowe. *Markets, Choice and Equity in Education.* Buckingham: Open University Press, 1995.

Halsey, A.H. *Decline of Donnish Dominion: The British Academic Professions in the Twentieth Century.* Oxford: Clarendon Press, 1992.

Henkel, M. *Academic Identities and Policy Change in Higher Education.* London: Jessica Kingsley, 2000.

Jarzabkowski, P. "Centralised or Decentralised? Strategic Implications of Resource Allocation Models." *Higher Education Quarterly* 56.1 (2002): 5–32.

Keat, R., N. Whiteley and N. Abercrombie (eds). *The Authority of the Consumer.* London: Routledge, 1994.

Kogan, M. and S. Hanney. *Reforming Higher Education.* London: Jessica Kingsley, 2000.

Kogan, M., I. Moses and E. El-Khawas. *Staffing Higher Education: Meeting New Challenges.* London: Jessica Kingsley, 1994.

Lave, J. and E. Wenger. *Situated Learning: Legitimate Peripheral Participation.* Cambridge: Cambridge University Press, 1991.

Mintzberg, H. *The Structuring of Organisations.* Englewood Cliffs: Prentice Hall, 1979.

Moodie, G. "Buffer, Coupling and Broker: Reflections on 60 years of the UGC." *Higher Education* 12.3 (1983): 331–347.

NCIHE (National Committee of Enquiry into Higher Education). *Main Report.* London: The Stationery Office, 1997.

Powell, W. and P. DiMaggio (eds). *The New Institutionalism in Organisational Analysis.* Chicago: University of Chicago Press, 1991.

Pratt, J. *The Polytechnic Experiment, 1965–1992.* Buckingham: Open University Press, 1997.

Reed, M. "New Managerialism, Professional Power and Organisational Governance in UK Universities: A Review and Assessment." In Amaral, A., G. Jones and B. Karseth (eds). *Governing Higher Education: National Perspectives on Institutional Governance.* Dordrecht: Kluwer Academic Publishers, 2002, 163–185.

Shattock, M. *The UGC and the Management of British Universities.* Buckingham: Open University Press, 1994.

Shattock, M. "The Academic Profession in Britain: A Study in the Failure to Adapt to Change." *Higher Education* 41.1–2 (2001): 27–47.

Slaughter, S. and L. Leslie. *Academic Capitalism: Politics, Policies and the Entrepreneurial University.* Baltimore: Johns Hopkins Press, 1997.

THES (Times Higher Education Supplement). "Resisting Reforms is a High-risk Strategy" (leading article). 7 March 2003, 16.

Trow, M. *Problems in the Transition from Elite to Mass Higher Education. Policies for Higher Education.* General Report to the Conference on the Future Structure of Post-secondary Education. Paris: OECD, 1974.

Trowler, P. *Academics Responding to Change: New Higher Education Frameworks and Academic Cultures.* Buckingham: Open University Press, 1998.

Webb, J. "Work and the New Public Service Class?" *Sociology* 33.4 (1999): 747–766.

Winter, R. "The University of Life plc: the 'Industrialisation' of Higher Education." In Smyth, J. (ed.). *Academic Work: The Changing Labour Process in Higher Education.* Buckingham: Open University Press, 1995, 129–143.

METHODOLOGICAL APPENDIX: RESEARCH DESIGN

The project was organised in three phases.

In Phase 1 we conducted 12 focus group discussions with academics, manager-academics and administrators from different UK-wide learned societies and representative bodies, including three generic organisations and learned societies from natural science, applied science/technology, management, social science and arts/humanities. The intention of this phase was to gather the views and perceptions of people from different universities about what they thought was happening to the management and running of UK universities. During the focus groups we explored views not only on managerialism and management but also changes to the context of UK higher education, notions of collegiality and accountability, and whether there was a 'glass ceiling' in the senior ranks of manager-academics.

In the second phase we carried out semi-structured interviews with a range of manager-academics from heads of department or school, through deans up to pro vice-chancellors and vice-chancellors, at each of 12 UK universities. Together with phase 3 interviews of a similar range of people, we finished with 135 usable interviews with manager-academics. (We also interviewed a much smaller number of senior professional administrators (normally two from each institution), resulting in 29 administrator interviews across phases 2 and 3. The intention of these interviews was to examine, albeit briefly, the ways in which administrators and manager-academics saw themselves working for common aims, and also to explore whether administrators were one source of private sector influences on higher education.) The manager-academic interviews covered academic and management careers (including selection mechanisms for the post currently held), training and support for management, work life and home life, management practices and routines, views about change, work anxieties and pleasures, views about the institution and about recent developments in the external context of UK higher education, and issues related to management and gender processes. In choosing universities, we paid attention to achieving a cross section of pre- and post-1992 universities, a range of locations across the UK, different academic emphases and different sizes of university.

In phase 3 we made use of our phase 2 data to decide on a small number of institutions for more detailed study. We rejected the possibility of deciding our choice on the basis of purely organisational factors (such as presence or absence of faculties, schools and departments) since it was already apparent that this made little difference to the interview responses. Instead, we made our choice of four universities based on size, type (pre- or post-92 institution), location and kind of site(s), mission and academic emphasis. We first conducted a similar range of interviews with manager-academics and senior administrators as in phase 2. We also collected and analysed documentation (e.g. missions and strategic plans, published teaching reviews, annual reports), attended some key meetings, conducted some general observation on site and carried out interviews and focus groups with a broad range of university staff, including support staff, ordinary academics and representatives of student unions. In this way we were able to collect contrasting views of the institutions and their management/organisation from those who were not in management positions.

V. LYNN MEEK

GOVERNANCE AND MANAGEMENT OF AUSTRALIAN HIGHER EDUCATION: ENEMIES WITHIN AND WITHOUT

1. INTRODUCTION

The question of how best to optimise the performance of the higher education sector continues to generate much debate both at the level of government and that of the individual institution. In part, the debate has been fuelled by the steep growth in higher education participation rates and the pressures on higher education institutions to find increasing proportions of their operating grants from sources other than the public purse. Concerns regarding the relevance of higher education to the labour market and to economic growth and prosperity have also put pressure on the sector. A common theme in the performance debate has been the adequacy of existing institutional governance and management structures and processes to meet stakeholder expectations (Meek and Wood 1997).

Nearly everywhere, higher education is being asked to be more accountable and responsive, efficient and effective and, at the same time, more entrepreneurial and self-managing. In this respect, Australia is an acknowledged leader in the reform of public sector management generally and that of higher education specifically (Harman 2003). At the sector level, the introduction of market mechanisms for the steering of higher education, on the one hand, and various accountability measures, on the other, have been largely successful. The Commonwealth government has been just as intent upon encouraging micro-reforms of governance and management at the level of individual institutions. However, government perceives that it has not been so successful in bringing about changes to university management practices, particularly with respect to productivity gains. Evidence of this is reflected in the fact that the reform of institutional governance and management has been prominent on the government's agenda for nearly two decades.

In Australia, as elsewhere, powerful groups both within and without the academy have come to view management as something too important to be left to academics. This is clearly the view of government. But the Australian Association for Tertiary Education Management (the main professional association for university administrators) also recently claimed that "the academic role has changed to such an extent where they cannot manage universities any more, but they do not yet trust administrators to carry out the task on their behalf" (2002: 3). The governance and management of Australian higher education have increasingly been characterised by

A. Amaral et al. (eds.), The Higher Education Managerial Revolution?, 179–201.
© 2003 Kluwer Academic Publishers. Printed in the Netherlands.

deepening conflict and bitterness between the managers and the managed. The way in which institutions have responded to this tension is the subject of this chapter.

The discussion starts with an outline of the history of the management reform push in Australian higher education. The next section examines the link between 'new managerialism' in higher education and public sector reform more generally. This is followed by a discussion of government attempts to reform institutional governance, which leads into an analysis of workplace reform and industrial relations in higher education.

One of the central arguments of the chapter is that concerns about university management are directly related to the centrality of higher education in the emerging knowledge-based, post-industrial economy – a centrality that Daniel Bell identified nearly four decades ago when he coined the phrase post-industrial society. Politicians, government bureaucrats and institutional leaders alike are attempting to realign management practices to ensure that universities optimise the commercialisation of their intellectual products. Nearly every Australian university has a Deputy/Pro Vice-Chancellor Research and a large research management office, often presided over by a professional administrator in the area of research management. The Deputy/Pro Vice-Chancellors Research, as a class of institutional managers, have progressively gained power and influence over the past decade. The penultimate section of the chapter examines how the commodification of knowledge generally and the recent introduction of a prioritised and finely targeted research funding regime more specifically are reshaping research management and internal relations in Australian higher education. The concluding section questions whether the threat of the new managerialism in Australian higher education to 'traditional' academic norms and values may in the long term actually weaken the contribution of academe to a knowledge-based economy and society.

2. HISTORY OF THE AUSTRALIAN MANAGEMENT REFORM PUSH

Throughout the 1970s and into the 1980s, Australian higher education policy makers and institutional leaders alike became increasingly concerned about effective and efficient management practices, culminating in the Commonwealth Tertiary Education Commission's (CTEC) 1986 *Review of Efficiency and Effectiveness in Higher Education*. Questions of efficiency and effectiveness have remained on the higher education reform agenda, but with the publication of the 1987 Green Paper (*Higher Education: A Policy Discussion Paper*) and the 1988 White Paper (*Higher Education: A Policy Statement*) they became subsumed in a broader push to make higher education more relevant to national economic needs and priorities. The White Paper initiated a dramatic transformation of Australian higher education which, amongst other things, led to the abolition of the 'binary' distinction between universities and colleges of advanced education (CAEs) and the creation of the Unified National System (UNS) in which there is now a much smaller number of significantly larger institutions, all called universities.

The White Paper made specific reference to the need to strengthen management practices at the institutional level and proposed a reduction in the size of institutional governing bodies (councils or senates). Some states took up the recommendation concerning the size of governing bodies while others did not. Nonetheless, government reforms have had a direct and powerful impact on institutional management, as was intended. The White Paper stated, for example, that "effective management at the institutional level will be the key to achieving many of the Government's objectives for the unified national system: growth in areas of national need; an effective partnership with other parties to the education and training process, including employers; improvements to equity and access to higher education; and efficiency of operation" (1988: 101). According to a report of the then Department of Employment, Education and Training (DEET 1993: 127–128), government should assist institutions to achieve:

- strong managerial modes of operation, removing barriers to delegation of policy implementation while maintaining a variety of inputs to policy determination;
- adequate levels of consultation with and accountability to government, employers, employees, students and the community;
- streamlined decision-making processes; and
- maximum flexibility in institutional capacity to implement new policies, with minimal timelag between making and implementing decisions.

Within the changed policy context, many responsibilities were devolved to individual universities. But, at the same time, institutions have been held more directly accountable for the effective and efficient use of the funding and other freedoms they enjoy. Moreover, institutions have increasingly been placed in a much more highly competitive environment, and considerable pressure has been brought to bear on universities to strengthen management, to become more entrepreneurial and corporate like.

Some of the more noticeable changes in management practice within universities include the considerable strengthening and expansion of the office of Vice-Chancellor. This has been coupled with a general devolution of financial and administrative responsibility to faculties, with each faculty treated as a separate cost centre. There has been considerable expansion of the management responsibilities of deans of faculty and heads of department. Deans of faculty in particular are now considered very much a part of management and are usually appointed rather than elected. For heads of department, the administrative burden has substantially increased in such areas as: staff supervision, budgeting and increasing outside earnings, student recruitment, quality assurance in both teaching and research, publicity, and in implementing a medley of university policies. Based on national survey data, Harman (2002) compares the profile of deans and heads for the years 1977 and 1997. Harman (2002: 67) concludes:

While there has been a recent move in many universities to the appointment rather than election or nomination of deans and heads and to place increased emphasis in selection processes on management expertise experience, deans and heads continue to be academics with superior qualifications and impressive research achievements. However, the gap between the research records of deans/heads and other academics has closed considerably since the 1970s whereas the gap has increased between deans/heads and professors. In 1977, deans and heads had published about five times as many scholarly papers as other academics while by 1997 they had published about twice as many.

While in 1977 university deans and heads had published about 90% as much as
professors by 1997 they had published only 66% as much.

While the differences between deans and heads in 1977 and 1997 are not as
pronounced as one might expect, it is likely that the gap between the managerial
dean/head and the 'traditional academic scholar' has continued to widen. Of course,
this begs the question of what are the attributes of a 'traditional academic scholar' (if
there ever was such a creature). But the point here, and developed further elsewhere
in the chapter, is that many academic roles in Australian higher education are being
redefined and, as Considine (2001: 146) argues, "these new norms buttress the most
rapid expansion of executive power in the history of the academy".

The 1995 Hoare Report (*Higher Education Management Review* 1995: 45)
maintained that "effective governance is a matter which needs to be reconsidered in
the light of the current and developing environment for higher education.
Universities can probably no longer rely on their traditional governance forms if
they are to operate fully effectively". The West Report (*Learning for Life* 1998: 111)
which was to follow three years later was even more categorical in condemning
traditional academic practices of self-governance:

> Sooner, rather than later, universities will need to address the essential incompatibility
> of a view of the world based on collegial decision making and an alternative view based
> on executive decision making and reflected in the size and style of operation of most
> business boards. The assertion by some within the university system that collegial
> decision making is desirable and natural is countered by the fact that decision making is
> often slow because of the time needed to resolve competing views.

Over the last decade, there has been considerable change in the governance and
management structures of Australian universities. Nonetheless, government has not
relented in its criticisms of these structures. At the beginning of 2002 another
Commonwealth review of higher education was begun under the general title of
Higher Education at the Crossroads. One of the issue papers released as part of the
Crossroads review entitled *Meeting the Challenges* was dedicated to governance
and management issues. *Meeting the Challenges* (2002: v) considered that at the
heart of many of the problems faced by higher education "are governance and
management structures, which are in some instances more appropriate to the past
than they are to serving the needs of Australia in the future". The issues paper is
particularly concerned that universities are given the latitude to operate as
commercial entities and states that "it is vital that they seize opportunities to
commercialise intellectual property of the university through royalties, trademarks,
licensing and equity ventures". As discussed in more detail below, the notion of
commercialisation and the commodification of knowledge is having an increasingly
strong influence on the governance and management structures of Australian
universities. But, first, the new management push in Australian higher education
needs to be analysed with respect to government's much broader public sector
reform agenda.

3. PUBLIC SECTOR REFORM AND THE 'NEW MANAGERIALISM' IN HIGHER EDUCATION

Since the mid-1970s, there has been strong national pressure to better integrate Australia into the global economy. This has impacted on higher education "to the extent that human capital investment came to be seen as being instrumental to economic reform" (Harman 2003: 3). The White Paper on higher education argued that "our industry is increasingly faced with rapidly changing international markets in which success depends on ... the conceptual, creative and technical skills of the labour force, the ability to innovate and be entrepreneurial" (1988: 6). Reform of the Australian economy has continued throughout the 1990s and into the new millennium.

As maintained by Harman (2003), economic reform has been coupled with new ideas about public sector management. A variety of public sector reforms, both developed locally (Wanna, O'Faircheallaigh and Weller 1992; Hilmer 1993) and subject to international influence (OECD 1987a, 1987b, 1995), has impacted on higher education. New public management in higher education was initially grounded on ideas of efficiency and effectiveness as was indicated above with respect to the 1980's CTEC review. "But from the early 1990s, the emphasis changed with the introduction of the concepts of competition and contestability, or more commonly market forces ... The important distinction to draw here ... is between these new concepts, on the one hand, and the traditional models based on coordination, collaboration and planned service provision, on the other" (Harman 2003: 5). Market forces and the concept of market steering have continued to shape the structure, function and character of Australian higher education for well over a decade, bringing in their train new ideas and approaches to university management (Meek 2001, 2002a).

Throughout the 1990s and into the new millennium, changes in the management practices of Australian universities did not reach an equilibrium between concentration of power in a small executive and more collaborative decision making involving a large proportion of academic staff. In fact, the exact opposite has occurred with an increasing sense of alienation by rank-and-file academic staff regarding the ways in which their institutions are governed and managed (NTEU 2000; Marginson and Considine 2000). As Winter and Sarros (2001: 19) maintain, "gaining the support of the 'managed' will not be an easy task when many academics feel personally threatened by the tenets and practices of managerialism". However, government reports on higher education governance and management repeatedly call for more concentration of power and decision making responsibility at the board and executive level, not less.

The 1988 White Paper proposed particular changes in higher education management at the institutional level, especially to strengthen the role of Vice-Chancellors and other senior executives, to speed up institutional decision making, and to enhance the capacity of institutions to respond quickly and effectively to new needs and opportunities. Fourteen years later, *Meeting the Challenges* (2002: x, xi, 24) stated that "boards, Councils or Senates often remain unwieldy structures, unable to provide the support and advice necessary to Vice-Chancellors managing a large-scale organisation"; "reforms are crucial to the success of Vice-Chancellors in managing the change processes that face the higher education sector in the years ahead"; "governing bodies could be given the flexibility to make appointments to ensure that ... they have the balance of capability, experience and business acumen that Vice-Chancellors need to draw upon in managing a large organisation". Surely, Vice-Chancellors require support as these statements indicate. But what is not contained in statements of this type is the traditional notion of Vice-Chancellors as first amongst equals – once a powerful myth if not reality in the Australian context. In the new management structures it does not appear that Vice-Chancellors have any equals. Harman (2003: 32) observes that:

> An ongoing problem in many universities is how to combine efficient management to meet the current highly competitive environment with substantial academic involvement in decisions that need to be based on high-level judgment. In many universities, there is a growing cultural gap between academics and senior management. This problem is being exacerbated with increasing academic workloads and pressures with respect to research and publication, and by the need for academics to undertake new teaching and administrative tasks related to income generating activities ... Academic communities have been split by arguments about entrepreneurialism and about the possible adverse effects of commercialism on academic values.

Australian universities are now placed in a much more highly competitive environment, and considerable pressure has been put on them to strengthen management, to become more entrepreneurial and corporate like. The large universities with more than 35,000 students, several campuses and annual budgets that run to hundreds of millions of dollars, rival in size and complexity many private corporations. Institutions must respond quickly and decisively to take advantage of market opportunities.

According to Scott (1993: 47) "the 'collegial' university governed by the academic guild assisted by low-profile administrators has been succeeded by the 'managerial' university dominated by an increasingly expert cadre of senior managers" which, according to him is caused in particular by the size of the present day institutions: "universities must be managed as businesses not because they are businesses but because they are on a corporate scale". While this may be true, a distinction needs to be drawn between 'management' as a set of practices and principles for the 'proper, effective and efficient' operation of an organisation, and management as a set of ideologically based control principles that favour a particular set of power configurations within institutions and between institutions and government.

There can be little doubt that the sheer size and complexity of Australian higher education demands strong and expert management at the institutional level. But what is at issue here is not expert management but 'managerialism' in the sense that Martin Trow uses the word. Managerialism "is not just a concern for the effective management of specific institutions in specific situations. The 'ism' points to an ideology, to a faith or belief in the truth of a set of ideas which are independent of specific situations" (Trow 1994: 11). Similar to what Trow has to say about the British case, managerialism in Australian higher education can be understood as a "substitute for a relationship of trust between government and universities, trust in the ability of institutions of higher education to broadly govern themselves" (1994: 11).

Trow (1994) distinguishes between two distinct approaches to managerialism in higher education: 'hard' and 'soft' management.[1] According to Trow (1994: 11): "... the 'soft' managerialists still see higher education as an autonomous activity, governed by its own norms and traditions, with a more effective and rationalised management still serving functions defined by the academic community itself". The hard managerialists:

> are resolved to reshape and redirect the activities of [the academic] community through funding formulas and other mechanisms of accountability imposed from outside the academic community, management mechanisms created and largely shaped for application to large commercial enterprises. Business models are central to the hard conception of managerialism; when applied to higher education ... the commitment is to transform universities into organisations similar enough to ordinary commercial firms so that they can be assessed and managed in roughly similar ways (Trow 1994: 12).

With respect to the British situation, it appears that the 'hard' concept of managerialism has been entrenched mainly with respect to the relationship between government and higher education institutions: "the withdrawal of trust in its universities by the British government has forced it to create bureaucratic machinery and formulas to steer and manage the universities from outside the system" (Trow 1994: 11).[2] Within British universities, the soft approach to managerialism seems to still prevail (Henkel 2002). In Australia, too, the hard managerialist approach originated in the transformation of the relationship between government and universities. However, it has increasingly permeated organisational boundaries and become characteristic of management relationships within institutions. Moreover, CEOs and other senior university managers often appear to be more comfortable with the values and management principles of senior government bureaucrats than with those of their academic colleagues.

Initially, the impetus for a corporate ethos within universities came from the federal government and the Senior Executive Service of the Commonwealth Public Service and the then Hawke Labor government's commitment to public sector reform and the introduction of private sector managerial practices into the public sector (Bessant 1995; cf. Williams 1988; Karmel 1989; Meek 1991, 2001). As an elite cadre of academic managers developed in Australian universities, they commenced to take on many of the characteristics of their private sector counterparts: for example, receiving attractive and individually negotiated salary packages and performance-based pay and bonuses.

The expansion and strengthening of the executive branch within higher education institutions question past conceptualisations of university management as organised anarchies (Cohen and Marsh 1974) or as political collectives (Baldridge 1971) or as a collegium (Moore and Langnecht 1986). At the same time, one needs to be cautious in adopting a linear view of the new management push in higher education. The new forms of management have not gone uncontested, nor have they become entirely institutionalised. Nonetheless, there has been a steady and consistent consolidation of power within the executive office of most universities with a corresponding diminution of academic professional authority and prestige.

However, it appears that government still thinks this process has yet to go far enough or fast enough (*Higher Education at the Crossroads* 2002).

4. INSTITUTIONAL GOVERNANCE

At least since the publication of the 1988 White Paper, the composition and size of university governing bodies have been regarded as significant. The White Paper considered that in terms of size and composition, appropriate models for university councils "can be drawn from boards of large private sector organisations" (1988: 103). The Hoare and West Reports said the same, and consistently the Commonwealth government has maintained that an appropriate size for university councils is between 10 and 15 members. The Hoare Report maintained that "governing bodies with more than 20 are likely to be unmanageable, particularly given the increased strategic focus that the bodies should have" (1995: 53). The committee was particularly concerned that council membership was not dominated by internal institutional representatives. The committee's chair, Mr David Hoare, was not an academic but the Chairman of Bankers Trust Australia.

These debates have continued into the new millennium. As mentioned above, *Meeting the Challenges* (2002: x) refers to councils, boards or senates as unwieldy structures, unable to provide necessary support and advice. While acknowledging some reduction in size of councils over the years, it is reported with some implied disgust that university councils "still average 21 members". *Meeting the Challenges* asks "Does the need to appoint a wide range of sectoral interests make governance structures too cumbersome? Do the methods of appointment undermine the fiduciary duty of governing members to always put the interests of the university above conflicting personal or institutional interests?" The report goes on to clearly indicate that it sees the answer to these questions in the affirmative. For example, it is stated that "effectiveness of university governing bodies is reduced by confusion about the role of some members ... Preventing conflicts of interest is important given growth in commercial activities" (2002: x). It was also suggested that council members be paid for their services, as is the case for most board members in the private sector. As an aside, it is interesting to note that according to Payette (2001: 17) the term 'fiduciary duty' is often used by those who do not really understand what it means, either accusingly to exhort a decision or action of some kind or evoked by "persons in a position of authority who use the term to justify or enhance a particular position or point of view when making a decision, usually controversial".

In Australia and elsewhere, the composition of the governing body is not without implications for the accountability of the institution to its various stakeholders. However, the argument here does not so much concern the size and composition of university councils per se, but the justifications used to limit size and restrict representation basically for commercial ends and to emulate boards of governors in the business sector.

The notion that universities would be more efficient and effective if governing bodies were more like those in the corporate sector cannot be accepted without question. In debates about higher education governance and management, the corporate model is consistently held up as the paragon of management virtue. But what is often not recognised is that the corporate sector has as many if not more governance and management problems as the university sector. For example, a study on corporate governance of Australia's top 100 listed companies sponsored by the Conference of Major Superannuation Funds concluded that the "preferred model of governance is being honoured more in breach than acceptance". The research was undertaken by the outgoing executive director of the Australian Institute of Superannuation Trustees and reported in the business section of the *Australian* newspaper under the heading 'Most top 100 boards fail on independence' (Owen 1996: 26). The study revealed that most boards failed the Australian Investment Managers Association independence test and that "just 35 of the nation's top 100 listed companies are run by boards with a majority of completely independent non-executive directors". More recent failures of Australian top companies have sponsored distrust in both corporate governing bodies and CEOs. The former head of one of Australia's leading insurance companies, for example, has recently been reported calling for "an overhaul of the way in which company boards are appointed", arguing that "too many are formed through personal relationships without sufficient scrutiny from investors" (Hughes 2002: 55). Corporate image has been tarnished to an even greater extent in countries like the United States where former leading CEOs have been paraded in front of the TV cameras in handcuffs.

Failings in corporate governance and management should not be used to justify those in universities. But it reflects a bit of a *cargo cult* mentality to assume that, by merely modelling university governing boards on those of the corporate sector, the independence and quality of advice and the more efficient and effective operation of the institution will automatically be ensured. This is not to argue that changes in the composition and function of university governing bodies are not necessary. But the need for such changes should be assessed in terms of the overall goals and purposes of higher education, rather than based on some vague notion of a corporate management efficiency and effectiveness gold standard.

Debates about governance structures in the corporate sector are primarily based on the interests of those who own the company (i.e. the shareholders). With respect to higher education, ownership issues are inherently more complex and extend to society at large and future generations. Those who call for more corporate like, commercially oriented university councils rarely take these broader issues into account. Moreover, it can be questioned whether there are any desirable intrinsic similarities between university and corporate boards of governors. Noam Chomsky (2002: 1) notes:

> After all, corporations are not benevolent societies. As Milton Friedman correctly says, though in slightly different words, the board of directors of a corporation actually has a legal obligation to be a monster, an ethical monster. Their legal obligation is to maximise profits for the shareholders, the stockholders. They're not supposed to do nice things. If they are, it's probably illegal, unless it's intended to mollify people, or improve market share, or something. That's the way it works. You don't expect corporations to be benevolent any more than you expect dictatorships to be benevolent. Maybe you can force them to be benevolent, but it's the tyrannical structure that's the problem, and as the universities move toward corporatisation you expect all of these effects.

Steane (2001: 1) drawing on research findings with respect to the operation of boards of governors in a variety of public and private sector organisations reaches more or less the same conclusion. According to Steane, two dimensions that differentiate charitable boards from boards in the corporate sector are that "the diverse nature of non-profit boards brings efforts to incorporate a representative slice of the organisation's members", and in non-profit boards there is a strong "link between values as a primary dimension in decision making at a level deemed strategic". Steane rejects the suggestion that there is convergence between profit and non-profit boards and that non-profit boards mimic the corporate sector. Of course, government and some institutional managers might attempt to claim that the governing boards of Australian universities are already located in the corporate sector.

5. THE HIGHER EDUCATION WORKPLACE REFORM PROGRAMME

The higher education industrial movement has contributed substantially to Australian academics being treated like any other employee group. This in turn has increased tension between academics and administrative staff over the very control of what is arguably the basis of the academic profession, that is, knowledge and the curriculum. The 'de-professionalisation' of academics has been coupled with a claim to professional status by administrative staff. Moreover, in Australia at least, this has recently taken an interesting if not perilous turn of events with some arguing that the roles of academics and administrators are merging to create a new type of professional in Australian higher education institutions – the academic/administrator hybrid.

In 1982, the then Federation of Australian University Staff Associations (later the Federated Australian University Staff Association – FAUSA) affiliated with the Australian Council of Trade Unions, and in 1983 higher education was effectively recognised as an industry by the then (federal) Conciliation and Arbitration Commission, with the subsequent registration of FAUSA (amalgamated in the early 1990s with other academic staff unions to become the National Tertiary Education Union – NTEU) as a union in November 1986 (Hancock 1989). In 1988, FAUSA was a party to the first negotiated industrial award for Australian academic staff – the Australian Universities' Academic Staff (Conditions of Employment) Award 1988, generally known as the Second Tier Wage Agreement/Award – and "for the first time academic unions ... had to give an undertaking on behalf of all Australian academics that certain steps would be taken to increase productivity in return for the 4% salary increase gained" (Lublin 1992: 74). This and all subsequent industrial awards have included reference to productivity gains and staff appraisal.

The 1988 White Paper and the Second Tier Wage Agreement envisaged a freeing up of industrial relations and award structures within individual institutions which was to be realised through such processes as enterprise bargaining. Enterprise bargaining at the local institutional level based on staff productivity was further enshrined in the Structural Efficiency Principle of the 1989 National Wage Case and the 1991 Academic Award Restructuring Agreement, and in subsequent wage agreements. But higher education institutions have not been able to exercise the expected degree of freedom to negotiate individual academic employment contracts. If anything, industrial relations within universities have become more rigid and bureaucratic.

The relationship between unions, employees and employers is changing throughout both the public and private sectors, and what is happening in higher education is only one aspect of a much broader industrial relations reform agenda. Many industries have shifted away from national wage agreements towards enterprise bargaining and negotiated productivity gains at the local level (although certainly not without a great deal of conflict in several instances).

There is a strong perception amongst politicians and government bureaucrats that, despite government efforts, higher education has largely escaped the public sector reforms that have occurred in other sectors. This is largely not true. Nonetheless, part and parcel of the growing alienation of academic staff is the way in which industrial relations have evolved in Australian higher education.

Further significant changes in workplace relations in Australian higher education have taken place since 1993. From 1994 onwards, salary increases were to be productivity related and, beginning in 1996, pay increases "had to be offset by higher productivity because they were unfunded" by the Commonwealth (*Meeting the Challenges* 2002: 33). Since 1993 there have been three rounds of enterprise bargaining in Australian higher education, each covering a three-year period and providing staff with about a 12.5% pay rise in each round of bargaining. Most of the agreements expired in early 2003. The unfunded pay increases have put Australian universities under considerable financial pressure and created much antagonism between management and rank-and-file staff at the institutional level.

The Commonwealth Workplace Reform Program (WRP) came into operation at the beginning of 2000. The WRP provides universities with about 2% of their salary increases if the institution meets a number of specified criteria, including performance management, cost savings, revenue diversification, productivity measures and a number of other management and administration issues. In a system strapped for cash, relatively small financial incentives can be used to lever large scale compliance in particular areas.

But, despite government's efforts to free up industrial relations at the institutional level and to introduce more flexible working conditions, "university bargaining has continued to yield relatively uniform outcomes largely because of union bargaining approaches" (*Meeting the Challenges* 2002: 35). "The NTEU effectively acts as a gatekeeper on agreement making at individual universities resulting in a pattern-bargaining approach across the sector" (2002: 36). Institutions 'theoretically' have the option of bargaining directly with staff. But those few universities that have tried to by-pass the unions have been largely unsuccessful.

There is an important paradox in all this for it seems that none of the parties has been able to achieve their intended goals. Neither university management nor the government has been able to achieve their goals of flexible working and salary conditions coupled with increased productivity. But academic staff have lost out as well, particularly with respect to professional autonomy.

It is important to recognise, with respect to industrial relations within higher education, that the interests of the academic union are not the same as the collegial interests of all academic staff who belong to a university. In fact, union advocacy can at once weaken the role of collegial decision making and strengthen that of senior management. The conditions under which industrial relations presently operate provide a great deal of power both to the unions and to senior management, and, at the local institutional level, many of the negotiations take place between a very small group of union executive officers and senior managers, often in secrecy. As one former Vice-Chancellor (Penington 1991: 12–13) prophetically commented more than a decade ago:

> Union action has increased the power of the central management of a university. As the institution must bargain with an outside agency (namely the union …), it must have an individual or small group which is given the authority to negotiate. The inevitable effect is that central managers, rather than collegial committees, become the effective decision-makers. This is not in the interests of staff members, who need to have some impact on decision-making through the collegial system.

The government's review document has echoed the calls for increased productivity and flexibility in industrial relations that have resounded through the sector at least since the 1988 White Paper. But, in its 2002 discussion paper, the government suggests a somewhat novel approach to the problem: "universities' need for greater flexibility in their staffing profiles concerns the need for 'new' employment types, rather than just maintenance of the traditional dichotomy of 'academic' and 'general' staff". While academics have always undertaken some administrative functions, this new push is more towards "professionally qualified general staff becoming involved in teaching and research functions" (*Meeting the Challenges* 2002: 41).

The 1997 Dearing Committee in the UK noted a blurring of roles between academic and non-academic staff. Coaldrake and Stedman (1999: 15) see the emergence of a new para-academic position in Australian universities emerging out of "equity units, staff development, learning support, and instructional design". They (Coaldrake and Stedman 1999: 16) consider that the blurring of roles "will continue to grow in significance as universities move into more flexible modes of delivery of teaching and learning and as they seek to support and reward staff for their skills, performance and potential rather than on the basis of job classifications". Pickersgill, van Barneveld and Gearfield's (1998) review and analysis of general and academic work in Australian universities also found "identifiable and increasing areas of overlap of 'academic' and general staff work". The Association for Tertiary Education Management (2002: 3) argues that "a single industrial award with a new range of classifications is needed that allows a university to recognise its particular context, while ensuring that all staff, irrespective of original professional training, receive the reward, recognition and professional development they need …".

How far the sector will go in blurring academic and administrative roles remains to be seen. However, the phenomenon is part and parcel of the trend away from treating academics as professionals for employment purposes, towards treating them like any other industrial group. Somewhat paradoxically, the unionisation of academe reinforces this trend. There appears to be an inverse relationship between the industrial power and the professional power of academic collectives. In Australia, general staff are starting to join the NTEU and, in the future, the NTEU may bargain for general and academic staff collectively. This may increase the power of the union, but its impact on the traditional culture and values of the academy is likely to be deleterious.

But, to be fair, one needs to ask whether it could have been otherwise; could academic associations in Australia have retained their professional character and mode of operation? Possibly yes, had the external environment remained more benign. But, against increasing external pressure to place higher education in an extremely competitive, market-driven environment, coupled with the demand to increase internal productivity (i.e. do more with less), professional norms and values provided little defence. Unions have attempted to preserve salaries and working conditions as best they can. Much has been lost in the process. As Considine (2001: 149) maintains, Australian universities "now seem less sure of themselves, less able to self-organise than ever before. Constantly being reinvented, they are less capable of genuine acts of self-production".

6. RESEARCH MANAGEMENT

Academic management cannot be adequately understood outside the context in which it occurs. This includes not only intra-institutional dynamics (each somewhat unique), but also the relationship between higher education institutions and the broader social environment. Many of the pressures with which academic managers must cope are not created by themselves, but originate from a number of external social, economic and political demands, often reflected in government policy. In Australia, probably in no other area is the macro-economic reform at the national level – particularly in making the nation more responsive to a global knowledge-based economy – so closely aligned with the micro-management reform at the institutional level than with respect to the management of research.

The increasing recognition of the importance of research and the training of a highly skilled workforce in positioning the nation in a global knowledge-based economy at once elevate the importance of higher education institutions and threaten many of their traditional values. The process is part and parcel of the advent of the post-industrial society and the commodification of knowledge – commodification taken here to mean "the phenomenon in which non-material activities are being traded for money" (Lubbers 2001). Neave (2002: 3) explains:

> Knowledge has always been power as well as a public good. Access to it and its role in innovation determine both the place of Nations in the world order and of individuals in society. But, commodification displaces the creation and passing on of knowledge from the social sphere to the sphere of production.

> Displacing and reinterpreting knowledge under these conditions raise fundamental questions for the University above all, in the area of academic freedom and in the 'ownership' of knowledge. They also pose questions about the ethical obligation to make knowledge freely available to those who seek it.

In the mid-1980s, Lyotard (1984: 5, cited in Roberts 1998: 1) hypothesised that "the status of knowledge is altered as societies enter what is known as the post-industrial age and cultures enter what is know as the post-modern age". According to Roberts, knowledge "is becoming 'exteriorised' from knowers. The old notion that knowledge and pedagogy are inextricably linked has been replaced by a new view of knowledge as a *commodity*". Or as Oliveira (2002: 1) puts it, "there is an essential difference between 'science as a search for truth' and 'science as a search for a response to economic and political interests'". Lyotard again (cited in Roberts 1998: 1–2):

> Knowledge is and will be produced in order to be sold, it is and will be consumed in order to be valorised in a new production: in both cases, the goal is exchange. Knowledge ceases to be an end in itself, it loses its 'use-value' …
> Knowledge in the form of an informational commodity indispensable to productive power is already, and will continue to be, a major – perhaps the major – stake in the worldwide competition for power.

The Australian government's approach to knowledge is largely a utilitarian one, with a concentration on commercialisation and economic return. University research managers by and large tend to translate government research policy directions and priorities into institutional practices. Research management as it is presently evolving has the potential to at once divide institutions and the sector as a whole into 'research haves', and 'teaching have-nots'. To fully understand the implications of present policy and research management practices, it is necessary to go into some detail about how they work.

6.1. Research Funding Policies

Most operating resources provided by the Commonwealth to the higher education sector are allocated by the Department of Education, Science and Training (DEST) as block operating grants based on student enrolments. For well over a decade, however, federal governments have encouraged competition amongst institutions, particularly with respect to research funding. The White Paper stated that "concentration and selectivity in research are needed if funding is to be fully effective" (1988: 90). The then Labor government's policies were put into effect in a number of ways. First, at the system level, an increasing proportion of recurrent grants was 'clawed back' from institutions and given to the Australian Research Council (ARC) for competitive re-allocation. This included the ARC Large Grant scheme funded directly by the ARC and the ARC Small Grant scheme funded in proportion to the institutions' success in winning ARC Large Grants and administered by the institutions themselves. Second, individual institutions were compelled to formulate research management plans for the competitive allocation to academic staff of research funds available within the institution. Third, institutional research performance was competitively assessed for funding purposes through the so-called Research Quantum (RQ). The RQ, representing about 6% of total operating grants, was based on quantitative performance indicators: number of competitive research grants attracted (80%), publications (10%) and postgraduate completion rates (10%). Fourth, institutions were provided with Research

Infrastructure Block Grants (RIBG) on the basis of a formula with allocations reflecting the relative success of each institution in attracting competitive research funds.

With the intention of increasing competition over research funding even further, in June 1999 the Liberal coalition federal government released a discussion paper on research and research training entitled *New Knowledge, New Opportunities*. The paper identified several deficiencies in the existing framework which were considered to limit institutional capacity to respond to the challenges of the emerging knowledge economy. These included: funding incentives that do not sufficiently encourage diversity and excellence; poor connections between university research and the national innovation system; too little concentration by institutions on areas of relative strength; inadequate preparation of research graduates for employment; and unacceptable wastage of resources associated with low completion rates and long completion times of research graduates. A particular concern was with research training and the funding of PhD and research masters students.

The government released its policy statement on research and research training, *Knowledge and Innovation: A Policy Statement on Research and Research Training* in December 1999. Major changes to the policy and funding framework for higher education research in Australia were identified in the policy statement. The principal ones were:

- a strengthened Australian Research Council and an invigorated national competitive grants system;
- performance-based funding for research student places and research activity in universities, with transitional arrangements for regional institutions;
- the establishment of a broad quality verification framework supported by Research and Research Training Management Plans; and
- a collaborative research programme to address the needs of rural and regional communities.

The policy statement re-introduced the requirement for formal submission to DEST of Research and Research Training Management Plans. Core elements that institutions were expected to report on annually include: research strengths and activities; details of research active staff; graduate outcomes both in terms of attributes and employment; linkages to industry and other bodies; and policies on commercialisation (Wood and Meek 2002a, 2002b).

These changes have been put into effect by two new performance-based block funding schemes. The approaches are intended to "reward those institutions that provide high quality research training environments and support excellent and diverse research activities". The Institutional Grants Scheme (IGS) supports the general fabric of institutions' research and research training activities. The scheme absorbs the funding previously allocated for the Research Quantum and the Small Grants Scheme.

Funding under the IGS is allocated on the basis of a formula. The components and weightings are as follows: success in attracting research income from a diversity of sources (60%); success in attracting research students (30%); and the quality and output of its research publications (10%). The government considers that institutions are likely to be more outwardly focused in their research when research income from all sources is equally weighted, unlike pre-2002 arrangements which gave greater weight to Commonwealth competitive research grants schemes.

Funding for research training is allocated on a performance-based formula through the Research Training Scheme (RTS). Institutions attract a number of funded Higher Degree Research (HDR) places based on their performance through a formula comprising three elements: numbers of all research students completing their degree (50%); research income (40%); and the revised publications measure (10%). The values for each element will be the average of the latest two years' data. The key aspect of the RTS is that it is essentially based on *quantitative criteria* (Wood and Meek 2002b).

The RTS replaces the Research HECS Exemptions Scheme. It provides Commonwealth-funded HDR students with an 'entitlement' to a HECS (Higher Education Contribution Scheme) exemption for the duration of an accredited HDR course, up to a maximum period of four years' full-time equivalent study for a doctorate by research and two years' full-time equivalent study for a masters by research.

The number of RTS places to be Commonwealth-funded at each institution in 2001 was based on each institution's share in 2000 of the then 21,500 HECS-exempt places plus the 'gap' places each institution had committed to the RTS. 'Gap' places are those additional HDR places offered by institutions in excess of their HECS-exempt allocation. The total RTS funding provided to the sector in 2001 established the base for future years.

There is a 'funding pool' into which funds freed up by net separations each semester are placed, and from which re-allocations are made on a relative performance basis each semester. Institutions may provide research training on a fee-paying basis to students not granted a HECS-exempt RTS place.

From 2002, the RTS assigned the total funding for net separations of students across the sector to the funding pool. Students lodging theses, withdrawing from or suspending their studies, transferring between institutions or exhausting their maximum entitlement contributed to the count of net separations. The funding pool was then re-allocated through the RTS formula which reflected each institution's performance as specified above.

Gallagher (2000: 12) succinctly summarises some of the consequences of the new funding formula:

> For many institutions the crucial matter has been the determination of their starting base in 2001 for the application of the performance-based funding formulae in subsequent years. Most recognised how exacting the formulae would be in rewarding shares of the composition of national performance and the rapidly spiraling character of the rewards. If an institution starts in a position it cannot sustain, by exposing to contestability a level of resources above which it is unlikely to win (unless having some transitional

protections) and subsequently declines in its performance, then the outcomes will be harsh for it: relative under-performers will contribute more to the national pool and gain less from its redistribution. A higher ratio of student separations to completions flows through the formula into fewer commencers; and a relative decline in the national share of research income similarly reduces commencing student allocations which, in turn, dilutes research strength and reduces attractiveness for investment.

6.2. The New Research Management Regime

Commonwealth changes to research funding has required Australian universities to rethink much of their approach to the management of research and research training. High on the agenda has been the need to identify priorities, concentrate research effort, and develop a set of performance indicators and sophisticated research management information systems (Wood and Meek 2002b).

Coupled with the introduction of new research funding mechanisms has been government intervention in the setting of research priorities. At the beginning of 2002, the government announced, as a result of a 'consultation' process that was far from transparent, that a portion (33%) of the Australian Research Council's (the largest non-medical research funding agency in Australia) funding would be targeted to research in the following four priority areas: nano- and bio-materials, genome/phenome research, complex/intelligent systems, and photon science and technology.

In May 2002, the government announced its intention to further set national research priorities for government-funded research. According to government, the priorities "will highlight research areas of particular importance to Australia's economy and society, where a whole-of-government focus has the potential to improve research, and broaden policy outcomes" (DEST 2002: 1).

It is interesting to note that state governments have also gotten into the act of research priority setting in the expectation that targeted research funding, particularly in such areas as biotechnology, will enhance their economic competitiveness. For example, the Queensland government in 1999 formulated a four-year innovation strategy, *Innovation – Queensland's Future*, designed to stimulate innovation and technology across universities, business, industry and the wider community. In accordance with this strategy, the Queensland government earmarked $270 million for biotechnology ventures over a ten-year period. The New South Wales government has tied its recent initiatives in the science and technology areas specifically to the field of biotechnology, even more so than Queensland. In 2001, the New South Wales government released *BioFirst*, a five-year strategy that sets out the government's initiatives to promote biotechnology in New South Wales. Similar initiatives are being promoted by state governments in Victoria and Western Australia and, to a lesser extent, the other states and territories (Meek 2002b).

Concentration and selectivity remain the key issues in research. This means that universities have to identify strengths and make hard decisions about allocating resources to some areas and not to others. It is fairly obvious that those areas best able to commodify their intellectual wares are the ones to stand to gain the most from the new funding regime. It is also fairly obvious that these areas are not randomly distributed across the academy. And it is just not science and technology who are the winners, but those sub-fields that can lay claim to short- to medium-term economic return on their efforts. There is a danger that basic science will be further ignored, and in particular those disciplines traditionally associated with basic research, such as chemistry and physics, will go into further decline.

Under the new research funding formula for research students, universities earn income not only through student load but also through rates of completion. This presents particular difficulty for faculties in the humanities and social sciences that often have a large number of research students who traditionally study part-time, take considerable time to complete their degrees and have low completion rates compared to other disciplines. While absorbing a large amount of initial RTS load allocation, such areas may lose their student load in the future if completion rates are outside the formula guidelines. In protecting its overall share of the national research student quota, a university may decide that some subjects in the arts, humanities and social sciences are ones that it can ill afford (Wood and Meek 2002b).

Either wittingly or unwittingly, management within universities is playing the research concentration and priority setting game with the potential result of segmenting academic staff into research haves and teaching staff have-nots. By directing research funds and infrastructure to priority areas, non-priority areas will have fewer resources to conduct research. This appears to be exactly what government intends:

> It seems timely to challenge the assumptions of the academic model of much of the past century, and validate alternative academic career paths. Some academics may choose to specialise in teaching, and become 'teaching-only' academics. Some academics may choose to specialise in research (*Striving for Quality* 2002).

In a similar vein with respect to the UK situation, Willmott (1998: 1) argues that the "significance of the Research Assessment Exercises ... does not reside primarily in their rationalisation of resources for research or in securing improvements in accountability for their expenditure, but, rather, in their contribution to legitimising the restructuring of higher education which has included the withdrawal of research funding from an increasing proportion of academics and departments". In both countries, the intention is not merely to decouple research from teaching, but to simultaneously tie research more closely to the needs of industry and the economy while reducing unit cost.

Bertelsen (2002: 1) observes that "the commodification of higher education to serve the market is revolutionising our entire practice, from institutional image through to management, jobs and curriculum". She goes on to state that:

> once they have conceded that knowledge is a commodity to be traded, universities become subject ... to the full and ruthless protocols of the market. Time-honoured principles of truth and intellectual rigour are rapidly superseded by cost-effectiveness and utility, and market rules are systematically applied. First, research is only done if it creates new products, and courses which don't feed job skills are a waste of time. So managers dutifully prioritise 'core business' and eliminate 'peripheral' activities, and funding becomes an investment decision based on short-term production goals.

While Bertelsen may overstate the case, there is nonetheless still a good deal of truth in what she has to say. In Australian universities, management in many institutions strongly promotes those areas of the enterprise that appear to turn a profit, while shedding investment in less lucrative activities, such as the humanities, ancient and some modern languages, etc. Given the decline of public funding and rising student numbers in a highly competitive and volatile market, institutional leaders may well indeed argue that they have no other choice.

It appears that the modern university has shifted its orientation from social knowledge to market knowledge and that the "development of a market oriented university supersedes academic decision making" (Buchbinder 1993: 335). According to Newson (1993: 298), "These new forms of decision making fundamentally undermine a conception of the university as an autonomous, self-directing, peer-review and professional-authority based institution, and thus changes the politics of how academic work is accomplished". For decades, if not centuries, the autonomy debate in higher education has mainly concerned the relationship between institutions and government (or church in past eras) and undue external political interference in academic affairs. But within the context of the post-industrial society, driven by the production and marketing of knowledge, government is just one of many elements in the autonomy and collegiality matrices, and higher education institutions may have as many 'enemies' within as without. Meek and Wood (1997: 58) argue that:

> appeals to academic freedom as a device to locate control over university affairs within a scholarly collegium will no longer do. Nonetheless, academics will strongly resist being treated like factory workers and there is substantial evidence to suggest that if they are, then the very knowledge productivity that has made universities so important to society will be diminished. And here lies the basic challenge for higher education management: how to exploit the knowledge products of their institutions without destroying the internal foundations on which the production of those products rest.

7. CONCLUSION

There is a view that in responding to market opportunities in a highly competitive global economic environment "traditional governance often works against making decisions fast enough to capitalise on new opportunities and avoid threats" (Green, Eckel and Barblan 2002: 9). In a similar vein, the Australian higher education review document *Meeting the Challenges* (2002: ix) states that "at present many universities feel constrained in the extent to which they can respond to, and capitalise on, business and innovation opportunities in timeframes appropriate to the commercial world. Governments ... need to consider the regulatory regime imposed on universities to provide more freedom to pursue commercial opportunities ...".

In Australian higher education as elsewhere, "the rise of executive power ... coincided with – and was mutually constitutive of – the growing role of market exchange and economic competition" (Considine 2001: 149). This has yet to result in the complete disappearance of academic self-management from the academy. Professors and students still participate in the governance and management of the university. But the significance of their role and degree of power over key decisions have been extensively curtailed. Similar to Delanty's (2002: 186) report on Canadian higher education, as a result of neo-managerialism, "academic self-governance is mostly ceremonial, lacking any real basis".

While market considerations are driving governance and management reforms in Australian higher education, the long-term efficiency of such an approach can be questioned. The 'new managerialism' may eventually entirely transform the professional culture and work practices of academe. But, at the moment, what seems to be happening is entrenchment of antagonism between managers and the managed – a situation highly unproductive for all concerned. Traditional norms and values of the academic profession carry little weight with the new managerialists, and academics themselves are having to increasingly question their professional credibility within society and their own institutions. Slaughter and Leslie (1997: 5) make a similar argument when they state that:

> Participation in the market began to undercut the tacit contract between professors and society because the market put as much emphasis on the bottom line as on client welfare. The *raison d'etre* for special treatment for universities, the training ground of professionals, as well as for professional privilege, was undermined, increasing the likelihood that universities, in the future, will be treated more like other organisations and professionals more like other workers.

New forms of governance and management of higher education are challenging academics' basic loyalties. In the past, academic loyalty was first and foremost to the discipline and to disciplinary norms concerning the definition and production of knowledge (Gouldner 1958; Becher 1989; Clark 1983). That loyalty has come under challenge from powerful groups both within and without the academy demanding loyalty first and foremost to the institution – that is, to the corporation that pays the bills. The Association for Tertiary Education Management (2002: 3), for example, argues that all university staff "need to be managed, recognised and rewarded on the basis of how well they contribute to the goals of a university ... We might then see a declining of tension ... and an increasing and converging focus on the future of the university". We may also see a decline in the very academic and professional values, norms and qualities that have placed the university at the centre of the emerging knowledge-based economy. Further entrenchment of the hard managerialist approach to higher education may 'kill the goose that lays the academic golden eggs'.

NOTES

[1]   Of course, soft managerialism can be regarded as an ideology as well. However, it is much more lenient towards notions of academic self-governance than hard managerialism.
[2]   Here, it appears that Trow is referring both to changes in types of higher education intermediary bodies, such as the replacement of the University Grants Committee by the Higher Education Funding Council, and the nature of their composition and power over the sector.

REFERENCES

Association for Tertiary Education Management. "Submission 106" to *Higher Education at the Crossroads: Ministerial Discussion Paper*. Canberra: Department of Education, Science and Training, 2002, http://www.dest.gov.au.
Baldridge, J. Victor. *Power and Conflict in the University*. New York: John Wiley, 1971.
Becher, Tony. *Academic Tribes and Territories*. Milton Keynes: Open University Press, 1989.
Bertelsen, Eve. "'Degrees 'R' Us' – The Marketisation of the University." 2002,

http://web.uct.ac.za/org/aa/chomsk.htm#Eve Bertelsen.

Bessant, B. "Corporate Management and its Penetration of University Administration and Government." *Australian Universities' Review* 38.1 (1995): 59–62.

Buchbinder, H. "The Market Oriented University and the Changing Role of Knowledge." *Higher Education* 26.3 (1993): 331–347.

Chomsky, Noam. "Assaulting Solidarity – Privatizing Education." 2002, http://www.uct.ac.za/org/aa/chomsk.htm.

Clark, Burton R. *The Higher Education System: Academic Organization in Cross-National Perspective.* Berkeley: University of California Press, 1983.

Coaldrake, Peter and Lawrence Stedman. *Academic Work in the Twenty-first Century: Changing Roles and Policies.* Canberra: Department of Employment, Education, Training and Youth Affairs, 1999.

Cohen, Michael D. and James G. Marsh. *Leadership and Ambiguity: The American College President.* New York: McGraw Hill, 1974.

Commonwealth Tertiary Education Commission (CTEC). *Review of Efficiency and Effectiveness: Report of the Committee of Enquiry.* Canberra: AGPS, 1986.

Considine, Mark. "The Tragedy of the Common-rooms? Political Science and the New University Governance." *Australian Journal of Political Science* 36.1 (2001): 146–156.

DEET. *National Report on Australia's Higher Education Sector.* Canberra: AGPS, 1993.

Delanty, Gerard. "The Governance of Universities: What is the Role of the University in the Knowledge Society?" *Canadian Journal of Sociology* 27.2 (2002): 185–198.

DEST. "National Research Priorities." Canberra: DEST, 2002, http://www.dest.gov.au/priorities/framework.htm#top.

Gallagher, Michael. *The Emergence of Entrepreneurial Public Universities in Australia.* DETYA Higher Education Division Occasional Paper Series 00/E. Canberra: DETYA, 2000.

Gouldner, A. "Cosmopolitans and Locals: Toward an Analysis of Latent Social Roles." *Administrative Science Quarterly* 2 (1958): 281–306; 444–467.

Green, M., P. Eckel and A. Barblan. *Brave New (and Smaller) World of Higher Education: A Transatlantic View.* Washington: ACEnet, 2002.

Hancock, K. "Industrial Relations in Tertiary Education." Paper presented at the *AITEA Conference,* Auckland, New Zealand, 26 August, 1989.

Harman, Grant S. "Academic Leaders or Corporate Managers: Deans and Heads in Australian Higher Education, 1977 to 1997." *Higher Education Management and Policy* 14.2 (2002): 53–70.

Harman, Grant S. "Introduction: A Perspective on a Decade of Change in Second National Report on Higher Education." Canberra: Department of Education, Science and Training, 2003 (forthcoming).

Henkel, Mary. "Academic Identity in Transformation? The Case of the United Kingdom." *Higher Education Management and Policy* 14.3 (2002): 137–145.

Higher Education: A Policy Discussion Paper (Green Paper). Canberra: AGPS, 1987.

Higher Education: A Policy Statement (White Paper). Canberra: AGPS, 1988.

Higher Education at the Crossroads: Ministerial Discussion Paper. Canberra: Department of Education, Science and Training, 2002.

Higher Education Management Review. Hoare Committee Report. Canberra: AGPS, 1995.

Hilmer, F. *National Competition Policy: Report by the Independent Committee of Inquiry.* Canberra: AGPS, 1993.

Hughes, Anthony. "Former NRMA Boss Wants to End Board Cronyism." *Sydney Morning Herald.* 18–19 May, 2002, 55.

Karmel, Peter. *Reflections on a Revolution, Australian Higher Education in 1989.* AVCC Papers. 1, 1989.

Knowledge and Innovation: A Policy Statement on Research and Research Training. Canberra: Department of Employment, Education, Training and Youth Affairs, 1999.

Learning for Life: Final Report, Review of Higher Education Financing and Policy. R. West, Chair of Committee. Canberra: AGPS, 1998.

Lubbers, Ruud. "Definition: Commodification." 2001, http://globalize.kub.nl/.

Lublin, J. "Staff Development, Staff Assessment and the Industrial Awards." *Higher Education Research and Development* 11.1 (1992): 73–83.

Lyotard, J-F. *The Post-modern Condition: A Report on Knowledge.* Minneapolis: University of Minnesota Press, 1984.

Marginson, S. and M. Considine. *The Enterprise University: Power, Governance and Reinvention in Australia.* Melbourne: Cambridge University Press, 2000.

Meek, V. Lynn. "The Transformation of Australian Higher Education: From Binary to Unitary System." *Higher Education* 21.4 (1991): 11–43.

Meek, V. Lynn. "Australian Public Sector Reform." In Nolan, Brendan (ed.). *Public Sector Reform: An International Perspective.* Palgrave: London, 2001, 34–47.

Meek, V. Lynn. "On the Road to Mediocrity? Governance and Management of Australian Higher Education in the Market Place." In Amaral, Alberto, Glen A. Jones and Berit Karseth (eds). *Governing Higher Education: National Perspectives on Institutional Governance.* Dordrecht: Kluwer Academic Publishers, 2002a, 253–278.

Meek, V. Lynn. "An Evaluation of Higher Education Programs and Initiatives in Australian States and Territories Other Than Victoria." Analytical paper prepared for the Higher Education Directorate of the Victoria Department of Education and Training, 2002b.

Meek, V. Lynn and Fiona Q. Wood. *Higher Education Governance and Management: An Australian Study.* Canberra: AGPS, 1997.

Meeting the Challenges: The Governance and Management of Universities. Canberra: Department of Education, Science and Training, 2002.

Moore, J. and L. Langnecht. "Academic Planning in a Political System." *Planning for Higher Education* 14.1 (1986): 1–5.

Neave, G. "Globalization: Threat, Opportunity or Both?" *International Association of Universities Newsletter* 8.1 (2002): 1–3.

New Knowledge, New Opportunities: A Discussion Paper on Higher Education Research and Research Training. Canberra: Department of Education, Training and Youth Affairs, 1999.

Newson, J. "Constructing the 'Post-industrial' University: Institutional Budgeting and University Corporate Linkages." In Altbach, P.G. and B.D. Johnstone (eds). *The Funding of Higher Education: International Perspectives.* Garland Studies in Higher Education, vol. Q. New York: Garland Publishing Inc., 1993, 285–304.

NTEU. *Unhealthy Places of Learning: Working in Australian Universities.* South Melbourne: National Tertiary Education Union, 2000.

OECD. *Universities Under Scrutiny.* Paris: Organisation for Economic Cooperation and Development, 1987a.

OECD. *Structural Adjustment and Economic Performance.* Paris: Organisation for Economic Cooperation and Development, 1987b.

OECD. *Governance in Transition: Management Reforms in OECD Countries.* Paris: Organisation for Economic Cooperation and Development, 1995.

Oliveira, Luisa. "Commodification of Science and Paradoxes in Universities." ISCTE, Lisbon: University of Lisbon, 2002, http://rektorat.unizg.hr/rk/Docs/uisa.html.

Owen, R. "Most Top 100 Boards Fail on Independence." *Australian.* 13 March, 1996, 26.

Payette, Dennis. "Fiduciary Responsibility of Board Trustees and Officers in Universities and Colleges." *Corporate Governance* 1.4 (2001): 12–19.

Penington, D. "Collegiality and Unions." *Journal of Tertiary Education Administration* 13.1 (1991): 7–18.

Pickersgill, Richard, Kristin van Barneveld and Sue Gearfield. *General and Academic Work: Are They Different?* Canberra: AGPS, 1998.

Roberts, Peter. "Rereading Lyotard: Knowledge, Commodification and Higher Education." *Electronic Journal of Sociology* 3.3, 1998, http://www.sociology.org/content/vol003.003/roberts.html.

Scott, P. "Respondent." *The Transition from Elite to Mass Higher Education.* DEET Higher Education Division Occasional Papers Series. Canberra: AGPS, 1993.

Slaughter, S. and L. Leslie. *Academic Capitalism: Politics, Policies and the Entrepreneurial University.* Baltimore: Johns Hopkins University Press, 1997.

Steane, Peter. "Governance: Convergent Expectations, Divergent Practices." *Corporate Governance* 1.3 (2001): 15–19.

Striving for Quality: Learning, Teaching and Scholarship. Canberra: Department of Education, Science and Training, 2002.

Trow, M. "Managerialism and the Academic Profession: The Case of England." *Higher Educational Policy* 7.2 (1994): 11–18.

Wanna, J., C. O'Faircheallaigh and P. Weller. *Public Sector Management in Australia.* South Melbourne: Macmillan, 1992.

Williams, Bruce. "The 1988 White Paper on Higher Education." *Australian Universities' Review* 2 (1988): 2–8.

Willmott, Hugh. "Commercialising Higher Education in the UK: The State, Industry and Peer Review." Paper (revised version) presented at the *Higher Education Close-Up Conference*, University of Central Lancashire, Lancashire, 6–8 July, 1998.

Winter, Richard and James Sarros. "Corporate Reforms to Australian Universities: Views From the Academic Heartland." Paper presented at the *Critical Management Conference*, Education Stream. Manchester School of Management, Manchester, 11–13 July, 2001,
http://www.mngt.waikato.ac.nz/ejrot/cmsconference/2001/Papers/Education/Winter.pdf.

Wood, Fiona Q. and V. Lynn Meek. "Over-reviewed and Under-funded? The Evolving Policy Context of Australian Higher Education Research and Development." *Journal of Higher Education Policy and Management* 24.1 (2002a): 7–25.

Wood, Fiona Q. and V. Lynn Meek. "Research Management – A Question of Scale and Focus at the University of Adelaide. A Case Study for the OECD/IMHE – Trends in Research Management and Support at the Institutional Level." Paris: OECD/IMHE, 2002b.

SHEILA SLAUGHTER AND GARY RHOADES

CONTESTED INTELLECTUAL PROPERTY: THE ROLE OF THE INSTITUTION IN UNITED STATES HIGHER EDUCATION

1. INTRODUCTION

In this chapter, we argue that, in the United States, an academic public good knowledge regime is shifting to an academic capitalist knowledge regime. The public good knowledge regime was characterised by valuing knowledge as a public good to which the citizenry has claims. Mertonian norms – such as communalism, universality, the free flow of knowledge and organised scepticism – were associated with the public good model. The public service regime paid heed to academic freedom, which honoured professors' rights to follow research where it led, and gave professors the right to dispose of discoveries as they saw fit (Merton 1942). The cornerstone of the public good knowledge regime was basic science that led to the discovery of new knowledge within the academic disciplines, serendipitously leading to public benefits. Mertonian values are often associated with the Vannevar Bush model, in which basic science that pushes back the frontiers of knowledge was necessarily performed in universities (Bush 1945). The discoveries of basic science always preceded development. Development occurred in federal laboratories and sometimes in corporations. It often involved building and testing costly prototypes. Application followed development and almost always took place in corporations. The public good model assumed a relatively strong separation between public sector and private sector.

The academic capitalist knowledge regime values knowledge privatisation and profit taking, in which institutions, inventor faculty and corporations have claims that come before the public's. Public interest in science goods are subsumed in the increased growth expected from a strong knowledge economy. Rather than a single, non-exclusively licensed, widely distributed product (e.g. vitamin D irradiated milk) serving the public good, the exclusive licensing of many products to private firms contributes to economic growth which benefits the whole society. Knowledge is construed as a private good, valued for creating streams of high technology products that generate profit as they flow through global markets. Professors are obligated to disclose their discoveries to their institutions which have the authority to determine how knowledge shall be used. The cornerstone of the academic capitalism model is basic science for use and basic technology, models that make the case that science is embedded in commercial possibility (Stokes 1997; Branscomb 1997; Branscomb et al. 1997). These models see little separation between science and commercial

A. Amaral et al. (eds.), The Higher Education Managerial Revolution?, 203–228.
© 2003 *Kluwer Academic Publishers. Printed in the Netherlands.*

activity. Discovery is valued because it leads to high technology products for a knowledge economy.

We look at state system and institutional intellectual property policies for three states to see if they indicate a shift from a public good to an academic capitalist knowledge regime. The questions we are particularly interested in answering are: What values are embedded or explicit in these policies? Have they changed over time? Have the organisations that frame the values changed? What is the direction of the change? What do these changes tell us about the relation between market, state and higher education, and how these are valued?

2. THEORY

There are several strands in the US literature on the norms and values of science. The first, which we will call the Mertonian strand, looks at values associated with science and scientists, sometimes not differentiating clearly between the two. The second, which we will call the critical and/or social constructionist strand, challenges the Mertonian. The third or university–industry collaboration strand takes the position that science is not value-free, but that it can accommodate both academic and market values. The fourth strand, which we call 'the commons', approaches science and values from the point of view of the public good. The four are closely related and some, particularly the commons strand, are currently counterpoising traditional academic values to market values. Very few deal with organisations (such as the university) that sustain science, with how the state and private sector interact with organisations that sustain science, and with how values are embodied in these organisational relations.

In the United States, the norms and values of science are taken to include not only the physical and biological sciences, but also the social sciences and any other field or discipline that makes claims to have science at its core, which includes most areas of study in the university. Robert K. Merton (1942) is generally regarded as offering an early and enduring formulation of scientific norms and values with his conception of science as open, communistic (later changed to communal), universal, disinterested, and characterised by a sceptical habit of mind. Open science spoke to the non-secret character of science. Communistic or communal meant non-commercial. Universal referred to the idea that there was no national cast to science and that knowledge flowed freely across borders. Disinterestedness addressed the stance of the scientist toward knowledge: objective, non-partisan, not committed to a particular outcome. Maintaining a sceptical habit of mind challenged scientists to always question results. (There is more than a little irony in Merton's conceptualisation of disinterested science, in that he associated science with democracy and wrote to challenge the rise of nationalistic, fascist Nazi science. Again, ironically, even as he envisioned democratic science as open, the advent of World War II, which spurred him to write, gave rise to secret or classified science, justified in terms of national security.) In the 1950s and 1960s, Merton's values were compressed into 'basic', or 'fundamental' science, and the value of science was that it was 'value-free' or 'objective'. These properties were often conceived of as embedded in science itself, and separate from the scientist, who nonetheless was value-free and objective because 'he' served science. In the Mertonian model, which was closely aligned with the Vannevar Bush model, academic science stood alone, not tied to the state or corporations. A necessary condition of excellent science was university autonomy. Basic science, unfettered by the state or commerce, preceded development, often accomplished in federal laboratories, which was then followed by application, which occurred in corporations. Independence from state and market was essential for excellent science.

The second or critical/social constructionist strand of values literature critiqued the idea of science as 'value-free' and 'objective'. Opponents of the Vietnam War saw science as the servant of war, the capitalist state, and the imperial ambitions of American leaders (Foreman 1987; Leslie 1993). Social constructionists challenged the notion that science was separate from the scientist or that it embodied pure and noble ideas (Latour and Woolgar 1979; Dasgupta and David 1987). Marxists, neo-marxists, post-marxists and critical materialists of many stripes always saw close connections between science and business, with the result that science often served commercial values and ends (Veblen 1935; Noble 1976; Soley 1995).

The third strand of values literature sees science as currently re-framing market and academic values so they are not in opposition. Both policy makers (Council on Competitiveness 1996) and social scientists (who are sometimes policy makers as well) argue that the connection between science and business should not necessarily be viewed critically (Stokes 1997; Branscomb 1997; Branscomb et al. 1997; Etzkowitz, Webster and Healey 1998; Mowery and Ziedonis 2002). They stress three points in making their case: (1) science has always been involved with the economy through application/use; (2) science is a crucial component of the new/information/knowledge economy; and (3) science can accommodate market and academic values. The third strand takes the insights of the second strand, which challenges an idealised science, and re-frames the ends of science from serving the (unspecified) public good to serving (unspecified) economic prosperity, redefined as the public good, which more easily enables the coexistence of market and academic values. Indeed, the market capabilities of higher education are highly valued. In this conception, academic science is closely related to the market, but the state is 'backgrounded' even though it supplies resources for partnerships between higher education and the market.

The fourth strand of values literature approaches science from a different direction, that of the public good. Scholars like Heller and Eisenberg (1998) and Bollier (2002) make the case that science is an 'intellectual commons' that must not be appropriated by the corporate or economic sector because to do so is against the interest of the public good or commonweal. The intellectual commons is a non-market space that is used for the public good or well being of society in much the same way that open pasturage was used by medieval communities for the good of the group as a whole. As the aristocracy enclosed common land in England, Scotland and other parts of the world, so the intellectual commons is now being appropriated by global corporations. The intellectual commons is sustained by an academic 'gift economy' which is open, free, non-alienable (and very Mertonian). It is these very properties that allow science to flourish. To 'enclose' the intellectual commons is to destroy it, wreaking havoc on the very system that created the science and technology which gave rise to the new information knowledge economy. Corporate values are understood as in opposition to the public good because they stress profit for individual firms rather then the well being of society as a whole.

Strands one and three are literatures that concentrate on science and technology rather than universities as organisations. (They sometimes address what makes university–industry collaborations work, but the focus is generally on the partnership rather than the university.) If they address policy or the state, it is almost always federal policy and a (mythic) state that honours the autonomy of science by giving money without strings attached. Strands one and three are concerned with two issues: (1) explaining and interpreting what values make (US) science excellent (the best in the world); and (2) raising funds to support US science. These two issues are not seen as contradictory, even from a values perspective. In both strands, the values elucidated by the scholar in post-hoc fashion are offered as the explanation for excellent science. As theory, strands one and three purport to interpret and explain why US science is excellent, and predict that dire consequences will come from lack of funding, although strand one calls for funding an idealised basic science, and strand three calls for funding an idealised entrepreneurial science.

Strand two in its Marxist (whether neo or post) aspect de-idealises science and is concerned with explaining how a non-autonomous and non-ideal science gained funding, power and authority through its links to corporations and the state, whether the military or medical industrial complex, and posits dehumanising imperial and/or capitalist values as dominating science. The social constructionist view de-idealises science by explaining how science is done, from construction of scientific facts to organisation of resources for research (Latour and Woolgar 1979; Dasgupta and David 1987). Much social constructionist work focuses on laboratory life, and the values and practices that animate and characterise it, such as competition for discovery, status and resources; as of yet, Science and Technology Studies scholars have largely overlooked the institutional context of colleges and universities. However, some have developed actor–network theory, exploring the agency of individual actors and groups, who through various complex networks are engaged in the social construction of practice, reality and policy (Callon 1986; Law and Callon 1992; Mulcahy 1999). Just as scientific facts are de-idealised through the analysis of their social construction, so too with the changing policies and structures within which science is enacted they are de-idealised by analysing their social construction according to the interests and interpretations of particular actors. Related constructs such as the social world's approach (Clarke and Fujimura 1992) and boundary organisations (see the Autumn 2001 issue of *Science, Technology and Human Values*) also are human agency and social construction centred; they note the changing boundaries and network dimensions of organisations, but leave the values effects to the contingencies of micro-level interactions and negotiations, not to larger structures of power embedded in the political economy of higher education (Kleinman 1998).

The fourth or intellectual commons strand, like the first and third strands, is concerned with explaining why science is excellent. It argues that the intellectual commons and academic gift economy are at the core of excellent science, and predicts that if they are destroyed by corporate predation, science itself, as well as the public good, will be irreparably harmed. The intellectual commons is presented as a form of social organisation, but it is an undefined space in terms of organisations and law. It draws authority from its connection to the public good, but the public good has always been an amorphous concept in that it purports to include everyone, or at least the greatest good for the greatest number, and an unspecified public good is very difficult to defend in an era that celebrates individual rights.

Most of the values literature does not look directly at values formation; instead, it seems to assume socialisation through scientific apprenticeship (strands one, three and four), or to assume values are defined by external resource holders (Marxist, neo and post, strand three) or are narrowly limited to the laboratory and scientific organisations (social constructionists, strand three). Yet there is a sub-text in the values literature that suggests that the organisation of science, and its location in relation to markets and the state, is very important. The Mertonian/Bush strand insists on an autonomous science, separate from state (development) or markets (application). The various Marxisms suggest that science and scientific values are very strongly shaped by interactions with the imperial state and the defence economy. The social constructionists concentrate on the micro-political level, suggesting that the effect of social structures and organisational arrangements in science and technology are contingent on the local activities of various social groups and individual actors, specific to the particular value choices and decisions in question. The commons theorists suggest that invisible organisations, such as the commons and the gift economy, are key organisational parameters for excellent science.

We too think organisations and policy play an important powerful intermediary part in values formation. However, we think these organisations are often outside scientific departments and disciplinary associations. For example, we see universities and state agencies as organisations that have an influence on scientific values through their formation of intellectual property policies. They intermediate between scientists in their laboratories, associations, federal granting agencies and the world of use, property and market actors, shaping values and concepts of excellence by the way they shape incentives and opportunities, permit close relations between market, state and higher education, and create new venues for assessment and judgment that are outside the peer review system.

3. DATA AND METHOD

We analysed state system and institutional intellectual property policies to examine embedded and explicit values and to analyse organisational intermediation in the values realm in order to see if and how the United States is changing from a public good to an academic capitalist knowledge regime. We chose to concentrate on states even though patents, copyright and trademarks are the province of the federal government because the states have authority over education, which is sometimes delegated to state systems of higher education, sometimes to the institutions themselves. State systems and public institutions higher education are arms of the state and have the authority to specify the treatment of intellectual property within these systems or institutions (Chew 1992).

That state policies are fertile grounds for investigating knowledge regime shifts and the changes in values associated with such shifts is suggested by statistics on university intellectual property activity. Partly in response to the Bayh-Dole Act (1980) which allowed colleges and universities to own patents discovered by faculty working on federal research grants, state systems and/or universities and colleges initiated or began to develop and change their intellectual property policies. Prior to 1981, fewer than 250 patents were issued to universities per year. Between fiscal year 1991 and fiscal year 1999, annual college and university invention disclosures increased by 63% (to 12,324). New patents filed increased by 77% (to 5,545) and new licences and options executed increased by 129% (to 3,914) (Council on Government Relations 1999). In 1978, several universities began to take equity in companies licensing their technology; by 2000, 70% of a sample of 67 research universities had participated in at least one equity deal (Feldman et al. 2002).

As universities' intellectual property activity has grown, states have changed their policies. They have moved from minimal policies to more expansive ones, some of which have dramatically changed the way intellectual property is handled. For example, in the past five years (1997–2002), approximately half of the states have adjusted their conflict of interest laws so that universities (as represented by administrators) and faculty (as inventors and advisors) can hold equity positions in private corporations even when those corporations do business with universities (Schmidt 2002). This is a major shift in the pattern of state conflict of interest laws, breeching the historic firewall between the public and private sectors.

We examined California, Utah and Texas. Both California and Texas have state system policies which govern research universities. Utah does not have a state system, so we examined the University of Utah's intellectual property policies because that university is the 'flagship' research institution. We focused on research universities because they generate the greatest amount of intellectual property. We do not make the claim that these are representative states. We think it difficult to claim that any particular state can stand for a number of others. Rather than trying to select 'representative' states, we chose states for specific reasons. We selected California because it has a long history of patenting and, as a system, holds more patents and earns more income from patents than any other state system. The University of California System (UC System) had the second highest two-year average income in 1999 at $80,363,000. Utah and Texas were selected because they are aggressively pursuing intellectual property as part of their state economic development plans. The University of Utah ranked 20th in 1999 in terms of its three-year average, and the several University of Texas System institutions ranked 30th, 35th and 64th. These universities generated much less income than those in California. The highest of the Texas System universities brought in only about $4,000,000 for a two-year average, and the University of Utah brought in approximately $3,000,000 (Association of University Technology Managers 1999). The states we selected offered a contrast between established intellectual property systems and ambitious ones.

We did not study private research universities, but do so elsewhere (Slaughter and Rhoades forthcoming). In this chapter we wanted to focus on organisational intermediation among markets, state and higher education. We thought this could be more clearly seen in public (state) institutions. We are aware that private institutions have multiple connections to the several states and federal government, but they are not governed by state law, making their links to the state less direct than public institutions.

The questions we are particularly interested in answering are: What values are embedded or explicit in these policies? Have they changed over time? Have the organisations that frame the values changed? What is the direction of the change? What do these changes tell us about the relation between market, state and higher education, and how these are valued?

To operationalise and test the models, we developed the following categories for patent analysis: patent policies; royalty splits; policy coverage; exceptions; academic capitalism; managerial capacity; oversight; licensing; academic freedom. Patent analysis specifies the types of intellectual property covered by the policy. The inclusion of more and more types of intellectual property suggests movement from one knowledge regime to another. Royalty splits tell us about incentives for faculty and institutions to participate in generating intellectual property; change signals shifts in intellectual property regimes. Policy coverage – additions of new categories of university members – that becomes more inclusive does the same. Elimination of exceptions to institutional ownership of patents – for example, faculty being able to claim patents if discovered on their own time – is also indicative of a shift. Increases in academic capitalist activity, which refers to the policies needed to make universities market actors – for example, rules governing start-up companies – is another indication. If universities develop their capacity to engage in academic capitalism, this indicates the elimination of the separation between markets, state and higher education posited in the Mertonian/Bush model and preferred in the commons/public good model. Managerial capacity is a sub-category of academic capitalism, as is oversight. Managerial capacity refers to the degree to which faculty and administrators are permitted to be involved in running corporations in which they or the university have an interest. Managerial capacity sheds light on the degree to which universities and faculty are involved with market and state. Oversight allows us to look at how university and faculty relations with market and state are regulated. Licensing refers to non-exclusive versus exclusive licensing. Finally, the public good category refers to policies and statements within policies that give voice to or create rules that foster public good knowledge regimes, which include Mertonian norms.

We review changes in state system intellectual property policies and the policies of individual institutions. The period of change considered is variable, given that states introduced intellectual property policies and changes at different times. Due to considerations of chapter length, we look only at the first and last document in each set, and do not consider the alterations and deletions that came in between. When there are institutional intellectual property policies that are different from the state system's, we look at them. We compared additions and deletions across time, focusing on the substance of the changes in the categories mentioned above.

4. STATE AND INSTITUTIONAL INTELLECTUAL PROPERTY POLICIES

4.1. California

The intellectual property policies of the UC System comprised our data set. UC System policies covered all institutions in the system. These are the UC Berkeley, UC Davis, UC Irvine, UCLA, UC Riverside, UC San Diego, UC Santa Barbara, UC Santa Cruz and UC San Francisco.

The UC System first developed a patent policy in 1963. This was revised in 1973. We have not yet acquired copies of these early patent policies, but know from Mowery and Ziedonis (2002) that these early policies required faculty to assign their patents to the system, although the system was not committed to aggressive development of intellectual property. The heart of our analysis is a comparison of the 1985 patent policy and 1997 revisions to this document. The 1997 revision refers to the UC equity policy (1996), so we briefly review this, and consider as well the 2002 guidelines on accepting and managing equity. The 1997 revision also refers to the 1974 conflict of interest policy, which we briefly examine.

The public interest and Mertonian norms. In 1985, all mention of the public appeared in the first four paragraphs of the policy, which constituted the preamble. The policy nodded to Mertonian norms, stating that research was conducted "primarily for the purpose of gaining new knowledge", which gave rise to applied research and "fortuitous by-products". The purpose of the patent policy was to find an equitable way to administer intellectual property for the public benefit, which included further support of research and education, while providing incentives for faculty and staff to use the patent system for discovery and invention. The wording about the public good remained the same in the 1997 policy.

Types of intellectual property claimed by the system. The patent policy covered only patents, and did not address other forms of intellectual property. These were covered in separate policies, such as the 1992 copyright policy, the trademark policy and the software policy. The UC System did not move to a unified intellectual property policy that covered all types.

Who owns intellectual property? In 1985, all UC employees had to sign a mandatory form that assigned their patents and agreements to the university. Persons not directly employed by the university but who used research facilities or who received gifts, grants or contract funds also had to sign. Agreement to assign meant disclosure, in this case, to the Director of the Patent, Trademark and Copyright Office. In 1997, the office to which persons disclosed changed to the Office of Technology Transfer.

Ownership rights. UC employees had rights to patents only when the university chose not to file a patent. Even then, such rights were contingent on the absence of any overriding obligation to outside research sponsors. When a patent was released to a faculty member or other university employee, the university assumed no further research or development would occur that involved university support and facilities. The university also expected a 'shop right' for itself when patents were released to employees. These provisions remained in effect in the 1997 policy.

Royalty splits and use of patent income within the system. In 1985, inventors received "50% of net royalties and fees, less the 15% thereof for administrative costs, and less the costs of patenting, protecting and preserving patent rights, maintaining patents, the licensing of patent and related property rights, and such other costs, taxes, or reimbursements as may be necessary or required by law" (University of California 1985). In the 1997 policy, inventors received 35% of the net royalties and fees. An additional 15% was to be allocated for research-related purposes on the inventor's campus or laboratory. Again, net royalties were defined as gross royalties and fees, less the costs of patenting and protecting.

In 1985, the university agreed to "give first consideration" to "support of research" when disposing of its 50% of net income from patents. What type of research was unspecified. By 1997, inventors lost 15% of patent income, but the inventor's campus or laboratory gained 15% for research, perhaps making the change in patent income more popular. The 15% was discretionary research money for each campus. Such discretionary research funds were probably appreciated because the remaining 50% of patent income was directed toward technology transfer activities and improving "inventions not earning income" (University of California 1997a). Applied or entrepreneurial research trumped any other kind of research when it came to disposal of patent income.

In 1997, a new clause was inserted: inventor income represented an employee benefit. While this may have been an accounting solution, it pointed to the variability of income (salary and benefits) among employees. Great variation in salaries has developed nationally since the mid-1980s (American Association of University Professors 2002), and specifically within the UC System (Chronicle of Higher Education 2002). However, variation in benefits was through employee choice among a number of benefit packages. Classifying income from patents as a benefit raised the possibility of variation in benefits that mirrored variation in salaries.

In 1985 and 1997, litigation costs were covered before patent income was distributed to the inventor. Indeed, the university could withhold distribution and impound royalties until litigation, 'actual or imminent', was resolved. Given that the UC System engaged in more patent litigation than any other university system, patent protection could easily absorb a great deal of any single inventor's royalty income. For example, the UC System had engaged in approximately 20 years of litigation with Genentech and Eli Lily over the human insulin patent, and had gone to the Supreme Court to secure 11th amendment relief against infringement claims from business competitors (Baez and Slaughter 2001). The UC System would likely benefit despite litigation costs because it had a large number of patents that provided licensing and royalty income. However, individual inventors might realise no income on their patents after litigation costs were covered.

Academic capitalism. We take rules and regulation related to academic capitalism to specify system, institutional and individual engagement with the market, specifically, in profit taking. We are aware that all the systems and institutions we consider are non-profit. Thus, the rules and regulations express a conundrum. They prescribe how profit-taking activity shall occur in a formally non-profit organisation.

In 1985, the Intellectual Property Advisory Council was the committee that advised the President on patent management. This committee was chaired by the Senior Vice-President of Academic Affairs. The Senior Vice-President evaluated inventions and discoveries, negotiated patent and equity agreements as well as licences and license option agreements, and negotiated prospective rights with research sponsors and federal agencies. In 1997, these responsibilities were shifted to the Senior Vice-President for Business and Finance. The Committee that advised the Senior Vice-President changed as well: it was the Technology Transfer Advisory Committee. Although the Provost, Senior Vice-President of Academic Affairs and head of the Faculty Senate were members of the new committee, the movement of the committee from the academic side to the business side represented a boundary shift. Business concerns were given primacy over academic. Research took a back seat to commerce when intellectual property was involved.

The UC System patent policy was succinct and comprehensive in both 1985 and 1997. It covered most contingencies the system might face with regard to our analytic categories. Details with regard to the management of intellectual property, which have a direct bearing on academic capitalism, were not spelled out. However, the 1997 policy stated that equity would be handled in accordance with the 1996 Policy on Accepting Equity When Licensing University Technology. This policy was elaborated in 2002 in Bulletin G-44 (University of California 2002). Together, these documents addressed some of the ways in which system officials should conduct themselves as academic capitalists.

The UC equity policy began by making the case that applied science could best benefit the general public through an active technology licensing programme. The UC sought licensees who were able to pay the costs of patenting, able to pay for developing and protecting patents, and able to pay to ensure fulfilment of regulatory requirements. Generally, the companies best able to meet such requirements were likely to be large corporations. However, small or start-up companies often pioneered new technologies. To meet its financial concerns, the UC accepted equity in such companies under certain circumstances.

The UC System claimed it selected technology to license on the basis of: "principles of openness, objectivity and fairness in decision-making, and preeminence of the education, research, and public service missions of the University over financial or individual personal gain", as specified in the University Guidelines on University–Industry Relations, the Conflict of Interest Policy and the University Policy on Integrity in Research. While the policy firmly put education, research and public service at the forefront, and fulfilment of university missions over financial or individual gain, the various sets of related policies on which this dictum was based suggest that business principles were often more important than academic considerations, and that when universities engaged in academic capitalism conflicts of interest and threats to the integrity of research were rife.

The university did not hold positions on the boards of directors of companies in which it held equity, nor did it exercise voting rights. According to Bulletin G-44 (University of California 2002), which provided guidelines for accepting and managing equity, employees could neither hold positions on boards in which the university had equity, nor exercise voting rights. However, they could hold observer rights and participate on scientific boards of the licensee. Whether an employee-inventor could hold a management position in a corporation in which they held equity was not addressed.

Although the UC System took the position that employee-inventors could not vote, they were allowed observer rights at board meetings, and were not prohibited from offering advice. They also were able to participate on scientific boards that offered advice to the company. Given these privileges, the prohibition against voting may not prevent faculty from wielding extensive influence in companies, given their stature as inventors of the licensed technology.

University investigators were able to perform clinical trials in companies in which the university held equity, provided review committees assessed 'real or perceived' conflict of interest. The equity policy articulated this position even though university researchers' performance of clinical trials for companies in which the university held equity seemed to offer *prima facie* instances of perceived conflict of interest.

The university generally did not hold more than a ten per cent share of equity in a licensee. The university took all equity, including the inventor's share, in its name. Decisions about equity were made "upon sound business judgment and publicly available information" (University of California 1996). Equity shares were the same as in the patent policy. As always, exceptions to any policies could be made, subject to scrutiny by review committees, and given presidential approval.

Bulletin G-44 (University of California 2002), which provided guidelines for accepting and managing equity, straightforwardly said that the university would manage equity in a 'businesslike manner'. In this document, business principles and research principles at best coexisted uneasily and sometimes came into sharp conflict. When making decisions about converting stocks to cash and exercising options, the university would give "no consideration ... to unpublished University research programs related to the technology or to company information uniquely available ... through ... technology program activities" (University of California 2002). While this was portrayed as 'sound business practice' which dictated that the university should work through 'publicly available information', it meant that the university could be aware that a better technology was available or that the technology to be licensed had severe problems, yet would not acknowledge this information. Given that universities, by definition, harbour a great deal of unpublished knowledge, the decision to abide by public information cut the business arm of the university off from the scientific, allowing business to occur without science informing it. Similarly, the treasurer was directed to evaluate technologies in which the university might take an equity position "in terms of the financial return to the University, neither in terms of the status of nor the need for support of the subject invention" (University of California 2002). Following this guideline, the university might reject an equity position in a company that wanted to build or rent a high energy physics testing facility or in a company proposing an HIV vaccine. While such decisions might not involve monetary conflict of interest, they did clash with traditional conceptions of university research, in which prestige was maximised and science was finally justified in terms of its service to humanity.

Another business practice that impinged on research was 'pipelining'. This referred to granting a licensee a licence in a new technology that was related to the already licensed technology. The university took the position that inventions should be licensed to the company best able to develop them. It noted that this stance did not preclude a company from developing more than one invention if it was best suited to bring 'successor' inventions to fruition. However, other companies' bids should be fairly considered. Yet, frequently, researchers had to be involved with future as well as current technology. As a means of successfully developing licensed technology, companies often wrote in future research support of the faculty member who was named on the patent. Despite concerns about pipelining, if the company paid for the research, they were able to negotiate a licence to it.

This dilemma gave rise to a variety of conflict of interest policies, some at the state level, others at the system level, and still others at the federal level. The state conflict of interest statute (1974) held that if a principal investigator had a financial interest in equity that exceeded $2,000 the conflict of interest policy came into play. Any project supported by the National Science Foundation (NSF) or the Public Health Service (which included the National Institutes of Health – NIH) required disclosure of financial information; if the inventor's equity interest exceeded $10,000, federal conflict of interest policies came into play. However, these policies had rather large loopholes. For the state policy, if the inventor did not directly accept an equity interest, and instead the university treasurer held that interest for future conversion to cash, then the equity interest did not 'constitute a positive disclosure' and the inventor was not subject to the various review committees. Although the inventor did not have an immediate cash interest in the company, they had strong future stakes which might easily influence their assessments of research. The same held true with regard to federal conflict of interest policy. Further, the UC System interpreted the federal conflict of interest policy to mean that "royalty payments made in the form of cash by The Regents to the inventor also are not discloseable financial interested related to NSF or PHS-sponsored projects" (Appendix D, University of California 2002).

Involvement with the market caused greater and greater elaboration of rules and regulation. The equity policy (1996) noted that licensing had to be conducted within the framework of "the University Guidelines on University–Industry Relations (1989), the Conflict of Interest Policy (1974), the University Policy on Integrity in Research (1990) and related University policies and guidelines". Each of these policies spawned their own series of memoranda and guidelines. For example, the equity policy (1996) gave rise to Memoranda G-44 in 2002, which provided 45 pages of guidelines for accepting and managing equity. This document provided two forms which inventors had to fill out and sign: a checklist and a model agreement. The management of intellectual property contributed to contractualisation and bureaucratisation, creating employment for managerial professionals, such as lawyers and administrators, whose increasing presence made faculty managed professionals (Rhoades c1998).

4.2. Texas

For the state of Texas, we examined intellectual property policies of the University of Texas System (UT System) which framed policy for its component institutions. Component institutions of the UT System include: UT Dallas, UT Tyler, UT Arlington, UT Southwestern Medical Center, UT Health Center-Tyler, UT El Paso, UT Permian Basin, UT Health Science Center-Houston, UT Austin, UT M.D. Anderson, UT San Antonio, UT Medical Branch, UT Health Science Center-San Antonio, UT Pan American and UT Brownsville. We also looked at the University of Texas at Austin (UT Austin), one of the component institutions, and arguably the most well known.

There are no readily available documents for the UT System prior to 1985. In 1985, the entire intellectual property policy was re-written, perhaps in response to the opportunities created by Bayh-Dole (1980), certainly in response to state laws requiring disclosure. In the years between 1985 and 2002, the system intellectual property rules were modified at least fifteen times, with a substantial re-write in 1992, and important changes in 2001. We compared the system policies at two points in time: 1985 and 2002 (University of Texas System 1985, 1987, 1992, 2002).

The public interest. The 1985 Regents' Rules and Regulations took the position that system exploitation of intellectual property was not a primary organisational purpose, but nonetheless necessary to ensure the public good. To that end, the Board of Regents promoted non-exclusive licensing, which made intellectual property developed within the system available to many companies simultaneously. Such a policy allowed more companies to access the intellectual property, but diminished the value of the property for any one company because another company could develop and market a competitive product, very likely lowering the profits of both (or more) companies. However, if product or process development had occurred on the part of more than one company, the public might well have benefited from lower pricing resulting from competition. The board apparently understood the difficulties created by non-exclusive licensing and made the case that the public interest could sometimes best be served by a "limited exclusive license or even an exclusive license for the period of the patent". By 2002, the board had changed to exclusive licensing.

Academic freedom and/or norms of science. Although universities historically have asserted some rights in patents, in American postsecondary education there were not specific policies governing the process of how discoveries reached the wider world. Traditionally, faculty published to assert primacy in new discoveries, sharing their knowledge with the academic community and the public. In 1985, the Texas Board of Regents conformed to that norm. They stressed that faculty should have "a major role in the ultimate determination of how it [potential intellectual property] is to be made public – by publication, by development and commercialization after securing available protection for the creation, or both" (University of Texas System 1985). Although the policy indicated that faculty could both publish and commercialise, that was an option only if faculty commercialised first. If faculty published first, they in effect could not commercialise because in the

US system knowledge became part of the public domain and as such lost novelty and therefore could not be patented. Giving faculty the option to publish first could potentially deprive the UT System of patents, and perhaps subsequent revenues from royalties.

By 2002, the system policy with regard to faculty determination of how a discovery should be made public had changed. The phrase "to permit the creator of intellectual property maximum freedom in respect to their creations" was dropped, as was the idea that faculty could 'both' publish and commercialise. Instead, the policy read: "Any person who as a result of his or her activities creates intellectual property ... should have a major role in the ultimate determination of how it is to be published; however, the component president will decide in his or her sole discretion whether to develop and commercialize an invention after securing available protection for the creation, if necessary" (University of Texas System 1985). In other words, creators of intellectual property still had a voice, but they could make decisions only after the president of their institution had decided whether they wanted to commercialise whatever the faculty had disclosed.

Types of intellectual property claimed by the system. In 1985, the Regents' Rules and Regulations focused specifically on patents. By 1987, patents were broadened to include "intellectual property of all types ... any invention, discovery, trade secret, technology, scientific or technological development, or computer software ... whether under patent, trademark or copyright law" (University of Texas System 1987). Although it made claims that included copyright, the board was clear that it would not "assert an interest in faculty produced textbooks, scholarly writing, art works, musical compositions and dramatic non-dramatic literary work".

In 2002, the Rules and Regulations read that "The Board shall assert its interest in scholarly or educational materials, art works, musical compositions and dramatic and non-dramatic literary works related to the author's academic or professional field, regardless of the medium of expression" (University of Texas System 2002). The board also expanded the categories with the term 'educational materials', which could be interpreted to refer to courseware, whether used at the institutional or system level, or over the Internet. Two sub-sections attenuated the board's sweeping claims. The first said these did not apply to "students, professionals, faculty, and nonfaculty researchers". However, these authors were urged to manage their copyright carefully because the board retained certain rights to those works: a 'shop right' to faculty scholarship. The second sub-section said the board "normally shall assert ownership in software as an invention", but that software which was closely linked to the content of creative work was not covered by the intellectual property policy. However, as with scholarly and creative work, the board retained rights that were enumerated in the new copyright policy. Generally, these rights were to royalty-free use of faculty works.

In 2002, the board also specified data as subject to system ownership. If an employee's research activities created data, they were owned by the board. In the instance of data, the board allowed employees a non-exclusive licence for use, so long as it was for non-profit educational, research or scholarly activities. Presumably, the board would assert its interest if a faculty member or employee attempted to market data.

Overall, the Regents moved from system claims to patents to assert ownership in all types of intellectual property. The board allowed faculty to continue to hold copyright to scholarly and creative work; indeed, the board expected faculty to copyright rather than cede intellectual property to journal and book publishers so that these scholarly materials would be freely available to the system. The copyright policy had a perverse logic, which made faculty academic capitalists by requiring commodification; even the system planned to use the materials without paying royalties to faculty.

Who owns intellectual property? In 1985, the Regents asserted that the intellectual property policy applied to "all persons employed by the component institutions of the system, to anyone using System facilities under the supervision of System personnel, and to postdoctoral and predoctoral fellows" (University of Texas System 1985). By 2002, "candidates for masters and doctoral degrees" as well as "part-time faculty and staff and visiting faculty members and researchers ... [and] ... undergraduates" were added. At first glance, 'all persons', seems encompassing. But, given the nature of the educational process, where work may be less than full time and faculty, such as visiting professors, may have allegiances elsewhere, the aim to control intellectual property emanating from the system required greater and greater degrees of specificity. Students are an especially interesting group because the component universities may not employ them, yet the system has decided to treat them like 'all employees', regardless of whether they receive wages or salaries.

Ownership rights. The bases of intellectual property ownership in the UT System were clear from the beginning. Individual employees owned intellectual property only if it were unrelated to their employment; if it were created on the individual's own time; and if it were created without support from the system. All other work had to be submitted to the Institutional Patent Committee, which determined whether the system would pursue a patent. By 2002, the creator of intellectual property was obliged to disclose to the president of their institution rather than to a patent committee. Institutions could then send disclosures to patent or other committees, but this was no longer necessary. When institutional patent committees were used, they had to conform to system guidelines. When intellectual property resulted from a grant or contract with the federal government or other external entity, whether non-profit or for-profit, the provisions of the contract stipulated to whom the intellectual property belonged. The system policy made no distinction between work for hire and traditional faculty work.

Royalty splits and use of patent income within the system. From 1985 until 2002, the royalty split in the UT System remained the same: 50% to the creator, 50% to the system. However, the component institutions had some discretion with regard to this split: they could adjust the creator's royalties or other income so that the creator received anywhere between 25–50%. Presumably the component institutions kept the difference for themselves. However, the discretionary clause gave them a fair amount of leeway in establishing incentives for faculty to patents. The discretionary clause also meant that there was not necessarily a uniform royalty split, so that each faculty member who patented had to become an academic capitalist, negotiating individually with the institution.

Use of income from intellectual property. In 1985, the system's first priority for its share of income from intellectual property was to defray the expenses of the System Intellectual Property Office. It drew down 100% of the income from licences and royalties until these costs were met. Then the system kept 50% of the income, and disbursed the remainder to those institutions where the creation originated. After distributing funds according to the (negotiable) royalty split, the component institution could create an endowment fund to be used as it wished so long as the board approved the purposes. In 2002, the rules about use of the income from intellectual property remained essentially the same. However, the policy was elaborated to cover ever more eventualities, for example, system allocation of royalties where one or more persons were entitled to share, but were unable to agree on the appropriate division.

Academic capitalism. The 1985 Regents' Rules and Regulations refer to, but do not specify, an Office of Asset Management, which presumably was involved in managing and marketing the system's intellectual property. The Office of Asset Management was to work with the Office of the General Counsel, creating model agreements between the system and various external entities. The model agreement noted that any contracts into which the system entered had to abide by the state conflict of interest laws.

By 2002, the system incorporated into its intellectual property policy sections on equity interests and business participation. The system was empowered to negotiate equity interests on behalf of employees. The system and employees of the system were allowed to receive equity in business interests as partial or total compensation for rights conveyed. Dividend income from equity interests was to be divided in the same way as royalties. Employees who were creators of property were not allowed to serve as members of the board of directors or as officers or employees of the business entity developing the property. However, employees were able to serve as consultants to such organisations. If the president of one of the component institutions thought that the benefits of a particular business agreement outweighed the disadvantages, they were allowed to make arrangements outside the system intellectual property policy, provided they secured Regental approval.

In 2002, the equity interest section of the policy allowed the system to receive monies from a company in which its employees held equity in return for creating the business entity. The system did not have to share these funds with faculty or other employees. If faculty held an equity interest in a business entity that had an agreement with the system, they had to abide by the conflict of interest management plan developed by their institution. If appropriate committees and institutional managers determined that the employee had a conflict, the employee might have to divest him/herself of the interest. No provisions were made for oversight of system or institutional management of equity interests.

Perhaps the most striking change in the 2002 policy was with regard to business participation. Prior to 1992, employees were not able to serve as members of the board or as officers of entities in which they held equity; in 2002, faculty were allowed to serve if they followed their institution's conflict of interest management plan. This change was made possible because the state changed its conflict of interest policy, partially due to heavy lobbying by Texas A&M University (Schmidt 2002).

The equity interest and business participation sections of system intellectual property policies allowed the system, component institutions and faculty as well as other employees to be market actors. The system was able to create corporations based on employee inventions and receive funds for doing so. The system was also able to negotiate and hold equity in companies created by external interests. The presidents of component institutions were able to disregard the system intellectual property rules if they could make a case that would win Regental approval, making presidents potential market actors above and beyond their role as specified by the policy. Faculty and other employees moved from not being able to serve on boards or act as officers of corporations in which they and the system had an equity interest to being able to hold such positions.

4.2.1. Institutional Conflict of Interest Management Plan at the University of Texas at Austin

In the 2002 intellectual property policy, the UT System gave its component institutions responsibility for overseeing conflict of interest when faculty served as board members or acted as officers of corporations in which they and the system had an equity interest. In assigning institutions responsibility for conflict of interest, the state intersected federal policy, making use of the Public Health Service and National Science Foundation requirements that institutions have conflict of interest plans. Although the UT Austin had no specific intellectual property policies, and was guided by the system rules and regulations, it did have a conflict of interest management plan because without one, it could not receive NIH or NSF research funding.

The UT Austin plan was developed to ensure sponsored research, whether done in cooperation with the federal government, a consortium or a private entity, would be conducted so "that there is no reasonable expectation that the design, conduct, and reporting of the research will be biased by any Significant Financial Interest" (University of Texas at Austin 2002). The onus for reporting was on the principal investigator, who was required to submit a financial disclosure statement that listed 'anything of monetary value' including salary, consulting fees, honoraria, equity interests and intellectual property rights, but only if they exceeded $10,000. Although the system intellectual property policy applied to all employees, the institutional conflict of interest management plan was directed toward faculty, researchers, graduate students and postdoctoral fellows, who presumably were the most likely to be principal investigators on research projects that yielded patentable discoveries.

The oversight committee for the conflict of interest management plan had a heavy representation of administrators. Following principal investigator disclosure of financial interest, the committee was able to monitor and modify research plans, request divestiture of financial interests, or "severance of relations that create actual or potential conflicts" (University of Texas at Austin 2002). Should principal investigators fail to comply with the plan, the oversight committee could advise the

Vice-President of Research on punishments ranging from a formal reprimand to termination.

The state and system created substantially more opportunities for conflict of interest to arise by changing policies so that faculty and system officials could serve as members of boards or directors of companies in which they held an equity interest based on patent rights. The system assigned management of such conflicts to the institutions. Ironically, the institutions had conflict of interest management plans in place because federal agencies had been concerned with maintaining researcher objectivity in the face of financial temptations. Researchers were the point at which policing took place. There were no provisions for monitoring system interests in and perhaps pressure on faculty.

4.3. Utah

In Utah, we reviewed the intellectual property policies of the University of Utah. Utah does not have a system policy; each university has its own policy. We analysed the first University of Utah policy, 1970, and the most recent, 1999.

Patent policies and coverage. In 1970, the patent policy covered 'all inventions, improvements and discoveries' owned by a faculty member or any person associated with the university if the discovery arose from employment or used the university's time, facilities, equipment or materials. In 1999, part-time faculty and staff as well as student employees were included. In 1970, all copyrightable material, other than videotapes, was 'reserved to the author', even though the author was a university employee. The university had limited rights to work that was available without charge or to work produced specifically for the university. In 2001, the university issued a separate copyright policy. All types of copyrightable work, including those arising from currently unforeseeable technologies, were claimed by the university on the grounds they were work for hire. Some rights were then granted back to employee authors.

Royalty splits. The royalty split remained the same throughout the various iterations of the policy. The inventor(s) received 40% of the first $20,000 in revenue, 35% of the next $20,000 and 30% of any additional revenue, after the university was reimbursed for developmental, marketing and related expenses. In 1999, the University of Utah Research Foundation could spend an unlimited amount of funds on development of intellectual property. The university 'permitted' inventors to pay for patenting and licensing, and, if they did so, the royalty or revenue shares were divided, 65% to the inventor and 35% to the university. Moreover, the inventor could be reimbursed for patent expenses.

In 1970, after costs were covered and royalties disbursed according to the patent agreement, revenue was used "to pay the inventor's royalties, and thereafter for technological and scientific research and development, and for other university purposes" (University of Utah 1970). In 1999, the University of Utah Research Foundation allocated any surplus funds from patent development to furthering the research and education programmes of the university.

Exceptions. From 1970 onward, the university was clear that it did not claim any invention made by employees in the course of private consulting services. In 1999, the policy stated that it was assumed university time, resources and facilities were used unless employees could prove otherwise. In 1999, the document noted that, when a faculty actively cooperated in the commercialisation process, deductions for development were decreased and royalties were increased, but the document was not clear whether a specific share of these increased royalties were designated for cooperative faculty members.

Academic capitalism. The area that changed the most over the years was academic capitalism. In 1970, the policy merely stated that the director of patent and product development handled all matters concerning intellectual property. A patent advisory committee advised the president and the director. By 1999, the University of Utah Research Foundation was "the instrument of the university that commercialised inventions". The Research Foundation purchased the services of the Director of the University Patent and Product Development Offices to prosecute patents, explore commercialisation and negotiate agreements. The director was located in the Technology Transfer Office. This office, not the Patent Review Committee, evaluated disclosures for patenting and commercialisation. The Patent Review Committee became an oversight committee rather than a decision-making committee. By 1999, the oversight function of this committee was underlined by a name change: it became the Technology Transfer Advisory Committee. The committee, upon request, advised the administration on disputes involving intellectual property.

The 1999 policy referred to two other documents: Remunerative Consultation and Other Employment Activities, and Faculty Profit-making Corporations. On the one hand, the consulting document stressed that faculty were full-time employees, and stipulated the days per month (two) they could work elsewhere, the need to abide by conflict of interest requirements, and the need to relieve the university of any liability. On the other hand, the document that dealt with Faculty Profit-making Corporations allowed university faculty and/or administrators to participate in corporations in which they held "substantial stock interest" as "consultants, employees, members of the board of directors or as chairman [sic] of the board of directors" if the full and proper conduct of their university assignments was not impaired and conflict of interest was avoided. How these responsibilities sat with two days a month for consulting was not directly addressed. However, a clause near the end of the document suggested that faculty involved in corporate R&D for firms in which they held an interest was done on "a time and material contract basis through the engineering experiment station. All work shall be on a full overhead basis and shall be subject to approval by the department head".

The document on University Faculty Profit-making Corporations opened with a general statement that endorsed energetic academic capitalism. University faculty members are increasingly becoming involved in profit-making corporations in which they hold substantial stock interest and in which they are active participants. These corporations may have a substantial beneficial influence on the economic growth of the state; and the associations derived by the faculty member from participation in the corporations may, in most cases, have a beneficial influence on their teaching and research capabilities. Consequently, it would not be in the university's interest to preclude this type of association.

The document required that inventions jointly produced by the university and a corporation in which a faculty member was financially involved become the exclusive property of the university, although the corporation could have a non-exclusive licence. The policy cautioned that faculty invention did not ensure university licensing to a corporation in which the faculty was an active member. If a faculty member's invention were given to a 'competing firm', under open bidding, the faculty member was obliged to give "full, unrestrained disclosure and assistance to the licensee firm". So, too, with regard to purchasing, open bid was the format, with care given to not making preferential purchases from a corporation in which a faculty member held an interest. But if the faculty-owned company won the open bid, the university could do business with the firm in which they had an interest.

Public good research model. The 1970 University of Utah policy saw its obligation to the public as administering inventions "in the best interests of the local and national public", unless federal or industrial contracts obligated them otherwise. From 1984 onward, the public interest was mentioned in the opening paragraph on general policy, making the case that, as a public institution, Utah had to "facilitate application of scientific and technical research for public use", as well as provide equitably for those involved in the invention process. The patent documents make no other mention of the public, nor do they invoke Mertonian norms. The policies do not use any of the rhetoric surrounding basic research, or even entrepreneurial science. The underlying model of science is applied.

5. DISCUSSION

Generally, the system patent policies in California and Texas and the institutional policy of the University of Utah do not sit well with Mertonian values: communalism, the free flow of knowledge, disinterestedness and organised scepticism. Rather than being shared, intellectual property is owned. The patent policies indicate that ownership precludes communalism (or the intellectual commons) in several ways. The object of patent policies is to contain or enclose knowledge, render it alienable. The patent policies detail the process of enclosure: obligatory disclosure, administrative review, advisory committee review, executive decision making. Once knowledge is enclosed or owned, it has to be managed, elaborating the enclosure process, and creating policies that deal with royalties, licensing, equity and conflict of interest, all of which more tightly fence in information. Rather than an intellectual commons, to which all members of the academic community have rights, intellectual property policies transform the academic community into a mine, in which faculty tunnel, with the help of a small crew, to unearth knowledge from veins or seams with commercial properties, which they present to technology licensing officials for evaluation.

Knowledge flows less freely when patent policies are in place. Obligatory disclosure means that administrative authorities are able to direct faculty to patent rather than publish, which keeps knowledge out of circulation for the period in which the patent is being proved, anywhere from three months to a year. In an era of telecommunications, electronic journals and pre-publications, this interruption of knowledge flow can slow discovery. As the patent process details, when knowledge is owned and commodified, it becomes valuable, and is no longer traded in a gift economy. Data sets are ownable, as are research tools, and faculty are charged for their use. As public–private partnerships built around exploitation of intellectual property owned by universities increase, knowledge about them decreases. A number of states have passed laws that make contracts that deal with intellectual property exempt from freedom of information requests (Schmidt 2002). (As a test of the degree to which restriction occurs, request copies of your university's contracts with corporations.)

Disinterestedness stresses that scientists should not have a stake in the outcome of their research. The intellectual property policies create an interest for scientists in outcomes by attaching monetary incentives to discovery. The policies give faculty large rewards, up to 50 per cent of royalty or licensing income, should an invention prove profitable. It is possible to argue that these incentives do not motivate faculty because so few discoveries result in profits. However, the steep curve of disclosures, patents, licences and equity agreements from 1980 to 2002 suggests otherwise. The proliferation of conflict of interest language and rules in all three policies is another indication of the death of disinterestedness.

Organised scepticism calls for scientists to question results and look for alternative approaches and answers. The intellectual property policies implicitly set up a system that rewards the opposite. If faculty and universities are rewarded through royalties derived from the licensing of products or processes, then faculty and administrators have no incentives to question the science on which the products or processes are built, nor any incentives to look for alternatives because alternatives, if better or more cleverly marketed, would pose a threat to their revenue stream. The presence of concern about 'pipelining', the licensing of technologies related to those already patented, in the UC System policies points to the possibility of faculty and institutional commitment to specific product and process lines, which makes faculty research or university sponsorship of alternatives unlikely.

We have documented and described the shift from a public good knowledge regime, associated with Mertonian values and the Vannevar Bush model of science, to an academic capitalist knowledge regime, associated with basic science for use and basic technology, concepts which their framers argue allow academic and commercial values to coexist, even if uneasily. But description is not explanation. What caused the values to shift? In this chapter, we are not concerned with underlying causes, such as the shift from a defence to a knowledge economy, but with proximal causes, namely organisation.

The sub-text of the Mertonian/Bush model was that organisational separation of universities from the state and the market was necessary for the values it espoused to prevail. Academic knowledge was valuable to society precisely because it offered disinterested expertise, removed from politics and economics. The Vannevar Bush model stressed separation of university science from state and economy: basic science done in the university preceded development, which occurred in federal laboratories, or application, accomplished by industry. Certainly these conceptions of the organisation of science were self-interested in that they called for a system that gave scientists unprecedented autonomy, state subsidy with no strings. While the system was at best relatively autonomous, it nonetheless reinforced a status and prestige system for science that was independent of the state and commerce. Status depended on discovery and reputation within an elaborated system of non-profit associations: scientific associations of disciplines, umbrella associations (such as the American Association for the Advancement of Science) and universities. These organised the work of science – peer review and journal publication – which was not tightly tied to remuneration. Science depended upon the federal government for funding, but a significant portion of that funding was awarded through peer review, which distanced science from the state. Science was involved in commercial activity, but application was not at the core of the status and prestige system, in large part because scientists had access to federal funds.

An academic capitalist knowledge regime to some degree reorganised science, changing the configuration of relations between university, state and market, the process of which changed values. Able to hold title and profit from inventions made by faculty working on federal grants, universities became market actors. As market actors, they moved to control or enclose faculty discovery through intellectual property policy, which, as some institutions began to generate substantial revenue streams, called for more extensive management of that property and more sustained involvement in the market by universities and faculty members. The universities are the state arm that dramatically shifted federal resources from the Merton/Bush model to an entrepreneurial model. Public universities' patent programmes dismantled the firewall between the state and the market, making less possible the autonomous science envisioned by the Merton/Bush model.

Although the various intellectual property policies make (uneven and sporadic) attempts to separate business from research, the two are embroiled because successful development of technology often depends on the continued involvement of university inventors or experts. Without them, technology development often flounders or fails. More and more universities officially encourage inventors to work closely with licensing professionals or potential licensees to better promote commercialisation. Although conflict of interest sections of the policies attempt to separate the university and faculty from too close an engagement in the market, a successful patent programme demands faculty and institutional market involvement. Indeed, the various patent policies provide powerful financial incentives for faculty to remain involved.

The status and prestige system that sustained the Merton/Bush model depended to some degree on the (relative) organisational autonomy of universities and science. From the end of World War II until roughly 1980, universities' engagement with the economy was primarily through the Department of Defense (DOD), and was structured through a division of research labour, initiated in part by the Vannevar Bush model, in which universities performed basic research, the federal laboratories were involved in development, and corporations focused on applied research. As part of the Keynesian welfare state, the DOD funded research generously, offering university scientists long-term grants for projects that did not have immediate payoff, and that, even though classified, were not closely supervised in day-to-day terms. Despite violation of Mertonian norms of secrecy and lack of national purpose, the DOD promoted a sense of (relative) autonomy among scientists. This system of organisation (implicitly endorsed by the intellectual commons model, sans the DOD connection), with its degrees of separation from state and economy, sustained (some) Mertonian values. The NSF was implicitly seen as the linchpin of this system, different from the mission agencies in that it sponsored basic science, able to support open, free, disinterested research. These organisational structures – an elaborate grant and contract system that functioned through peer review and at least one federal agency not directly committed to a specific (state) mission with economic implications – in a sense made Mertonian values possible.

As universities became more involved with the economy, the organisational structure surrounding research changed. Universities were major actors in the process, responding to the opportunity structure created by Bayh-Dole and an array of federal legislation supported by a bi-partisan competitiveness coalition in the US Congress that began in the 1980s, the end of the Cold War, and the rise of a global economy (Slaughter and Rhoades 1996; Slaughter and Leslie 1997). The NSF, in response to the competitiveness coalition, began to support university–industry partnerships, initially in engineering (Feller, Ailes and Roessner 2002). The NSF moved further away from funding basic research when it took on the job of organising the Internet for privatisation (Slaughter and Rhoades forthcoming). Periodic and severe fiscal crises in the several states encouraged state legislators to work with university administrators to pass laws that made disclosure obligatory and public–private partnerships possible (Eisinger 1988; Isserman 1994; Chew 1992). As we have seen in our review of university intellectual property policies, these policies began to reorganise research by dismantling the firewall that had separated the state (universities) from the economy. The process of patenting and copyrighting enclosed knowledge, commodified it as property to be licensed to corporations in return for royalties, making universities market actors. The royalty splits provided powerful economic incentives for institutions and faculty. With anywhere from one-third to one-half of the royalty stream as their reward for patenting, entrepreneurial faculty became part of a compensation system that was more like that of CEOs paid 300 times that of their workers than like faculty on merit or market-based salaries, governed by the norms of their disciplines. Simultaneously, and ironically, the patent policies also made faculty more like all other workers, in that the institution, intent on generating revenue streams, over the period considered, came to claim virtually all intellectual property from all members of the university community, making faculty, staff and students less like university professionals and more like corporate professionals whose discoveries are considered work-for-hire, the property of the corporation, not the professional. The patent policies also evidence the creation of organisational capacity to engage the market: the development of technology transfer offices that handle licensing, the creation of equity procedures and agreements that allow universities to act as venture capitalists and faculty as state-subsidised entrepreneurs, and conflict of interest policies to regulate the increasingly porous boundary between state and market. In sum, the patent policies restructure the organisation of research so it is closer to a commercial system.

Currently, the Mertonian/Bush and academic capitalist knowledge regimes coexist and sometimes overlap. However, the values of both systems depend in part on the organisational structures which sustain the cultures of research. The academic status and prestige system is still concerned with discovery, fundamental (broad) scientific questions, pushing back the frontiers of knowledge, and recognition as reward. However, we think that system can be sustained only if there continues to be an organisational infrastructure that supports it: a degree of separation from a (relatively autonomous) state and a degree of separation from the market. The academic capitalist knowledge system is setting up an alternative system of rewards, one in which discovery is valued because of its commercial properties and economic rewards, broad scientific questions are framed so that they are relevant to commercial possibilities (biotechnology, telecommunications, computer grids), knowledge is regarded as a commodity rather than a free good, and universities have the organisation capacity (and are permitted by law) to license and invest and profit from these commodities.

Thus far, the academic capitalist knowledge regime has developed around science and engineering, which lends itself to patenting, and touches a relatively small number of research university faculty. However, the passage of the Digital Millennium Copyright Act, and the rapid development of university copyright policies in the 1990s, suggest that the academic capitalist knowledge regime may touch the lives of all faculty. Copyright policies cover software, courseware, making what is taught a commercial property.

REFERENCES

American Association of University Professors. *The Annual Report on the Economic Status of the Profession 2001–02.* 2002, http://www.aaup.org/surveys/02z/z02rep.htm.

Association of University Technology Managers. *FY 2000 Annual AUTM Licensing Survey.* 1999, http://www.autm.net/surveys/99/survey99A.pdf.

Baez, B. and S. Slaughter. "Academic Freedom and Federal Courts in the 1990s: The Legitimation of the Conservative Entrepreneurial State." In Smart, J. and W. Tierney (eds). *Handbook of Theory and Research in Higher Education.* Bronx, NY: Agathon Press, 2001, 73–118.

Bollier, D. *Silent Theft: The Private Plunder of Our Common Wealth.* New York: Routledge, 2002.

Branscomb, L. "From Technology Politics to Technology Policy." *Issues in Science and Technology* 13 Spring (1997): 41–48.

Branscomb, L., R. Florida, D. Hart, J. Keller and D. Boville. *Investing in Innovation, Toward a Consensus Strategy for Federal Technology Policy.* Cambridge: Center for Science and International Affairs, Harvard University, 1997.

Bush, V. *Science–The Endless Frontier: A Report to the President on a Program for Postwar Scientific Research.* Washington, DC: National Science Foundation, 1990 (1945).

Callon, M. "The Sociology of an Actor–network: The Case of the Electric Vehicle." In Callon, Michael, John Law and Arie Rip (eds). *Mapping the Dynamics of Science and Technology.* Basingstoke, UK: Macmillan, 1986, 19–34.

Chew, P.K. "Faculty-generated Invention: Who Owns the Golden Egg?" *Wisconsin Law Review* 259 (1992).

Chronicle of Higher Education. *The Chronicle Almanac 2002–03: California.* 30 August 2002.

Clarke, A.E. and J.H. Fujimura (eds). *The Right Tools for the Job: At Work in Twentieth Century Life Sciences.* Princeton, NJ: Princeton University Press, 1992.

Council on Competitiveness. *Endless Frontier, Limited Resources: U.S. R&D Policy for Competitiveness.* Washington, DC: Council on Competitiveness, 1996.

Council on Governmental Relations. *A Tutorial on Technology Transfer in US Colleges and Universities.* 1999, http://www.cogr.edu/techtransfertutorial.htm.

Dasgupta, P. and P. David. "Information Disclosure and the Economics of Science and Technology." In Feiwel, G. (ed.). *Arrow and the Ascent of Modern Economic Theory.* New York: New York University Press, 1987, 519–542.

Eisinger, P.K. *The Rise of the Entrepreneurial State: State and Local Economic Development Policy in the United States.* Madison: University of Wisconsin Press, 1988.

Etzkowitz, H., A. Webster and P. Healey. *Capitalizing Knowledge: New Interactions of Industry and Academia.* Albany: State University of New York Press, 1998.

Feldman, M., I. Feller, J. Bercovitz and R. Burton. "Equity and the Technology Transfer Strategies of American Research Universities." *Management Science* 48.1 (2002): 105–121.

Feller, I., C.P. Ailes and J.D. Roessner. "Impacts of Research Universities on Technological Innovation in Industry: Evidence From Engineering Research Centers." *Research Policy* 31.3 (2002): 457–475.

Foreman, P. "Behind Quantum Electronics: National Security as a Basis for Physical Research in the United States, 1940–1960 (Part 1)." *Historical Studies in the Physical and Biological Sciences* 18 (1987): 149–229.

Heller, M.A. and R.S. Eisenberg. "Can Patents Deter Innovation? The Anticommons in Biomedical Research." *Science* 5364 (1998): 698–701.

Isserman, A.M. "State Economic Development Policy and Practice in the United States: A Survey Article." *International Regional Science Review* 16.1/2 (1994): 49–100.

Kleinman, D.L. "Untangling Context: Understanding a University Laboratory in the Commercial World." *Science, Technology and Human Values* 23.3 (1998): 285–314.

Latour, B. and S. Woolgar. *Laboratory Life: The Social Construction of Scientific Facts.* Beverly Hills: Sage, 1979.

Law, J. and M. Callon. "The Life and Death of an Aircraft: A Network Analysis of Technological Change." In Bijker, Wiebe and John Law (eds). *Shaping Technology, Building Society.* Cambridge, Mass: MIT Press, 1992, 21–52.

Leslie, S. *The Cold War and American Science: The Military–Industrial–Academic Complex at MIT and Stanford.* New York: Columbia, 1993.

Merton, R.K. *The Sociology of Science: Theoretical and Empirical Investigations.* Chicago: University of Chicago Press, 1973 (1942).

Mowery, D.C. and A.A. Ziedonis. "Academic Patent Quality and Quantity Before and After the Bayh-Dole Act in the United States." *Research Policy* 31 (2002): 399–418.

Mulcahy, D. "(Actor-net) Working Bodies and Representations: Tales From a Training Field." *Science, Technology and Human Values* 24.1 (1999): 80–104.

Noble, D.F. *America by Design: Science, Technology and the Rise of Corporate Capitalism.* New York: Knopf, 1976.

Rhoades, G. *Managed Professionals: Unionized Faculty and Restructuring Academic Labor.* Albany: State University of New York Press, c1998.

Schmidt, P. "States Push Public Universities to Commercialize Research." *Chronicle of Higher Education.* 29 March 2002, A26–27.

Science, Technology and Human Values. Special Issue on Boundary Organizations in Environmental Policy and Science. 26.4 (2001).

Slaughter, S. and L. Leslie. *Academic Capitalism: Politics, Policies and the Entrepreneurial University.* Baltimore: Johns Hopkins University Press, 1997.

Slaughter, S. and G. Rhoades. "The Emergence of a Competitiveness Research and Development Policy Coalition and the Commercialization of Academic Science and Technology." *Science, Technology and Human Values* 21.3 (1996): 303–339.

Slaughter, S. and G. Rhoades. *More Academic Capitalism: Markets, State and Higher Education.* Baltimore, MA: Johns Hopkins University Press, forthcoming.

Soley, L. *Leasing the Ivory Tower: The Corporate Takeover of Academia.* Boston: South End Press, 1995.

State of California. *The State of California Political Reform Act of 1974.* 1974.

Stokes, D. *Pasteur's Quadrant: Basic Science and Technological Innovation.* Washington, DC: Brookings Institution Press, 1997.

University of California. *University of California Patent Policy.* 1985, http://www.ucop.edu/ott/patentpolicy/patentp1.html.

University of California. *University Guidelines on University–Industry Relations.* 1989, http://www.ucop.edu/raohome/cgmemos/89-20.html.

University of California. *Revision of the University of California Patent Policy.* 1990a.

University of California. *University Policy on Integrity in Research.* 1990b, http://www.ucop.edu/raohome/cgmemos/90-01S1.html.

University of California. *University of California Policy on Copyright Ownership.* 1992, http://www.ucop.edu/ucophome/uwnews/copyr.html.

University of California. *Policy on Accepting Equity When Licensing University Technology.* 1996, http://www.ucop.edu/ott/equi-pol.html.

University of California. *University of California Patent Policy.* 1997a, http://www.ucop.edu/ott/patentpolicy/patentpo.html#pol.

University of California. *Summary of Changes to the Patent Policy.* 1997b.

University of California. *Business and Finance Bulletin G-44 on Accepting Equity.* 2002, http://patron.ucop.edu/ottmemos/docs/ott02-01.html.

University of Texas System. *The University of Texas System History of Board of Regents' Rules and Regulations and Other Policies on Intellectual Property Rules, 1985–Present.* 1985, http://www.utsystem.edu/OGC/Intellectualproperty/contract/IPhistory.htm.

University of Texas System. *The University of Texas System History of Board of Regents' Rules and Regulations and Other Policies on Intellectual Property Rules, 1985–Present.* 1987, http://www/utsystem.edu/ogc/intellectualproperty/contract/iphist-rr3.htm.

University of Texas System. *The University of Texas System History of Board of Regents' Rules and Regulations and Other Policies on Intellectual Property Rules, 1985–Present.* 1992, http://www.utsystem.edu/ogc/intellectualproperty/contract/iphist-rr7.htm.

University of Texas System. *Regents' Rules and Regulations. Part Two, Chapter XII, Intellectual Property.* 2002, http://www.utstyem.edu/OGC/IntellectualProperty/2xii.htm.

University of Texas at Austin. *Original Handbook of Operating Procedures.* 2002, http://www.utexas.edu/policies/hoppm/h0511.html.

University of Utah. *Patent, Inventions and Copyrights Policy.* 1970.

University of Utah. *Patents and Inventions (Policy #6–4).* 1999, http://www.admin.utah.edu/ppmanual/6/6-4.html.

Veblen, T. *The Higher Learning in America: A Memorandum on the Conduct of Universities by Business Men.* New York: Viking Press, 1935.

NICO CLOETE AND TEMBILE KULATI

MANAGERIALISM WITHIN A FRAMEWORK OF COOPERATIVE GOVERNANCE?

1. INTRODUCTION

This chapter draws on research and case studies from South Africa to demonstrate the complexities of the ways in which institutions, and particularly institutional management, respond to an increasingly perplexing set of demands from their own staff, government, society and global developments. The chapter begins with a discussion of the evolution of the governance debate in South Africa and the emergence of new governance models with the demise of the apartheid era. The next section details contemporary changes in institutional governance and leadership, followed by an analysis of various pressures that may be pushing South African higher education governance and management towards 'managerialism', within a policy framework of cooperative governance. The concluding section argues that managerialism can be found either everywhere or nowhere, depending on one's perspective. Indeed, while there are global characteristics to the managerial movement in higher education, a complete picture of what is happening with governance and management in specific countries cannot be understood without reference to the complexity of local governance relationships.

2. THE CONTOURS OF THE GOVERNANCE DEBATE

In examining the evolution of the governance debate in higher education in South Africa, it is important to recognise that the struggles for the transformation of higher education governance predate the promulgation of the new higher education legislative framework by a number of years (White Paper, Department of Education 1997). The debate on leadership and management in higher education institutions was subsumed under the broader struggles for governance transformation, with very little, if any, engagement with questions and issues relating to the management and role of leadership in institutional change.

The genesis of the debate on governance transformation in South African higher education can be traced to the education struggles of the 1980s that were led by the organisations affiliated to the National Education Co-ordinating Committee (NECC), and in particular the student formations belonging to the Mass Democratic Movement (MDM). Much of the emphasis of these struggles was centred on the demand for the democratisation of institutional governance structures, in particular

A. Amaral et al. (eds.), The Higher Education Managerial Revolution?, 229–251.
© 2003 Kluwer Academic Publishers. Printed in the Netherlands.

the councils, and the establishment of alternative structures of institutional governance, namely the broad transformation forums.

The launch of the NECC in March 1986 signalled a strategic shift from the earlier phase of the education struggles, which was focused on making the apartheid state structures ungovernable, to one whose objective was to develop 'People's Education for People's Power', the slogan around which the NECC waged its struggle for democratic participation. The political strategy of People's Education, which began as an attempt to shift the balance of educational power such that a "people's [educational] authority is established alongside the existing [apartheid] state authority", went through several stages of development (Obery interview with Ihron Rensburg cited in Levin 1991).

Although these stages arose in the context of the struggle for the control of township schools, they were also reflected in the demands of student organisations at higher education institutions, especially in the black universities. The first stage, whose objective was to shift the balance of educational power in schools from the state to the community, centred around the need to develop alternative structures and programmes within the schools. The shift in strategy in the second stage focused on the need to gain control of governance structures in schools and higher education institutions, as a key element in the 'dual power' strategy to gaining state power.

Mohamed and Cloete (1996) have, not unlike Levin (1991), attempted to periodise the education struggles relating to the transformation of higher education governance into three phases. The first phase focused on the demand for the establishment of alternative democratic governance structures, namely the broad transformation forums, that would challenge the authority of what were considered to be illegitimate and unrepresentative governance structures, in particular the councils and senates. Change was to be achieved through changing the composition of council and senate to ensure that marginalised groups and constituencies were represented in institutional decision making.

The second phase had as its focus the legitimation of the institutional management structures. This was to be achieved through the replacement of the discredited appointees of the apartheid state in university administrations with progressive institutional leaders, appointed democratically.

The third phase centred on the demand for the processes of governance and decision making to be more participatory and accountable. At some institutions, mainly historically disadvantaged universities and some English-medium institutions, this process started well before 1994; in others the process continued long after the principles and framework for democratic institutional governance had been embodied in the legislation.

The focus of the governance debate was on issues relating to structural reform and, to a lesser extent, on the substantive challenge of participatory decision making. There was hardly any discussion of how higher education institutions – once transformed at the level of representation in governance structures – ought to be organised and managed, and what role institutional managers could play in the unfolding transformation processes.

In terms of the relationship between institutions and the government, South Africa has a peculiarly mixed history. While the apartheid period is commonly perceived to be repressive, with little or no autonomy, the apartheid state in regulating higher education produced contradictory effects. In certain areas, some universities acquired a remarkable degree of autonomy and freedom whilst in other areas racist legislation and the use of state security apparatuses turned some of the universities into ideological and physical battlefields (Moja, Muller and Cloete 1996). Initially the governance model for black institutions was clearly a state control model, that is, control by legislation backed up by central government administrative and executive powers with respect to the composition of management, administrative and academic structures, access, student affairs and funding as well as the appointment of all senior members of staff.

In contrast, the Van Wyk De Vries Commission (1974) recommended strong institutional autonomy for the historically white institutions, which during the 1980s achieved an unprecedented degree of autonomy. The South African Post Secondary Education funding model contained elements of a weak state supervision model. Weak supervision was gradually supplemented with irregular state interference, targeting particularly the black institutions and individual students and staff.

2.1. A New Governance Model

Influenced by the history of the problematic relationship between the government and higher education institutions, and taking into account international debates of the early 1990s, the National Commission on Higher Education (NCHE) (1996), appointed by President Mandela in 1994, proposed a model of cooperative governance. Cooperative governance as conceptualised in the NCHE is framed within the notion of the new state. The cooperative governance approach made a clear choice between three models of government/higher education interaction.

The first model, namely *state control*, is premised on effective and systematic state administration of higher education executed by a professional and competent civil service – the 'Continental model' characteristic of Western Europe in the twentieth century. *State supervision*, which constitutes the second model, is founded on less centrist forms of control. The locus of power shifts from 'centralised control' to 'steering' in which governments provide the broad regulatory framework, and, through the use of instruments such as planning and funding, institutions are 'steered' to produce the outputs governments' desire. Steering is seen as an interactive process between government and institutions and it is the current preferred model in many countries, albeit with widely divergent mechanisms and levels of steering. The third model, *state interference,* is based on control in higher education that is neither systematic (model one) or 'regulation through steering' (model two) but which is based on arbitrary forms of intervention. This model operates in many developing countries, Africa in particular (Kraak 2001).

Cooperative governance was located within a state supervision model, with academic freedom guaranteed by the constitution; autonomy was to be exercised within a framework of government leadership through funding and planning. The government accepted the framework of the NCHE and the 1997 White Paper (Section 3.6) states that:

Recognising the need to transcend the adversarial relations between state and civil society arising from the apartheid era, the Ministry of Education adopts a model of co-operative governance for higher education in South Africa based on the principle of autonomous institutions working co-operatively with a proactive government and in a range of partnerships.

The White Paper (Section 3.6) further states that:

The transformation of the structures, values and culture of governance is a necessity, not an option, for South African higher education. Higher education institutions are vital participants in the massive changes which our society is undergoing, and in the intellectual, economic and cultural challenges of the new world order. For the first time in their history, our higher education institutions have the opportunity to achieve their full potential, but they will not do so until their system of governance reflects and strengthens the values and practices of our new democracy.

The transformation of governance was to be achieved through a system of cooperative governance that is based on a number of assumptions, namely, that:

- no single actor can effect change;
- there are complementary and competing interests;
- new structures are established to promote cooperative behaviour among institutional stakeholders; and
- the responsibilities of different partners are clarified.

The new legislation stipulates the main governance structures to be the council, the senate, and the institutional forum. The council is the supreme governing body in public higher education institutions, and is responsible for ensuring good governance within an institution. As the White Paper (Section 3.6) puts it: "Councils are the highest decision-making bodies of public institutions. They are responsible for the good order and governance of institutions and for their mission, financial policy, performance, quality and reputation". The senate is the highest decision-making body in relation to the "academic and research functions of the public higher education institution and must perform such other functions as may be delegated or assigned to it by the Council" (Higher Education Act 1997, Section 28 (1)).

Institutional forums are new structures that have been set up to broaden participation in institutional governance. Forums are meant to act as 'shock absorbers' to the transformation process by providing an arena for issues that pertain to the broad transformation agenda of the institution to be openly debated and discussed. They have also been established to advise councils on a number of issues, including the mediation of conflicts among campus stakeholders, and in making an input into the process of appointing senior executive management of the institution.

During the consultative phase that the Department of Education embarked upon prior to the promulgation of the legislation, there was general agreement with the concept and principles of cooperative governance. However, as the implementation process began to unfold, it became clear that 'agreement in principle' does not translate into 'unity in practice'. Firstly, it seems that there are two competing – although not uncomplementary – notions about democracy in South African higher education. The first position posits that the key transformation issue is about the participation of previously excluded groups in the restructured governance structures – thus the main democratisation task is to get more blacks and women into existing decision-making structures. The second position argues for the transformation of the governance processes themselves – in other words, putting more blacks and women into the institutional council is not enough; the role and functions of the council itself must change. The key changes have to do with democratic participation, transparency and accountability.

Democratising governance was not the only transformation task. The White Paper proposed the introduction of a single coordinated system with major demands for improvements with regards to equity and efficiency. At the same time that the education White Paper was being written and consulted about, the new government introduced a new macro-economic policy framework called Growth, Employment and Redistribution (GEAR) (Department of Finance 1996). This policy closely followed the so-called Washington consensus that expects countries who want to join the global economy to apply macro-economic discipline, reduce the balance of payments and curb government spending – a strong overall focus on efficiency, accountability and good governance as a means to attract foreign investment and stimulate growth.

The new legislative framework, which coupled market competition with the emergence of new public management, put enormous pressure on institutions to devise new ways of managing what were becoming more diverse and very complex institutions. Within the space of five years, higher education institutions were confronted with many challenges, including the need to:

- dramatically improve access and success for the previously excluded;
- diversify their income streams while doing more, and different, things with increasingly less reliance on the fiscus (most institutions receive less than 50% of their income from direct state subsidy);
- reconfigure institutional missions and the ways in which they traditionally produced, packaged and disseminated their primary product – knowledge – in order to meet the challenges of a diversifying student population, as well as an increasingly technologically oriented, and globalising, economy;
- forge new kinds of relationships with other knowledge producers within and outside higher education, especially in industry and the private sector; and
- bring about transformation in a democratic, consultative manner (Kulati 2000).

The emphasis on institutional effectiveness, efficiency and responsiveness within the new economic and legislative framework positioned the role of leadership, the vice-chancellor and the administration centre stage in institutional change. How this would square with more participative, consultative decision making is the main part of the story that follows.

3. CHANGES IN INSTITUTIONAL GOVERNANCE AND LEADERSHIP

A recent major study on South African higher education governance (Hall, Symes and Luescher 2002), which was commissioned by the Council on Higher Education, has developed a typology of institutional governance, which is based on a combination of three criteria that the study claims is required for good governance practice. These criteria are: the degree of representivity in governance structures; the extent of delegation of authority and responsibilities; and the ability of institutions to implement governance and management decisions.

From a survey of 12 higher education institutions, the study identified four categories of governance, as manifested in institutional practice (Hall, Symes and Luescher 2002: 23). These are:

- *Contested institutions*: In this category there is limited representivity in governance and poorly developed systems of delegation. These tend to be institutions in crisis, or institutions that are vulnerable to crisis if their present leadership loses legitimacy. They are a particular consequence of South Africa's history, in that issues inherited from the apartheid years are still dominant (25% of the sample fell into this category).
- *Management-focused institutions*: Universities and technikons in this group share a focus on management issues, either because they have made the explicit decision to adopt models from the corporate sector, or because systems of internal organisation that were better suited to previous years now present substantial obstacles to institutional adaptation. These institutions have inwardly focused systems of governance with well-developed capacity for administration and the delegation of authority. They are at risk from factional interests pursuing sectoral issues that are not in the interests of the institution as a whole (33% of the sample).
- *Democratic institutions*: These institutions combine broad representivity with shallow systems of delegation. They are the classic defenders of academic participation in governance. However, their poorly developed formal systems of delegation make them vulnerable to institutional gridlock if consensus cannot be reached on key issues (33% of institutions).
- *Democratic, well-managed institutions*: Institutions in this category have achieved an impressive record in governance through combining the strengths of participatory governance with the advantages of well-developed, formal systems of delegation of authority and responsibility (9% of institutions).

The governance framework developed in this study suffers from a number of weaknesses, however. The first is that the matrix of governance arrangements does not incorporate the criterion of implementation capacity as one of its variables, although this is highlighted as one of the key constituent criteria of effective governance. Another weakness is that there is a conflation of causal relationships between the criteria that have been outlined and their effect on governance behaviour. For example, it is assumed that the more limited the representivity in governance structures, the more prone to crisis an institution will be. Of course, the converse is also true, in that with more stakeholders represented on governance structures, there is also the likelihood – especially in the context of a relatively young democracy – that tensions between stakeholders might have a deleterious effect on governance effectiveness.

The main strength of the report is that it adds further insight to the 'styles of leadership' developed by Kulati and Moja (2002) and elaborates the governance indicators developed by Cloete, Bunting and Bunting (2002). Another important contribution is a different approach in understanding the two dimensions of representivity (and the extent to which governance becomes self-referential) and delegation as two axes of a matrix that plots an interaction between functional/effective and dysfunctional/unstable governance.

The study referred to earlier by Kulati and Moja (2002) identifies three leadership approaches to institutional governance that emerged during the post-1994 period. Two of the approaches discussed in the chapter, namely managerial and transformative leadership will be discussed below, while the third, crisis management, is more of an institutional condition than an emerging leadership style.

3.1. Managerial Leadership

The strategic objective of this approach is to reconfigure the institution to become more competitive and market oriented through the vigorous adaptation of corporate management principles and techniques to the higher education setting.

Thus the change agenda within these institutions is driven by a strong, decisive centre (usually located in the office of the vice-chancellor) that is buttressed by sophisticated management-support systems and structures, and which is staffed by a highly competent middle management layer. The leadership style is characterised by a rapid-response management ethos. Where others talk in terms of threats and survival in the face of globalisation and fierce competition from the emerging private higher education sector, the buzz here is about exploiting niches and developing partnerships.

Stumpf (2001) describes the way in which many of these institutions have become less reliant on government subsidy funding by devising various strategies to generate private income. These institutions have become increasingly entrepreneurial in their orientation, as reflected in the way in which many of them (especially the historically white research institutions) have established specific structures to package and patent their intellectual property. Another approach to increasing income has been to move into flexible modes of educational delivery. Apart from introducing modularised postgraduate programmes on a large scale, these institutions also entered the field of distance education for undergraduate programmes. This they did in partnership with private providers and thus saved themselves massive set-up and logistical costs.

Some of these institutions have also established spin-off companies in which staff members who had a direct interest in the development of a particular piece of intellectual property, would have a shareholding along with the institution and private sector shareholders. Others have established structures to advance institutional/private sector cooperation in a variety of ways and adjusted their internal allocation mechanisms to reward performance in the field of partnerships with the private sector and in the generation of their own income.

In response to the increasing importance of strategic management, many institutions invested in management training for their senior administrators and established offices of institutional research. Apart from taking care of the formal information requirements of government, these units have usually been responsible for other forms of quantitative (and sometimes even qualitative) planning support to management. In many cases sophisticated systems of performance management were established, based on institutional management information systems. Institutions in which these offices function well are, in general, well poised to respond quickly to new challenges and new opportunities, thereby creating for themselves a competitive edge in the face of increasing competition for students from overseas' institutions entering the South African market and the declining pool of available students (Stumpf 2001).

Two sub-categories can be delineated within the broader classification of managerial approaches to institutional change, namely *strategic managerialism* and *unwavering entrepreneurialism*. These sub-categories are derived from the distinction that has been made between the 'soft' and 'hard' approaches to managerialism. The 'soft managerialists', although applying management techniques in order to run their institutions more efficiently and effectively, still see higher education institutions as distinct from businesses, governed by their own norms and traditions. This is in contrast to the 'hard' approach to managerialism, where institutional management has "resolved to reshape and redirect the activities [of their institutions] through funding formulas and other mechanisms of accountability imposed from outside the academic community – management mechanisms created, and largely shaped, for application to large commercial enterprises" (Trow 1994: 12).

The leadership challenge for strategic managerialists is to get the institution to think and act more strategically, and to convince the academics that 'being managed', and working in an institution that is run on sound management principles, does not constitute a threat to the traditional values of the academy, such as academic freedom.

According to the strategic managerialists, being a first-rate academic with a good understanding of business principles ought not to be a contradiction in terms. As one South African vice-chancellor put it: "The vice-chancellor has to be an academic with a business sense. It also depends on what type of institution you're aspiring to be: for a research/comprehensive university, you must have a strong research background; if you don't have it you can't run senate. And if you can't run senate, you're dead".[1]

For strategic managerialists, globalisation and the market are not viewed as threats, but as opportunities to be exploited in order to make the institution more competitive internationally. Consequently, the managerialists have been more successful in exploiting the fairly loose legislative framework to the advantage of their institutions, having established strong relationships with international funders, developed partnerships with the private sector and parastatal research agencies, recruited top academics from abroad, and built strong links with universities in Africa.

Further along the continuum of the corporatisation of higher education institutions are the *unwavering entrepreneurs*. For this group the higher education institution is seen as being a business, as opposed to being run like a business. Institutions are thus in the business of providing their clients – the students – with goods and services that are sold at a competitive price. The institutions have, or try to develop, strong links with industry, and generally lack a collegial tradition. The institutions falling under this category are mostly from the polytechnic sector (technikons), although a few universities can also be found within this category.

For them, the transformation project is about developing useful products for the market, in other words producing employable graduates. The challenge is to gear-up the institution so that it is responsive to rapidly changing customer needs and expectations. The approach is characterised by an unquestioning application of private sector management procedures and techniques. The executive management, whose central concern is to ensure that the institution is run efficiently, believes in leading from the front, being in the driving seat of institutional change (Kulati interviews).

The 'unwavering entrepreneurs' regard the government's regulatory framework as an inconvenience; it is seen as failing to appreciate the demands and challenges facing modern higher education institutions. Government is viewed as not being generally supportive of institutional leadership, and although policies such as cooperative governance are regarded as necessary, they are seen as a nuisance.

3.2. Transformative Leadership

Transformative leadership is not a homogeneous category; nor does it imply one single notion of transformation. Rather, it is regarded as transformative in the South African context because it combines elements of leadership, which are broadly recognised as being successful, with features of cooperative governance. An in-depth case study (Cloete, Bunting and Bunting 2002) of two institutions (University of Port Elizabeth and Peninsula Technikon) revealed the following as some of the key elements of cooperative transformative processes followed by the leadership in those institutions:

- *Critical self-reflection*: A process often initiated by the vice-chancellor, where a wide range of members of staff engaged in critical self-reflection on the transformation process. This included more than one attempt to rethink the mission of the institution. In some cases members of the executive leadership wrote regularly about the successes and weaknesses of the processes.

- *Negotiated transformation*: A process where agreement – on issues such as the new mission of the institution – was reached through a protracted negotiations process involving various internal and external stakeholders.
- *Active forums*: A feature of some institutions where the institutional forum had an active agency role, meaning that they met regularly, discussed issues such as gender discrimination or affirmative action and made recommendations to the institutional leadership or the council.
- *Role differentiation*: The development of an understanding and acceptance of distinctions between governance functions and roles. Considering the lack of clarity in the policy about the role of leadership, a key task was to reach agreement about who has authority over what. This included the acceptance that neither the council nor the institutional forum should try to manage the institution, and that leadership must implement decisions which had been agreed upon in these structures.
- *Expanded leadership core*: The establishment of an expanded management group which in some cases included the president of the student representative council, and the development of a common vision for the institution and a shared discourse of the change process.
- *Trust*: An essential component of the change process which enabled the different constituencies to allow management to implement decisions and to lead.
- *Directive leadership with consultation*: An approach that helped manage the tension between leading and consulting. The manner and sequence of consultation varied according to leadership style and institutional culture.
- *Constructive/critical relationship between the chairperson of council and the vice-chancellor*: Central to holding the transformation process together was a supportive and critical working relationship between the chair of council and the vice-chancellor, based on a clearly understood complementarity of functions and skills.

It must be stressed that putting these processes in place in the two institutions did not depend on a specific leadership style. At one institution the leader can be described as a philosopher who steered from behind rather than leading from the front: "Nothing gets done without consultation" (Kirsten, University of Port Elizabeth, interview). At the other institution a charismatic engineer led from the front, but still within the framework of the elements described above: "I had to shake the institution out of its complacency at being 'the best technikon' and therefore not needing to change much; in other words, to get staff to realise it is not 'business as usual' ... to get [the] institution to realise that the value framework that it (once) cherished cannot be sustained" (Figaji, Peninsula Technikon, interview). In both institutions, the central characteristic of transformative leadership was the management of the tension between leading and consulting (Cloete, Bunting and Bunting 2002).

The features and processes mentioned above are illustrative of managerial and political responses to transformation pressures. It is within this context that two related, but distinct, approaches to transformative leadership can be described.

The first approach, referred to as *reformed collegialism*, starts from the premise that at the centre of the transformation project of the institution lies the intellectual agenda of higher education, which is non-negotiable. Thus part of the transformation agenda is to reclaim and reassert the centrality of the intellectual traditions of higher education institutions. The starting point of the institutional change strategy is to be sensitive to, and work within, the confines and limits of the prevailing institutional culture, rather than going to war against it (Birnbaum 1992). This can be achieved through remoulding the institution so that it is better able to respond and adapt to the new demands that it faces, while holding on to the central tenets of the academic tradition of the university, namely the pursuit of truth, disinterested enquiry etc. In other words, the leadership challenge is about facilitating academic excellence by supporting, managing, nurturing and inspiring one's academic colleagues. Collegialists would concur with Ramsden (1998: 13) that "deep at the heart of effective leadership is an understanding of how academics work".

'Reformed' refers to the fact that even the most devoted collegialists are not oblivious to the pressures of democracy and global trends on academia. By responding to these pressures, however, tensions develop between collegiality and management strategies for change.

While acknowledging the importance of the new, participatory governance principles, the second approach, referred to as *transformative managerialism*, is characteristic of leaders who put more emphasis on 'driving' transformation from the centre. The challenge for the transformative managerialists is to transform the culture of the institution from an authoritarian to a more democratic one, whilst ensuring that the institution is managed more efficiently, in line with policy principles or market pressures.

In order to push the transformation agenda through the institution, decision making is centralised, decentralised and re-centralised. This is done by expanding the 'top' leadership group to include executive deans and certain professionals, such as finance or human resource directors. Key strategic decisions are taken by this group, and the deans become the implementers at the faculty level. Traditionally, the deans are supposed to represent and defend faculty interests. Whilst the executive dean and their faculty may have an autonomous budget and control over the appointment of new colleagues, the budget parameters and employment equity targets are set centrally. When taking the faculty decisions back to top management where the decisions could be overturned, the dean is placed in a very complex relationship within management, of which they are part, and faculty, which they are supposed to represent. This is even further complicated by the fact that in many cases the self-image of the dean is that of a faculty member, and not that of a manager.

This role confusion can be described as a position of 'in-betweenity', meaning that the dean is always located, and often trapped, between the faculty and management, between the faculty and students, and between the institution and the external communities. In a number of institutions, particularly those with strong academic cultures, a few deans have fallen foul of this role schizophrenia which Du Toit argues is currently a greater threat to academic freedom than the state. For example, he states that "it is not clear how an executive deanship could be compatible with a 'collegial' approach to the conduct of faculty governance in any serious sense" (2001: 5).

In summary, while transformative leadership grapples with the new demands for participation and responses to the market, major tensions are emerging, accentuated by the academic culture of the institution and the urgency for change. In some instances the institutions may lean more towards collegial styles of management; in others towards a centralised approach to management.

The above shows that, while there are certain commonalties regarding governance and leadership at the institutional level, there are also major differences in the ways that institutions respond to these.

4. PRESSURES TOWARDS MANAGERIALISM

In a wide-ranging overview of institutional adaptation to demands for managerial reform, Gumport and Sporn (1999) attribute the expanding role of administration to three interdependent dynamics: resource dependency that is primarily motivated by organisational survival; institutional isomorphism that is motivated by legitimacy concerns; and professional authority that is motivated by a struggle for professional identity. Two more recent, and very informative, reviews of change that contribute to a managerial approach are by Amaral and Magalhães (2002) and Maassen (2002).

Primarily, management is responsible for maintaining the organisation's exchange relationship, whether it be a bridge or a buffer, it must transverse an increasingly complex environment that is not only government and business, but also an escalating range of 'stakeholders' (Neave 2002). It must meet compliance with environmental demands and cultivate alternative resources to reduce existing dependencies. Management becomes more important because they are mainly responsible for the development of strategies that increase existing sources of income, tap into new income sources and help to reduce existing dependency relationships.

A key resource is legitimacy, and it is increasingly important that institutions be seen to be responding, in a business-like manner, to demands for reform. Symbolic activity is as important as real activities in order to sustain existing resources and to gain access to new sources. Presenting a more unified and business-like front, an expanded management core is much better positioned to represent the institution than the often fractious collegiality.

The literature on the sociology of the professions explains how a dynamic is put into place that will promote a tendency amongst professional, or pre-professional, groups, to gain greater authority and improved benefits, both financially and in terms of control over their domain of work. Gumport and Sporn (1999) describe the effects of this as a shift in the authority structure within higher education organisations that entails an expanding domain for the administrators and the leadership and a narrowing authority domain for the academic faculty.

The above mentioned factors come into play very forcibly when, as has been the case in South Africa in the post-1994 period, institutions are faced with a sudden increase in demands for reform from the government and society, and an unleashing of market forces by both the government and a burgeoning local and global private higher education sector (Cloete and Maassen 2002).

As is indicated by Gumport and Sporn (1999) there are many factors that put pressures on higher education to become more business-like and, by implication, more managerial, but we want to explore two specific factors in the South African context. The first is that, despite a formal policy of cooperative, participative governance, some of the reforms of the national government have, intentionally and unintentionally, promoted managerialism rather than greater democratisation. Secondly, through a process of mimetic and normative isomorphism, institutional management's notions of 'successful' institutions have been exchanged, mimicked and adopted through professional networks who are, on the one hand, responding to resource and legitimacy demands, and on the other hand to promoting their position.

4.1. Effects of Government Reforms

4.1.1. Shifts Towards a More Centralised Reform Process

The new Minister of Education, appointed after the second democratic election in 1999, declared that implementation, and not more policy, was a priority. Implementation requires very specific policy, which was not available, since most of the post-1994 policies were symbolic, attempting to bring about new frameworks and greater unity (Cloete and Maassen 2002). Making policy trade-offs between different interests could not be made in the same consultative manner as developing symbolic policy, and the ministry did not have much experience in negotiating trade-offs. The new phase of more centralised decision making and less 'broad consultation' was not peculiar to education; it had started with the Minister of Finance declaring in 1997 that the new macro-economic policy was not up for consultation or negotiation.

A series of institutional crises and a lack of confidence in higher education leadership – a critical component of governance – led to numerous amendments to the 1997 Higher Education Act. Examples of this gradual transition from a steering to an increasingly centralised approach to the management of the higher education reform process are to be found in the following amendments:

- Higher Education Amendment Act 55 of 1999 – allows the Minister to appoint administrators to a higher education institution where there is financial or other maladministration of a serious nature.
- Higher Education Amendment Act 54 of 2000 – allows the Minister to determine the scope and range of operations of an institution, and determines that an institution may not, without the approval of council and under certain circumstances without the concurrence of the Minister, enter into a loan or overdraft agreement or develop infrastructure.

- Higher Education Amendment Act 23 of 2001 – includes a provision for the indefinite appointment of the administrator and the repeal of private acts (Olivier 2001).

Concurrent with the legislative changes, the method of 'steering' also altered. Initially, planning and funding were regarded as an interactive approach to determine goals and targets (Department of Education 1998). However, the ministry shifted to a view that in order to implement the transformation programme an increasing use of the executive powers vested in him by the Higher Education Act would be required. A key example is the proposed new funding model which, in the words of one of the authors: "will be a top-down one. It will come into operation only when the government has determined what total of public funds should be spent in a given year on universities and technikons and what the key policy goals should be for that year" (Bunting 2001: 4). This model is not an interactive steering approach, but is much closer to the centralised state control approach rejected in the White Paper as a model for governance.

The latest reform policy is a decision that the number of higher education institutions will be reduced from 36 to 23 institutions through a process of mergers – some of these mergers will be voluntary since the affected institutions have agreed to merge, others will be 'involuntary'. In a memo to the president about mergers (Department of Education 2002), the ministry lists equity, efficiency and development as the key principles that are driving the need for change. Democracy, a key principle in all previous government policy documents, is not mentioned. Also the process of bringing about the mergers is perceived to be a leadership and management-driven one, since the interim councils, which will be appointed by the Minister, will have no representation from students or staff.

It is not only the Minister who has acquired new powers and shifted to a more 'top-down' model, but also the Council on Higher Education (CHE) has adopted a more centralised approach. Writing about the proposals formulated by the CHE Task Team on 'Size and Shape', Kraak (2001) argues that the proposals represent a shift in the conception of the role of the state from that founded on a model of 'state supervision' to that of 'state interference'. The solutions to the dysfunction and endemic crisis in the higher education system sought by the CHE are found in the articulation of a 'state interference' model – a bureaucratic, weak and arbitrary form of intervention based on prescriptive fiat and rigid rules and procedures. The affinities between this form of state intervention and the proposals of the CHE are self-evident. They represent a view of the state as unable to attain the sophistication required for 'steering', and, as a consequence, necessitating a reversal to a conception of the state as bureaucratic and prescriptive (Kraak 2001: 30).

Trying to justify this shift, Hall, Symes and Luescher (2002), in a commissioned study for the CHE, argue that "the concept of co-operative governance, as defined in the earlier 1990s, is now in danger of becoming a hindrance that confuses policy and inhibits the development of good practice" and should be replaced by a notion of 'conditional autonomy' (p. 108). The report argues that the National Plan for Higher Education (Department of Education 2001) marks the path of change to a "system of conditional autonomy in which substantive autonomy (academic freedom) continues to be guaranteed while the state exercises increasing control over procedures of funding and academic accreditation" (Hall, Symes and Luescher 2002: 19).

The argument is flawed because the decision that 10 mergers and four incorporations must happen, whether the institutions agree or not, violates the first condition of conditional autonomy set out in the report, namely "the right of individual institutions to determine their primary goals". The apartheid regime also had a model of conditional autonomy, the difference being that under apartheid the conditions were very clear, while under the new Minister the conditions are unspecified and keep shifting, which makes the propagation of such a model potentially very dangerous (Moja, Cloete and Olivier forthcoming).

The effects of increasing centralised reform and less consultation at the national level create a climate that promotes top-down decision making, both from the national government and from institutional leadership. Responding to the extraordinary amount of new legislation and policies requires an enormous managerial/administrative capacity,[2] which on the one hand distracts academics from teaching and research, and on the other demands a more sophisticated and expanded administrative capacity.

The merger process in particular, aiming to achieve efficiency gains that will necessitate the reduction of staff and programmes, will require strong management. It could thus be concluded that a combination of a strong equity and efficiency agenda will, intentionally and unintentionally, provide a drive for more leadership and management authority.

The Changing Role of the Senate

An alarming development in the past five years has been the growing marginalisation of the senate in institutional governance. Hall, Symes and Luescher (2002) in their study on governance in South African higher education, argue that senates are not carrying out their function of being the premier governance structure in relation to academic governance, noting that many senates are "reactive (and sidelined) bodies" (p. 25). The study, however, does not provide an explanation of this declining role of the senate in institutional governance, merely attributing poor attendance as one possible factor. We would like to submit that there are possibly three factors that have given rise to the marginalisation of the senate.

The evidence to support these claims is anecdotal, as it arises from informal interactions the authors had with senior academics from a few institutions. The first is that in the face of more assertive councils – a function of the incorporation of hitherto excluded stakeholders and increasing vigilance of council in relation to their fiduciary responsibilities – and executive management (a process that has been accentuated by the emergence of executive deanship as a critical layer in institutional management), senates have not taken an active role in the strategic decisions of the institution.

A second reason is that many senior professors and academics at the research universities have been under pressure – in the light of the declining government subsidy – to raise more private income through contract research (see Table 1 below). Consequently, many professors have come to regard their involvement in institutional (governance) issues as of secondary importance, with the result that attendance of senate meetings has declined markedly. The declining interest in getting involved in institutional matters can also be attributed to the emergence of moonlighting in academia. Increasingly, many senior academics are working as consultants to government and the private sector to supplement their declining salaries.

Table 1. Trends in contract income at four institutions 1995–2000 (rands millions)

Institution	1995–96	1998	2000	% increase from 1995 to 2000
Pretoria	27	61	92	480
Stellenbosch	46	78	119	258
Natal	46	83	138	300
Cape Town	102	139	190	186

Source: Bawa and Mouton 2002

Two recent incidents highlight a third possible reason for the marginalisation of the senate. As was indicated in the previous section regarding a new governance model, the 1997 Higher Education Act draws a clear distinction between the role of councils and senates. Councils, as the highest decision-making bodies of public institutions, are given responsibility for the mission, financial policy and overall institutional performance. The senate on the other hand is the highest decision-making body in relation to academic and research functions. This attempts to draw too 'hard' a distinction between functions that are not so clearly demarcatable in governance terms. Reed, Meek and Jones (2002) describe this as the differentiation of functions (separating academic and financial decision-making arenas) and, conversely, the blurring or de-differentiation of separate and autonomous institutional spheres.

At both the Universities of Natal and Witwatersrand, conflict has developed around the relationship between the council, the vice-chancellor and the senate. During 2002, the University of Natal Senate passed an unprecedented resolution accusing the Council of "acting arbitrarily and illegitimately in proceeding with the appointment of a Vice-Chancellor by ignoring the required support from Senate" (University of Natal Senate Resolution 5/6/2002).

In announcing her resignation, the Vice-Chancellor of the University of Witwatersrand, stated that: "there will be searching questions asked about the powers assumed by the Wits Council and its chairperson and the sidelining of the people who appointed me; the Senate, students and staff associations and the 100,000 strong convocation" (Norma Reid, *Business Day*, November 2002).

In both the above cases, discussions with academics reveal a concern, in some cases outrage, that the council is expanding its jurisdiction over financial matters to the appointment, or dismissal, of the vice-chancellor without adequately involving the senate, not to mention other stakeholders.

The effect of the increasingly marginal role that the senate is playing at certain institutions is that there is an absence of a countervailing voice to the centralisation of decision-making powers. Many of the important decisions concerning the strategic direction of the institution are bypassing what is meant to be a key governance structure in higher education institutions, with many senates now being pre-occupied with narrow academic matters – becoming, in the words of a senior professor, the 'cheerleaders of the curriculum'.

4.1.2. Institutional Isomorphism

Despite the much vaunted independence of thought of higher education staff, there is much evidence towards isomorphism. Mimetic isomorphism is the result of institutions mimicking the behaviour of each other in order to minimise risk in highly competitive environments. When institutions are highly dependent upon a narrow range of resource providers, such as an education ministry or a very homogeneous population, they will tend to have similar programmes, structures and operating norms. Coercive isomorphism is the result of pressures from the environment, principally government policies, that force institutions to become more similar, thus reducing diversity in a higher education system. Governments might act in this way in order to promote efficiency, on the assumption that too much diversity is inefficient (Meek et al. 1996).

An example of mimetic isomorphism is the issue of the outsourcing of support service functions. A study by Van der Walt et al. (2002: 20) shows that "outsourcing has been strongly favoured by public sector university managements: every single public sector in South Africa has introduced outsourcing over the last decade". Outsourcing cuts across categories such as historically advantaged or disadvantaged institutions and a managerial or a transformative leadership style – although one institution (Peninsula Technikon) followed a very different approach (Cloete, Bunting and Bunting 2002).

The study showed that that for the 16 (out of 21) institutions that responded to the survey, 80% chose to adopt outsourcing in order to reduce costs. Slightly less than half (40%) of these institutions hoped that outsourcing would also improve the efficiency of support services. A substantial number of universities also considered their decision to adopt outsourcing to be part of a broader vision of improving the competitiveness of their institutions: for eight institutions (53%), the support services were outsourced on the grounds that they were 'non-core' functions within the university. Three of the institutions regarded the decision to outsource as in line with government policy.

The reduction of costs may be attributed to the general financial squeeze on the public sector universities arising from declining government subsidies, and falling revenue from student enrolments. In open-ended questions, respondents spoke of the need to make their institutions 'leaner', to 'do more with less', to 'reduce overheads', and to restructure due to 'financial considerations' and a lack of 'sufficient resources'.

Van der Walt reports that the paradigm of university marketisation has had an impact on university strategy, respondents citing the need to focus upon 'core' activities as a rationale for support service outsourcing. Whilst the historically advantaged institutions more often cited increased competitiveness as a reason, the historically under-resourced disadvantaged institutions responded more to the new context in order to survive financially – thus more a case of survivalism than marketisation.

As Van der Walt's survey suggests, there were different reasons for responding to financial austerity and institutions had different goals that they were trying to achieve. That so many picked on the workers as a source of savings clearly has to do with power; another group pushed to the limit during this period were students whose fees were substantially increased over the period (Bunting 2002).

Outsourcing is both a feature of new public management and of the globalisation of labour practices associated with global trends described by Carnoy (2001). According to Carnoy, businesses are trying to transform themselves by looking to increase productivity and reduce labour costs. A key to this is flexibility, meaning that work, and workers, can be constantly adapted and changed to produce new products for new markets. Flexibility means conditions of employment, more short-term staff and self-programmable skills, meaning the ability not only to learn on the job, but also to redefine the job. Another major aspect is networking, by which Carnoy (2001: 25) means:

> A new logic of the firm, where changing hierarchies and organisational forms are based on interactive connections between different layers and positions within the firm, between firms, and within the market. New information technologies allow for greater flexibility and networking; and globalisation emphasises interdependence, interaction, and constant adaptation to an ever changing environment. This environment affects workers in firms, creating a culture of individual networking across companies. Individual networking is a way both to learn about working conditions, projects, and innovations in other firms and to make strategic job moves in a flexible labour market.

What is rather remarkable is that a common solution was imported by higher education leadership. This is arguably the only time that all institutions tried to implement a similar reform; it was not a government policy, but an international 'best' practice they mimicked.

This raises the important point that global practices are often enthusiastically imported as best or 'universal' practice solutions for problems by people within the nation state, and not surreptitiously imposed by Washington as many conspiracy theorists often proclaim.

Some institutions, albeit a minority, have, through a policy of absorbing outsourced workers and defending the packages of those who join outsourcing enterprises, maintained a sense of institutional ownership. The negotiated employment policy seems to have resulted in an institution such as Peninsula Technikon being one of the few institutions in South Africa that has managed to retain a sense of campus community (Cloete, Bunting and Bunting 2002).

Not only have the conditions of work of lower skilled employees changed dramatically, the differential between a service worker and a vice-chancellor increased from 20:1 in 1986 to 25:1 in 2000 (Gibbon and Kabaki 2002). Service workers whose jobs were outsourced, and who the contracting companies subsequently hired, had their packages halved (on average). This means that in the post-apartheid era the differential between the vice-chancellor and certain service workers could be as high as 50:1, in contrast with 20:1 under the apartheid government. Whilst the managerial 'class' did disproportionately well in the new South Africa, the fate of the service workers was less fortunate.

There is increasing evidence that there has not only been a widening gap between workers and management, but also between management and academics (see Table 2). The gap between senior managers, with 'market-related' packages, and senior teaching and research staff seems to have widened significantly over the past few years (from a ratio of about 2:1 during the late 1980s to a ratio of 4.5:1 in the late 1990s (Gibbon and Kabaki 2002).

Table 2. Salary ratios: Regulation and deregulation

Level	Late 1980s Government Regulation	2000 Deregulation at a Leading University
Vice-Chancellor	2.0	4.5
Deputy Vice-Chancellor	1.6	3.5
Professor	1.3	1.3
Senior Lecturer*	1.0	1.0

*The SAPSE funding formula uses senior lecturer level as the basis for salary comparisons
Source: SAPSE Return for 2000, University of Cape Town

At one of South Africa's leading institutions, which is not unrepresentative of the South African system, there are now seven salary bands, with more than 30 directors, deans, managers and deputy vice-chancellors above the professorial level. Unlike the situation in the US and other countries, there are no academic super-professors who earn packages equivalent to those of executive deans or deputy vice-chancellors. Some institutions have introduced the category of senior professors who are offered substantially larger packages than those of their colleagues, but they are still not comparable with the salary packages of top managers (Gibbon and Kabaki 2002).

The management at higher education institutions claims that market-related packages are necessary in order to attract and keep senior executives. These packages, in other words, are a consequence of the intense competition for highly qualified executives, particularly those who are black and/or female. But, unlike executives in the private sector environment, senior executives in higher education are rarely tied to performance clauses in their contracts. There are two points worth making here. One is that these packages relate to competition at the high end of the labour market but have little to do with the other ways in which institutions have to make themselves market-competitive. Generally speaking, it is the academic staff, particularly the senior academic staff, who attract students, research grants and consultancy contracts. This is the group that is operating in the market, but who are not rewarded in a market-related manner even though it would not be difficult to build a market reward into the packages of entrepreneurial academics (Gibbon and Kabaki 2002).

The second point is that the remuneration packages of senior executives are not necessarily an effect of, or directly connected to, more managerial approaches to higher education administration. In fact, some of the highest paid vice-chancellors in the country do not appear to be pursuing entrepreneurial or managerial style leadership approaches at all.

5. MANAGERIALISM EVERYWHERE?

It could be argued that the pressures for an expanding role for management and administration in the post-1994 period are not that dissimilar to what Gumport and Sporn (1999) described: institutional adaptation influenced by resource dependency that is primarily motivated by organisational survival; institutional isomorphism that is motivated by legitimacy concerns; and professional authority that is motivated by a struggle for professional identity. The effects of all three factors are evident in the South African context. At one level, the South African higher education governance landscape is thus reassuringly 'global', but the above picture of governance at council, leadership, senate and worker levels reveals a very complex governance set of interrelationships that can be understood in different ways.

One approach could be to start from an assumption that managerialism, like chicken man,[3] is everywhere and then to look for evidence of the ascendancy of globalising managerialism. Another approach, and the one followed here, is to first describe new developments within a particular higher education context and then to look for trends and issues.

As we have shown, the pressures towards managerialism come from intentional and unintentional effects of government reform policies, from what is regarded as global best practices, from a management cadre promoting their own interests and from academics relinquishing power in pursuit of other interests.

Within a policy framework of cooperative governance accepted by government and institutions, both government and higher education institutions are behaving in ways that undermine the policy. Certain government policies, intended and unintended, promote aspects of managerialism. According to the Hall, Symes and Luescher (2002) study, at least 33% of the institutions are 'management focused'. However, what is quite remarkable in higher education is that more than 40% can be classified as 'democratic' or 'democratically well managed'. It could be argued that considering that since 1998 the Minister has consistently increased his powers, institutions may have taken the policy of cooperative governance somewhat more seriously than government itself.

What seems quite self-evident from the range of responses is that within one country, with a national policy framework, a large range of governance arrangements has developed. To label this 'a historic march to managerialism' is to obscure, and miss, some very interesting responses emerging amongst different groups of institutions. The different governance and leadership styles may contain many elements of what is being described as managerialism; however, institutions with a more collegial history seem to be developing a range of 'democratic', managerial, practices. What a label of managerialism will obscure is the interesting new forms of consultation and participation that are emerging under conditions of demands for greater efficiency and accountability.

In many of the debates about managerialism, the traditional collegial model is implicitly or explicitly held to as an alternative. In South Africa this model was thoroughly discredited during the initial phases of the demands for greater democratisation. Firstly, it was assumed to be too exclusive, and regarded as inimical to the transformation agenda of higher education. Secondly, the majority of the 'colleagues' were white men aligned, directly or indirectly, to the apartheid regime. It is also very difficult to make a case for an unreformed collegial model when the external and internal environments are changing so drastically. However, as was demonstrated with the case about outsourcing, a simplistic mimetic isomorphism is hardly a palatable alternative.

In conclusion, the task ahead seems not to be to counter managerialism with a knee-jerk return to collegiality, but to start identifying lessons from some of the very innovative strategies and structures that are developing in different countries and amongst different institutional cultures in response to the new changing world, that is, in the words of Manuel Castells (2001: 6), not calm waters with an occasional wave, but more like the 'bubbly world of sparkling water'.

NOTES

[1] Tembile Kulati conducted a number of interviews with vice-chancellors during the course of 2000 as part of a broader project on governance.

[2] A report by the South African University Vice-Chancellors Association lists over 30 change initiatives from various government departments that currently demand higher education management time and financial resources (SAUVCA 2002).

[3] During the 1960s the BBC world radio service had a famous comic figure called chicken man. Some days chicken man was 'everywhere, everywhere' and some days chicken man was 'nowhere, nowhere'.

REFERENCES

Amaral, A. and A. Magalhães. "The Emergent Role of External Stakeholders in European Higher Education Governance." In Amaral, A., G.A. Jones and B. Karseth (eds). *Governing Higher Education: National Perspectives on Institutional Governance.* Dordrecht: Kluwer Academic Publishers, 2002, 1–21.

Bawa, A. and J. Mouton. "Research." In Cloete, N., R. Fehnel, P. Maassen, T. Moja, H. Perold and T. Gibbon (eds). *Transformation in Higher Education: Global Pressures and Local Realities in South Africa.* Cape Town: Juta, 2002, 296–339.

Birnbaum, R. *How Academic Leadership Works: Understanding Success and Failure in the College Presidency.* San Francisco: Jossey Bass, 1992.

Bunting, I. "The Relationship Between State and Public Higher Education Institutions." CHET Paper, 2001 (unpublished).

Bunting, I. "Funding." In Cloete, N., R. Fehnel, P. Maassen, T. Moja, H. Perold and T. Gibbon (eds). *Transformation in Higher Education: Global Pressures and Local Realities in South Africa.* Cape Town: Juta, 2002, 115–146.

Carnoy, M. "The Role of the State in the New Global Economy." In Muller, J., N. Cloete and S. Badat (eds). *Challenges of Globalisation: South African Debates with Manuel Castells.* Cape Town: Maskew Miller Longman, 2001, 22–34.

Castells, M. "The New Global Economy." In Muller, J., N. Cloete and S. Badat (eds). *Challenges of Globalisation: South African Debates with Manuel Castells.* Cape Town: Maskew Miller Longman, 2001, 2–21.

Cloete, N., L. Bunting and I. Bunting. *Transformation Indicators Applied to Two South African Higher Education Institutions.* Pretoria: CHET Publications, 2002.

Cloete, N. and P. Maassen. "The Limits of Policy." In Cloete, N., R. Fehnel, P. Maassen, T. Moja, H. Perold and T. Gibbon (eds). *Transformation in Higher Education: Global Pressures and Local Realities in South Africa.* Cape Town: Juta, 2002, 447–490.

Department of Education. *Education White Paper 3: A Programme for the Transformation of Higher Education.* General Notice 1196 of 1997. Pretoria, 1997.

Department of Education. *National and Institutional Planning Framework for the Higher Education System.* Pretoria, 1998.

Department of Education. *National Plan for Higher Education.* Pretoria, 2001.

Department of Education. *Memorandum to the President of Clarification on Transformation and Mergers in Higher Education.* Pretoria, 2002.

Department of Finance. *Growth, Employment and Redistribution: A Macroeconomic Strategy.* Pretoria, 1996.

Du Toit, A. "Revisiting Academic Freedom in Post-apartheid South Africa: Current Issues and Challenges." CHET Commissioned Paper, 2001, http://www.chet.org.za/papers.asp.

Gibbon, T. and J. Kabaki. "Staff." In Cloete, N., R. Fehnel, P. Maassen, T. Moja, H. Perold and T. Gibbon (eds). *Transformation in Higher Education: Global Pressures and Local Realities in South Africa.* Cape Town: Juta, 2002, 186–229.

Gumport, P. and B. Sporn. "Institutional Adaptation: Demands for Management Reform and University Administration." In Stuart, J. and W. Tierney (eds). *Handbook of Theory and Research, vol. xiv.* New York: Agathon Press, 1999, 103–145.

Hall, M., A. Symes and T. Luescher. *Governance in South African Higher Education.* Council on Higher Education. Pretoria, 2002.

Higher Education Act 1997, Section 28 (1). *Government Gazette.* vol. 390, December 1997.

Kraak, A. "Policy Ambiguity and Slippage: Higher Education Under the New State, 1994–2001." CHET Commissioned Paper, 2001, http://www.chet.org.za/papers.asp.

Kulati, T. "Governance, Leadership and Institutional Change in South African Higher Education: Grappling with Instability." *Tertiary Education and Management* 6.3 (2000): 177–192.

Kulati, T. and T. Moja. "Leadership." In Cloete, N., R. Fehnel, P. Maassen, T. Moja, H. Perold and T. Gibbon (eds). *Transformation in Higher Education: Global Pressures and Local Realities in South Africa.* Cape Town: Juta, 2002, 230–291.

Levin, R. "People's Education and the Struggle for Democracy in South Africa." In Unterhalter, E., H. Wolpe, T. Botha, S Badat, T. Dlamini and B. Khotseng (eds). *Apartheid Education and Popular Struggles.* London: Zed, 1991.

Maassen, P. "Organisational Strategies and Governance Structures in Dutch Universities." In Amaral, A., G.A. Jones and B. Karseth (eds). *Governing Higher Education: National Perspectives on Institutional Governance.* Dordrecht: Kluwer Academic Publishers, 2002, 23–41.

Meek, V.L., Leo Goedegebuure, Osmo Kivinen and Risto Rinne (eds). *The Mockers and Mocked: Comparative Perspectives on Diversity, Differentiation and Convergence in Higher Education.* Oxford: Pergamon, 1996.

Mohamed, N. and N. Cloete. "Transformation Forums as Revolutionary Councils, Midwives to Democracy or Forums for Reconstruction and Innovation." Research Report, 1996 (unpublished).

Moja, T., N. Cloete and N. Olivier. "Is Moving from Co-Operative Governance to Conditional Autonomy a Contribution to Effective Governance?" *Kagisano.* Pretoria: Council on Higher Education, forthcoming.

Moja, T., J. Muller and N. Cloete. "Towards New Forms of Regulation in Higher Education: The Case of South Africa." *Higher Education* 32 (1996): 129–155.

National Commission on Higher Education. *A Framework for Transformation.* Pretoria: Department of Education, 1996.

Neave, G. *On Stakeholders, Chesire Cats and Seers: Changing Visions of the University.* The CHEPS Inaugurals. Enschede: University of Twente, 2002.

Olivier, N. *The Relationship Between the State and Higher Education Institutions with Reference to Higher Education Policy Documentation and the Legislative Framework.* CHET Paper, 2001, http://www.chet.org.za/papers.asp.

Ramsden, P. *Learning to Lead in Higher Education.* London: Routledge, 1998.

Reed, M.I., V.L. Meek and G.A. Jones. "Introduction." In Amaral, A., G.A. Jones and B. Karseth (eds). *Governing Higher Education: National Perspectives on Institutional Governance.* Dordrecht: Kluwer Academic Publishers, 2002, xv–xxxi.

Reid, Norma. *Business Day.* November 2002.

SAUVCA (South African University Vice-Chancellors Association). *A New Vision.* 2002.

Stumpf, R. *Higher Education Funding in the Period 1994–2001.* CHET Paper, 2001, http://www.chet.org.za/papers.asp.

Trow, M. "Managerialism and the Academic Profession: The Case of England." *Higher Education Policy* 7.2 (1994): 11–18.

Van der Walt, L., C. Bolsman, B. Johnson and L. Martin. "Globalisation and the Outsourced University in South Africa." Final Report for CHET. University of Witwatersrand. 2002, http://www.chet.org.za/publications/outsourced.pdf.

Van Wyk De Vries Commission. *Main Report of the Inquiry Into Universities.* Pretoria: Government Printer, 1974.

DENISE LEITE

INSTITUTIONAL EVALUATION, MANAGEMENT PRACTICES AND CAPITALIST REDESIGN OF THE UNIVERSITY: A CASE STUDY

1. INTRODUCTION

This chapter is a product of reflections on continuing research projects[1] concerning institutional evaluation. The evaluation processes of nine universities[2] from four countries were researched. I worked in partnership with colleagues from these countries and was supported mainly by CNPq (National Council for Scientific and Technological Development) and FAPERGS (Foundation for Support of Research in the State of Rio Grande do Sul). The main objective of the project was to understand the impact and changes associated with university evaluations. I focused on pedagogical innovation. The theory that sustains the cases researched is based on Buchbinder's conceptions (1993) about 'market-oriented universities', on Cowen's (1996) discussions about 'performative universities' and on Barrow's (1996) conception about the university of 'selective excellence'. As background, I used the Portuguese social theorist B.S. Santos'(1994) notion of the 'university of ideas' instead of the 'idea of the university'. This allowed me to examine the cases with respect to their contradictions and differences instead of their similarities. At the beginning, I was in search of participative practices as an innovative evaluation methodology. But when discussing the performance results of the evaluation processes I realised that another important change was occurring – the capitalist redesigning of universities. This redesigning is associated with the improvement of management of corporate boards, aiming at the markets and the resolution of institutional problems. Once the problems are identified – along with more competitive issues – strategies are articulated. These strategies are internally directed to the boundaries of efficiency and effectiveness with the central scope of 'doing more with less' and externally directed to new publics and to the market visibility of the institution. The changes cannot be understood as a linear and direct result of internal evaluations. Many factors are relevant to this new university performance, including the introduction of educational reforms and national evaluation and accreditation processes, institutionalised in the 1990s, in Latin American higher education. International pressures on universities can also be identified as a factor affecting internal change.

Big, costly, complex public universities have adopted a policy of 'good' administration which can reorganise and transform them. In the construction of a

A. Amaral et al. (eds.), The Higher Education Managerial Revolution?, 253–273.
© 2003 Kluwer Academic Publishers. Printed in the Netherlands.

knowledge society, the redesigning of institutions is occurring through a process of strategic planning which includes a very special kind of organisational learning. In order to present my argument, I will describe some general examples of capitalist redesign observed in the case studies. After that, I will concentrate on one Brazilian case study of institutional evaluation that is illustrative of the transformations. Following this, universities as learning organisations in the global economy will be discussed. To introduce the themes I will provide a brief summary of Latin American reforms of higher education occurring during the 1990s.

2. THE 1990 REFORMS

Analysing the cases of institutional evaluation in Latin American universities and in one European university it was possible to observe that the relations between state, university and society, especially in Latin American countries, are changing. This occurs through the effect of reforms of the higher education system, including university evaluation processes. Introduced by the respective governments, the reforms follow similar paths in each Latin American country. The Latin American governments have tended to imitate each other with respect to policy reform. They seem to accept and advance change in an unquestionable manner, since they feel pressured by the political agendas of the multilateral agencies such as the International Monetary Fund (IMF), the World Bank and other international organisations such as UNESCO (United Nations Educational, Scientific and Cultural Organization) (Rodriguez Gómez and Santuario 2000).[3] Globalisation and its ideologies seem to be co-participants in the processes of change. In general, with respect to the evaluation and accreditation procedures, ownership belongs to the Ministry of Education, as in Brazil and Chile. In Argentina, the Ministry of Culture and Education and a buffer agency called CONEAU[4] are in charge of accreditation and evaluation processes. In Uruguay the evaluation is a university responsibility.

The reforms of the Latin American higher education systems have been examined by several authors (Krotsh 1997; Sguissardi 1997; Kent 1997, 2001; Arocena and Sutz 2000; Leite 2000, 2002; Fanelli 2000; and Mollis 2001, 2002) and are characterised as the Nineties Neo-liberal Reforms. They have some factors in common: (a) a starting date in the 1990s; (b) the political centralisation of legislative reforms (LOCE 1990, Chile; LES 1995, Argentina; and LDB 1996, Brazil); (c) the introduction of 'national' evaluation and accreditation procedures; and (d) the diversification of the universities' mission.

Under the framework of 'state modernisation', the educational reforms brought about similar results in the different countries. These included the expansion of the system (especially the private sector); the payment of enrolment fees, even in public universities; a salary differentiation among academics through the introduction of teachers' evaluation and a merit-pay system; and the re-location of public resources, altering the universities' budgeting.

The following table shows the expansion and diversification of institutions of higher education (1970–80 and 1997–98) and the allocation of budgeting percentage for higher education in Argentina, Brazil, Chile and Uruguay. The data from different sources are mainly illustrative. Chile is included in order to present the transformation of the systems.

Table 1. Number of higher education institutions and percentage of GNP

	Argentina	Brazil	Chile	Uruguay
Number and type of Institutions	1970 10 Public Univ. 21 Private Univ.	1980 34 Federal Public Univ.	1980 08 Public Univ.	1980 01 Public Univ.
	1997 41 Public Univ. 48 Private Univ. 5 University. Institute Public 5 University. Institute Private 1700 Higher Education Inst.	1998 69 Public Univ. 86 Private Univ. 93 Colleges, Univ. Centres 727 Isolated Institutes	1999 67 Universities 73 Profession. Institutes 127 Centres for Technical Formation	1998 01 Public Univ. 02 Private Univ.
Investments	1998 GNP 4.1% Education	1997 GNP 4.7% Education	1998 GNP 3.6% Education	1998 GNP 2.7% Education
	0.9 Tertiary 2.8 Other levels	1.1 Tertiary 3.1 Other levels	0.6 Tertiary 2.7 Other levels	0.6 Tertiary 1.9 Other levels

Source: MCyE 1999 (Argentina); MEC/INEP 2001 (Brazil); MCE 2001 (Chile); Udelar 2002 (Uruguay); OECD 2001

In Table 1, the percentage of the national GNP to education corresponds to 4.5% in Argentina with 0.9% to higher education institutions; in Brazil 4.7% of GDP for all levels of education and 1.1% for higher education institutions; in Chile this percentage is 3.6% for all levels and 0.6% for higher education institutions; in Uruguay the percentages are 2.7% and 0.6% respectively (OECD 2001). The national budget allocated to higher education is smaller than that going to other educational levels. This corresponds to the policy emphasis of international financing organisations such as the IMF.

Table 2 summarises the main reforms. These include differentiation of resources; public policies for expansion of institutions and enrolments; and mission diversification, academic diversification (services and consultancies) and salary diversification with evaluations of merit and productivity, including a merit-pay system in Brazil – GED (Teachers Gratification Stimulus) for public university teachers. The table condenses the quality evaluation and accreditation systems which include internal evaluation by universities following higher education legislation and an external evaluation that strengthens government power to recognise or accredit higher education institutions' undergraduate and graduate courses. The evaluation processes are under state supervision in the Argentinian and

Chilean cases, and under direct state control in Brazil (Ministry of Education). The processes belong exclusively to the university in the Uruguayan case.

Table 2. Higher education institution reforms

	Argentina	Brazil	Chile	Uruguay
Resources	*Public budgeting *Payment of enrolment	*Public budgeting *Other funds *Payment for specialisations and MBAs in public universities	*Public budgeting *Payment of enrolment	*Public budgeting
Public Policies	*Increase in the number of private institutions *Improvement in enrolments *Mission diversification *Diversification of academic functions *Consultancy and advisory services *Salary differentiation for academics – researchers	*Increase in the number of private institutions *Improvement in enrolments *Mission diversification *Diversification of academic functions *Consultancy and advisory services *Salary differentiation for academics – merit-pay system in public universities (GED)	*Dismantle of public system *Improvement in enrolments *Mission diversification *Diversification of academic functions *Consultancy and advisory services *Salary differentiation for academics	
Evaluation of Higher Education	*Internal: University *External: CONEAU: Evaluation and accreditation of universities and postgraduate courses *Ownership: CONEAU and MCyE	*Internal: University *External: Authorisation (licensing), acknowledgement and credential MEC/INEP – undergraduate MEC/CAPES – postgraduate * Ownership: MEC	*Internal: University *External: Accreditation (licensing, examination, supervision) CNAP and CONAP *Ownership: CSE Consejo Superior de Educación	*Internal: University *External: University *Ownership: University

Source: Kent 1997, 2001; Leite 2002; Leite, Mollis and Contera 2002

It is interesting to note that the reforms were initiated within a context of university autonomy in Argentina, Chile and Uruguay. This was not the case in Brazil. Brazil has a centralised federal administration of education, where the public universities have partial autonomy and the state has strong control over the total system, even over private universities.

Table 3. Funds distribution in public and private tertiary institutions (%)

Sources	Argentina (1998)	Brazil (1998)	Chile (1998)	Uruguay (1998)	Country Averages OECD (1999)
Public sources	74.33	–	24.23	100	77.29
Private sources	25.67	–	75.77	N/A	22.71
Private subsidies	–	–	6.73	N/A	4.81

Source: OECD 2001

In Table 3 it is possible to observe the higher education public and private funding proportions, apart from Uruguay where the single public university is totally state subsidised. The higher education systems in Argentina (74% public funds and 26% private funds) and Chile (24% public funds and 76% private funds) have less public funding then the OECD average percentage (77% public). Unfortunately, the Brazilian data were not available.

Table 4. Enrolment rates – Participation rates (%)

Country	1998–99	1999–00
Argentina	46.94	47.96
Brazil	13.58	14.83
Chile	33.76	37.52
Uruguay	34.75	33.60

Note: World average 25.38%

Source: OECD 2001

When talking about reforms, it is important to see their effect on enrolment rates. Taking into account only one interval at the end of the 1990s, total enrolment rates in three countries (between 1998–99 and 1999–00) have increased (see Table 4). Uruguay did not follow the same pattern, even with respect to the expansion of private institutions, though in 2002 there were four private higher education institutions in the country. Brazil in 2002 exceeded three million enrolments in higher education.

3. REFORMS AND EVALUATIONS: SOME EXAMPLES OF THE CAPITALIST REDESIGN OF UNIVERSITIES

The binomial equation of reforms and evaluations preceded by international pressures on universities, produced a contradictory approach. On one side of the equation one can understand institutional university evaluation as an *instrument of social responsibility*. On the other side, it can be understood as an *instrument of capitalist redesign* of universities.

Evaluation can merely be regarded as a *qualified organiser* which transforms valid data into useful information in a methodic and value-added way that, in itself, does not carry the strength of change. Institutional evaluation can also be regarded as a tool of *democratic responsibility*, stimulating critical thought in the university community and autonomous action of managers and rectors, as observed in one of the case studies – UDELAR (Uruguayan case) – and with less intensity in other cases – UNIJUI and UFRGS (Brazilian cases). As demonstrated by Santos (1994) evaluation is part of a democratic and emancipatory model of a university of ideas. As was pointed out by one of the participants interviewed, the tool of democratic responsibility is part of autonomous evaluation procedures. That occurs when the university forms a new type of link with the public sector, with governmental spheres, with public opinion in general; when it establishes a new type of link which is supported by transparent and true information about itself, making clear what its compromises are, its real results and its internal quality control process. In this respect, a political requirement is satisfied. Institutional evaluation appears as an important tool of democratic responsibility (Leite 2000; Leite, Mollis and Contera 2002).

However, institutional evaluation procedures can also contribute to the *capitalist redesign of universities,* a kind of institutional performance marked by characteristic traces of a certain specialised knowledge, science and services commodification and by a new management of campuses where private commercialisation (for profit) is taking place. These aspects – in part or in combination – were observed locally in some of the nine universities which were the object of the case studies: UNISINOS, UNESP, UFRGS, UFPEL (Brazilian cases); URF, UNSJ (Argentinian cases). With varying degrees of intensity, these cases confirmed what was previously presented by Barrow (1996), Cowen (1996) and Buchbinder (1993).

In the internal changes taking place in the university context it was possible to observe the kind of movement I call a capitalist redesign. As stated in the introduction to this chapter, this can be explained by certain characteristics being assumed by universities such as 'market-oriented goals' (Buchbinder 1993), 'performativity' (Cowen 1996) and the search for 'selective excellence' (Barrow 1996) with respect to evaluation processes. It may be useful to briefly summarise the main concerns of each of the selected authors.

Buchbinder, in the early 1990s, examined the changing role of knowledge production in universities in the context of global competition. He discussed, in a well-known paper, the kind of development of corporate–university linkages that was occurring in the information society facing the globalisation of capital. Examining the market-driven university in Canada, he explained the market-oriented goals and objectives of higher education which come together so that the centralisation of management reduces collegial and democratic possibilities.

> The objectives of higher education which are expressed as the production and transmission of knowledge as a social good are replaced by an emphasis on the production of knowledge as a market good, a saleable commodity. Simultaneously, the development of a market oriented university supersedes academic decision making (Buchbinder 1993: 335).

By performativity in the post-modern university, Cowen, supported by previous studies of Lyotard on post-modernity, mainly examines useful knowledge production in universities. For him it is important to see the double meaning of performativity as an epistemological condition and at the same time as a political project:

(...) as both an epistemological condition and, when it comes to the relations of higher education and the state, as an explicit political project. Performativity has to be socially constructed. It is stimulated by an external, extra national challenge and framed by the political decision that universities are the correct locus and arena for the interlinking of business–industry–state concerns for performativity (Cowen 1996: 252).

Following Cowen's and Buchbinder's thoughts, Barrow (1996), referring to the American system of higher education, describes the strategy of selective excellence which can push institutional redesign to better take advantage of global competition. In response to fiscal crises, universities engage in a reform process. Such reforms include a shift from institutional emulation to differentiation; a shift from basic to applied research and to interdisciplinary and multidisciplinary studies; and a shift from departments to centres and institutes. For Barrow, the strategy of selective excellence involves a consensus among decision makers and policy makers. Downsizing processes are central to this strategy that is "designed to rationalize the American system of higher education by further differentiating the missions of individual institutions, eliminating programs that do not support that mission and by shifting research activities into interdisciplinary applied research centers" (Barrow 1996: 447).

In research in the Latin American countries, the existence of market-oriented goals and of performativity and selective excellence are observed along with the presence of a market within the universities, with stores and companies on the campus site. Evidence includes private sponsorship for all activities; utilitarian or applied research and other financed activities by non-traditional entities; professorial entrepreneurs who are able to seize external resources for their research and laboratories; and undergraduate and graduate course fees, even those offered in the public universities which are state supported. Other aspects of redesigning were confirmed, even though more apparent in some countries and universities than in others. On a continuum, Brazil is more involved with these shifts than Argentina, which might be more involved than Portugal or Uruguay.

Some other understated aspects, concerning the capitalist redesign of universities, are as follows (Leite 2000, 2002).

- Graded evaluations – the most complete example is Brazil with the well-known national courses examination (National Study Diplomas Evaluation), the Provão.[5] The examination provides information on curricula coherence and flexibility. It influences decisions about the kind of knowledge to be taught. There is a set minimum study content for each professional career, which is mainly defined by experts outside the academy or by the assessment materials themselves. The examinations produce institutional rankings which stimulate intensive competition amongst different institutions. Merit-pay systems and competition for research grants do the same amongst teachers and researchers.
- Evaluations produced by agencies outside the universities, in a top-down system, like CONEAU in Argentina and INEP[6] in Brazil (and Chile) also contribute to the capitalist redesign of the academy. The Ministry in Brazil sets policy and carries out evaluation and accreditation of courses. The results

of evaluations are publicised in the media where institutions are ranked accordingly. Much of this publicity raises doubts amongst the public about the academic, pedagogic, administrative and financial quality of the universities. A low ranking of a certain programme of study at the national level seriously threatens the status of the institution as a whole, and may reduce its ability to obtain additional resources.

- Academic capitalism[7] is another factor where professorial entrepreneurs, in obtaining resources for their research, have to search for national and international visibility and prestige. Activities, such as courses and seminars, are put on the market by the best-selling names in a particular field. National and international specialists, or commissions of 'specialists', sell advisory and consultative services, suggesting transformations of the curricula and internal evaluations, which in turn affect external evaluations. The influence of the specialised professorial entrepreneur tends to be stronger in the most developed countries or regions in one single country (in Argentina, Brazil and Uruguay).

- Top-down decisions (taken in the light of central government measures) are internally processed by managers and institutional governing bodies. In the university, these decisions, especially those about the graded evaluation, are made in an inexplicable absence of public criticism from the faculty members (in Brazil).

- Decisions of a managerial character are common in Latin American systems, either central or local, inducing constraint in costs, such as salary cuts or the reduction of teaching posts. Early retirement of qualified professors or technicians is a common occurrence. Temporary employment with low salary and a heavy teaching load is also frequent. New recruits, employees with precarious work contracts or those at the base of their careers, tend either to normalise the changes or consider these changes as a part of the context. It is as if they had always been present, a natural characteristic of the system. Some people appreciate the merit evaluation as a way of increasing their salary (in Brazil and Argentina).

- Governance decisions merge with strategic planning and alter the way universities are managed. The central management team, which may be a small group, sometimes listens to external constituents and supercedes collegial management in order to 'accelerate' decision making and to control communication flows and costs. Drastic course and department cuts are seen, even in public universities. The decisions can also include the reduction and re-utilisation of teaching and technician posts. The wide financial activity of the public universities' foundation is combined with a certain degree of centralised decision making, sometimes without accountability.[8] Wide and special powers are given to management teams including the selling and renting of the institution's patrimonial property. These teams, sometimes, work with external members from specialised market enterprises. Often times events occur, frequently without academic control (in Argentina and Brazil).

- There are the more entrepreneurial universities with an active or moderate role in the knowledge market, including partnerships between staff and students in forming their own businesses, the development of company incubators, national and international patent registration etc. Registered products are put on the market. Technology parks, and other similar activities, are established on campus (especially in Brazil).
- There is the establishment of local branch campuses involving campus expansion over different locations (Brazil, Argentina, Uruguay), counties or regions in search of potential consumers. There is the offering of classroom-based and virtual courses, singularly or in association with other institutions (twinning arrangements) with a strong bias towards the administration, finance, computer and engineering areas.

This set of characteristics forms a new epistemology that suggests that universities are setting new course directions and redesigning their profile. In order to further illustrate what is occurring, the following section presents one of the evaluation case studies. But, first, a summary of the Brazilian evaluation system will be presented in order to set the scene.

4. THE BRAZILIAN HIGHER EDUCATION SYSTEM AND THE EVALUATION SYSTEM

In order to talk about evaluation in Brazil it is necessary to illustrate the size and diversity of the system. The publication by O Estado de São Paulo of 23 November 2002 about the 'Future of Higher Education' provides a useful summary:

> The Census of Higher Education shows that a number of students who started courses at this level in Brazil grew 16.46% between 2000 and 2001. Last year, 1,206,273 new students were admitted in higher education institutions against 1,035,750 in the previous year. The goal of 3 million enrolled was already exceeded and 69.9% of university students are in private institutions. (...) The private system, as shown in the Census, was much more efficient than the public to assist the demand for higher education. From the 395,000 students graduating in 2001, 260,000 attended private colleges. Among these undergraduate students there is a strong number in some careers: 44,000 were in Law, 37,000 in Pedagogy and 35,000 in Business. Brazil has had also, since 2001, more than 8,000 doctors and, curiously, more than 12,767 journalists. These data indicate a tenuous balance between the type of diploma offered and market absorption.

The size of the Brazilian system of higher education can be seen in Table 5. On offer are about 10,585 undergraduate courses (study diplomas) with 2,694,245 enrolled students whose main choice is professional careers in Social Sciences, Business and Law (41.6%), followed by careers in Education (21.7%), Health and Social Welfare (12%), Science, Math and Computer Science (8.7%) and Engineering, Production and Construction (8.7%). Staff qualifications are different for public and private sectors. In public institutions, almost 70% of the teachers have masters and doctorate degrees; in the private institutions, 32.1% have a masters degree and 11.3% a doctorate degree. The teacher/student ratio is 1:11 in the federal and regional public institutions and 1:17.3 in the private ones. The ratio of candidate per vacancy is close to 10 in public institutions and 2.0 in private ones.

Table 5. Undergraduate numbers – Brazil 2000

	Total	Administrative Categories			
		Federal	State	Municipal	Private
Institutions	1,180	61	61	54	1,004
Courses	10,585	1,996	1,755	270	6,564
Enrolments	2,694,245	482,750	332,104	72,172	1,807,219
Concluders	324,734	59,098	43,757	9,596	212,283
Active Teachers	183,194	43,739	30,836	4,137	104,482
Active Civil Servants	198,074	67,001	43,879	2,693	84,501
Vestibular (Entrance examinations):					
Offered Vacancies	1,100,224	115,272	94,441	28,269	862,242
Enrolments	3,826,293	1,129,749	951,594	59,044	1,685,906
Admissions	829,706	113,388	90,341	23,428	602,549
Enrolments (%):					
Evening classes	56.1	23.1	44.6	75.6	66.2
Females	56.2	50.6	57.9	56.9	57.4
Enrolment per Area (%):					
Education	21.7	20.6	43.3	30.7	17.7
Human Sciences and Arts	3.4	7.4	4.6	1.8	2.0
Social Sciences, Business and Law	41.6	24.4	19.9	43.7	50.1
Sciences, Mathematics and Computer Science	8.7	12.2	8.1	7.5	7.9
Engineering, Production and Construction	8.7	14.4	10.7	6.6	6.9
Agriculture and Veterinary	2.3	5.9	3.6	1.6	1.2
Health and Social Welfare	12.0	14.5	9.4	7.5	12.0
Services	1.6	0.6	0.4	0.6	2.2
Teachers Total (%):					
With Masters	31.4	34.5	25.4	24.6	32.1
With Doctorate	20.6	33.4	33.1	9.6	11.3
Teacher/Student Ratio	14.7	11.0	10.8	17.4	17.3
Candidates per Vacancy	3.5	9.8	10.1	2.1	2.0

Source: MEC/INEP 2000

Considering the diversity and complexity of the system, it is possible to imagine the variable quality of higher education institutions in Brazil. Thus, many evaluative approaches were introduced by the Ministry of Education in comprising a quality evaluation system. As stated by Amaral and Polidori (1999: 82):

> Besides the unequal distribution of resources across the country, the Brazilian HE system is also extremely heterogeneous as regards the quality of education, some universities being of very high quality and with an excellent research reputation, while many others are little more than secondary schools.

The evaluation of higher education institutions in Brazil has been occurring since 1970, through CAPES (Coordination of Higher Education Personnel Improvement) which is concerned with research and postgraduate education. But it was in the 1990s that the process of global evaluation of institutions, students, teachers and professional careers, especially at the undergraduate level, began.

The international movement towards quality evaluation of universities, especially the Thatcherian neo-liberal model, caught the attention of Brazilian rectors, universities and the Ministry of Education. Between 1992 and 1996 many actors began to play a similar role. The rectors of federal universities, through ANDIFES (National Association of Federal Universities) with the acquiescence of ANDES (National Higher Education Teachers Association) proposed to the Ministry of Education a programme of evaluation based on the CAPES experience and on the Dutch evaluation model. This had wide repercussions in the academic environment. Known as PAIUB (Program of Institutional Evaluation of Brazilian Universities), it began operation in 1993. Almost simultaneously, teachers, students and corporations began to discuss the principles and interests involved in quality evaluation and accreditation. The Health Sciences planned and executed their own programme, the CINAEM (National Council for Evaluation of Medical Education), to the schools of Medicine. The state, as the main actor, was involved in the discussions throughout the implementation of an evaluation system whose main focus was on student examination verification: the Provão (discussed above). The Provão was initiated in 1995 by the Secretary of Higher Education in the Ministry of Education and is presently the responsibility of INEP/MEC (National Institute for Educational Study and Research/Ministry of Education). Recently, the rectors of CRUB (Council of Brazilian Rectors Association), which constitutes private, communitarian, confessional and public institutions, entered the scene by proposing a model of evaluation that was more independent and along the lines initially proposal by PAIUB.

As Kells (1996) maintains, the intensive involvement of different actors pushed Brazil to the front of what was happening in Latin America in higher education in the 1990s. Brazil provided the greatest contribution to the development of institutional evaluation in this part of the world, especially through the accumulated experience of CAPES which established a pioneer programme of research and postgraduate evaluation.

However, the diversity of the higher education system in Brazil with a great number of universities and higher education institutions of different types made the establishment of a unitary evaluation process very difficult. At the end of the 1990s, the evaluation system of higher education, supported by pertinent legislation (Magna Law, Art. 84, Inc. IV and V; Law 4024/61; Law 9131/95; Law 9394/96 and Decree 3860/01), comprised:

a) general system evaluation through higher education indicators produced from data of the Annual Census of Higher Education Institutions (by region, unit of the federation, fields of knowledge and type of higher education institution), by INEP/MEC;

b) institutional evaluation of higher education institutions (Institutional Self-evaluation and Internal Evaluation) modelled on PAIUB, or CRUB or MEC, by the institution;

c) external evaluation of institutions and of the undergraduate formation through the ENC (National Examination of Study Diploma), a national courses examination called Provão, plus the 'Teaching Conditions Offer' of each educational institution examined by ministry specialists (a field peer review), by INEP/MEC. The data from these two evaluations will comprise the national ranking of higher education institutions;

d) external evaluation of research and postgraduate courses by CAPES/MEC; the data from this evaluation classifies the Brazilian programmes on a numerical scale (1 to 7);

e) evaluation of federal university teachers, a self-evaluation by teachers and special commissions in universities – GED (Teachers Gratification Stimulus); it comprises a merit-pay system in order to increase salaries.

The results of the evaluations are considered for licensing, recognition and accreditation of the higher education institutions. Institutions must also present their PDI, a plan of institutional development.

Given the above as background, I will now present a case study of institutional evaluation, the Case Study of UNISINOS (the University of Rio dos Sinos Valley). This is a confessional and communitarian university that participated in the evaluation called PAIUB between 1994 and 1996, after which it engaged in the evaluation proposed by MEC – Provão. It also used the CAPES evaluation.

As part of the main research project, the methodology for the case study followed the orientation of Bogdan and Biklen (1982) and Miles and Huberman (1994) for qualitative research in education; of Leonardos, Gomes and Walker (1992) for case studies applied to educational innovation; and Yin (1994) for case studies in general. I argue that a case study about a lived situation can be of great interest for educators and managers because it "illuminate[s] a decision or a set of decisions: why they are taken, how they were implemented, and with what result" (Yin 1994: 12).

5. CASE STUDY: INSTITUTIONAL EVALUATION OF UNISINOS

The University of Rio dos Sinos Valley – UNISINOS – is located in São Leopoldo, Rio Grande do Sul, Brazil. It is a private, not-for-profit, confessional institution, owned by the 'Sociedade Antônio Vieira da Companhia de Jesus'. Its origins date from 1869 when the first Jesuits – Spanish, Austrian and German – arrived in the state of Rio Grande do Sul to administer to the European settlers. The Jesuits also assumed an educative mission, founding a school for new priests. At this school in 1953 the colleges of Philosophy, Sciences and Arts were created. In 1958, new higher education courses began. In 1969 UNISINOS was authorised by the Ministry of Education (Decree 722/69). The institution has had a difficult history. Between 1986 and 1990, there were problems with strikes, reduction in enrolments and financial restrictions that made the institution mortgage part of its heritage. The number of student enrolments dropped from 22,348 in 1990 to 18,812 in 1991 and to 16,602 in 1992. These factors led the new university to search for a new profile and to invest in new planning and evaluation approaches (UNISINOS 1998). Main changes involved the structure of university units and the administrative management of the university. From the original centralised structure – pro-rectories, schools, study programmes and departments – the institution began to decentralise. Teaching centres were established each with a collegiate administrative staff comprising a director, an administrative pro-director and an extension, research and teaching pro-director. The centres subsumed previous departments. They were grouped by field of knowledge and had the function of organising and executing teaching, research and services. The centres were as follows: Centre of Human Sciences, of Law Sciences, of Economic Sciences, of Math and Exact Sciences and of Technological Sciences. The rector was nominated by the Jesuit order. The centres' directors were elected. The rector can be successively re-appointed to the position. UNISINOS has four main administrative branches: Academic, Financial Resources, Human Resources and Grounds and Facilities.

The institutional evaluation programme was installed, integrating PAIUB (UNISINOS 1994). This programme was part of the strategic plan whose implementation had been presenting difficulties due to lack of acceptance by teachers. Most of the principles defined by the plan caused fear because teachers foresaw new forms of organisation – the centres – and new forms of work distribution. It was necessary to have an organisational reconfiguration.

In 1994 when UNISINOS adhered to PAIUB, strategic planning became more participative and gained the teachers' trust. It added new goals to the evaluation in addition to those in the original strategic plan. "We were not participating on the institutional evaluation because of PAIUB's pressure. We were hitched to our strategic plan and because of that there were no difficulties to join PAIUB because we had already gone a long way" (Interview 1999). The main objectives of the evaluation programme in phase I were: (a) "guide the university towards the acknowledgement of its potential in the search for innovative perspectives; (b) guarantee the constant improvement of quality; (c) promote a self-knowledge process to rethink goals, forms of action and results on the perspective of a UNISINOS adjusted to its own strategic project; (d) propose and implement changes on activities of teaching, research and extension services and on processes of management, contributing to the reformulation of projects" (UNISINOS 1995). The phases of PAIUB – sensibilisation (sensibilização), internal and external evaluation and re-evaluation – were met. The management of the evaluation process was decentralised – committees of institutional evaluation (CAI and NACs) were created. These committees, one general and one for each centre, were composed of members from the teachers' board, students, former students, employees, experts on evaluation and one member of the Strategic Planning Group. The evaluation methodology, drawn from PAIUB, was as follows: (a) presentation of the project to the internal community and creation of NACs; (b) sensibilisation with seminars, conferences and publications on the theme; (c) diagnosis (data collected on undergraduate studies); (d) analysis of the data collected for each course of the six centres followed by reports (self-evaluation); (e) constitution of committees for external evaluation (reports on internal evaluation were sent to external evaluators who came to the institution and discussed the evaluation with representatives of the centres' courses and presented suggestions about quality improvement); (f) decision making based on reflections about the process of evaluation through seminars; discussion and spread of documents; projections on the future with improvement measures; and data dissemination to appropriate units to improve decision making (UNISINOS 1995: 26, 27). The external evaluation was applied to three courses: History, Social Services and Geology. The evaluation of other courses, after 1995, was undertaken by the Specialists Committee which since the advent of Provão was part of the National Brazilian System of Evaluation of the Ministry of Education.

The participants of the first evaluation phase reported through interviews the difficulties in conducting an evaluation programme: "The proposal to evaluate, initially, was understood as a proposal of change and that caused a certain distrust of the teachers and a certain anxiety in students; there was no time for writing, for registering the evaluation history; there was only a simple analysis of the data without profundity due to the lack of time of the teams; a characteristic of the process – the dissemination of data within each Center, showed some analysis very distant of its real meaning; showed the absence of a whole perspective, a perspective of totality" (Interview 1999). The interviewees (1999) reported the changes accomplished by evaluation and strategic planning. A special budget rubric was created for evaluation, there was no lack of resources; in the centres' environment it was observed that the students were complaining less about their teachers; an integration of the nuclei in the centres was also observed: "... the NAC is now a part of the coordination collegiate of the Center". Some of the students' requests were accommodated. There was more pedagogical support for teachers and the establishment of a unit to assist students with financial or other special needs such as the physically handicapped. There were changes to curricula, organisational structure (mentioned above), infrastructure (mainly libraries), management practices and communication inside and outside the campus. The students perceived the evaluation process as a channel of communication with the institution through the 'public hearing audience' when the results of evaluations were returned to them: "We gathered all data in an exhibition in the corridors" (Interview 1999). A project on the use of new technologies in teaching and for the training of technicians and employees was approved. Investments in services were intensified reaching municipalities near the campus. This meant an opening up to the outside community, and new relations with the society. This can be seen in the Technological Pole, InfoPole, Project Bravo São Leopoldo, communitarian activities in some centres, nature preservation activities and actions, and the creation of the EGT (Office of Management and Technology) to bring the labour market closer. For the latter, an information system and a databank were implemented. The articulation between different proposals should be emphasised: "... from the strategic planning we have a provision and from that we have the changes in curricula; so, the Centers have their structure ... there has been an internal change and we [teachers] moved to the Centers and the Centers have their proposal adjusted to the strategic planning, mainly with the mission and the religious creed of the university" (Interview 1999).

The transformations happened together in a participative process that gained the confidence of the staff. Even pedagogical projects began to refer to the strategic planning and to the evaluation: "The Pedagogical Project for us, to reach the changing terms, must have its references on the rectorship or on the strategic planning, [because] on it is defined the *mission purposes, the creed, the vision of the university. The Center in this case gave us a sort of filter. In 'filtering' it reaches the curriculum ... it really made this articulation"* (Interview 1999).

In 1996, the university commenced phase II of undergraduate evaluation through the National Examination of Study Diploma. The graduate evaluation was still conducted by CAPES. These processes, as seen in the previous section about the Brazilian system of evaluation, aim at the acknowledgement of disciplinary courses and the accreditation of the institution.

From 1999 to 2002 many innovations took place. New courses including distance education and several initiatives based on regional needs were offered. Among them are included new teaching technologies, curricula flexibility, modular structure and partial diplomas and the search for new educational market niches. The niches include: Studies in Audio-Visual Media – Movies, TV, Documentary, Photography, Animation, Games, Internet; Computer Sciences applied to Engineering and Management for Leadership and Innovation in Business. The campus was opened to the community of the region creating the UniCity (UniCidade) with a convenience centre (shopping malls, food court, amphitheater, services, cinema, restaurants, health assistance), a knowledge centre (library – open day and night, art gallery, concert hall, bookshop, cybercafe, exhibitions and video room) and a sports and leisure centre (humanist leisure concept for all ages). The UNISINOS, with a radio station and TV channel, turned out to be one of the largest universities in Brazil. In 2001 the institution enrolled 30,667 students in undergraduate courses, 1,432 in graduate programmes and 7,115 students in extension courses. It has 1,065 teachers, 21% with PhDs and 48% with masters degrees. In 2002 the university had five courses with A grade, seven with B grade and five with C grade at the Provão and two graduate programmes with grade 5 from CAPES, two with grade 4, and eight programmes with grade 3 CAPES all from the MEC evaluation.

6. ANALYSIS OF THE UNISINOS CASE

The case study emphasises 'strategic planning' as a tool of administrative–academic management. In contrast to some experiences elsewhere, at UNISINOS the process involved wide participation of the community and had its strength assured by the evaluation. UNISINOS integrated PAIUB at the right time because it served as an element of belief, of trust in the changes that were being led by the central university administration via external consultancy. This strategy was used as a resource to introduce changes that were either felt or perceived as necessary in the face of threats to survival. From 1986 to 1990 the particular problems that led the institution to mortgage part of its heritage forced the need for change. People longed for strategic planning as an instrument to bring about change. But it was the 'strategic evaluation', the seminars 'Challenges of Changes' and the participative methodology that compelled the community to accept the strategic planning process. Institutional evaluation became a way of knowing how best to improve, of learning and acquiring competence to change pedagogically and administratively.

What was observed next was a radical transformation of the university. The institution eliminated departments, schools and units and implemented the university centres. The first signs of change came from the evaluation process. The coordination of institutional development began to concentrate the functions of evaluation together with the teams of each centre (NACs). In that way, the institutional evaluation process began to be decentralised and was conducted on an annual basis.

How can one understand the evaluation and its influence on management in this individual university? In the team's own words, UNISINOS worked with a 'strategic evaluation'. It is strategic because it served to integrate information, to search for quality with a rationalisation of resources and with the participation of the community. In this manner strategic evaluation contributed to the project of organisational re-configuration that had a real and effective impact towards change and innovation. The evaluation was not the only accelerator of change but was essential for it. This case makes us think about universities that are oriented by the strategy of selective excellence that, according to Barrow (1996), look for differentiation in their institutional mission, eliminating programmes or activities which can no longer be supported. They try to coordinate activities of teaching and research in interdisciplinary programmes. It can be asked, with respect to selective excellence, if in this case the intention was to downsize the institution in the face of the budgetary crisis – understood as imminent in the globalised recession and losses of clients (students) – or was it only a local economical and organisational strategy?

The case study can also be understood in terms of the market-oriented university model and performativity model centred on information, services and technology as part of the post-industrial economy. The university invests in information and the evaluation constitutes one aspect of this. It invests in services, including specialised assistance to students; in a wide sense it captures markets and invests in technology. Its objective, however, seems to be closer to the model of selective excellence since, as Barrow (1996: 453) says: "... a common theme in strategic master plans and restructuring proposals is the idea that individual institutions must sharpen their mission by concentrating on specialized areas of institutional strength or on areas of high market demand". In some institutions, the author says, the idea of a traditional multiversity is often rejected. In the Report of External Evaluation of the Rectors from HRK (1998), ordered by the state government of Rio Grande do Sul, the institution is seen as a typical regional higher education structure that does not concentrate on innovative courses that answer the needs of the market. This option could confirm the model of specialisation by differentiation.

However, the UNISINOS Case supports Barrow because it shows that the institutional evaluation was co-author of the strategic process of change. Selective excellence "depends on a clarification of institutional mission, the identification of mission-oriented programs, and the identification of comparatively weak academic programs, along with areas of low student demand on a campus" (Barrow 1996: 454).

In studying the UNISINOS Case, one can see what Barrow terms as interrelated structural reforms and non-traditional organisational structures in the examples of change that evolve from mission differentiation to basic research, to applied research; from disciplinary studies to interdisciplinary ones; and from organised activities in departments to the matrix of centres. These transformations are identifiable, especially in the creation of the centres, as indicators of a shrinkage in the management organisational structure. A large number of teachers in the centres suffered a loss of identity in relation to the former department-based organisational structure. But it should be noted that the same evaluation procedure that permitted the strategic change 'was the institutional evaluation previously agreed'. The evaluation process (PAIUB phase I) was mainly responsible for a participative methodology which created communication links between the academic community and the institution; a return to the 'public hearing audience' that provides managers with the possibility of adjustments and articulation of their institutions' mission, in a process to support decisions. What differentiates UNISINOS from other universities which used the same PAIUB evaluation methodology are the paradigms supporting it. The process is innovative in its wide spectrum because it aligns competence with a vision of a consensually agreed future probably shared by the academic community.

As the participative methodology of institutional evaluation has been exhausted in recent years and the institution has assumed the external evaluation of MEC, which utilises a totally opposite methodology, it is possible to identify a strong swing in the direction of the market, in order to cope with competition. Considering the elements which characterise the capitalist redesign of universities, it is possible to observe in this case a new set of investments: curricula and pedagogical changes, flexible curriculum (aimed at the market) such as the new courses in Audio-Visual, Engineering and Management, and distance education programmes. The marketable use of the national examination results from the rankings of MEC (Provão and CAPES), products of a classificatory evaluation (phase II), are also observed.

So long as a process of evaluation sets the pace, the institution maintains the reformist spirit. At the beginning, evaluation phase I, even top-down decisions were widely discussed with the academic community through the institutional evaluation mechanisms. However, during phase II, MEC evaluation was not always consensual, neither voted on in collegiate bodies nor were the results of evaluation always shared with the academic community.

This case study shows a typical institution in search of expansion through a wide and careful engagement with the community, internal and external (strategic evaluation). One can ask: How long will these strategies be productive? While there has been a 'paradigm shift' towards the market, internal and external, selective excellence was also evidenced by the data collected. What attracts attention in this case is the evaluation process in different surroundings, that is, the conduct of evaluation in a strategic manner, in the apparently double-sided relationship of the academic and administrative community. If this 'surroundings of evaluation' cannot be maintained, will the institution transform itself in the direction of an entrepreneurial, redesigned university?

By supporting change based on strategic evaluation and planning involving a participative methodology, the institution, in less than 10 years, has moved from a time when problems and debts were severe to a time when social learning and technical capital were enhanced. The capitalist redesign – a humanist redesign in the interviewees' words – may be understood in terms of the evaluative procedures that have contributed to institutional learning.

7. UNIVERSITIES AS LEARNING ORGANISATIONS

Apparently, the *capitalist redesigning* of universities has been configuring itself as a preferential path, post-evaluation. Aiming at the reorientation of their mission, universities improve their governance practices. It can be observed, as in the UNISINOS Case, that many of the organisational structures and communication flows become better understood after evaluation processes because the institutional data were better organised and documented. The performance criteria based on specific quantitative indicators, including the national rankings, lead the institution to search for efficiency and efficacy of administrative management with profound repercussions for the academic management of teaching, research and extension. This was observed in the case study.

Traditionally, universities were non-profit institutions, collegially oriented with academics managing the production, storage and dissemination of knowledge with state or church support. The idea of knowledge as an intangible asset was widely disseminated. However, the capitalist mode of production, itself expanding, carries in its globalising path knowledge, services and the institutions that produce them. The clearest example is the World Trade Organisation's intentions (through GATS – General Agreement on Trade in Services) to commodify services – the expansion of capital forces, the search for new markets. Presently, capitalist ownership is being extended to services and knowledge which were previously considered in the public domain.

Universities are contributing to these new markets by redesigning their mission in new directions, searching for diversification. If they didn't know how to do this in the past, they are certainly learning now, where evaluations have taught them more about themselves (internal evaluations) and about their external image (external evaluations and rankings). Nobody can say that universities are engaging in the new globalisation era in the absence of their own efforts: universities are engaging in the new era as learning organisations.

In a simple and utopian way, one can state that a learning organisation, especially the university, involves a group of people which holds common values and objectives, putting themselves at the disposal of institutional development and improvement. The university is a very special organisation, though. People who make it what it is today are not the same people who constituted the academy in the past. Still, they espouse the preservation of a certain 'soul' or common spirit that crosses the centuries. People presently at universities find different solutions to their problems; they represent various groups and interests based on gender and cultural, religious, ethnic and social status diversity. They are at the same time part and parcel of a given social structure within the same institution.

Universities (independently of their original model – Humboldtian, Napoleonic, Latin American) also share features that tie them to the past and make them resist some of the imposed external pressures. This resistance is, in part, based on what remains of academic freedom. Academic freedom helps explain the preservation of the university organisation over the centuries, and distinguishes them from other corporate organisations associated with knowledge production.

In opposition to these corporate institutions, the university has a product (if we can call it that) of long maturation. It is an institution oriented to the long term. It is a work-intensive institution, not a capital-intensive one (Santos 1994). However, in a society of knowledge and information, the flow of products needs to be quicker. These products require compatible action strategies as well as management and evaluation. Therefore, when I mention a learning organisation, I mean that learning is being processed at a certain speed in terms of a post-evaluation option. But the university must be up-to-date with what happens regularly at other institutions, companies and governments. Evaluation processes can be regarded as links in the chain of happenings flowing in national and international contexts, having as a starting point the expansion of information in the knowledge-based society. This all spreads out to regional and local levels through the educational reforms led by attentive governments. The commodification of universities' services and products, and their entrance into the marketplace in the most various ways as shown in the UNISINOS Case Study, put universities closer to being companies when they are after immediate profits to survive. Obviously, there are benefits and losses.

The knowledge society rhetoric is confronted by a market reality in the universities, both public and private, where the professorial entrepreneur is the key figure. The entrepreneurial university is the recognised body; evaluation is the mechanism that establishes a market differential through rankings. The main products are knowledge, science and technology. Universities in a knowledge society are, as is the case with other human organisations, in a learning process: learning to live in a global economy.

NOTES

[1] The research projects are: Leite, D., M. Mollis and C. Contera. *Inovação e avaliação institucional: efeitos e mudanças na missão das universidades contemporâneas* (Br, Uy, Arg). Porto Alegre, Evangraf Editora, 2002. Report supported by CNPq, FAPERGS; Santiago, R. *Evaluation, Institutional Self-analysis and Higher Education Management*. Aveiro, Pt, FCT, Sapiens Project, 2002; Leite, D. et al. *Avaliação, auto-análise e gestão das universidades: um estudo conjunto Brasil-Portugal*. Porto Alegre, Br–Aveiro, Pt, 2002. Final Report supported by CNPq–ICCTI, FAPERGS.

[2] The case studies of institutional evaluation were conducted at: (a) public universities: UFRGS, UFPEL and UNESP, Brazil; UNSJ and UCPBas, Argentina; UDELAR, Uruguay; University of Aveiro, Portugal; and (b) private or communitarian universities: UNISINOS and UNIJUI, Brazil; Universidad Rene Favaloro, Argentina.

[3] National education policy is often influenced by the interests of the international financing institutions, see: WB (1993) *Argentina: From Insolvency to Growth*; WB (1994) *O ensino superior: lições da experiência*; Winkler, D. (1994) *La educación superior en América Latina*; WB (1996)

Higher Education in Latin America and the Caribbean: A Strategy Paper; WB (1996) Social Program Division, IDB, Draft 11/06/1996; WB (2000) *Higher Education in Developing Countries: Peril or Promise*; IMF *(2001) IMF 01/2001 Report – Brazil*. The financial agencies' 'recommendations', or desirable features for Latin American higher education, expressed by the different authors cited above are: 1) differentiation of institutions; 2) fiscal funding with results; 3) diversification of financial sources; 4) re-definition of the management of higher education; 5) quality and equity; 6) reduction of curricula (in years of study); and 7) performance criteria for the allocation of public resources. More recently, some of the 'recommendations' of best practice include: 1) reduction of the total amount of the countries' external debts (loans) in relation to a systemic reform of the higher education systems; 2) systemic reform of the higher education systems; 3) flexible curricula; 4) system expansion; 5) more openness to market forces; 6) mixed funding models; 7) improvement of institutions' governance and management; and 8) cooperation and competition for physical and human capital (Leite 2002).

[4]   CONEAU – National Commission for University Evaluation and Accreditation – is a decentralised evaluation agency which operates under the supervision of 12 members appointed by the National Inter-university Council, Private Universities' Rectors Council, National Academy of Education, Ministry of Education and designated by the National Congress.

[5]   Provão is a national disciplinary examination, ruled by law – MP1018/95; LDB9394/96; Port.249/96; Dec.2026/96; Dec.3860/01. It is compulsory (since 1995) for undergraduate students in their last year of studies. Its main objective is to measure student learning aiming at an external evaluation of the quality of the study programme and the educational provision offered by each higher education institution. The student's grades are used only to classify the student's programme of study in the national Brazilian ranking of higher education institutions.

[6]   The INEP (National Institute for Educational Study and Research) of the Ministry of Education (MEC) headed by its Directory of Higher Education Access and Evaluation (DAAES) is the external agency in charge of the execution and application of Provão to public and private higher education institutions. Until 2000, about 18 knowledge areas were assessed: law, economy, journalism, medicine (health), veterinary, odontology, psychology, agrarian sciences, biology, chemistry, physics, languages, business administration, civil engineering, electric engineering, mechanical engineering, chemical engineering. Until 2000, 191,000 students from the total national territory were assessed corresponding to 2,888 disciplinary courses. Examinations are held annually.

[7]   "Academic capitalism, or academic entrepreneurism or entrepreneurial activity – define the reality of a nascent environment of public research universities, an environment full of contradictions, in which faculty and professional staff expend their human capital stocks increasingly in competitive situations. In these situations, university employees are employed simultaneously by the public sector and are increasingly autonomous from it. They are academics who act as capitalists from within the public sector; they are state subsidized entrepreneurs" (Slaughter and Leslie 1999: 9).

[8]   In the Brazilian public sector the financial administration of public entities is controlled by the Tribunal de Contas da União. But in the public universities, special agencies, who are faster and more flexible, manage financial resources, especially competitive research funds, in an autonomous way – they are the universities' foundation.

REFERENCES

Amaral, A. and M. Polidori. "Quality Evaluation in Brazil: A Competency Based Approach?" *Higher Education Policy* 12 (1999): 177–199.

Arocena, R. and J. Sutz."La nueva reforma universitaria vista desde el Uruguay." *Separata Revista Avaliação* 3.10 (2001): 5–15.

Barrow, C. "The Strategy of Selective Excellence: Redesigning Higher Education for Global Competition in a Post-modern Society." *Higher Education* 41 (1996): 447–469.

Bogdan, R. and S.K. Biklen. *Qualitative Research for Education*. Boston: Allyn and Bacon, 1982.

Buchbinder, H. "The Market Oriented University and the Changing Role of Knowledge." *Higher Education* 26 (1993): 331–347.

Cowen, R. "Performativity, Post-modernity and the University." *Comparative Education* 32.2 (1996): 245–258.

Fanelli, A.M.G. "Los indicadores de las políticas de reforma universitaria Argentina: balance de la situación actual y perspectivas futuras." *Seminario Regional Taller: Gestión, evaluación y acreditación de instituciones de educación superior.* Buenos Aires: FLACSO, 6–10 November, 2000, 1–35.

HRK (Hocshschul Rektoren Conferenz). *Relatório de um grupo de consultores da HRK acerca da situação e do desempenho das IES no estado do Rio Grande do Sul, Brasil e das perspectivas de uma política estadual coordenadora de fomento.* Bonn, Germany: HRK, 1998.

Kells, H.R. "Higher Education Evaluation Systems for Latin America: An Analysis of Recent Experiences and Formulation of a Generalized Model." *Higher Education Policy* 9 (1996): 239–253.

Kent, Rollin (Comp.). *Los temas críticos de la educación superior en América Latina vol. 2: Los años 90. Expansión privada, evaluación y posgrado.* México: Fondo de Cultura Economica, 1997.

Kent, Rollin. *Experiencias de reforma de la educación superior en América Latina: los años 90.* México: Plaza y Valdez, 2001.

Krotsh, P. "El peso de la tradición y las recientes tendencias de privatización en la universidad Argentina: hacia una relación público-privado." *Revista Avaliação* 2.4 (1997): 31–43.

Leite, D. "Avaliação institucional e a produção de novas subjetividades." In Dias, J. and D. Ristoff (eds). *Universidade desconstruída: avaliação institucional e resistência.* Florianópolis: Ed. Insular, 2000, 129–147.

Leite, D. "Avaliação institucional, reformas e redesenho capitalista das universidades." *Revista Avaliação* 7.2 (2002): 29–48.

Leite, D., M. Mollis and C. Contera. *Inovação e avaliação institucional: efeitos e mudanças na missão das universidades contemporâneas.* Porto Alegre: Evangraf Editora, 2002.

Leite, D., R. Santiago, M.C. Loréa Leite and C. Sarrico. *Avaliação, auto-análise e gestão das universidades: um estudo conjunto Brasil-Portugal.* Final Report. Porto Alegre, Br–Aveiro, Pt: CNPq–ICCTI, FAPERGS, 2002.

Leonardos, Ana, C.A. Gomes and Robert Walker. "Estudo de caso aplicado às inovações educacionais: uma metodologia." Brasília, INEP, Série Documental: Inovações, n.1, dez., 1992.

Miles, Mathew and A.M. Huberman. *Qualitative Data Analysis.* 2nd edn. London: Sage Publications, 1994.

Mollis, M. *La universidad Argentina en tránsito.* Buenos Aires: Fondo de Cultura Economica, 2001.

Mollis, M. "La privatización de la educación superior desde la perspectiva del sur que no habla inglés." *Revista del IICE* 19 (2002): 13–21, Marzo.

OECD. *Education at a Glance. Indicators 2001.* Paris: OECD, 2001.

O Estado de São Paulo. Editorial. *O futuro do ensino superior.* São Paulo, SP, 23 November 2002, 2.

Rodriguez Gómez, Roberto and Armando Alcantara Santuario. "La reforma de la educación superior en América Latina en la perspectiva de los organismos internacionales." *Revisa Española de Educación Comparada* 6 (2000): 177–207.

Santiago, R. *Evaluation, Institutional Self-analysis and Higher Education Management.* Research Project. Aveiro, Pt, FCT and Sapiens Project, 2002.

Santos, B.S. *Pela Mão de Alice. O social e o político na pós-modernidade.* Porto: Afrontamento, 1994.

Sguissardi, W. *Avaliação universitária em questão. Reformas do estado e da educação superior.* São Paulo: Autores Associados, 1997.

Slaughter, S. and L.L. Leslie. *Academic Capitalism. Politics, Policies and the Entrepreneurial University.* Baltimore: The John Hopkins University Press, 1999.

UNISINOS. Gianotti, Suzana (Org.) *Projeto de avaliação institucional.* São Leopoldo: UNISINOS, 1995.

UNISINOS. *Missão e perspectivas 1994–2003.* São Leopoldo: UNISINOS, 1994.

UNISINOS. *Relatório de Atividades 97.* São Leopoldo: UNISINOS, 1998.

Yin, Robert K. *Case Study Research: Design and Methods.* 2nd edn. London: Sage Publications, 1994.

ALBERTO AMARAL, OLIVER FULTON AND
INGVILD M. LARSEN

A MANAGERIAL REVOLUTION?

1. INTRODUCTION

In the early days of higher education, the university was in general "a guild organisation of masters or students or of masters and students combined, having a high degree of juridical autonomy, the right to elect its own officers, statutory making powers, and a communal seal" (Cobban 1975: 32). This formed the origin of their characteristic governance system based on collegial decision making.[1]

The idea that academics are particularly gifted to manage their own affairs has been accepted over the centuries, either in the name of academic freedom or in recognition of the difficulties that lay people would experience in managing an institution characterised by a very strong emphasis on professionalisation along the lines of distinct 'disciplinary specialisms' (Clark 1983a). The idea of the Humboldtian university clearly rests on the need to protect individual academic freedom, an idea that was echoed by Karl Jaspers, as cited by Kenneth Wilson (1989: 38):

> The university is a community of scholars and students engaged in the task of seeking truth. It derives its autonomy from the idea of academic freedom, a privilege granted to it by state and society which entails the obligation to teach truth in defiance of all internal and external attempts to curtail it.

These "views on academic freedom and the right of academic self-government" (Fulton 2002: 206) were strongly supported by the UK's Robbins Committee:

> We are convinced also that such freedom is a necessary condition of the highest efficiency ... and that encroachments upon their liberty, in the supposed interests of greater efficiency, would in fact diminish their efficiency and stultify their development (Robbins Report 1963: 228).

Moodie and Eustace (1974: 233), less than thirty years ago, defended academics' predominance in university management on the basis of their very specific professional qualifications:

> The supreme authority, providing that it is exercised in ways responsive to others, must therefore continue to rest with the academics, for no one else seems sufficiently qualified to regulate the public affairs of scholars.

This view was later endorsed by Clark (1983a), among others, in a classical Mertonian formulation suggesting that "universities firmly based on the development of disciplinary specialisms could only be effectively governed by experts in those disciplines" (Fulton 2002: 207).

A. Amaral et al. (eds.), The Higher Education Managerial Revolution?, 275–296.
© 2003 *Kluwer Academic Publishers. Printed in the Netherlands.*

Since the 1980s this model has been under increasing attack. Maassen recalls in his chapter presented in this volume that as early as 1983 Clark pointed to the separation of academic and administrative cultures and roles. Duke (1992: 12) states that:

> There are two assumptions behind all this: that universities are inefficient; and that their efficiency will be improved by a series of external interventions, implemented largely top-down, and drawn in the main from the management practices and reward systems of other kinds of organisations.

The result has been that, instead of the traditional rhetoric in support of academic self-government, notions of managerialism, efficiency and even more alien concepts such as total quality management or value for money, have come to replace the former and long-lasting academic values of scientific excellence and academic freedom, although as Maassen reports the reform has not (at least yet) resulted in permanent and stable arrangements.

Van Vught (1989: 54) calls our attention to the fact that attempts to control universities may destroy the institution's quality:

> The fundamental characteristics of higher education institutions suggest that these institutions can only be controlled from outside, when the organisational variety is greatly reduced and when the professional autonomy is greatly restrained. However, when such an external control is imposed, it should be realised that the professional tasks these institutions perform may be severely damaged.

However, as argued by Meek in the introductory essay to this volume and Amaral, Magalhães and Santiago in their chapter, it is important to distinguish between, on the one hand, 'managerialism' as an ideology for strategic change of public services and, on the other, the quite commonly accepted need to provide institutions with more flexible and effective administration, on the understanding that any new management tools and processes remain instruments at the service of the institution and its academic leadership. This distinction is not always straightforward or easily maintained. An example is given by Clark, who felt compelled to clarify his position following misinterpretations of his book on the creation of entrepreneurial universities (Clark 1998). He states very clearly (Clark 2000: 118):

> Entrepreneurial character in universities does not stifle the collegial spirit; it does not make universities handmaidens of industry; and it does not commercialize universities and turn them into all-purpose shopping malls. On all three counts it moves in the opposite direction ...

> This [entrepreneurial] narrative is much needed as a counter-narrative, one that challenges both the simplistic understanding of the university as a business, about which we hear so much these days, and the simplistic depiction of universities as passive and helpless instrumentalities whose fate is determined by irresistible external demands.

This probably explains why a range of instruments and processes which can be seen as characteristic of managerialism may be supported by some academics, as no one in their senses will raise their voice against the idea that higher education institutions should be efficiently run. Some academics see the functioning of collegial bodies as cumbersome, time consuming and inefficient (Smith 2000). And if they are engaged in 'academic capitalism' (in the sense that their individual activities, especially as researchers, outweigh their concerns for the corporate life of their university) then they may well favour the concentration of power at the central institutional level, on the basis that this will release them from many hours of tiresome debates, mostly dealing with problems in other departments or disciplines and as such of little interest – always provided that the increased concentration of power at the central level does not mean increased interference with the daily life of their own self-contained academic world.

It is also true that, in some countries, the more conservative academics would like to see movement away from what they consider 'democratic excesses' following the May 1968 student rebellions, in order to reinforce a more meritocratic vision of the academy. De Boer observes that in the Netherlands the WUB-Act of 1970 with its emphasis on internal and external democratisation attracted criticism from the beginning while Amaral, Magalhães and Santiago observe in their chapter that in Portugal there is a general view that students are over represented in governing bodies and that university management is too corporatist.

Leite's chapter reports the contribution of institutional evaluation procedures to the 'capitalist redesign' of universities, and presents a case study of a Brazilian university where strategic evaluation was used as a tool for organisational reconfiguration. Pechar states in his essay that in some cases the initiative for management reforms "came from a group of academics (even if it was a small group and many other academics opposed the initiative), not from the government ...". Slaughter and Leslie (1997: 230) list some conditions which favour the concentration of power at the central level:

> in a stressful financial environment there is greater willingness by organizational stakeholders to vest in central management the power to deal with external agents. The demand is for increased central coordination of efforts and reporting mechanisms – in short, greater centralization of efforts to manage the environment on behalf of the larger organization, because, as Pfeffer and Salancik put it, 'solutions ... require the concentration of power' (1978: 284).

> In the competitive environment, staff perceive that the university is at risk and that resources are inadequate to maintain existing functions ... Institutional preservation requires that central administration be granted authority to deal with the external environment ... as operating units generate more and more of their own resources ... staff may perceive that in the new financial environment the central administration must have greater freedom to act, anyhow.

Internal criticism does not only come from academic staff. Smith (2000: 39) comments that "shared governance ... is perhaps the single most criticized aspect of higher education by non-academic institutional insiders. Such insiders include members of boards of trustees and overseers, senior administrators, and a host of ex-academic consultants". Smith (2000: 49) adds: "internal dissidents and critics are commonly the source of the most negative portraits of an institution's management principles and practices".

On the other hand, governments with a neo-liberal ideology, having selected new public management as their tool for replacing the slow, inefficient decision-making processes of academic collegiality by the "fast, adventurous, carefree, gung-ho, open-plan, computerised, individualism of choice, autonomous enterprises and sudden opportunity" (Ball 1998: 124) could hardly condone a system of institutional governance that did not allow for top-down decision making, and where institutional responsibility and accountability were diluted in a maze of collegial decision-making bodies which obscure the clear definition of individual responsibilities for the fate of the institution. This has led some governments to introduce or promote reforms that have concentrated power at the central level, reinforcing decision-making power in the hands of the individual leader of the institution (rector, vice-chancellor or president) and fostering the greater participation of outside 'stakeholder' constituencies in governing bodies. Leite refers in her chapter to the reforms of the 1990s in Latin America where under the pressure of the political agendas of international agencies such as the IMF and World Bank the different countries were forced to adopt similar managerial practices.

This has resulted in changes in university governance structures, with a decline in collegial governance and the streamlining and professionalisation of institutional management. "The traditional university pattern of a Senate which lumbered to decisions on new courses, and frequently saw fit not to approve innovative suggestions" (Eggins 1989: 128) is no longer compatible with new pressures for more effective and efficient, corporate-like management modes. Chris Duke (1992: 2) refers to the frenzied search for short-term results which has pervaded our societies over the last few decades under the name of the information society:

> A subtler cultural conflict also exists: between the long time horizons of the university ethos and the 'culture of the microsecond' which compels stock exchanges to install circuit breakers against information technology-induced disaster.

But despite some cases of enthusiasm or even infatuation with some of the measures aimed to increase management efficiency, there can be little doubt that in general academics are highly suspicious of new developments which they see as threatening their academic freedom. In those countries where increased autonomy has been granted to universities, the locus of power for the daily running of the institutions has been moved from the fuzzy location of (often inattentive) ministerial offices to a far more threatening proximity in the offices of the rector and central administration. And as institutions have been given greater autonomy, ostensibly a repatriation of authority to a sphere much closer to the academics themselves, many of the latter believe that they are now confronted with increasing attacks on their academic freedom and with closer control of their work – thus underlining Meek's point in the introductory essay that institutional autonomy is quite distinct from academic freedom. As rectors, vice-chancellors and presidents proudly proclaim the increased autonomy of their institutions, many academics complain that their own academic autonomy, or more precisely their academic freedom, is being curtailed (Magalhães and Amaral 2000). This has led to the kind of resistance movements that we analyse in section 4.

2. ISOMORPHISM OR DIVERSITY?

At the level of higher education systems, it appears that broadly similar political reform packages are taking place all over the world. Criticisms of traditional academic norms and values, the reinforcement of the economic role of higher education, the emergence of managerialism, an increasing role for external stakeholders, diversification of funding sources and the rolling-back of public funding constitute a common picture that cannot be explained solely by "the functional, national-cultural or rational-instrumental theories that have dominated the study of education systems or the curriculum hitherto" (Dale 2000: 431).

To explain the emergence of institutional and organisational similarities in social/political systems across the world, 'world institutionalists'[2] (e.g. Meyer et al. 1997; Finnemore 1996) have developed the argument that the institutions of the nation-state, including the state itself, are moulded at a supranational level by the dominant values and processes of Western ideology, rather than being autonomous and specific national creations. Røvik (1996) has traced how some such ideas travel fast and far, and within a short period of time come to be seen internationally as the best approach. As an example, Fuller and Rubinson (1992) explain the worldwide spread of the 'idea of the education system' on the basis of the same argument, that is, that globalisation takes effect in education through the operations of a universalistic culture and transnational actors. Others, like Dale (2000: 436), favour an alternative explanation based on a more economic approach to globalisation which they see as "a set of political-economic arrangements for the organisation of the global economy, driven by the need to retain the capitalist system rather than [by] any set of values".

However, other authors contend that there are strong local and national characteristics that play against uniformity. For instance Halpin and Troyna (1995: 304) state that "countries seem to be doing similar things, but on closer examination they are not as similar as it first appeared". Czarniawska and Sevòn (1996: 9) described how the distance between the model-organisation and the one which follows the model opens up a space for translations and diverse interpretation. Consequently, meanings ascribed to and copied from the models are edited in accordance with situational circumstances and limitations. And some authors believe that 'globalisation' is not incompatible with some forms of diversity:

> The logic of globalisation tolerates, indeed requires, the promotion of cultural (and possibly political) difference and diversity. Globalisation will build on diversity and needs to work through patterns that seem paradoxical – both global and decentred – forms of social organisation which convey powerful symbolic images of choice, freedom and diversity (Jones 1998: 149).

This second volume of the Douro series aims to provide some answers to questions about the emergence of managerialism in higher education. Is a managerial revolution really taking place, fatally usurping the governance structures of higher education institutions or, on the contrary, is managerialism mainly or only a rhetorical political device to encourage adaptations to new circumstances? Is managerialism such a powerful and convincing ideology that most higher education systems and their institutions are changing in a convergent direction that will lead to isomorphic outcomes, or are the responses of systems and their institutions still largely influenced by strong local and national characteristics that prevent uniformity? Is managerialism just another management fad, or will it produce a drastic and irreversible transformation of traditional forms of collegial academic decision making and even of the academic profession?

From the different contributions in this new volume of the Douro series we can obtain a picture of substantial diversity, ranging from situations in which most of the key characteristics of managerialism are absent to situations where the managerial paradigm seems to have been largely adopted.

In his chapter, designed to provide empirically based comparisons across three systems, De Boer argues that his case studies justify a critical attitude towards the 'managerial claim' of offering a single paradigm for the management of public organisations. This view can certainly be supported by reviewing the conclusions of the various national case studies in this volume. For example, in the instance of Portugal, Amaral, Magalhães and Santiago, claim that:

> the emergence of managerialism is not yet established in Portuguese higher education ... This is confirmed by the absence of legislation imposing a 'market' or 'market-like' behaviour on public universities, despite the presence of an important private higher education sector and some opinions and comments propagated by the more neo-liberal press. ... if managerialism exists, it is present at a rhetorical level.

This may be the result of both the 1974 revolutionary movement to democracy and a weak industrial fabric. A very weak presence of managerialism is also observed by De Boer in the case of France:

> respondents did not perceive a fundamental change in the role of academics in decision making. Only a few ... suggested that there has been a shift towards a managerial approach. Many perceived collegiality as the main feature (in particular at the lower levels).

France, with its tradition of intrinsic Republican values dating from the days of the French Revolution, as argued by De Boer, is probably the only country where a respondent would express his preference for elected leadership in the following terms:

> It goes without saying. We didn't go through the whole French Revolution and cut off the heads of our kings only to end up today with a system where the former President chooses the next one. Heavens no, this is absolutely unthinkable!

In Norway, despite some of De Boer's respondents perceiving "a shift towards managerialism" and believing that "the role of academics in decision making has diminished", many replied that "there remains a strong culture of democracy and collegiality"; "colleague-based decision making [is] evident at each level: central, faculty and department"; and "democracy is valued for its own sake". Larsen in her chapter endorses this general picture by referring to "democratic decision-making processes", the promotion of "consensus within the community", and sensitivity to "traditional values according to the collegial model" as well as to "consultation and persuasion rather than use of incentives" and concludes that "this study has demonstrated that the traditional model in many respects is still applicable". She adds, however, that there are also some tendencies that point towards the opposite.

Norwegian higher education could be at a turning point. During 2003 a comprehensive reform for higher education will be implemented which could reinforce a shift towards managerialism: the introduction of a new performance-based funding system, more external members in the central governing body, the possibility to appoint rather than elect academic leaders, and the abolition of the university council, all point in that direction.

Pechar presents a much more decisive movement towards managerialism in Austria, externally imposed by a government led by a coalition of conservatives and right wing populists, applying 'speed kills' techniques to public policy implementation. Pechar states that "for better or worse, the new act [UG 2002] brings Austria far ahead in the 'managerial revolution' on the European continent"; but it still remains to be seen how thoroughly the reforms will be implemented in practice, due to "the mistrust which was aroused during the reform debates" and which was reinforced among junior faculty as a consequence of new legislation on academic employment.

For Salminen, the Finnish national case is an example of the relatively successful implementation of managerial reform. Accountability based on performance indicators, "funding based on results", the replacement of collegial by individual leadership, "governance of universities based on ... results/performance management steering ... marketisation, commercialisation and the like" are many of the ingredients of a more managerial approach to university governance. In contrast to this general picture, however, Salminen still emphasises that "universities are, in the first place, professional organisations, including the ethical behaviour of the organisations", even though "as organisations, universities have to change from old to new management practices and processes".

De Boer presents the Dutch case as another example of significant penetration of managerialism in university governance: "The overwhelming majority of the respondents of the University of Twente answered that there had been [a] shift towards managerialism". The abolition of collegial decision-making bodies, ministerial appointment of the *raad van toezicht* (supervisory board), abolition of the powerful *vakgroepen* (departments), power concentration and a "new hierarchical management system based on appointment [rather than on election]" are some of the salient elements of this system's movement towards managerialism.

The UK is probably the Western European country where managerialism has emerged in its most virulent form. Fulton, describing the outcomes of a research project based at Lancaster University, reports that in general respondents consistently considered not only that accountability pressures, bureaucracy and management had increased, but that management had changed "in a way consistent with ideas about efficiency, performance monitoring, target setting, private sector models of running organisations and a decline in trust and discretion". Almost all decisions are now ostensibly finance-driven.

However, in each of those countries where managerialist practices appear to have taken hold there are also accounts of counter-movements that have opposed a straightforward *veni, vidi, vinci* takeover of higher education. This will be analysed in more detail in section 4 when we turn to elements of 'resistance'.

Outside Western Europe, South Africa offers a good example of exceptionalism, in the sense that its particular historical background and the recent dramatic political changes have very strongly influenced the reactions and perceptions of institutions and academic communities to external political steering. Certain universities (at the time nicknamed 'bush colleges') established by the apartheid regime for people classified 'Coloured', and frequently seen as one of many forms of humiliation imposed by white domination, had become the seedbeds of the struggle against the apartheid government and were subjected to continual strife and disruption that destroyed most of the elements of academic authority. At the same time, a number of traditionally white institutions, specifically those of Afrikaans culture and language, had gained a profound racial connotation during the second half of the last century, presenting the image of very conservative institutions which have inherited from the former apartheid regime a number of distortions which are difficult to eliminate. Cloete and Kulati report in their chapter that one of the first post-apartheid struggles consisted in challenging "the authority of what were considered to be illegitimate and unrepresentative governance structures".

South African changes have thus developed under the combined influence of calls for democratisation and redress, the Mandela government's political model of cooperative governance and, at the same time, the implementation of a macro-economic policy framework – 'Growth, Employment and Redistribution' – that followed closely the dictates of the Washington consensus, thus placing strong emphasis on "efficiency, accountability and good governance". According to Cloete and Kulati that is why "some of the reforms of the national government have, intentionally and unintentionally, promoted managerialism rather than greater democratisation".

Australia is one of the non-European countries in which managerialism seems to have gained a relatively profound grip. In his chapter on the Australian situation, Meek describes the strengthening and expansion of the office of vice-chancellor, the appointment (rather than election) of deans, a reduction in size of institutional governing bodies combined with a new predominance of external representatives on university councils, streamlined and more efficient decision-making processes, increased accountability, the marketisation and commodification of knowledge, the "de-professionalisation of academics", a loss of professional autonomy, and a "shift from social knowledge to market knowledge" with a "prioritised and finely targeted research funding regime". However, he also refers to resistance movements (see section 4), the displacement of academic loyalties and the "entrenchment of antagonism between managers and managed", together with some 'mostly ceremonial' remnants of academic self-governance.

Denise Leite reports that in Latin America one can observe the emergence of policies of 'good' administration aimed at increased efficiency and effectiveness. These polices are the result of the pressure of evaluation exercises and are supported by concepts such as 'market-oriented goals' (Buchbinder 1993), 'performativity' (Cowen 1996) and 'selective excellence' (Barrow 1996), assumed by universities within the context of evaluation processes.

Finally, the United States constitutes a case in itself. Coming from a long tradition of strong central administration and control by 'boards of trustees' and without a strong tradition of the university as fundamentally a self-governing community of academics and students, American institutions never gave their academic senates such a wide-ranging role as their European and Australian counterparts. Slaughter and Rhoades present in their chapter a picture of a "shift from a public good knowledge regime, associated with Mertonian values and the Vannevar Bush model of science, to an academic capitalist regime, associated with basic science for use and basic technology, concepts which their framers argue allow academic and commercial values to coexist, even if uneasily". They suggest that whatever the claims of coexistence, the reality is that this movement is making "faculty more like all other workers".

Our general conclusion must be that, whatever progress the onward march of managerialism may be making within specific systems, and granting that there are important similarities between some of these, taken as a whole these different case studies present a picture of continuing diversity at the national level. It cannot (at least yet) be convincingly argued that there is a multinational convergence towards new methods and processes of management, paved by the brutal expansion of the new managerialist ideology. We should also recognise that there is considerable variation within national systems. This is evident, for example, in Pechar's description of the opposite behaviour of universities and *Fachhochschulen* in Austria. And while Fulton reports that, in contrast, his research did not reveal systematic differences between established universities and former polytechnics, neither did it show any clear evidence of isomorphism or convergence on a single model. This is broadly consistent with Henkel's (2000: 237) identification of distinct value patterns according to institutional type: "Overall, the more traditional the university, the less likely were individuals to identify themselves as managers, even if they saw those at the centre of the university in these terms". And Cloete and Kulati state that:

> within one country, within a national policy framework, a wide range of governance arrangements have developed, and to suggest that there is an inevitable 'historic march to managerialism' is to obscure, and miss, some very interesting responses emerging amongst different groups of institutions. The different governance and leadership styles may contain many elements of what is being described as managerialism, but … institutions with a more collegial history seem to be developing a range of 'democratic' practices.

Thus the broad picture is one of diversity of behaviours and responses, both at system level and at institutional level within systems. In the following section, however, we nevertheless attempt to generalise about some characteristics that seem to present a more convergent pattern in some of the national case studies presented in this book.

3. ACADEMICS VS ADMINISTRATORS

It seems to be the case that, in general, there is widespread resentment among academics of recent changes in governance. Smith (2000: 83–91) refers to increased tension between faculty and administration, to negative, sometimes uncooperative, faculty behaviour, and to conflict between administrators and faculty. Slaughter and

Leslie (1997: 230) are of the opinion that "tensions between academic staff and central administrators are likely to grow". Henkel (2000: 239) reports complaints that "there is quite an antagonistic feeling developing in the department between Them (the managers) and Us (the workers)". Cloete and Kulati writing in this volume consider that "there has not only been a widening gap between workers and management, but also between management and academics" and Meek refers to "deepening conflict and bitterness between the managers and the managed".

This resentment is no doubt in large part the consequence of the reduced distance between the 'managers' and the 'managed', with the inevitable sensation that an increasingly intrusive 'Big Brother' is peering over one's academic shoulder. This feeling of discontent is further aggravated by micro-management mechanisms that are increasingly used by institutions in order to respond to outside pressures which promote the new values and demands of "economy, efficiency, utility, public accountability, enterprise and various definitions of quality" (Henkel 2000: 47).

The resentment of academics finds obvious targets not only in central administrations but also in the fast-breeding species of academic administrators. Reed (2002: 167) considers that this may result from "more intrusive and pervasive performance management, [placing] a consistent emphasis on the detailed monitoring and evaluation of 'quality' standards in service delivery [as] outcomes emerge as the overriding priority". As has often been observed of bureaucracies, central administrations tend to cling to power, and even when they nominally decentralise responsibilities to operating units, they may still try to retain ultimate control. Notably, central administrations sometimes decentralise 'responsibility' while keeping the associated resources at central level (Slaughter and Leslie 1997: 230), and operating units complain that "they have not quite let go of the budgetary reins in the way they will need to do to give us proper devolved authority" (Henkel 2000: 241). Fulton considers that the clearest example is when the freedom to recruit new personnel is not devolved, as is commonly the case. But there are other obvious sources of resentment such as price setting of central services or the imposition of large financial overheads on research grants. In the new entrepreneurial culture, money earned through contracts is seen as the property of those who have raised it, and the idea of paying an overhead, especially if this appears to include an element of support for those who are less capable, arouses strong feelings against an 'unfair' strategy which would be more appropriate to traditional 'welfare-based' university cultures.

One of the consequences of the new public management policies appears to have been a strong attack on the professions, and specifically on the academic profession which has undoubtedly lost prestige and social standing – albeit this has occurred in the wake of massification and changes in the nature and value of knowledge, and not only of new management processes. In any event, Scott (1989: 9–10) states that "the academy no longer enjoys great prestige on which higher education can build a successful claim to political autonomy", while Halsey (1992) refers to:

> The gradual proletarianization of the academic professions – an erosion of their relative class and status advantages as the system of higher education is propelled towards a wider admission of those who survive beyond compulsory schooling.

However, in the view of some authors, it was only after the emergence of new managerialism that there occurred "a much more direct ideological and political attack on institutional and professional autonomy" (Reed 2002: 172). Slaughter and Leslie (1997: 5) considered that "participation in the market began to undercut the tacit contract between professors and society". In the present volume, Slaughter and Rhoades restate that argument:

> Simultaneously and ironically ... patent policies also made faculty more like all other workers, in that the institution, intent on generating revenue streams, over the period considered, came to claim virtually all intellectual property from all members of the university community, making faculty, staff and students less like university professionals and more like corporate professionals whose discoveries are considered work-for-hire, the property of the corporation, not the professional.

In their chapters, both Meek and Fulton refer to the perceived de-professionalisation of academics, or the proletarianisation of the academic profession (Halsey 1992) and routinisation of the labour process (Winter 1995). And Leicht and Fennell (2001), as cited by Reed (2002: 179), offer an analysis of an emerging situation in which "elite managers are becoming the 'new professionals', while professionals are being captured by organisational stakeholders that consume and pay for professional services".

Academics and managers express mutual feelings of resentment. On the academics' side, faculty members tend to "resent that significant sums of money are being spent to support activities that they do for free" (Smith 2000: 90), while many criticise 'their' managers implicitly by insisting that "you must have people who empathise with the values of people in universities and who know how hard it is to do research" (Henkel 2000: 239), or as reported by Meek complain of "an increasing sense of alienation by rank-and-file academic staff regarding the ways in which their institutions are governed and managed". Cloete and Kulati in their chapter "reveal a concern, in some cases outrage, that the council is expanding its jurisdiction over financial matters to the appointment, or dismissal, of the vice-chancellor without adequately involving the senate, not to mention other stakeholders".

To make things worse, "this new managerial class rapidly evolved its own interests and agenda, which were and are often unrelated to those of faculty and students" (Smith 2000: 83). Meek notes that academics have quickly grasped the new stark reality: "the 'collegial' university governed by the academic guild assisted by low-profile administrators has been succeeded by the 'managerial' university dominated by an increasingly expert cadre of senior managers", with whom "traditional norms and values of the academic profession carry little weight".

Managers, for their part, see themselves as essential professional contributors to the successful functioning of the contemporary university. They complain that academics are frequently uncooperative, refusing to accept that current demands for increased efficiency, effectiveness and greater accountability, coupled with the much greater complexity of the manager's job, are no longer compatible with the amateur approach to management characteristic of "a senior professor of patriarchal structure ... with the role assumed by people who were good at that sort of thing and also had established academic reputations" (interviewee quoted in Henkel 2000: 236).

Meek argues in this volume that "the 'de-professionalisation' of academics has been coupled with a claim to professional status by administrative staff". This point is well illustrated in a recent article by Lauwerys (2002: 93–97), a successful professional manager with experience in several English higher education institutions, who offers a personal reflection "on the characteristics of a profession … and the extent to which higher education administration is developing towards having true professional standing". Lauwerys comments that thirty years ago administrators were "very much expected to operate in a subservient supportive role to the academic community, very much in a traditional Civil Servant mould". He presents a list of current grievances: lack of institutional support for administrative staff development, being "undervalued by their institution in general and their academic colleagues in particular" and seeing "senior posts going to those appointed from other sectors or to senior academics who switch careers".

A Norwegian study suggests that administrative staff are simultaneously enhancing their professionalism and experiencing feelings of uncertainty about their role. Administrators sense that their function and role are undervalued within the academic community while they know that the university cannot run smoothly without their managerial expertise. In the Norwegian context, administrative personnel see themselves as inconspicuous, exercising anonymous functional power. University administrators find themselves subject to a number of conflicting pressures associated with professional pride, the struggle for recognition, humbleness and loyalty to the organisation (Gornitzka and Larsen forthcoming). The administrative tension investigated in the Norwegian study was more a conflict between levels than direct dispute between academics and administrators. Tensions are noticeably lower at the departmental level than higher up within the administrative hierarchy. University departments are in general transparent, and there is considerable interaction and cooperation between administrative staff and head of department (Gornitzka, Kyvik and Larsen 1998).

4. RESISTANCE

The national case studies show that the implementation of new forms of academic governance has on occasions resulted in considerable resistance from the academic community. Such resistance has taken different forms. Henkel (2000) refers to collective resistance in the form of deliberate distortion of policy requirements (e.g. into compliant paper-chasing) or even of 'wilful misunderstanding', while Kogan (1999) speaks of the opportunities created by 'constructive ambiguity'. Maassen (2002: 26) describes how "by combining neo-institutional and resource dependence theories, Oliver [1991: 152] identifies five organisational strategies for dealing with environmental pressures: acquiescing, compromising, avoiding, defying, and manipulating". Trowler (1998) offers a rather similar list of coping strategies with which academics have responded to external pressures to become more effective, efficient, relevant and accountable.

De Boer cites Pressman and Wildavsky (1974) to remind us that "reforms do not by definition lead to the intended results", a problem that has long been recognised in research on higher education (Cerych and Sabatier 1986). To support his claim that "many authors [have come] to the conclusion that, generally speaking, government-initiated reforms in higher education systems must fail", Van Vught (1989: 58) quotes Becher and Kogan (1980: 121):

> [In the case of higher education systems] we are not dealing with a hierarchical system, where change can be decreed from above, but rather with a negotiative one, in which individuals, basic units and institutions each regard themselves as having the right to decide what is best for them. It follows that any innovative proposal has to be finally sanctioned by those who are in a position to put it into effect.

De Boer maintains in this volume that externally enforced reforms "tend to increase resistance to change even further, especially when they go against the wishes of those undergoing the reform".

A number of the chapters in this book report on resistance from academic staff. Pechar reports a pattern of systematic opposition to governmental reforms in the case of Austria, where the Humboldtian model has produced a caste of powerful 'academic mandarins': "A majority of the academic oligarchy opposed the higher education reforms ..." and "the critique from the academic side was passionate".

Meek reports that: "The new forms of management have not gone uncontested, nor have they become entirely institutionalised" and adds: "government perceives that it has not been so successful in bringing about changes to university management practices, particularly with respect to productivity gains. Evidence of this is reflected in the fact that the reform of institutional governance and management has been prominent on the government's agenda for nearly two decades".

Fulton observes that in the UK "there was also resistance to attempts to impose directive management which excluded academic staff", and that "there were some sharp contrasts between the often quite optimistic and positive stories of achievement and change told by manager-academics, especially at senior levels, and the accounts given by ordinary academics, support staff and students union officers". He adds: "nor have academics and manager-academics easily absorbed new managerialism – for each one who had, we found three who felt uncomfortable".

In South Africa, Cloete and Kulati consider that "the collegial model was thoroughly discredited during the initial phases of the demands for greater democratisation", and despite government reforms that "have, intentionally and unintentionally, promoted managerialism rather than greater democratisation ... new forms of consultation and participation are emerging under conditions of demands for greater efficiency and accountability". Larsen reports that "departmental heads in Norwegian universities are defenders of democratic processes for decision making [which are] sensitive to traditional values according to the collegial model" and in which the central leadership tools "are still consultation and persuasion rather than the use of incentives".

In the USA there are reports of examples of strong resistance from the academic community. Smith (2000: 91), for instance, states that "negative, sometimes uncooperative, faculty behaviour is the heavy cost that many institutions of higher education pay as a result of the new administrative class's attempt at domination" or, even worse, that the result "is a faculty that simply retreats ... When the faculty withdraws the institution loses not only its sight, its hearing, its touch, its smell, its taste, but also most of its common sense".

It is interesting that both in Australia, and particularly in the UK, where managerialism has assumed some of its most virulent forms, the implementation in higher education of reforms associated with new managerialism has been rather more ambiguous, contested and contradictory than the advocates or theorists anticipated. In general, managerialism seems to have been far more successful in other parts of the public sector such as national health services than when applied to higher education. In his chapter Fulton offers an explanation in the British context by stressing that "Unlike the British National Health Service, where early reforms introduced massive organisational changes, in universities new managerialism has developed within existing organisational forms". Reed (2002: 175) makes a similar point:

> The implementation of new managerialist discourse and strategy within UK universities
> ... has been significantly different from, say, the NHS (Ferlie et al., 1996), local
> government (Kean and Scase 1998) and social services (Jones 1999).

While in other social systems the new top 'managers' were generally recruited from outside the system – for instance, within the British NHS early reforms introduced a new cadre of general managers from outside the health service (Reed and Anthony 1993)[3] – this was not the case for British higher education institutions in which, for instance, over 90% of the vice-chancellors were appointed after careers in academia, and of those appointed since 1981 nearly a third had been Oxbridge[4] undergraduates (Smith et al. 1999). This was confirmed by Kogan (1999: 269):

> In virtually all higher education institutions there are mixtures of collegial, academic-
> based decision making, and bureaucratic/hierarchical working. Those operating the
> bureaucratic lines can be, however, either academics or professional administrators.

Using the results of his research project Fulton, based on the evidence of the observation of potentially competing discourses "both at the level of official policy discourse and in the narratives of manager-academics themselves", considers "that this indicates, not a successful hybridisation, but a contested and still unpredictable discursive struggle between competing views of university-based knowledge workers".

Manager-academics are at the front line in the struggle, or at least the tension, of working with incompatible sets of values: on the one hand, those traditional academic values that are linked to collegial decision making, to the "disinterested search for truth, and the certification of knowledge on the criteria of logic, evidence and demonstrability" (Kogan 1999: 269) and, on the other hand, the new and distinctive set of values linked to a managerial role, such as public accountability, economic efficiency, customer satisfaction and even "advancing the university beyond the good of individual academics or their departments" (Kogan 1999: 269). Different authors (see for instance Henkel 1998, 2000; Kogan 1999; Smith et al. 1999; Leicht and Fennell 2001; Reed 2002; and Fulton in this volume) have analysed this problem as experienced by the managers themselves. For example,

Reed (2002: 175, 180) speaks of a group of 'reluctant managers' who "continued to exhibit strong personal commitment to traditional academic values", and who "seem rather unwilling to fulfil the historical destiny that the ideology and practice of new managerialism has scripted for them". Henkel (2000: 249) describes how the "ambiguities of their organisational environment, the emergent nature of their roles, and the lack of systematic preparation for them laid a heavy onus on individuals to negotiate their way into them", and reports that some managers:

> made a distinction between being a manager and being managerial, an epithet against which, it was implied, it would self-evidently be necessary to defend oneself, even if its meanings were various. For our respondents these meanings included authoritarian, coercive, lacking respect for academics, and obsessed with efficiency, productivity and costs (p. 237).

Fulton reports in this volume that from the self-descriptions of the present identities of manager-academics it is evident that:

> many of the elements which Henkel (2000), Altbach (1996) and others note about academic identities (especially the continued commitment to both teaching and research ...) were strongly evident. Nor, generally, did these identities disappear once an interviewee had embarked on major management roles ...

This tension between what are fundamentally 'incompatible imperatives' (Reed 2002) has important consequences at the level of institutional management. While Meek (2002: 249) considers that "[the tension] is widespread and contributes significantly to staff alienation which, in turn, may undermine commitment to the very corporate planning processes that the managerial approach is intended to accomplish", Maassen in this volume refers to "institutional managers ... caught between the horizontal academic decision-making practices and the hierarchical administrative traditions". Henkel (2000: 54) refers to the emergence of ambiguity "between management for control and management for innovation, centralisation and decentralisation; bureaucratic and post-bureaucratic management, managerial and academic values; reduced and enhanced autonomy", and Reed (2002: 175) states that:

> the dominant theme in the implementation of new managerialist discourse and strategy within UK universities, as of the UK public sector as a whole, is one of 'hybridisation' – of institutional structures, organisational forms, occupational cultures and control technologies.

He sums up by suggesting that:

> Again, unlike other sectors, the control strategies and mechanisms deployed by HE manager-academics to try to secure required levels of individual and organisational performance, seem, in relative terms at least, rather muted and less crudely coercive than elsewhere within the public sector system as a whole.

5. CHANGING LOYALTIES

In an address during the celebrations of the 900th anniversary of the University of Bologna, Giovanni Agnelli (1988: 11) declared that:

> from their very beginning universities were free institutions, even in societies ruled by despots; they were disinterested, for their task was not imposed on them from outside, but chosen by themselves, and that task was the pursuit of knowledge. And from the first they were international in spirit. Even in the most intolerant and difficult times they held that knowledge should be free and universal.

In truth, this statement is an evident exaggeration, a generous contribution from industry to a university celebration. During its long and troubled history, academic freedom was many times abused, through the interventions of the Catholic Church (several researchers paid their tribute to academic freedom by being burned at the stake) or by the controls which different Protestant denominations imposed on the first American colleges.

The situation changed for the better with the advent of the modern university. According to Nybom (forthcoming) the tremendous problem that Humboldt succeeded in solving was:

> How is it possible to construct and then secure the necessary autonomous institutional order – or framework – to modern science and the pursuit of qualified knowledge and, at the same time, prevent it from being corrupted or even destroyed by other mighty and legitimate forces in society such as politics, economy, and religion?

Neave and Van Vught (1994: 271) similarly argue that what is characteristic of the 'state control' model is "the state's underwriting of non-interference by external interests in the individual freedom to teach and to learn, [by guaranteeing] a monopoly of access to curricular pathways leading to public service or [through] the [university's] administrative subordination to a powerful central ministry".

Through the power which it conferred on professionals, this concept of the university served as the foundation for institutions which developed their own unique organisational form. Universities were described by Mintzberg (1979) as professional bureaucracies, where the real power lies at the level of classrooms and research laboratories. According to Allen (1988: 26):

> universities are a unique form of organisation because of their multiplicity of missions and the absence of a single absolute authority. They are a genus apart, a non-organisation or an organised anarchy, characterised by ambiguity, but not therefore 'illegitimate, immoral or ineffective'.

The primacy of knowledge, regarded as free and universal, and the emphasis on individual academic freedom, conditioned the primary loyalties of academics. According to Clark (1983a) the loyalty of academics was first and above all to their own discipline, then to their department, sometimes to the faculty (or school) and even less frequently to the university itself.

This situation is apparently changing. Meek states in his chapter that "In the past, academic loyalty was first and foremost to the discipline and to disciplinary norms concerning the definition and production of knowledge ... That loyalty has come under challenge from powerful groups both within and without the academy demanding loyalty first and foremost to the institution – that is, to the corporation that pays the bills".

Slaughter and Rhoades argue that the traditional idea of free and universal knowledge has been replaced by the idea that "rather than being shared, intellectual property is owned", while "the proliferation of conflict of interest language and rules [in intellectual property policies] is another indication of the death of disinterestedness". Leite reports on "capitalist ownership being extended to services and knowledge which were previously considered in the public domain".

As universities are forced to look for alternative sources of funding, they become increasingly aware of the potential market value of innovation and new knowledge. In the USA, Slaughter and Rhoades demonstrate the 'obligatory disclosure' legislation which has been passed in a number of states allowing universities "to direct faculty to patent rather than publish", thus converting the traditional Mertonian values of American university research – communalism, the free flow of knowledge, disinterestedness and organised scepticism – into a thing of the past. Moreover, Slaughter and Rhoades report that following the recent passage of the Digital Millennium Copyright Act and the development of university copyright policies which cover software and courseware (thus clearly aimed at controlling e-learning materials), the other primary asset of the academic's ingenuity – what is taught – will also increasingly be converted into commodifiable property.

All this is transforming the academic from a professional, both protected from the marketplace and morally committed to professional practice (Freidson 2001: 34), into a more and more 'normal' employee of an enterprise which happens to be a university. In this sense, and whatever the precise forms of governance and management, the claim that the academic profession is becoming proletarianised may indeed be justified. As academics cross the boundary of the marketplace, whether as creators of marketable knowledge or as providers of teaching services to their student clients, their qualities of altruism and probity are slowly eroded, and the way is open to the accusation that corporatism has superseded the traditional loyalties and modes of working of academic life. Or, in the words of Michael Reed (2002: 177–178):

> No longer seen as the disinterested guardians of esoteric disciplinary knowledge guaranteeing expert status as recognised 'professionals' but as 'knowledge producers or workers' routinely engaged in generating and communicating socially relevant and economically useful skills or techniques, academics seem adrift on a 'sea of utilitarian pragmatism'.

As universities increase their penetration of the marketplace, academics will increasingly be seen as 'intellectual workers', forced to direct their loyalty, not to their academic peers in their department or discipline, but to the institutions that pay their salaries and demand the lion's share of the economic value they produce.

6. CONCLUSION

On the basis of the different authors' contributions to this second volume of the Douro series, we have concluded that managerialism as an ideology has not imposed a single, convergent model of behaviour on higher education systems and their institutions. Maassen notes that "there has not been a one-time-only introduction of new management structures". Governments have espoused managerialism, whether as ideology or as practice, to different degrees or not at all, and institutions have responded in very different ways, largely influenced by their historical, economic and social backgrounds. Cloete and Kulati offer sound advice to researchers with their warning, *a propos* developments in South Africa that "what a label of managerialism will obscure is the interesting new forms of consultation and participation that are emerging under conditions of demands for greater efficiency and accountability". Likewise, Meek in the introduction draws our attention to the fact that in this volume "a unified theoretical template has not been imposed on the country contributors. In our judgment, the cases are too diverse and the state of theoretical development in the field too meagre to warrant such a measure". And Maassen in his theoretical considerations emphasises that "it is not assumed that all new governance models with respect to higher education are market models, nor that all management developments in higher education institutions concern variations on NPM or new 'managerialism'".

However, despite the evident diversity, it also seems that there are some generally detectable patterns. These include: growing financial strictures, which have developed an increasing awareness among academics of financial limits and of the need for more efficient financial management; the growth in power of central administrations; and a growing awareness among academics of a loss of social standing, of proletarianised working conditions, and even of their loss of the moral trappings of professionalism: "to many academics on campus, eventually, the chase for the dollar would no longer be questionable behaviour" (Slaughter and Leslie 1997: 233). And Maassen in his chapter discusses "the changes in institutional management structures in higher education ... from the perspective of shifts in system-level governance arrangements".

The chapters also reveal that the attempted imposition of new managerial culture and values has been met almost everywhere by counter-movements of resistance, and that these have so far averted the complete victory of the new ideology, even in those countries where its emergence was more virulent. Fulton considers that this has been made easier by the fact that, even in those countries where managerialism was imposed as part of a new ideology of public service as a whole, higher education has been somewhat protected from its full force because the existing organisational forms have not been wholly uprooted and replaced. But this is not to downplay the problems, notably that an inevitable by-product of academic resistance has been an increasing tension between academics and managers.

What remains to be seen is whether the new ideology will turn out to herald a permanent change, or will it fade into organisational history as a new but transitory management fad. Reed (2002: 175) demonstrates how seriously he takes managerialist ideology in voicing his scepticism that it will be short-lived:

> But the longer-term impact and significance of these, more incremental, subtle and supposedly continuity-facilitating reforms should not be underestimated. The inherent contradictions, tensions and stresses remain; in many respects they seem to be intensifying. As usual, much depends on where you stand within a public sector system in a permanent state of flux and uncertainty where today's 'change masters' are tomorrow's 'change-casualties or victims'.

However, it is not only the potential 'victims' who have their reservations about the benefits of new managerial practices. In particular, a number of well-known analysts have questioned whether an absolute commitment to economic efficiency is an appropriate value to impose on universities. According to Clark (1983b), as Amaral and Magalhães (2003) observe, a more desirable

> model of university organisation consists in loose coupling between schools, departments, laboratories and professorial chairs. This model of organisation induces some disorder and allows for some inefficiency in the use of resources. On the other hand, it makes it possible for individuals and research teams to liberate their inventive capacity and to produce innovative ideas thus contributing to an effectiveness that is impossible within institutions with a formal and hierarchical chain of command.

Likewise, the Brazilian scholar Luís Cunha (1999) considers that "organisations are effective only when they are able to maximise their own abilities. Universities are effective when they are able to promote the initiatives and amplify the options of different and conflicting groups belonging to them". Others, such as Michael Shattock (2002), the former Registrar of the University of Warwick, have argued convincingly that in the UK, when improprieties and breakdowns occurred, they were not centred on the academic community but on governing bodies and the executive. Shattock also declares that there is little hard evidence that 'new managerialism' has been successful in delivering academic success, and he recommends a shift in the balance of modern concepts of university governance so that governing bodies should not be kept too remote from the internal academic discourse.

Recent scandals, such as those resulting from the bankruptcies of ENRON, WorldCom and other companies listed on the New York stock exchange or the criminal behaviour of auditing companies such as Arthur Andersen, have demonstrated the lack of efficient and reliable financial control in some of the most significant global corporations – and have cast justifiable doubt on the much-proclaimed 'evident supremacy' of management practices in the private sector. Meek reports in his chapter that recent research on corporate governance in Australia has demonstrated that "the corporate sector has many if not more governance and management problems than the university sector". Shattock (2002: 240) summarises his balanced arguments by concluding that:

> Jarratt and others may have been right to see the academic community as a force for slowing down decision-making and being indecisive, but it cannot stand accused of the kind of abuses that have attracted the attention of the National Audit Office.

We agree with Neave (1995: 9) when he states that "Looking into the future is a risky activity, as prophets and seers have found to their cost throughout the ages". The future of managerialism in higher education is beyond the divinatory powers of the most sibylline oracle. What we need is far more research on these questions, research which, we may hope, will help to shed light on the benefits and costs of a range of alternative possibilities for the governance and management of such a complex social organisation as the university.

NOTES

[1] This guild-like organisation was never implemented in the American university where the initial colleges were "meant to be the orthodox instrument of the community and its faith" (Hofstadter 1996: 81).

[2]   This designation is explained by Dale (2000: 429): "The work has been developed over twenty years through a wide range of publications put out by a group of scholars who may be referred to as 'world institutionalists' since their work develops on a world scale some tenets of what has become known as sociological institutionalism [Powell and DiMaggio 1991, Finnemore 1996, Hall and Taylor 1996]".

[3]   In Portugal, too, a recent reform of the hospitals integrated in the National Health Service has resulted in the appointment of all the presidents of the executive boards from outside the medical profession. These people were selected for their reputation as private sector managers, and generally had no previous knowledge of health administration.

[4]   The point is that Oxford and Cambridge are generally regarded as the most collegiate (and under-managed) of UK universities. Smith et al. (1999) emphasise that "When postgraduate and academic/teaching experience is taken into account Oxbridge influence increases still further".

REFERENCES

Agnelli, G. "Industry's Expectations of the University." *CRE-action* 83 (1988): 11–17.
Allen, M. *The Goals of Universities*. Milton Keynes: Open University Press, 1988.
Altbach, P. (ed.). *The International Academic Profession: Portraits of Fourteen Countries*. Princeton: Carnegie Foundation for the Advancement of Teaching, 1996.
Amaral, A and A. Magalhães. "The Triple Crisis of the University and its Reinvention." *Higher Education Policy* 2003 (forthcoming).
Ball, C. and H. Eggins (eds). *Higher Education into the 1990s: New Dimensions*. Buckingham: Society for Research into Higher Education and Open University Press, 1989.
Ball, S.J. "Big Policies/Small World: An Introduction to International Perspectives in Education Policy." *Comparative Education* 34.2 (1998): 119–130.
Barrow, C. "The Strategy of Selective Excellence: Redesigning Higher Education for Global Competition in a Post-modern Society." *Higher Education* 41 (1996): 447–469.
Becher, T. and M. Kogan. *Process and Structure in Higher Education*. London: Heinemann, 1980.
Buchbinder, H. "The Market Oriented University and the Changing Role of Knowledge." *Higher Education* 26 (1993): 331–347.
Cerych, L. and P. Sabatier. *Great Expectations and Mixed Performance: The Implementation of Higher Education Reforms in Europe*. Trentham: Trentham Books, 1986.
Clark, B.R. "Governing the Higher Education System." In Shattock, M. (ed.). *The Structure and Governance of Higher Education*. Guilford: Society for Research into Higher Education, 1983a, 19–42.
Clark, B.R. *The Higher Education System. Academic Organization in Cross-National Perspective*. Berkeley: University of California Press, 1983b.
Clark, B.R. *Creating Entrepreneurial Universities*. London: Pergamon Press, 1998.
Clark, B.R. "The Entrepreneurial University: New Foundations for Collegiality, Autonomy and Achievement." *Beyond the Entrepreneurial University? Global Challenges and Institutional Responses* (CD-ROM). IMHE General Conference 11–13 September. Paris: OECD, 2000, 118–127.
Cobban, A.B. *The Medieval Universities: Their Development and Organization*. London: Methuen, 1975.
Cowen, R. "Performativity, Post-modernity and the University." *Comparative Education* 32.2 (1996): 245–258.
Cunha, L.A. "O público e o privado na educação superior brasileira: uma fronteira em movimento." In Trindade, H. (ed.). *Uma Universidade em ruínas – Na República dos Professores*. Petrópolis: Editora Vozes, 1999, 39–56.
Czarniawska, B. and G. Sevòn (eds). *Translating Organizational Change*. Berlin: de Gruyter, 1996.
Dale, R. "Globalization and Education: Demonstrating a 'Common World Educational Culture' or Locating a 'Globally Structured Educational Agenda'?" *Educational Theory* 50.4 (2000): 427–448.
Duke, C. *The Learning University. Towards a New Paradigm?* Buckingham: Open University Press, 1992.
Eggins, H. "Conclusions." In Ball, C. and H. Eggins (eds). *Higher Education into the 1990s: New Dimensions*. Buckingham: Society for Research into Higher Education and Open University Press, 1989, 124–132.

Ferlie, E., L. Ashburner, L. Fitzgerald and A. Pettigrew. *The New Public Management in Action*. London: Sage, 1996.

Finnemore, M. *National Interests in International Society*. Ithaca: Cornell University Press, 1996.

Freidson, E. *Professionalism: The Third Logic*. Cambridge: The Pollity Press, 2001.

Fuller, B. and R. Rubinson (eds). *The Political Construction of Educational Expansion: The State, School Expansion and Economic Change*. New York: Praeger, 1992.

Fulton, O. "Higher Education Governance in the UK: Change and Continuity." In Amaral, A., G.A. Jones and B. Karseth (eds). *Governing Higher Education: National Perspectives on Institutional Governance*. Dordrecht: Kluwer Academic Publishers, 2002, 187–211.

Gornitzka, Å., S. Kyvik and I.M. Larsen. "The Bureaucratisation of Universities." *Minerva* 36.1 (1998): 21–47.

Gornitzka, Å. and I.M. Larsen. "Towards Professionalisation? Restructuring of the Administrative Work Force in Universities." *Higher Education* forthcoming.

Hall, P. and R. Taylor. "Political Science and the Three New Institutionalisms." *Political Studies* 44.4 (1996): 936–957.

Halpin, D. and B. Troyna. "The Politics of Policy Borrowing." *Comparative Education* 31 (1995): 303–310.

Halsey, A.H. *Decline of the Donnish Dominion: The British Academic Professions in the Twentieth Century*. Oxford: Clarendon Press, 1992.

Henkel, M. "Higher Education." In Laffin, M. (ed.). *Beyond Bureaucracy: The Professionals in the Contemporary Public Sector*. Ashgate: Aldershot, 1998, 183-200.

Henkel, M. *Academic Identities and Policy Change in Higher Education*. London: Jessica Kingsley, 2000.

Hofstadter, R. *Academic Freedom in the Age of the College*. New Brunswick: Transaction Publishers, 1996.

Jones, C. "Social Work: Regulation and Managerialism." In Exworthy, M. and S. Halford (eds). *Professionals and the New Managerialism in the Public Sector*. Buckingham: Open University Press, 1999, 37–49.

Jones, P.W. "Globalisation and Internationalism: Democratic Prospects for World Education." *Comparative Education* 34.2 (1998): 143–155.

Kean, L. and R. Scase. *Local Government Management: The Rhetoric and Reality of Change*. Buckingham: Open University Press, 1998.

Kogan, M. "Academic and Administrative Interface." In Henkel, M. and B. Little (eds). *Changing Relationships Between Higher Education and the State*. London, Jessica Kingsley Publishers, 1999, 263–279.

Lauwerys, J. "The Future of the Profession of University Administration and Management." *Perspective* 6.4 (2002): 93–97.

Leicht, K. and M. Fennell. *Professional Work: A Sociological Approach*. London: Blackwell, 2001.

Maassen, P. "Organisational Strategies and Governance Structures in Dutch Universities." In Amaral, A., G.A. Jones and B. Karseth (eds). *Governing Higher Education: National Perspectives on Institutional Governance*. Dordrecht: Kluwer Academic Publishers, 2002, 23–41.

Magalhães, A. and A. Amaral. "Portuguese Higher Education and the Imaginary Friend: The Stakeholders Role in Institutional Governance." *European Journal of Education* 35.4 (2000): 439–448.

Meyer, J., J. Boli, G. Thomas and F. Ramirez. "World Society and the Nation-State." *American Journal of Sociology* 103.1 (1997): 144–181.

Mintzberg, H. *The Structuring of Organizations*. Englewood Cliffs: Prentice-Hall, 1979.

Moodie, G. and R. Eustace. *Power and Authority in British Universities*. London: Allen and Unwin, 1974.

Neave, G. "On Visions, Short and Long." *Higher Education Policy* 8.4 (1995): 9–10.

Neave, G. and F.A. van Vught. "Conclusion." In Neave, G. and F.A. van Vught (eds). *Government and Higher Education Relationships Across Three Continents – The Winds of Change*. London: Pergamon, 1994, 269–271.

Nybom, T. "The Humboldt Legacy. Reflections on the Past, Present and Future of European Higher Education." In DeCorte, Eric (ed.). *Excellence in Higher Education*. London: Portland Press, forthcoming.

Oliver, C. "Strategic Responses to Institutional Processes." *Academy of Management Review* 16 (1991): 145–179.

Pfeffer, J. and G.R. Salancik. *External Control of Organizations: A Resource Dependence Perspective.* New York: Harper and Row, 1978.

Powell, W. and P. DiMaggio (eds). *The New Institutionalism in Organizational Analysis.* Chicago: University of Chicago Press, 1991.

Pressman, J.L. and A. Wildavsky. *Implementation: How Great Expectations in Washington are Dashed in Oakland; Or, Why It's Amazing That Federal Programs Work At All.* Berkeley: University of California Press, 1974.

Reed, M. "New Managerialism, Professional Power and Organisational Governance in UK Universities: A Review and Assessment." In Amaral, A., G.A. Jones and B. Karseth (eds). *Governing Higher Education: National Perspectives on Institutional Governance.* Dordrecht: Kluwer Academic Publishers, 2002,163–185.

Reed, M. and P. Anthony. "Between an Ideological Rock and an Organisational Hard Place: NHS Management in the 1980's and 1990's." In Clarke, T. and C. Pitelis (eds). *The Political Economy of Privatisation.* London: Routledge, 1993, 185–204.

(Robbins Report) *Higher Education: Report of the Committee Appointed by the Prime Minister Under the Chairmanship of Lord Robbins 1961–63.* Cmnd. 2154. London: HMSO, 1963.

Røvik, K.A. "Deinstitutionalization and the Logic of Fashion." In Czarniawska, B. and G. Sevòn (eds). *Translating Organisational Change.* Berlin: De Gruyter, 1996, 139–172.

Scott, P. "The Power of Ideas." In Ball, C. and H. Eggins (eds). *Higher Education into the 1990s: New Dimensions.* Buckingham: Society for Research into Higher Education and Open University Press, 1989, 7–16.

Shattock, M. "Re-balancing Modern Concepts of University Governance." *Higher Education Quarterly* 56.3 (2002): 235–244.

Slaughter, S. and L. Leslie. *Academic Capitalism: Politics, Policies and the Entrepreneurial University.* Baltimore: John Hopkins Press, 1997.

Smith, C.S. *Market Values in American Higher Education – The Pitfalls and Promises.* Lanham, Maryland: Rowan and Littlefield, 2000.

Smith, D., P. Scott, J. Bocock and C. Bargh. "Vice-Chancellors and Executive Leadership in UK Universities. New Roles and Relationship?" In Henkel, M. and B. Little (eds). *Changing Relationships Between Higher Education and the State.* London: Jessica Kingsley Publishers, 1999, 280–306.

Trowler, Paul R. *Academics Responding to Change: New Higher Education Frameworks and Academic Cultures.* Buckingham: Society for Research into Higher Education and Open University Press, 1998.

Van Vught, F.A. "Innovations and Reforms in Higher Education." In Van Vught, F.A. (ed.). *Government Strategies and Innovation in Higher Education.* London: Jessica Kingsley Publishers, 1989, 47–72.

Wilson, K. "The Pattern, Range and Purpose of Higher Education: A Moral Perspective." In Ball, C. and H. Eggins (eds). *Higher Education into the 1990s: New Dimensions.* Buckingham: Society for Research into Higher Education and Open University Press, 1989, 38–50.

Winter, R. "The University of Life plc: the 'Industrialization' of Higher Education." In Smyth, J. (ed.). *Academic Work: The Changing Labour Process in Higher Education.* Buckingham: Open University Press, 1995, 129–143.

Higher Education Dynamics

1. J. Enders and O. Fulton (eds.): *Higher Education in a Globalising World.* 2002
   ISBN Hb 1-4020-0863-5; Pb 1-4020-0864-3
2. A. Amaral, G.A. Jones and B. Karseth (eds.): *Governing Higher Education: National Perspectives on Institutional Governance.* 2002　　ISBN 1-4020-1078-8
3. A. Amaral, V.L. Meek and I.M. Larsen (eds.): *The Higher Education Managerial Revolution?* 2003　　ISBN Hb 1-4020-1575-5; Pb 1-4020-1586-0

KLUWER ACADEMIC PUBLISHERS – DORDRECHT / BOSTON / LONDON